Computer Networks
And Internets

FIFTH EDITION

DOUGLAS E. COMER

Cisco Research
Cisco, Inc.
San Jose, CA 95138

and

Department of Computer Sciences
Purdue University
West Lafayette, IN 47907

PEARSON
Prentice
Hall

Pearson Education International

Editorial Director, Computer Science and Engineering: Marcia J. Horton
Editorial Assistant: Melinda Haggerty
Director of Marketing: Margaret Waples
Marketing Manager: Christopher Kelly
Senior Managing Editor: Scott Disanno
Production Editor: Irwin Zucker
Art Director: Kenny Beck
Art Editor: Gregory Dulles
Manufacturing Manager: Alan Fischer
Manufacturing Buyer: Lisa McDowell

UNIX is a registered trademark of The Open Group in the U.S. and other countries. Microsoft Windows is a trademark of Microsoft Corporation. Microsoft is a registered trademark of Microsoft Corporation. Windows 95 is a trademark of Microsoft Corporation. Windows 98 is a trademark of Microsoft Corporation. Windows NT is a trademark of Microsoft Corporation. Solaris is a trademark of Sun Microsystems, Incorporated. Sniffer is a trademark of Network General Corporation. Java is a trademark of Sun Microsystems, Incorporated. JavaScript is a trademark of Sun Microsystems, Incorporated. AdaMagic is a trademark of Intermetrics, Incorporated. Sparc is a trademark of Sun Microsystems, Incorporated. Alpha is a trademark of Digital Equipment Corporation. Pentium is a trademark of Intel Corporation X Window System is a trademark of X Consortium, 1ncorporated.Smartjack is a trademark of Westell, Incorporated.

The author and publisher of this book have used their best efforts in preparing this book. These efforts include the development, research, and testing of the theories and programs to determine their effectiveness. The author and publisher make no warranty of any kind, expressed or implied, with regard to these programs or the documentation contained in this book. The author and publisher shall not be liable in any event for incidental or consequential damages in connection with, or arising out of, the furnishing, performance, or use of these programs.

Pearson Education Ltd., *London*
Pearson Education Singapore, Pte. Ltd.
Pearson Education Canada, Inc.
Pearson Education—*Japan*
Pearson Education Australia PTY, Limited
Pearson Education North Asia, Ltd., *Hong Kong*
Pearson Educación de Mexico, S.A. de C.V.
Pearson Education Malaysia, Pte. Ltd.
Pearson Education *Upper Saddle River, New Jersey*

PEARSON
Prentice
Hall

10 9 8 7 6 5 4 3

ISBN 10: 0-13-504583-5
ISBN 13: 978-0-13-504583-1

To Packets Everywhere

Contents

Chapter 3   Internet Applications And Network Programming   27

Chapter 4   Traditional Internet Applications   49

PART II   Data Communication Basics   83

Chapter 5   Overview Of Data Communications   85

Chapter 6   Information Sources And Signals   93

Chapter 9   Transmission Modes   153

Chapter 10   Modulation And Modems   165

PART III Packet Switching And Network Technologies 219

Chapter 13   Local Area Networks: Packets, Frames, And Topologies   221

Chapter 14   The IEEE MAC Sub-Layer   241

Chapter 15   Wired LAN Technology (Ethernet And 802.3)   255

Chapter 16   Wireless Networking Technologies   267

PART IV Internetworking   333

Chapter 20 Internetworking: Concepts, Architecture, and Protocols   335

Chapter 21 IP: Internet Addressing   345

Chapter 22   Datagram Forwarding   **363**

Chapter 23   Support Protocols And Technologies   **381**

PART V   Other Networking Concepts & Technologies 469

Preface

Previous editions of *Computer Networks And Internets* have received incredibly positive reviews; I especially thank readers who have taken the time to write to me personally. In addition to students who use the text in courses, networking professionals have written to praise its clarity and describe how it helped them pass professional certification exams. Many enthusiastic comments have also arrived about foreign translations. The success is especially satisfying in a market glutted with networking books. This book stands out because of its breadth of coverage, logical organization, explanation of concepts, focus on the Internet, and appeal to both professors and students.

In response to suggestions from readers and recent changes in networking, the new edition has been completely reorganized, revised, and updated. Descriptions of older technologies has been reduced or eliminated. Material on data communications, which is becoming an essential staple of networking courses, has been expanded and placed in Part II of the text. The networking chapters build on the data communication basics, and describe both wired and wireless networking. In addition, to emphasize the new 802.11 wireless standards, the discussion of wireless includes cellular telephone technologies because cellular systems currently offer data services and will soon be adopting Internet protocols.

Recent discussions about networking courses have engendered a debate about the bottom-up or top-down approach. In bottom-up, a student learns the lowest-level details, and then learns how the next higher levels use the lower-levels to provide expanded functionality. In top-down, one starts with a high-level application and only learns enough of the next lower layer to understand how the application can operate. This text combines the best of each. The text begins with a discussion of network applications and the communication paradigms that the Internet offers. It allows students to understand the facilities the Internet provides to applications before studying the underlying technologies that implement the facilities. Following the discussion of applications, the text presents networking in a logical manner so a reader understands how each new technology builds on lower layer technologies.

The text is intended for upper-division undergraduates or beginning graduate students, who have little or no background in networking. It does not use sophisticated mathematics, nor does it assume a knowledge of operating systems. Instead, the text defines concepts clearly, uses examples and figures to illustrate how the technology operates, and states results of analysis without providing mathematical proofs.

The text answers the basic question "how do computer networks and internets operate?" in the broadest sense. It provides a comprehensive, self-contained tour through all of networking that describes low-level details such as data transmission and wiring, network technologies such as LANs and WANs, internetworking protocols, and applications. It shows how protocols use the underlying hardware and how applications use the protocol stack to provide functionality for users.

The text is divided into five parts. The first part focuses on uses of the Internet and network applications. It describes protocol layering, the client-server model of interaction, the socket API, and gives examples of application-layer protocols used in the Internet.

The second part (Chapters 5—12) explains data communications and gives background on both the underlying hardware and concepts such as modulation, multiplexing, and channel coding. Chapters discuss transmission modes, and define terms such as *bandwidth* and *baud*. The final chapter in the second part presents access and interconnection technologies used in the Internet, and explains how each technology implements concepts from previous chapters.

The third part (Chapters 13—19) focuses on packet switching and packet switching technologies. Chapters give the motivation for using packets, introduce the IEEE model for layer 2 protocols, and consider wired and wireless networking technologies. The third part also introduces the four basic categories: LAN, MAN, PAN, and WAN, and discusses routing in WANs. The final chapter presents examples of network technologies that have been used in the Internet.

The fourth part (Chapters 20—27) focuses on the Internet protocols. After discussing the motivation for internetworking, the text describes Internet architecture, routers, Internet addressing, address binding, and the TCP/IP protocol suite. Protocols such as IP, TCP, UDP, ICMP, and ARP are reviewed in detail, allowing students to understand how the concepts relate to practice. Chapter 26 on TCP covers the important and deep topic of reliability in transport protocols.

The final part of the text (Chapters 28—32) considers topics that cross multiple layers of a protocol stack, including network performance, network security, network management, bootstrapping, and multimedia support. In each case, the chapter draws on topics from previous parts of the text. The placement of these chapters at the end of the text follows the approach of defining concepts before they are used, and does not imply that the topics are less important.

The text is ideally suited for a one-semester introductory course on networking taught at the junior or senior level. Designed for a comprehensive course, it covers the entire subject from wiring to applications. I encourage instructors to engage students with hands-on assignments. In the undergraduate course at Purdue, for example, students are given weekly lab assignments that span a wide range of topics: from network measurement and packet analysis to network programming. By the time they finish our course, each student is expected to: know how an IP router uses a table to forward IP datagrams; describe how a datagram crosses the Internet; identify and explain fields in an Ethernet frame; know how TCP identifies a connection and why a concurrent Web server can handle multiple connections to port 80; compute the length of a single bit as it travels across a gigabit Ethernet; explain why TCP is classified as end-to-end; and know why DSL can send data over wires that are also being used for an analog telephone call.

The goal of a single course is breadth, not depth — to cover the subject, one cannot focus on a few technologies or a few concepts. Thus, the key to a successful course lies in maintaining a quick pace. To cover the most important topics in a semester, the lower-layer material in Part 2 can be condensed, and the sections on networks and internetworking can be allocated four weeks each, leaving two weeks for the introductory material on applications and topics such as network management and security. The details of socket programming can be covered in programming exercises.

Instructors should impress on students the importance of concepts and principles: specific technologies may become obsolete in a few years, but the principles will remain. In addition, instructors should give students a feeling for the excitement that pervades networking.

Although no single topic is challenging, students may find the quantity of material daunting. In particular, students are faced with a plethora of new terms. Networking acronyms and jargon can be especially confusing; students spend much of the time becoming accustomed to using proper terms. In classes at Purdue, we have found that a weekly vocabulary quiz helps students to learn terminology as the semester proceeds.

Because programming and experimentation are crucial to helping students learn about networks, hands-on experience is an essential part of any networking course†. At Purdue, we begin the semester by having students construct client software to access the Web and extract data (e.g., write a program to print the current temperature). Appendix 1 is extremely helpful in getting started: the appendix explains a simplified API. The API, which is available on the web site, allows students to write working code before they learn about protocols, addresses, sockets, or the (somewhat tedious) socket API. Later in the semester, of course, students learn socket programming. Eventually, they are able to write a concurrent web server (support for server-side scripting is optional, but most students complete it). In addition to application programming, students use our lab facilities to capture packets from a live network, write programs that decode packet headers (e.g., Ethernet, IP, and TCP), and observe TCP connections. If advanced lab facilities are not available, students can experiment with free software, such as *Ethereal*.

Giving students access to a network builds enthusiasm and encourages experimentation — our experience shows that students who have access to a live network understand and appreciate the subject better. Thus, if a dedicated packet analyzer is not available, an analyzer can be created by installing appropriate shareware software on a standard PC.

The web site for the text contains materials that make teaching easier and help readers understand the material. For students without access to networking facilities, the web site contains examples of packet traces; students can write programs that read a trace and process packets as if they have been captured from the network. For instructors, the web site contains course materials, figures from the text that can be used in

---

†A lab manual, *Hands-On Networking*, is available that describes possible experiments and assignments that can be performed on a variety of hardware, including a single computer or a set of computers on a local area network.

presentations, and animated figures that help clarify the concepts. The site also contains materials not in the text, including photographs of network wiring and equipment as well as files of data that can be used as input to student projects. The web site is:

http://www.netbook.cs.purdue.edu

I thank all the people who have contributed to this edition of the book. Fred Baker and Dave Oran at Cisco suggested topics of importance. Lami Kaya suggested the overall reorganization, helped formulate the content of the data communications chapters, reviewed the text, and made many other valuable suggestions. Lami has agreed to manage the web site. Special thanks go to my wife and partner, Christine, whose careful editing and helpful suggestions made many improvements throughout.

Douglas E. Comer

March, 2008

About The Author

Dr. Douglas Comer is an internationally recognized expert on TCP/IP protocols, computer networking, and the Internet. One of the researchers who contributed to the Internet as it was being formed in the late 1970s and 1980s, he was a member of the Internet Architecture Board, the group responsible for guiding the Internet's development. He was also chairman of the CSNET technical committee, a member of the CSNET executive committee, and chairman of DARPA's Distributed Systems Architecture Board.

Comer has consulted for industry on the design of computer networks. In addition to giving talks in US universities, each year Comer lectures to academics and networking professionals around the world. Comer's operating system, Xinu, and implementation of TCP/IP protocols (both documented in his textbooks), have been used in commercial products.

Comer is a Distinguished Professor of Computer Science at Purdue University. He is currently on leave from Purdue, serving as VP of Research Collaboration at Cisco Systems. Recently, Comer has taught courses on networking, internetworking, computer architecture, and operating systems. He has developed innovative labs that provide students with the opportunity to gain hands-on experience with operating systems, networks, and protocols. In addition to writing a series of best-selling technical books that have been translated into sixteen languages, he served as the North American editor of the journal *Software — Practice and Experience* for twenty years. Comer is a Fellow of the ACM.

Additional information can be found at:

www.cs.purdue.edu/people/comer

Enthusiastic Comments About
Computer Networks And Internets

"The book is one of the best that I have ever read. Thank you."

Gokhan Mutlu
Ege University, Turkey

"I just could not put it down before I finished it. It was simply superb."

Lalit Y. Raju
Regional Engineering College, India

"An excellent book for beginners and professionals alike — well written, comprehensive coverage, and easy to follow."

John Lin
Bell Labs

"The breadth is astonishing."

George Varghese
University of California at San Diego

"It's truly the best book of its type that I have ever seen. A huge vote of thanks!"

Chez Ciechanowicz
Info. Security Group, University Of London

"The miniature webserver in Appendix 1 is brilliant — readers will get a big thrill out of it."

Dennis Brylow
Marquette University

"Wow, what an excellent text book."

Jaffet A. Cordoba
Technical Writer

(continued on next page)

More Comments About
Computer Networks And Internets

"The book's great!"

Peter Parry
South Birmingham College, UK

"Wow, when I was studying for the CCNA exam, the clear explanations in this book solved all the problems I had understanding the OSI model and TCP/IP data transfer. It opened my mind to the fascinating world of networks and TCP/IP."

Solomon Tang
PCCW, Hong Kong

"An invaluable tool, particularly for programmers and computer scientists desiring a clear, broad-based understanding of computer networks."

Peter Chuks Obiefuna
East Carolina University

"The textbook covers a lot of material, and the author makes the contents very easy to read and understand, which is the biggest reason I like this book. It's very appropriate for a 3-credit class in that a lot of material can be covered. The student's positive feedback shows they too appreciate using this textbook."

Jie Hu
Saint Cloud State University

"Despite the plethora of acronyms that infest the discipline of networking, this book is not intimidating. Comer is an excellent writer, who expands and explains the terminology. The text covers the entire scope of networking from wires to the web. I find it outstanding."

Jennifer Seitzer
University of Dayton

Other Books In the Internetworking Series
from Douglas Comer and Prentice Hall

Internetworking With TCP/IP Volume I: Principles, Protocols and Architectures, 5th edition: 2005, ISBN 0-13-187671-6

The classic reference in the field for anyone who wants to understand Internet technology, Volume I surveys the TCP/IP protocol suite and describes each component. The text covers protocols such as IP, ICMP, TCP, UDP, ARP, SNMP, and RTP, as well as concepts such as Virtual Private Networks and Address Translation.

Internetworking With TCP/IP Volume II: Design, Implementation, and Internals (with David Stevens), 3rd edition: 1999, ISBN 0-13-973843-6

Volume II continues the discussion of Volume I by using code from a running implementation of TCP/IP to illustrate all the details.

Internetworking With TCP/IP Volume III: Client-Server Programming and Applications (with David Stevens)

Linux/POSIX sockets version: 2000, ISBN 0-13-032071-4
AT&T TLI Version: 1994, ISBN 0-13-474230-3
Windows Sockets Version: 1997, ISBN 0-13-848714-6

Volume III describes the fundamental concept of client-server computing used to build all distributed computing systems, and explains server designs as well as the tools and techniques used to build clients and servers. Three versions of Volume III are available for the socket API (Linux/POSIX), the TLI API (AT&T System V), and the Windows Sockets API (Microsoft).

Network Systems Design Using Network Processors, Intel 2xxx version, 2006, ISBN 0-13-187286-9

A comprehensive overview of the design and engineering of packet processing systems such as bridges, routers, TCP splicers, and NAT boxes. With a focus on network processor technology, *Network Systems Design* explains the principles of design, presents tradeoffs, and gives example code for a network processor.

The Internet Book: Everything you need to know about computer networking and how the Internet works, 4th Edition 2007, ISBN 0-13-233553-0

A gentle introduction to networking and the Internet that does not assume the reader has a technical background. It explains the Internet in general terms, without focusing on a particular computer or a particular brand of software. Ideal for someone who wants to become Internet and computer networking literate; an extensive glossary of terms and abbreviations is included.

For a complete list of Comer's textbooks, see:

www.comerbooks.com

PART I

Introduction To Networking And Internet Applications

An overview of networking and the interface that application programs use to communicate across the Internet

Chapters

Chapter Contents

1

Introduction And Overview

1.1 Growth Of Computer Networking

Computer networking has grown explosively. Since the 1970s, computer communication has changed from an esoteric research topic to an essential part of the infrastructure. Networking is used in every aspect of business, including advertising, production, shipping, planning, billing, and accounting. Consequently, most corporations have multiple networks. Schools, at all grade levels from elementary through post-graduate, are using computer networks to provide students and teachers with instantaneous access to online information. Federal, state, and local government offices use networks, as do military organizations. In short, computer networks are everywhere.

The growth and uses of the global Internet† are among the most interesting and exciting phenomena in networking. In 1980, the Internet was a research project that involved a few dozen sites. Today, the Internet has grown into a production communication system that reaches all populated countries of the world. Many users have high-speed Internet access through cable modems, DSL, or wireless technologies.

The advent and utility of networking has created dramatic economic shifts. Data networking has made telecommuting available to individuals and has changed business communication. In addition, an entire industry emerged that develops networking technologies, products, and services. The importance of computer networking has produced a demand in all industries for people with more networking expertise. Companies need workers to plan, acquire, install, operate, and manage the hardware and software systems that constitute computer networks and internets. In addition, computer programming is no longer restricted to individual computers — network programming is re-

---

†Throughout this text, we follow the convention of writing *Internet* with an uppercase "I" to denote the global Internet.

quired because all programmers are expected to design and implement application software that can communicate with applications on other computers.

1.2 Why Networking Seems Complex

Because computer networking is an active, exciting field, the subject seems complex. Many technologies exist, and each technology has features that distinguish it from the others. Companies continue to create commercial networking products and services, often by using technologies in new unconventional ways. Finally, networking seems complex because technologies can be combined and interconnected in many ways.

Computer networking can be especially confusing to a beginner because no single underlying theory exists that explains the relationship among all parts. Multiple organizations have created networking standards, but some standards are incompatible with others. Various organizations and research groups have attempted to define conceptual models that capture the essence and explain the nuances among network hardware and software systems, but because the set of technologies is diverse and changes rapidly, models are either so simplistic that they do not distinguish among details or so complex that they do not help simplify the subject.

The lack of consistency in the field has produced another challenge for beginners: instead of a uniform terminology for networking concepts, multiple groups each attempt to create their own terminology. Researchers cling to scientifically precise terminology. Corporate marketing groups often associate a product with a generic technical term or invent new terms merely to distinguish their products or services from those of competitors. Thus, technical terms are easily confused with the names of popular products. To add further confusion, professionals sometimes use a technical term from one technology when referring to an analogous feature of another technology. Consequently, in addition to a large set of terms and acronyms that contains many synonyms, networking jargon contains terms that are often abbreviated, misused, or associated with products.

1.3 The Five Key Aspects Of Networking

To master the complexity in networking, it is important to gain a broad background that includes five key aspects of the subject:

- Network Applications And Network Programming
- Data Communications
- Packet Switching And Networking Technologies
- Internetworking With TCP/IP
- Additional Networking Concepts And Technologies

1.3.1 Network Applications And Network Programming

The network services and facilities that users invoke are each provided by application software — an application program on one computer communicates across a network with an application program running on another computer. Network application services span a wide range that includes email, file transfer, web browsing, voice telephone calls, distributed databases, and audio and video teleconferencing. Although each application offers a specific service with its own form of user interface, all applications can communicate over a single, shared network. The availability of a unified underlying network that supports all applications makes a programmer's job much easier because a programmer only needs to learn about one interface to the network and one basic set of functions — the same set of functions are used in all application programs that communicate over a network.

As we will see, it is possible to understand network applications, and even possible to write code that communicates over a network, without understanding the hardware and software technologies that are used to transfer data from one application to another. It may seem that once a programmer masters the interface, no further knowledge of networking is needed. However, network programming is analogous to conventional programming. Although a conventional programmer can create applications without understanding compilers, operating systems, or computer architecture, knowledge of the underlying systems can help a programmer create more reliable, correct, and efficient programs. Similarly, knowledge of the underlying network system allows a programmer to write better code. The point can be summarized:

> *A programmer who understands the underlying network mechanisms and technologies can write network applications that are more reliable, correct, and efficient.*

1.3.2 Data Communications

The term *data communications* refers to the study of low-level mechanisms and technologies used to send information across a physical communication medium, such as a wire, radio wave, or light beam. Data communications is primarily the domain of Electrical Engineering, which studies how to design and construct a wide range of communication systems. Data communications focuses on ways to use physical phenomena to transfer information. Thus, many of the basic ideas are derived from the properties of matter and energy that have been studied by physicists. For example, we will see that the optical fibers used for high-speed data transfer rely on the properties of light and its reflection at a boundary between two types of matter.

Because it deals with physical concepts, data communications may seem somewhat irrelevant to our understanding of networking. In particular, because many of the terms and concepts refer to physical phenomena, the subject may only seem useful for engineers who design low-level transmission facilities. For example, modulation techniques that use physical forms of energy, such as electromagnetic radiation, to carry information appear to be irrelevant to the design and use of protocols. However, we will see that several key concepts that arise from data communications influence the design of many protocol layers. In the case of modulation, the concept of bandwidth relates directly to network throughput.

As a specific case, data communications introduces the notion of multiplexing that allows information from multiple sources to be combined for transmission across a shared medium and later separated for delivery to multiple destinations. We will see that multiplexing is not restricted to physical transmission — most protocols incorporate some form of multiplexing. Similarly, the concept of encryption introduced in data communications forms the basis of most network security. Thus, we can summarize the importance:

> *Although it deals with many low-level details, data communications provides a foundation of concepts on which the rest of networking is built.*

1.3.3 Packet Switching And Networking Technologies

In the 1960s, a new concept revolutionized data communications: packet switching. Early communication networks had evolved from telegraph and telephone systems that connected a physical pair of wires between two parties to form a communication circuit. Although mechanical connection of wires was being replaced by electronic switches, the underlying paradigm remained the same: form a circuit and then send information across the circuit. Packet switching changed networking in a fundamental way, and provided the basis for the modern Internet: instead of forming a dedicated circuit, packet switching allows multiple senders to transmit data over a shared network. Packet switching builds on the same fundamental data communications mechanisms as the phone system, but uses the underlying mechanisms in a new way. Packet switching divides data into small blocks, called packets, and includes an identification of the intended recipient in each packet. Devices throughout the network each have information about how to reach each possible destination. When a packet arrives at one of the devices, the device chooses a path over which to send the packet so the packet eventually reaches the correct destination.

In theory, packet switching is straightforward. However, many designs are possible, depending on the answers to basic questions. How should a destination be identified, and how can a sender find the identification of a destination? How large should a packet be? How can a network recognize the end of one packet and the beginning of another packet? If many computers are sending over a network, how can they coordinate to insure that each receives a fair opportunity to send? How can packet switching be adapted to wireless networks? How can networking technologies be designed to meet various requirements for speed, distance, and economic cost? Many answers have been proposed, and many packet switching technologies have been created. In fact, when one studies packet switching networks, a fundamental conclusion can be drawn:

> *Because each network technology is created to meet various requirements for speed, distance, and economic cost, many packet switching technologies exist. Technologies differ in details such as the size of packets and the method used to identify a recipient.*

1.3.4 Internetworking With TCP/IP

In the 1970s, another revolution in computer networking arose: the concept of an Internet. Many researchers who investigated packet switching looked for a single packet switching technology that could handle all needs. In 1973, Vinton Cerf and Robert Kahn observed that no single packet switching technology would ever satisfy all needs, especially because it would be possible to build low-capacity technologies for homes or offices at extremely low cost. The solution, they suggested, was to stop trying to find a single best solution, and instead, explore interconnecting many packet switching technologies into a functioning whole. They proposed that a set of standards be developed for such an interconnection, and the resulting standards became known as the *TCP/IP Internet Protocol Suite* (usually abbreviated *TCP/IP*). The concept, now known as *internetworking*, is extremely powerful. It provides the basis of the global Internet, and forms an important part of the study of computer networking.

One of the primary reasons for the success of TCP/IP standards lies in their tolerance of heterogeneity. Instead of attempting to dictate details about packet switching technologies, such as packet sizes or the method used to identify a destination, TCP/IP takes a virtualization approach that defines a network-independent packet and a network-independent identification scheme, and then specifies how the virtual packets are mapped onto each possible underlying network.

Interestingly, TCP/IP's ability to tolerate new packet switching networks is a major motivation for the continual evolution of packet switching technologies. As the Internet grows, computers become more powerful and applications send more data, especially graphic images and video. To accommodate increases in use, engineers invent new technologies that can transmit more data and process more packets in a given time. As they are invented, new technologies are incorporated into the Internet along with extant technologies. That is, because the Internet tolerates heterogeneity, engineers can experiment with new networking technologies without disrupting the existing networks. To summarize:

> *The Internet is formed by interconnecting multiple packet switching networks. Internetworking is substantially more powerful than a single networking technology because the approach permits new technologies to be incorporated at any time without requiring the replacement of old technologies.*

1.4 Public And Private Parts Of The Internet

Although it functions as a single communication system, the Internet consists of parts that are owned and operated by individuals or organizations. To help clarify ownership and purpose, the networking industry uses the terms *public network* and *private network*.

1.4.1 Public Network

A *public network* is run as a service that is available to subscribers. Any individual or corporation who pays the subscription fee can use the network. A company that offers communication service is known as a *service provider*. The concept of a service provider is quite broad, and extends beyond *Internet Service Providers (ISPs)*. In fact, the terminology originated with companies that offered analog voice telephone service. To summarize:

> *A public network is owned by a service provider, and offers service to any individual or organization that pays the subscription fee.*

It is important to understand that the term *public* refers to the general availability of service, not to the data transferred. In particular, many public networks follow strict government regulations that require the provider to protect communication from unintended snooping. The point is:

> *The term* public *means a service is available to the general public; data transferred across a public network is not revealed to outsiders.*

1.4.2 Private Network

A *private network* is controlled by one particular group. Although it may seem straightforward, the distinction between public and private parts of the Internet can be subtle because control does not always imply ownership. For example, if a company leases a data circuit from a provider and then restricts use of the circuit to company traffic, the circuit becomes part of the company's private network. The point is:

> *A network is said to be* private *if use of the network is restricted to one group. A private network can include circuits leased from a provider.*

Networking equipment vendors divide private networks into four categories:

- Consumer
- Small Office / Home Office (SOHO)
- Small-To-Medium Business (SMB)
- Large Enterprise

Because the categories relate to sales and marketing, the terminology is loosely defined. Although it is possible to give a qualitative description of each type, one cannot find an exact definition. Thus, the paragraphs below provide a broad characterization of size and purpose rather than detailed measures.

Consumer. One of the least expensive forms of private network consists of a LAN owned by an individual — if an individual purchases an inexpensive LAN switch and uses the switch to attach a printer to a PC, the individual has created a private network. Similarly, a wireless router constitutes a private network that a consumer might purchase and install.

Small Office/Home Office (SOHO). A SOHO network is slightly larger than a consumer network. A typical SOHO network connects two or more computers, one or more printers, a router that connects to the Internet, and possibly other devices, such as a cash register. Most SOHO installations include a battery-backup power supply and other mechanisms that allow them to operate without interruption.

Small-To-Medium Business (SMB). An SMB network can connect many computers in multiple offices in a building, and can also include computers in a production facility (e.g., in a shipping department). Often an SMB network contains multiple Layer-2 switches interconnected by routers, uses a broadband Internet connection, and may include wireless access points.

Large Enterprise. A large enterprise network provides the IT infrastructure needed for a major corporation. A typical large enterprise network connects several geographic sites with multiple buildings at each site, uses many Layer-2 switches and routers, and has two or more high-speed Internet connections. Enterprise networks usually include both wired and wireless technologies.

To summarize:

> *A private network can serve an individual consumer, a small office, a small-to-medium business, or a large enterprise.*

1.5 Networks, Interoperability, And Standards

Communication always involves at least two entities, one that sends information and another that receives it. In fact, we will see that most packet switching communication systems contain intermediate entities (i.e., devices that forward packets). The important point to note is that for communication to be successful, all entities in a network must agree on how information will be represented and communicated. Communication agreements involve many details. For example, when two entities communicate over a wired network, both sides must agree on the voltages to be used, the exact way that electrical signals are used to represent data, procedures used to initiate and conduct communication, and the format of messages.

We use the term *interoperability* to refer to the ability of two entities to communicate, and say that if two entities can communicate without any misunderstandings, they *interoperate* correctly. To insure that all communicating parties agree on details and follow the same set of rules, an exact set of specifications is written down. To summarize:

> *Communication involves multiple entities that must agree on details ranging from the electrical voltage used to the format and meaning of messages. To insure that entities can interoperate correctly, rules for all aspects of communication are written down.*

Following diplomatic terminology, we use the term *communication protocol, network protocol*, or *protocol* to refer to a specification for network communication. A given protocol specifies low-level details, such as the type of radio transmission used in a wireless network, or describes a high-level mechanism such as the messages that two application programs exchange. We said that a protocol can define a procedure to be followed during an exchange. One of the most important aspects of a protocol concerns situations in which an error or unexpected condition occurs. Thus, a protocol usually explains the appropriate action to take for each possible abnormal condition (e.g., a response is expected, but no response arrives). To summarize:

> *A communication protocol specifies the details for one aspect of computer communication, including actions to be taken when errors or unexpected situations arise. A given protocol can specify low-level details, such as the voltage and signals to be used, or high-level items, such as the format of messages that application programs exchange.*

1.6 Protocol Suites And Layering Models

A set of protocols must be constructed carefully to ensure that the resulting communication system is both complete and efficient. To avoid duplication of effort, for example, each protocol should handle a part of communication not handled by other protocols. How can one guarantee that protocols will work well together? The answer lies in an overall design plan: instead of creating each protocol in isolation, protocols are designed in complete, cooperative sets called *suites* or *families*. Each protocol in a suite handles one aspect of communication; together, the protocols in a suite cover all aspects of communication, including hardware failures and other exceptional conditions. Furthermore, the entire suite is designed to allow the protocols to work together efficiently.

The fundamental abstraction used to collect protocols into a unified whole is known as a *layering model*. In essence, a layering model describes how all aspects of a communication problem can be partitioned into pieces that work together. Each piece is known as a *layer*; the terminology arises because protocols in a suite are organized into a linear sequence. Dividing protocols into layers helps both protocol designers and implementors manage the complexity by allowing them to concentrate on one aspect of communication at a given time.

Figure 1.1 illustrates the concept by showing the layering model used with the Internet protocols. The visual appearance of figures used to illustrate layering has led to the colloquial term *stack*. The term is used to refer to the protocol software on a computer, as in "does that computer run the TCP/IP stack?"

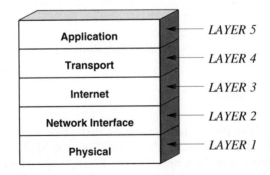

Figure 1.1 The layering model used with the Internet protocols (TCP/IP).

Later chapters will help us understand layering by explaining protocols in detail. For now, it is sufficient to learn the purpose of each layer and how protocols are used for communication. The next sections summarize the role of the layers; a later section examines how data passes through layers when computers communicate.

Layer 1: Physical

Protocols in the *Physical* layer specify details about the underlying transmission medium and the associated hardware. All specifications related to electrical properties, radio frequencies, and signals belong in layer 1.

Layer 2: Network Interface†

Protocols in the *Network Interface* layer specify details about communication between higher layers of protocols, which are usually implemented in software, and the underlying network, which is implemented in hardware. Specifications about network addresses and the maximum packet size that a network can support, protocols used to access the underlying medium, and hardware addressing belong in layer 2.

Layer 3: Internet

Protocols in the *Internet* layer form the fundamental basis for the Internet. Layer 3 protocols specify communication between two computers across the Internet (i.e., across multiple interconnected networks). The Internet addressing structure, the format of Internet packets, the method for dividing a large Internet packet into smaller packets for transmission, and mechanisms for reporting errors belong in layer 3.

Layer 4: Transport

Protocols in the *Transport* layer provide for communication from an application program on one computer to an application program on another. Specifications that control the maximum rate a receiver can accept data, mechanisms to avoid network congestion, and techniques to insure that all data is received in the correct order belong in layer 4.

Layer 5: Application

Protocols in the top layer of the TCP/IP stack specify how a pair of applications interact when they communicate. Layer 5 protocols specify details about the format and meaning of messages that applications can exchange as well as procedures to be followed during communication. Specifications for email exchange, file transfer, web browsing, telephone services, and video teleconferencing all belong in layer 5.

---

†Some publications use the term *Data Link* in place of *Network Interface*. In a later section, we will see that ambiguity can arise because another layering model uses *Data Link* for layer 2.

1.7 How Data Passes Through Layers

Layering is not merely an abstract concept that helps one understand protocols. Instead, protocol implementations follow the layering model by passing the output from a protocol in one layer to the input of a protocol in the next layer. Furthermore, to achieve efficiency, rather than copy an entire packet, a pair of protocols in adjacent layers pass a pointer to the packet. Thus, data passes between layers efficiently.

To understand how protocols operate, consider two computers connected to a network. Figure 1.2 illustrates layered protocols on the two computers. As the figure shows, each computer contains a set of layered protocols. When an application sends data, the data is placed in a packet, and the outgoing packet passes down through each layer of protocols. Once it has passed through all layers of protocols on the sending computer, the packet leaves the computer and is transmitted across the underlying physical network†. When it reaches the receiving computer, the packet passes up through the layers of protocols. If the application on the receiving computer sends a response, the process is reversed. That is, a response passes down through the layers on its way out, and up through the layers on the computer that receives the response.

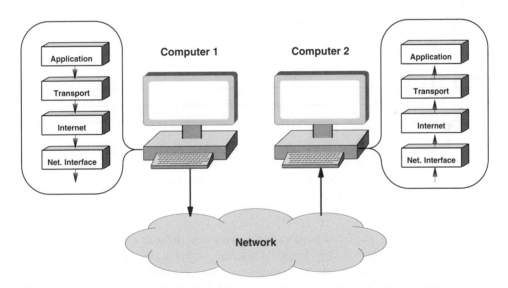

Figure 1.2 Illustration of how data passes among protocol layers when computers communicate across a network. Each computer has a set of layered protocols, and data passes through each layer.

---

†The figure shows only one network. When we study Internet architecture, we will learn about intermediate devices called *routers* and see how layered protocols operate in an Internet.

1.8 Headers And Layers

We will learn that each layer of protocol software performs computations that insure the messages arrive as expected. To perform such computation, protocol software on the two machines must exchange information. To do so, each layer on the sending computer prepends extra information onto the packet; the corresponding protocol layer on the receiving computer removes and uses the extra information.

Additional information added by a protocol is known as a *header*. To understand how headers appear, think of a packet traveling across the network between the two computers in Figure 1.2. Headers are added by protocol software as the data passes down through the layers on the sending computer. That is, the Transport layer prepends a header, and then the Internet layer prepends a header, and so on. Thus, if we observe a packet traversing the network, the headers will appear in the order that Figure 1.3 illustrates.

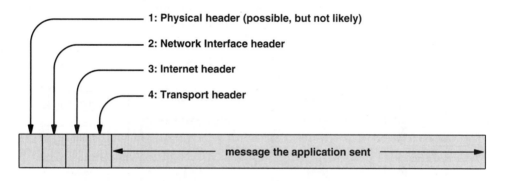

Figure 1.3 The nested protocol headers that appear on a packet as the packet travels across a network between two computers. In the diagram, the beginning of the packet (the first bit sent over the underlying network) is shown on the left.

Although the figure shows headers as the same size, in practice headers are not of uniform size, and a physical layer header is optional. We will understand the reason for the size disparities when we examine header contents. Similarly, we will see that the physical layer usually specifies how signals are used to transmit data. Thus, one does not expect to find a Physical layer header.

1.9 ISO and the OSI Seven Layer Reference Model

At the same time the Internet protocols were being developed, two large standards bodies jointly formed an alternative reference model. They also created a set of internetworking protocols. The organizations are:

- International Organization for Standardization (ISO)
- International Telecommunications Union, Telecommunication Standardization Sector (ITU-T)†,

The ISO layering model is known as the *Open Systems Interconnection Seven-Layer Reference Model*. Confusion arises in terminology because the acronym for the protocols, OSI, and the acronym for the organization, ISO, are similar. One is likely to find references to both the *OSI seven-layer model* and to the *ISO seven-layer model*. Figure 1.4 illustrates the seven layers in the model.

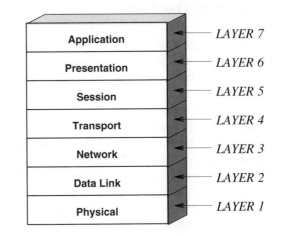

Figure 1.4 The OSI seven-layer model standardized by ISO.

1.10 The Inside Scoop

Like most standards organizations, ISO and the ITU use a process that accommodates as many viewpoints as possible when creating a standard. As a result, some standards can appear to have been designed by a committee making political compromises rather than by engineers and scientists. The seven-layer reference model is controversial. It did indeed start as a political compromise. Furthermore, the model and the OSI protocols were designed as competitors for the Internet protocols.

ISO and the ITU are huge standards bodies that handle the world-wide telephone system and other global standards. The Internet protocols and reference model were

---

†When the standard was first created, the ITU was known as the *Consultative Committee for International Telephone and Telegraph (CCITT)*.

created by a small group of about a dozen researchers. It is easy to see why the standards organizations might be confident that they could dictate a set of protocols and everyone would switch away from protocols designed by researchers. At one point, even the U.S. government was convinced that TCP/IP should be replaced by OSI protocols.

Eventually, it became clear that TCP/IP technology was technically superior to OSI, and in a matter of a few years, efforts to develop and deploy OSI protocols were terminated. Standards bodies were left with the seven-layer model, which did not include an Internet layer. Consequently, for many years, advocates for the seven-layer model have tried to stretch the definitions to match TCP/IP. They argue that layer three could be considered an Internet layer and that a few support protocols might be placed into layers five and six. Perhaps the most humorous part of the story is that many engineers still refer to applications as *layer 7 protocols*, even when they know that layers five and six are unfilled and unnecessary.

1.11 Remainder Of The Text

The text is divided into five major parts. After a brief introduction, chapters in the first part introduce network applications and network programming. Readers who have access to a computer are encouraged to build and use application programs that use the Internet while they read the text. The remaining four parts explain how the underlying technologies work. The second part describes data communications and the transmission of information. It explains how electrical and electromagnetic energy can be used to carry information across wires or through the air, and shows how data is transmitted.

The third part of the text focuses on packet switching and packet technologies. It explains why computer networks use packets, describes the general format of packets, examines how packets are encoded for transmission, and shows how each packet is forwarded across a network to its destination. The third part of text also introduces basic categories of computer networks, such as Local Area Networks (LANs) and Wide Area Networks (WANs). It characterizes the properties of each category and discusses example technologies.

The fourth part of the text covers internetworking and the associated TCP/IP Internet Protocol Suite. The text explains the structure of the Internet and the TCP/IP protocols. It explains the IP addressing scheme, and describes the mapping between Internet addresses and underlying hardware addresses. It also discusses Internet routing and routing protocols. The fourth part includes a description of several fundamental concepts, including: encapsulation, fragmentation, congestion and flow control, virtual connections, address translation, bootstrapping, IPv6, and various support protocols.

The fifth part of the text covers a variety of remaining topics that pertain to the network as a whole instead of individual parts. After a chapter on network performance, chapters cover emerging technologies, network security, and network management.

1.12 Summary

The large set of technologies, products, and interconnection schemes make networking a complex subject. There are five key aspects: network applications and network programming, data communications, packet switching and networking technologies, internetworking with TCP/IP, and topics that apply across layers, such as security and network management.

Because multiple entities are involved in communication, they must agree on details, including electrical characteristics such as voltage as well as the format and meaning of all messages. To insure interoperability, each entity is constructed to obey a set of communication protocols that specify all details needed for communication. To insure that protocols work together and handle all aspects of communication, an entire set of protocols is designed at the same time. The central abstraction around which protocols are built is called a *layering model*. Layering helps reduce complexity by allowing an engineer to focus on one aspect of communication at a given time without worrying about other aspects. The TCP/IP protocols used in the Internet follow a five-layer reference model; the phone companies and International Standards Organization proposed a seven-layer reference model.

EXERCISES

1.1   List ten industries that depend on computer networking.

1.2   Provide a brief history of the Internet describing when and how it was started.

1.3   List the layers in the TCP/IP model, and give a brief explanation of each.

1.4   What is a protocol suite, and what is the advantage of a suite?

1.5   Describe the TCP/IP layering model, and explain how it was derived.

1.6   Provide reasons for Internet growth in recent years.

1.7   What is interoperability, and why is it especially important in the Internet?

1.8   According to the text, is it possible to develop Internet applications without understanding the architecture of the Internet and the technologies? Support your answer.

1.9   To what aspects of networking does *data communications* refer?

1.10 What is a communication protocol? Conceptually, what two aspects of communication does a protocol specify?

1.11 List major standardization organizations that create standards for data communications and computer networking.

1.12 Give a brief explain of the layers in the ISO Open System Interconnection model.

1.13 What is packet-switching, and why is packet switching relevant to the Internet?

1.14 Explain how headers are added and removed as data passes through a layered model.

Chapter Contents

2

Internet Trends

2.1 Introduction

This chapter considers how data networking and the Internet have changed since their inception. The chapter begins with a brief history of the Internet that highlights some of the early motivations. It describes a shift in emphasis from sharing centralized facilities to fully distributed information systems.

Later chapters in this part of the text continue the discussion by examining specific Internet applications. In addition to describing the communication paradigms available on the Internet, the chapters explain the programming interface that Internet applications use to communicate.

2.2 Resource Sharing

Early computer networks were designed when computers were large and expensive, and the main motivation was *resource sharing*. For example, networks were devised to connect multiple users, each with a screen and keyboard, to a large centralized computer. Later networks allowed multiple users to share peripheral devices such as printers. The point is:

> *Early computer networks were designed to permit sharing of expensive, centralized resources.*

17

In the 1960s, the *Advanced Research Projects Agency (ARPA†)*, an agency of the U.S. Department of Defense, was especially interested in finding ways to share resources. Researchers needed powerful computers, and computers were incredibly expensive. The ARPA budget was insufficient to fund many computers. Thus, ARPA began investigating data networking — instead of buying a computer for each project, ARPA planned to interconnect all computers with a data network and devise software that would allow a researcher to use whichever computer was best suited to perform a given task.

ARPA gathered some of the best minds available, focused them on networking research, and hired contractors to turn the designs into a working system called the *ARPANET*. The research turned out to be revolutionary. The research team chose to follow an approach known as *packet switching* that became the basis for data networks and the Internet‡. ARPA continued the project by funding the Internet research project. During the 1980s, the Internet expanded as a research effort, and during the 1990s, the Internet became a commercial success.

2.3 Growth Of The Internet

In less than 30 years, the Internet has grown from an early research prototype connecting a handful of sites to a global communication system that extends to all countries of the world. The rate of growth has been phenomenal. Figure 2.1 illustrates the growth with a graph of the number of computers attached to the Internet as a function of the years from 1981 through 2008.

The graph in Figure 2.1 uses a linear scale in which the y-axis represents values from zero through five hundred fifty million. Linear plots can be deceptive because they hide small details. For example, the graph hides details about early Internet growth, making it appear that the Internet did not start to grow until approximately 1994 and that the majority of growth occurred in the last few years. In fact, the average rate of new computers added to the Internet reached more than one per second in 1998, and has accelerated. In 2007, more than two computers were added to the Internet each second. To understand the early growth rate, look at the plot in Figure 2.2, which uses a log scale.

---

†At various times, the agency has included the word *Defense*, and used the acronym *DARPA*.
‡Chapter 13 discusses packet switching.

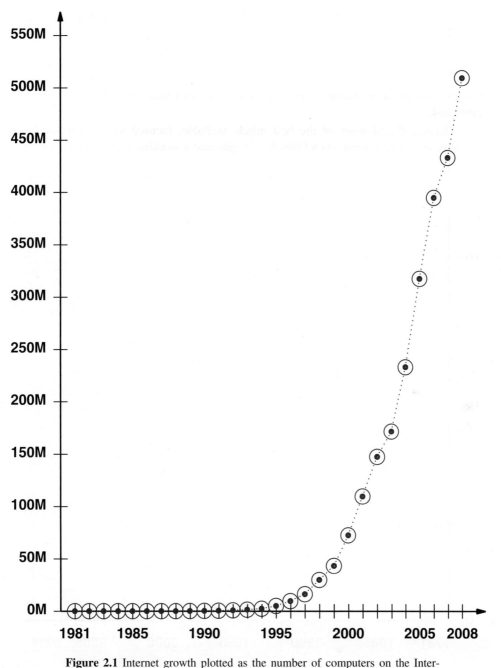

Figure 2.1 Internet growth plotted as the number of computers on the Internet.

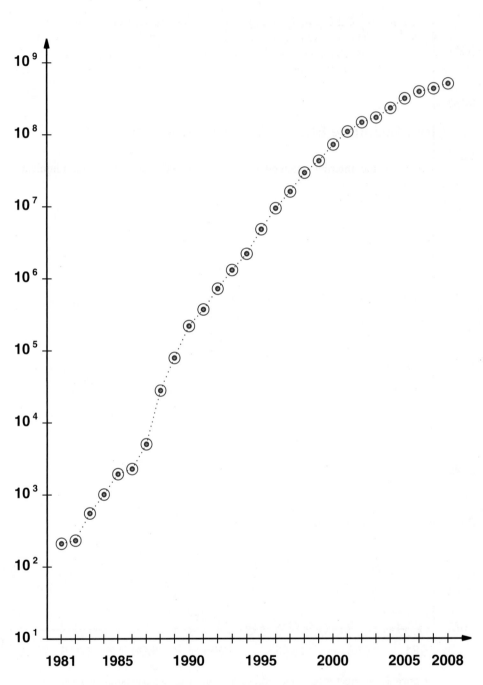

Figure 2.2 Internet growth plotted on a log scale.

The plot in Figure 2.2 reveals that the Internet has experienced exponential growth for over 25 years. That is, the Internet has been doubling in size every nine to fourteen months. Interestingly, the exponential growth rate has declined slightly since the late 1990s as a significant percentage of the population in developed countries gained access.

2.4 From Resource Sharing To Communication

As it grew, the Internet changed in two significant ways. First, communication speeds increased dramatically — a backbone link in the Internet can carry 100,000 times as many bits per second as a backbone link in the original Internet. Second, new applications arose that appealed to a broad cross-section of society. The second point is obvious — the Internet is no longer dominated by scientists and engineers, scientific applications, or access to computational resources.

Two technological changes fueled a shift away from resource sharing to new applications. On one hand, higher communication speeds enabled applications to transfer large volumes of data quickly. On the other hand, the advent of powerful, affordable, personal computers provided the computational power needed for complex computation and graphical displays, eliminating most of the demand for shared resources.

The point is:

> *The availability of high-speed computation and communication technologies shifted the focus of the Internet from resource sharing to general-purpose communication.*

2.5 From Text To Multimedia

One of the most obvious shifts has occurred in the data being sent across the Internet. Figure 2.3 illustrates one aspect of the shift.

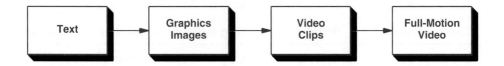

Figure 2.3 A shift in the type of data users send across the Internet.

As the figure indicates, Internet communication initially involved textual data. In particular, email messages were limited to text displayed in fixed-width font. By the

1990s, computers had color screens capable of displaying graphics, and applications arose that allowed users to transfer images easily. By the late 1990s, users began sending video clips, and full-motion videos became feasible. Figure 2.4 illustrates that a similar transition has occurred in audio.

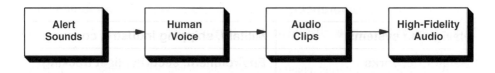

Figure 2.4 A shift in the audio that users send across the Internet.

We use the term *multimedia* to characterize data that contains a combination of text, graphics, audio, and video. Much of the content available on the Internet now consists of multimedia documents. Furthermore, quality has improved as higher bandwidths have made it possible to communicate high-resolution video and high-fidelity audio. To summarize:

> *Internet use has transitioned from the transfer of static, textual documents to the transfer of high-quality multimedia content.*

2.6 Recent Trends

Surprisingly, new networking technologies and new Internet applications continue to emerge. Some of the most significant transitions have occurred as traditional communication systems, such as the voice telephone network and cable television, moved from analog to digital and adopted Internet technology. In addition, support for mobile users is accelerating. Figure 2.5 lists some of the changes.

Topic	Transition
Telephone system	Switch from analog to Voice over IP (VoIP)
Cable television	Switch from analog delivery to Internet Protocol (IP)
Cellular	Switch from analog to digital cellular services (3G)
Internet access	Switch from wired to wireless access (Wi-Fi)
Data access	Switch from centralized to distributed services (P2P)

Figure 2.5 Examples of transitions in networking and the Internet.

One of the most interesting aspects of the Internet arises from the way that Internet applications change even though the underlying technology essentially remains the same. For example, Figure 2.6 lists types of applications that have emerged.

Application	Significant For
High-quality teleconferencing	Business-to-business communication
Navigation systems	Military, shipping industry, consumers
Sensor networks	Environment, security, fleet tracking
Social networking	Consumers, volunteer organizations

Figure 2.6 Examples of popular applications.

The availability of high-quality teleconferencing systems such as Cisco's *TelePresence* is significant for businesses because such systems permit meetings to occur without travel expense. In many businesses, reducing travel expenses lowers costs significantly.

Social networking applications such as Facebook, Second Life, and YouTube are fascinating because they have created new social connections — sets of people know each other only through the Internet. Sociologists suggest that such applications will enable more people to find others with shared interests, and will foster small social groups.

2.7 Summary

The Advanced Research Projects Agency (ARPA) funded much of the early investigations into networking as a way to share computation resources among ARPA researchers. Later, ARPA shifted its focus to internetworking and funded research on the Internet, which has been growing exponentially for decades.

With the advent of high-speed personal computers and higher-speed network technologies, the focus of the Internet changed from resource sharing to general-purpose communication. The type of data sent over the Internet shifted from text to graphics, video clips, and full-motion video. A similar transition occurred in audio, enabling the Internet to transfer multimedia documents.

Internet technologies impact society in many ways. Recent changes include the transition of voice telephones, cable television, and cellular services to use digital Internet technologies. In addition, wireless Internet access and support for mobile users has become essential.

Although the underlying Internet technology has remained virtually unchanged, new applications continue to emerge that provide enhanced experiences for Internet users. Businesses use high-end teleconferencing systems to reduce travel costs. Sensor networks, maps, and navigation systems enable environmental monitoring, security, and easier travel. Social networking applications encourage new social groups and organizations.

EXERCISES

2.1 Describe the evolution in audio that has occurred in the Internet.

2.2 Assume that one hundred million new computers are added to the Internet each year. If computers are added at a uniform rate, how much time elapses between two successive additions?

2.3 Describe Internet applications that you use regularly that were not available to your parents when they were your age.

2.4 Why was sharing of computational resources important in the 1960s?

2.5 What shift in Internet use occurred when the World Wide Web first appeared?

2.6 The plot in Figure 2.1 shows that Internet growth did not start until after 1995. Why is the figure misleading?

2.7 List the steps in the transition in graphics presentation from the early Internet to the current Internet.

2.8 What Internet technology is the telephone system using?

2.9 Extend the plot in Figure 2.2, and estimate how many computers will be connected to the Internet by 2020.

2.10 What impact is Internet technology having on the cable television industry?

2.11 List four new Internet applications, and tell the groups for which each is important.

2.12 Why is the switch from wired Internet access to wireless Internet access significant?

Chapter Contents

3

Internet Applications And Network Programming

3.1 Introduction

The Internet offers users a rich diversity of services that include web browsing, email, text messaging, and video teleconferences. Surprisingly, none of the services is part of the underlying communication infrastructure. Instead, the Internet provides a general purpose communication mechanism on which all services are built, and individual services are supplied by application programs that run on computers attached to the Internet. In fact, it is possible to devise entirely new services without changing the Internet.

This chapter covers two key concepts that explain Internet applications. First, the chapter describes the conceptual paradigm that applications follow when they communicate over the Internet. Second, the chapter presents the details of the *socket Application Programming Interface* (socket API) that Internet applications use.

The chapter demonstrates that one does not need to understand the details of data communication or network protocols to write innovative applications — once a programmer masters a few basic concepts, it is possible to construct applications that communicate over the Internet. The next chapter continues the discussion by examining example Internet applications such as email.

Although programmers can get started easily, and it is possible to create Internet applications without knowing how networks operate, understanding network protocols and technologies allows a programmer to write efficient and reliable code that enables

27

applications to scale across many sites. Later parts of the text provide the necessary information by explaining data communications and protocols used to form the Internet.

3.2 Two Basic Internet Communication Paradigms

The Internet supports two basic communication paradigms: a *stream* paradigm and a *message* paradigm. Figure 3.1 summarizes the differences.

Stream Paradigm	Message Paradigm
Connection-oriented	Connectionless
1-to-1 communication	Many-to-many communication
Sequence of individual bytes	Sequence of individual messages
Arbitrary length transfer	Each message limited to 64 Kbytes
Used by most applications	Used for multimedia applications
Built on TCP protocol	Built on UDP protocol

Figure 3.1 The two paradigms that Internet applications use.

3.2.1 Stream Transport In The Internet

The term *stream* denotes a paradigm in which a sequence of bytes flows from one application program to another. In fact, the Internet's mechanism arranges two streams between a pair of communicating applications, one in each direction. For example, a browser uses the stream service to communicate with a web server: the browser sends a request and the web server responds by sending the page. The network accepts input from either application, and delivers the data to the other application.

The stream mechanism transfers a sequence of bytes without attaching meaning to the bytes and without inserting boundaries. In particular, a sending application can choose to generate one byte at a time, or can generate blocks of bytes. The network chooses the number of bytes to deliver at any time. That is, the network can choose to combine smaller blocks into one large block or can divide a large block into smaller blocks. The point is:

> *Although it delivers all bytes in sequence, the stream paradigm does not guarantee that the chunks of bytes passed to a receiving application correspond to the chunks of bytes transferred by the sending application.*

3.2.2 Message Transport In The Internet

The alternative Internet communication mechanism follows a *message paradigm* in which the network accepts and delivers messages. Each message delivered to a receiver corresponds to a message that was transmitted by a sender; the network never delivers part of a message, nor does it join multiple messages together. Thus, if a sender places exactly *n* bytes in an outgoing message, the receiver will find exactly *n* bytes in the incoming message.

The message paradigm allows unicast, multicast, or broadcast delivery. That is, a message can be sent from an application on one computer directly to an application on another, the message can be broadcast to all computers on a given network, or the message can be multicast to some of the computers on a network. Furthermore, applications on many computers can send messages to a given application. Thus, the message paradigm can provide 1-to-1, 1-to-many, or many-to-1 communication.

Surprisingly, the message service does not make any guarantees about the order in which messages are delivered or whether a given message will arrive. The service permits messages to be:

- Lost (i.e., never delivered)
- Duplicated (more than one copy arrives)
- Delivered out-of-order

A programmer who uses the message paradigm must insure that the application operates correctly, even if packets are lost or reordered†. Because most applications require delivery guarantees, programmers tend to use the stream service except in special situations, such as video, where multicast is needed and the application provides support to handle packet reordering and loss. Thus, we will focus on the stream paradigm.

3.3 Connection-oriented Communication

The Internet stream service is *connection-oriented*, which means the service operates analogous to a telephone call: before they can communicate, two applications must request that a *connection* be created. Once it has been established, the connection allows the applications to send data in either direction. Finally, when they finish communicating, the applications request that the connection be terminated. Algorithm 3.1 summarizes the interaction.

---

†Later chapters explain why such errors can occur.

Algorithm 3.1

Purpose:

Interaction over a connection-oriented mechanism

Method:

A pair of applications requests a connection

The pair uses the connection to exchange data

The pair requests that the connection be terminated

Algorithm 3.1 Communication over a connection-oriented mechanism.

3.4 The Client-Server Model Of Interaction

The first step in Algorithm 3.1 raises a question: how can a pair of applications that run on two independent computers coordinate to guarantee that they request a connection at the same time? The answer lies in a form of interaction known as the *client-server model*. One application, known as a *server*, starts first and awaits contact. The other application, known as a *client*, start second and initiates the connection. Figure 3.2 summarizes the interaction.

Server Application	Client Application
Starts first	Starts second
Does not need to know which client will contact it	Must know which server to contact
Waits passively and arbitrarily long for contact from a client	Initiates a contact whenever communication is needed
Communicates with a client by both sending and receiving data	Communicates with a server by sending and receiving data
Stays running after servicing one client, and waits for another	May terminate after interacting with a server

Figure 3.2 A summary of the client-server model.

Subsequent sections describe how specific services use the client-server model. For now, it is sufficient to understand:

*Although it provides basic communication, the Internet does not ini-
tiate contact with, or accept contact from, a remote computer; application programs known as a clients and severs handle all services.*

3.5 Characteristics Of Clients And Servers

Although minor variations exist, most instances of client-server interaction have
the same general characteristics. In general, client software:

- Is an arbitrary application program that becomes a client temporari-
  ly when remote access is needed, but also performs other computa-
  tion
- Is invoked directly by a user, and executes only for one session
- Runs locally on a user's personal computer
- Actively initiates contact with a server
- Can access multiple services as needed, but usually contacts one re-
  mote server at a time
- Does not require especially powerful computer hardware

In contrast, server software:

- Is a special-purpose, privileged program dedicated to providing one
  service that can handle multiple remote clients at the same time
- Is invoked automatically when a system boots, and continues to ex-
  ecute through many sessions
- Runs on a large, powerful computer
- Waits passively for contact from arbitrary remote clients
- Accepts contact from arbitrary clients, but offers a single service
- Requires powerful hardware and a sophisticated operating system

3.6 Server Programs And Server-Class Computers

Confusion sometimes arises over the term *server*. Formally, the term refers to a
program that waits passively for communication, and not to the computer on which it
executes. However, when a computer is dedicated to running one or more server programs, the computer itself is sometimes called a *server*. Hardware vendors contribute to
the confusion because they classify computers that have fast CPUs, large memories, and
powerful operating systems as *server* machines. Figure 3.3 illustrates the definitions.

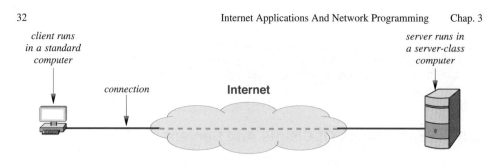

Figure 3.3 Illustration of a client and server.

3.7 Requests, Responses, And Direction Of Data Flow

The terms *client* and *server* arise from which side initiates contact. Once contact has been established, two-way communication is possible (i.e., data can flow from a client to a server or from a server to a client). Typically, a client sends a request to a server, and the server returns a response to the client. In some cases, a client sends a series of requests and the server issues a series of responses (e.g., a database client might allow a user to look up more than one item at a time). The concept can be summarized:

> *Information can flow in either or both directions between a client and server. Although many services arrange for the client to send one or more requests and the server to return responses, other interactions are possible.*

3.8 Multiple Clients And Multiple Servers

A client or server consists of an application program, and a computer can run multiple applications at the same time. As a consequence, a computer can run:

- A single client
- A single server
- Multiple copies of a client that contact a given server
- Multiple clients that each contact a particular server
- Multiple servers, each for a particular service

Allowing a computer to operate multiple clients is useful because services can be accessed simultaneously. For example, a user can have three windows open simultaneously running three applications: one that retrieves and displays email, another that connects to a chat service, and a third running a web browser. Each application is a client that contacts a particular server independent of the others. In fact, the technology allows a user to have two copies of a single application open, each contacting a server (e.g., two copies of a web browser).

Allowing a given computer to operate multiple servers is useful because the hardware can be shared. In addition, a single computer has lower system administration overhead than multiple computer systems. More important, experience has shown that the demand for a server is often sporadic — a server can remain idle for long periods of time. An idle server does not use the CPU while waiting for a request to arrive. Thus, if demand for services is low, consolidating servers on a single computer can dramatically reduce cost without significantly reducing performance. To summarize:

> *A single, powerful computer can offer multiple services at the same time; a separate server program is needed for each service.*

3.9 Server Identification And Demultiplexing

How does a client identify a server? The Internet protocols divide identification into two pieces:

- An identifier for the computer on which a server runs
- An identifier for a particular service on the computer

Identifying A Computer. Each computer in the Internet is assigned a unique 32-bit identifier known as an *Internet Protocol address (IP address)*†. When it contacts a server, a client must specify the server's IP address. To make server identification easy for humans, each computer is also assigned a name, and the Domain Name System described in Chapter 4 is used to translate a name into an address. Thus, a user specifies a name such as *www.cisco.com* rather than an integer address.

Identifying A Service. Each service available in the Internet is assigned a unique 16-bit identifier known as a *protocol port number* (often abbreviated *port number*). For example, email is assigned port number 25, and the web is assigned port number 80. When a server begins execution, it registers with its local system by specifying the port number for the service it offers. When a client contacts a remote server to request service, the request contains a port number. Thus, when a request arrives at a server, software on the server uses the port number in the request to determine which application on the server computer should handle the request.

Figure 3.4 summarizes the discussion by listing the basic steps a client and server take to communicate.

---

†Chapter 21 explains Internet addresses in detail.

- **Start after server is
  already running**

- **Obtain server name
  from user**

- **Use DNS to translate
  name to IP address**

- **Specify that the
  service uses port N**

- **Contact server and
  interact**

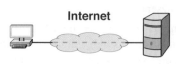

Internet

- **Start before any of
  the clients**

- **Register port N with
  the local system**

- **Wait for contact
  from a client**

- **Interact with client
  until client finishes**

- **Wait for contact from
  the next client...**

Figure 3.4 The conceptual steps a client and server take to communicate.

3.10 Concurrent Servers

The steps in Figure 3.4 imply that a server handles one client at a time. Although a *serial* approach works in a few trivial cases, most servers are *concurrent*. That is, a server uses more than one *thread of control†*, to handle multiple clients at the same time.

To understand why simultaneous service is important, consider what happens if a client downloads a movie from a server. If a server handles one request at a time, all clients must wait while the server transfers the movie. In contrast, a concurrent server does not force a client to wait. Thus, if a second client arrives and requests a short download (e.g., a single song), the second request will start immediately, and may finish before the movie transfer completes.

The details of concurrent execution depend on the operating system being used, but the idea is straightforward: concurrent server code is divided into two pieces, a main program (thread) and a handler. The main thread merely accepts contact from a client, and creates a thread of control for the client. Each thread of control interacts with a single client, and runs the handler code. After handling one client, the thread terminates. Meanwhile, the main thread keeps the server alive — after creating a thread to handle a request, the main thread waits for another request to arrive.

Note that if *N* clients are simultaneously using a concurrent server, *N+1* threads will be running: the main thread is waiting for additional requests, and *N* threads are each interacting with a single client. We can summarize:

> *A concurrent server uses threads of execution to handle requests from multiple clients at the same time.*

---

†Some operating systems use the term *thread of execution* or *process* to denote a thread of control.

3.11 Circular Dependencies Among Servers

Technically, any program that contacts another is acting as a client, and any program that accepts contact from another is acting as a server. In practice, the distinction blurs because a server for one service can act as a client for another. For example, before it can fill in a web page, a web server may need to become a client of a database. A server may also become the client of a security service (e.g., to verify that a client is allowed to access the service).

Of course, programmers must be careful to avoid circular dependencies among servers. For example, consider what can happen if a server for service X_1 becomes a client of service X_2, which becomes a client of service X_3, which becomes a client of X_1. The chain of requests can continue indefinitely until all three servers exhaust resources. The potential for circularity is especially high when services are designed independently because no single programmer controls all servers.

3.12 Peer-To-Peer Interactions

If a single server provides a given service, the network connection between the server and the Internet can become a bottleneck. Figure 3.5 illustrates the architecture.

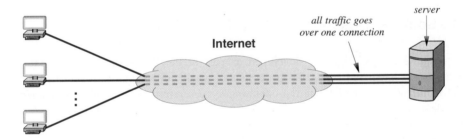

Figure 3.5 The traffic bottleneck in a design that uses a single server.

The question arises, "can Internet services be provided without creating a central bottleneck?" One way to avoid a bottleneck forms the basis of file sharing applications. Known as a *peer-to-peer (p2p)* architecture, the scheme avoids placing data on a central server. Conceptually, data is distributed equally among a set of N servers, and each client request is sent to the appropriate server. Because a given server only provides $1/N$ of the data, the amount of traffic between a server and the Internet is $1/N$ as much as in the single-server architecture. Thus, server software can run on the same computers as clients. Figure 3.6 illustrates the architecture.

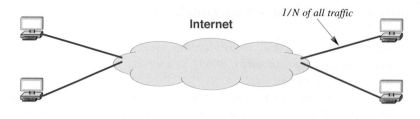

Figure 3.6 Interaction in a peer-to-peer system.

3.13 Network Programming And The Socket API

The interface an application uses to specify communication is known as an *Application Program Interface (API)*†. Although the exact details of an API depend on the operating system, one particular API has emerged as the de facto standard for software that communicates over the Internet. Known as the *socket API*, and commonly abbreviated *sockets*, the API is available for many operating systems, such as Microsoft's Windows systems as well as various UNIX systems, including Linux. The point is:

The socket API is a de facto standard for Internet communication.

3.14 Sockets, Descriptors, And Network I/O

Because it was originally developed as part of the UNIX operating system, the socket API is integrated with I/O. In particular, when an application creates a *socket* to use for Internet communication, the operating system returns a small integer *descriptor* that identifies the socket. The application then passes the descriptor as an argument when it calls functions to perform an operation on the socket (e.g., to transfer data across the network or to receive incoming data).

In many operating systems, socket descriptors are integrated with other I/O descriptors. As a result, an application can use the *read* and *write* operations for socket I/O or I/O to a file. To summarize:

When an application creates a socket, the operating system returns a small integer descriptor that the application uses to reference the socket.

---

†Appendix 1 contains a simplified API (with only seven functions) and example code that demonstrates how such an API can be used to create Internet applications, including a working web server.

3.15 Parameters And The Socket API

Socket programming differs from conventional I/O because an application must specify many details, such as the address of a remote computer, the protocol port number, and whether the application will act as a client or as a server (i.e., whether to initiate a connection). To avoid having a single socket function with many parameters, designers of the socket API chose to define many functions. In essence, an application creates a socket, and then invokes functions to specify details. The advantage of the socket approach is that most functions have three or fewer parameters; the disadvantage is that a programmer must remember to call multiple functions when using sockets. Figure 3.7 summarizes key functions in the socket API.

Name	Used By	Meaning
accept	server	Accept an incoming connection
bind	server	Specify IP address and protocol port
close	either	Terminate communication
connect	client	Connect to a remote application
getpeername	server	Obtain client's IP address
getsockopt	server	Obtain current options for a socket
listen	server	Prepare socket for use by a server
recv	either	Receive incoming data or message
recvmsg	either	Receive data (message paradigm)
recvfrom	either	Receive a message and sender's addr.
send (write)	either	Send outgoing data or message
sendmsg	either	Send an outgoing message
sendto	either	Send a message (variant of sendmsg)
setsockopt	either	Change socket options
shutdown	either	Terminate a connection
socket	either	Create a socket for use by above

Figure 3.7 A summary of the major functions in the socket API

3.16 Socket Calls In A Client And Server

Figure 3.8 illustrates the sequence of socket calls made by a typical client and server that use a stream connection. In the figure, the client sends data first and the server waits to receive data. In practice, some applications arrange for the server to send first (i.e., *send* and *recv* are called in the reverse order).

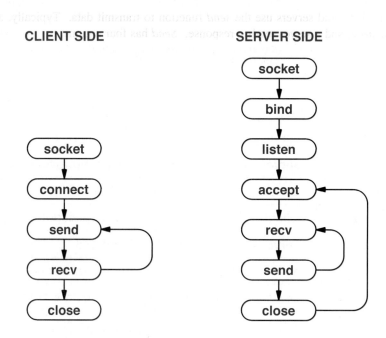

Figure 3.8 Illustration of the sequence of socket functions called by a client and server using the stream paradigm.

3.17 Socket Functions Used By Both Client And Server

3.17.1 The Socket Function

The *socket* function creates a socket and returns an integer descriptor:

$$descriptor = socket(protofamily, type, protocol)$$

Argument *protofamily* specifies the protocol family to be used with the socket. The identifier *PF_INET* specifies the TCP/IP protocol suite used in the Internet. Argument *type* specifies the type of communication the socket will use: stream transfer is specified with the value *SOCK_STREAM*, and connectionless message transfer is specified with the value *SOCK_DGRAM*.

Argument *protocol* specifies a particular transport protocol used with the socket. Having a *protocol* argument in addition to a *type* argument, allows a single protocol suite to include two or more protocols that provide the same service. The values that can be used with the *protocol* argument depend on the protocol family.

3.17.2 The Send Function

Both clients and servers use the *send* function to transmit data. Typically, a client sends a request, and a server sends a response. *Send* has four arguments:

send(socket, data, length, flags)

Argument *socket* is the descriptor of a socket to use, argument *data* is the address in memory of the data to send, argument *length* is an integer that specifies the number of bytes of data, and argument *flags* contains bits that request special options†.

3.17.3 The Recv Function

A client and a server each use *recv* to obtain data that has been sent by the other. The function has the form:

recv(socket, buffer, length, flags)

Argument *socket* is the descriptor of a socket from which data is to be received. Argument *buffer* specifies the address in memory in which the incoming message should be placed, and argument *length* specifies the size of the buffer. Finally, argument *flags* allows the caller to control details (e.g., to allow an application to extract a copy of an incoming message without removing the message from the socket). *Recv* blocks until data arrives, and then places up to *length* bytes of data in the buffer (the return value from the function call specifies the number of bytes that were extracted).

3.17.4 Read And Write With Sockets

On some operating systems, such as Linux, the operating system functions *read* and *write* can be used instead of *recv* and *send*. *Read* takes three arguments that are identical to the first three arguments of *recv*, and *write* takes three arguments that are identical to the first three arguments of *send*.

The chief advantage of using *read* and *write* is generality — an application program can be created that transfers data to or from a descriptor without knowing whether the descriptor corresponds to a file or a socket. Thus, a programmer can use a file on a local disk to test a client or server before attempting to communicate across a network. The chief disadvantage of using *read* and *write* is that a program may need to be changed before it can be used on another system.

---

†Many options are intended for system debugging, and are not available to conventional client and server programs.

3.17.5 The Close Function

The *close* function tells the operating system to terminate use of a socket†. It has the form:

close(socket)

where *socket* is the descriptor for a socket being closed. If a connection is open, *close* terminates the connection (i.e., informs the other side). Closing a socket terminates use immediately — the descriptor is released, preventing the application from sending or receiving data.

3.18 The Connection Function Used Only By A Client

Clients call *connect* to establish a connection with a specific server. The form is:

connect(socket, saddress, saddresslen)

Argument *socket* is the descriptor of a socket to use for the connection. Argument *saddress* is a *sockaddr* structure that specifies the server's address and protocol port number‡, and argument *saddresslen* specifies the length of the server address measured in bytes.

For a socket that uses the stream paradigm, *connect* initiates a transport-level connection to the specified server. The server must be waiting for a connection (see the *accept* function described below).

3.19 Socket Functions Used Only By A Server

3.19.1 The Bind Function

When created, a socket contains no information about the local or remote address and protocol port number. A server calls *bind* to supply a protocol port number at which the server will wait for contact. *Bind* takes three arguments:

bind(socket, localaddr, addrlen)

Argument *socket* is the descriptor of a socket to use. Argument *localaddr* is a structure that specifies the local address to be assigned to the socket, and argument *addrlen* is an integer that specifies the length of the address.

Because a socket can be used with an arbitrary protocol, the format of an address depends on the protocol being used. The socket API defines a generic form used to

---

†Microsoft's *Windows Sockets* interface uses the name *closesocket* instead of *close*.

‡The combination of an IP address and a protocol port number is sometimes called an *endpoint address*.

represent addresses, and then requires each protocol family to specify how their protocol addresses use the generic form. The generic format for representing an address is defined to be a *sockaddr* structure. Although several versions have been released, most systems define a sockaddr structure to have three fields:

```
struct sockaddr {
        u_char  sa_len;         /* total length of the address */
        u_char  sa_family;      /* family of the address       */
        char    sa_data[14];    /* the address itself          */
};
```

Field *sa_len* consists of a single octet that specifies the length of the address. Field *sa_family* specifies the family to which an address belongs (the symbolic constant *AF_INET* is used for Internet addresses). Finally, field *sa_data* contains the address.

Each protocol family defines the exact format of addresses used with the *sa_data* field of a *sockaddr* structure. For example, Internet protocols use structure *sockaddr_in* to define an address:

```
struct sockaddr_in {
        u_char   sin_len;        /* total length of the address */
        u_char   sin_family;     /* family of the address       */
        u_short  sin_port;       /* protocol port number        */
        struct   in_addr sin_addr;/* IP address of computer      */
        char     sin_zero[8];    /* not used (set to zero)      */
};
```

The first two fields of structure *sockaddr_in* correspond exactly to the first two fields of the generic *sockaddr* structure. The last three fields define the exact form of an Internet address. There are two points to notice. First, each address identifies both a computer and a protocol port on that computer. Field *sin_addr* contains the IP address of the computer, and field *sin_port* contains the protocol port number. Second, although only six bytes are needed to store a complete address, the generic *sockaddr* structure reserves fourteen bytes. Thus, the final field in structure *sockaddr_in* defines an 8-byte field of zeroes, which pad the structure to the same size as *sockaddr*.

We said that a server calls *bind* to specify the protocol port number at which the server will accept contact. However, in addition to a protocol port number, structure *sockaddr_in* contains a field for an address. Although a server can choose to fill in a specific address, doing so causes problems when a computer is multi-homed (i.e., has multiple network connections) because the computer has multiple addresses. To allow a server to operate on a multi-homed host, the socket API includes a special symbolic constant, *INADDR_ANY*, that allows a server to specify a port number while allowing contact at any of the computer's addresses. To summarize:

> *Although structure* sockaddr_in *includes a field for an address, the socket API provides a symbolic constant that allows a server to specify a protocol port at any of the computer's addresses.*

3.19.2 The Listen Function

After using *bind* to specify a protocol port, a server calls *listen* to place the socket in passive mode, which makes the socket ready to wait for contact from clients. *Listen* takes two arguments:

listen(socket, queuesize)

Argument *socket* is the descriptor of a socket, and argument *queuesize* specifies a length for the socket's request queue. An operating system builds a separate request queue for each socket. Initially, the queue is empty. As requests arrive from clients, each is placed in the queue. When the server asks to retrieve an incoming request from the socket, the system extracts the next request from the queue. Queue length is important: if the queue is full when a request arrives, the system rejects the request.

3.19.3 The Accept Function

A server calls *accept* to establish a connection with a client. If a request is present in the queue, *accept* returns immediately; if no requests have arrived, the system blocks the server until a client initiates a request. Once a connection has been accepted, the server uses the connection to interact with a client. After it finishes communication, the server closes the connection.

The *accept* function has the form:

newsock = accept(socket, caddress, caddresslen)

Argument *socket* is the descriptor of a socket the server has created and bound to a specific protocol port. Argument *caddress* is the address of a structure of type *sockaddr*, and *caddresslen* is a pointer to an integer. *Accept* fills in fields of argument *caddress* with the address of the client that formed the connection, and sets *caddresslen* to the length of the address. Finally, *accept* creates a new socket for the connection, and returns the descriptor of the new socket to the caller. The server uses the new socket to communicate with the client, and then closes the socket when finished. Meanwhile, the server's original socket remains unchanged — after it finishes communicating with a client, the server uses the original socket to accept the next connection from a client. Thus, the original socket is only used to accept requests, and all communication occurs over the new socket created by *accept*.

3.20 Socket Functions Used With The Message Paradigm

The socket functions used to send and receive messages are more complicated than those used with the stream paradigm because many options are available. For example, a sender can choose whether to store the recipient's address in the socket and merely send data or to specify the recipient's address each time a message is transmitted. Furthermore, one function allows a sender to place the address and message in a structure and pass the address of the structure as an argument, and another function allows a sender to pass the address and message as separate arguments.

3.20.1 Sendto and Sendmsg Socket Functions

Functions *sendto* and *sendmsg* allow a client or server to send a message using an unconnected socket; both require the caller to specify a destination. *Sendto* uses separate arguments for the message and destination address:

sendto(socket, data, length, flags, destaddress, addresslen)

The first four arguments correspond to the four arguments of the *send* function; the final two specify the address of a destination and the length of that address. Argument *destaddress* corresponds to a *sockaddr* structure (specifically, *sockaddr_in*).

The *sendmsg* function performs the same operation as *sendto*, but abbreviates the arguments by defining a structure. The shorter argument list can make programs that use *sendmsg* easier to read:

sendmsg(socket, msgstruct, flags)

Argument *msgstruct* is a structure that contains information about the destination address, the length of the address, the message to be sent, and the length of the message:

```
struct  msgstruct {                     /* structure used by sendmsg */
        struct sockaddr *m_saddr;  /* ptr to destination address */
        struct datavec  *m_dvec;   /* ptr to message (vector)    */
        int     m_dvlength;        /* num. of items in vector    */
        struct access   *m_rights; /* ptr to access rights list  */
        int     m_alength;         /* num. of items in list      */
};
```

The details of the message structure are unimportant — it should be viewed as a way to combine many arguments into a single structure. Most applications use only the first three fields, which specify a destination protocol address, a list of data items that constitute the message, and the number of items in the list.

3.20.2 Recvfrom And Recvmsg Functions

An unconnected socket can be used to receive messages from an arbitrary set of clients. In such cases, the system returns the address of the sender along with each incoming message (the receiver uses the address to send a reply). Function *recvfrom* has arguments that specify a location for the next incoming message and the address of the sender:

> recvfrom(socket, buffer, length, flags, sndraddr, saddrlen)

The first four arguments correspond to the arguments of *recv*; the two additional arguments, *sndraddr* and *saddrlen*, are used to record the sender's Internet address. Argument *sndraddr* is a pointer to a *sockaddr* structure into which the system writes the sender's address, and argument *saddrlen* is a pointer to an integer that the system uses to record the length of the address. Note that *recvfrom* records the sender's address in exactly the same form that *sendto* expects, making it easy to transmit a reply.

Function *recvmsg*, which is the counterpart of *sendmsg*, operates like *recvfrom*, but requires fewer arguments. It has the form:

> recvmsg(socket, msgstruct, flags)

where argument *msgstruct* gives the address of a structure that holds the address for an incoming message as well as locations for the sender's Internet address. The *msgstruct* recorded by *recvmsg* uses exactly the same format as the structure required by *sendmsg*, making a reply easy.

3.21 Other Socket Functions

The socket API contains a variety of support functions. For example, after a server accepts an incoming connection request, the server can call *getpeername* to obtain the address of the remote client that initiated the connection. A client or server can also call *gethostname* to obtain information about the computer on which it is running.

Two general-purpose functions are used to manipulate socket options. Function *setsockopt* stores values in a socket's options, and function *getsockopt* obtains the current option values. Options are used mainly to handle special cases (e.g., to increase the internal buffer size).

Two functions provide translation between Internet addresses and computer names. Function *gethostbyname* returns the Internet address for a computer given the computer's name. Clients often call *gethostbyname* to translate a name entered by a user into a corresponding IP address. Function *gethostbyaddr* provides an inverse mapping — given an IP address for a computer, it returns the computer's name. Clients and servers can use *gethostbyaddr* to translate an address into a name a user can understand.

3.22 Sockets, Threads, And Inheritance

The socket API works well with concurrent servers. Although the details depend on the underlying operating system, implementations of the socket API adhere to the following inheritance principle:

> *Each new thread that is created inherits a copy of all open sockets from the thread that created it.*

The socket implementation uses a *reference count* mechanism to control each socket. When a socket is first created, the system sets the socket's reference count to *1*, and the socket exists as long as the reference count remains positive. When a program creates an additional thread, the thread inherits a pointer to each open socket the program owns, and the system increments the reference count of each socket by *1*. When a thread calls *close*, the system decrements the reference count for the socket; if the reference count has reached zero, the socket is removed.

In terms of a concurrent server, the main thread owns the socket used to accept incoming connections. When a connection request arrives, the system creates a new socket for the new connection, and the main thread creates a new thread to handle the connection. Immediately after a thread is created, both threads have access to the original socket and the new socket, and the reference count of each socket is *2*. The main thread calls *close* for the new socket, and the service thread calls *close* for the original socket, reducing the reference count of each to *1*. Finally, when it finishes interacting with a client, the service thread calls *close* on the new socket, reducing the reference count to zero and causing the socket to be deleted. Thus, the lifetime of sockets in a concurrent server can be summarized:

> *The original socket used to accept connections exists as long as the main server thread executes; a socket used for a specific connection exists only as long as the thread exists to handle that connection.*

3.23 Summary

In the Internet, all services are supplied by applications, which use either a stream paradigm or a message paradigm to communicate. The stream paradigm guarantees to deliver a sequence of bytes in order, but can choose how many bytes to pass to a receiver in each batch. The message paradigm preserves boundaries, but allows messages to be lost, duplicated, or delivered out-of-order.

The basic communication model used by network applications is known as the client-server model. A program that passively waits for contact is called a server, and a program that actively initiates contact with a server is called a client.

Each computer is assigned a unique address, and each service, such as email or web access, is assigned a unique identifier known as a protocol port number. When a server starts, it specifies a protocol port number; when contacting a server, a client specifies the address of the computer on which the server runs as well as the protocol port number the server is using.

A single client can access more than one service, a client can access servers on multiple machines, and a server for one service can become a client for other services. Designers and programmers must be careful to avoid circular dependencies among servers.

An Application Program Interface (API) specifies the details of how an application program interacts with protocol software. Although details depend on the operating system, the socket API is a *de facto* standard. A program creates a socket, and then invokes a series of functions to use the socket. A server using the stream paradigm calls socket functions: *socket*, *bind*, *listen*, *accept*, *recv*, *send*, and *close*; a client calls *socket*, *connect*, *send*, *recv*, and *close*.

Because many servers are concurrent, sockets are designed to work with concurrent applications. When a new thread is created, the new thread inherits access to all sockets that the creating thread owned.

EXERCISES

3.1   Why is symbolic constant *INADDR_ANY* used?

3.2   What are the two basic communication paradigms used in the Internet?

3.3   Implement the simplified API in Appendix 1 using socket functions.

3.4   Give six characteristics of Internet message communication.

3.5   What is the difference between a server and a server-class computer?

3.6   If a sender wants to have copies of each data block being sent to three recipients, which paradigm should the sender choose?

3.7   Can all computers run multiple services effectively? Why or why not?

3.8   List the steps a client uses to contact a server after a user specifies a domain name for the server.

3.9   Once a socket is created, how does an application reference the socket?

3.10 Does a client ever use *bind*? Explain.

3.11 What basic operating system feature does a concurrent server use to handle requests from multiple clients simultaneously?

3.12 Give six characteristics of Internet stream communication.

3.13 Give the typical sequence of socket calls used by a client and by a server.

3.14 Compare and contrast a client and server application by summarizing characteristics of each.

3.15 List the possible combinations of clients and servers a given computer can run.

3.16 Suppose a socket is open and a new thread is created. Will the new thread be able to use the socket?

3.17 Examine the web server in Appendix 1, and build an equivalent server using the socket API.

3.18 If a sender uses the stream paradigm and always sends 1024 bytes at a time, what size blocks can the Internet deliver to a receiver?

3.19 Give the general algorithm that a connection-oriented system uses.

3.20 Can data flow from a client to a server? Explain.

3.21 What are the three surprising aspects of the Internet's message delivery semantics?

3.22 What two identifiers are used to specify a particular server?

3.23 To what socket functions do *read* and *write* correspond?

3.24 What performance problem motivates peer-to-peer communication?

3.25 When two applications communicate over the Internet, which one is the server?

3.26 Name two operating systems that offer the socket API.

3.27 Is *sendto* used with a stream or message paradigm?

3.28 What are the main functions in the socket API?

Chapter Contents

4

Traditional Internet Applications

4.1 Introduction

The previous chapter introduces the topics of Internet applications and network programming. The chapter explains that Internet services are defined by application programs, and characterizes the client-server model that such programs use to interact. The chapter also covers the socket API.

This chapter continues the examination of Internet applications. The chapter defines the concept of a transfer protocol, and explains how applications implement transfer protocols. Finally, the chapter considers standard Internet applications, and describes the transfer protocol each uses.

4.2 Application-Layer Protocols

Whenever a programmer creates two applications that communicate over a network, the programmer specifies details, such as:

- The syntax and semantics of messages that can be exchanged
- Whether the client or server initiates interaction
- Actions to be taken if an error arises
- How the two sides know when to terminate communication

In specifying details of communication, a programmer defines an *application-layer protocol*. There are two broad types of application-layer protocols that depend on the intended use:

- *Private communication*. A programmer creates a pair of applications that communicate over the Internet with the intention that the pair is for private use. In most cases, the interaction between the two applications is straightforward, which means a programmer may choose to write code without writing a formal protocol specification.

- *Standardized service*. An Internet service is defined with the expectation that many programmers will create server software to offer the service or client software to access the service. In such cases, the application-layer protocol must be documented independent of any implementation, and the specification must be precise and unambiguous so that all clients and servers can *interoperate* correctly.

The size of a protocol specification depends on the complexity of the service; the specification for a trivial service can fit into a single page of text. For example, the Internet protocols include a standardized application service known as *DAYTIME* that allows a client to find the local date and time at a server's location. The protocol is straightforward: a client forms a connection to a server, the server sends an ASCII representation of the date and time, and the server closes the connection. For example, a server might send a string such as:

Sat Sep 9 20:18:37 2008

The client reads data from the connection until an *end of file* is encountered.

To summarize:

> *To allow applications for standardized services to interoperate, an application-layer protocol standard is created independent of any implementation.*

4.3 Representation And Transfer

Application-layer protocols specify two aspects of interaction: representation and transfer. Figure 4.1 explains the distinction.

Aspect	Description
Data Representation	Syntax of data items that are exchanged, specific form used during transfer, translation of integers, characters, and files between computers
Data Transfer	Interaction between client and server, message syntax and semantics, valid and invalid exchange error handling, termination of interaction

Figure 4.1 Two key aspects of an application-layer protocol.

For a basic service, a single protocol standard can specify both aspects; more complex services use separate protocol standards to specify each aspect. For example, the DAYTIME protocol described above uses a single standard to specify that a date and time are represented as an ASCII string, and that transfer consists of a server sending the string and then closing the connection. The next section explains that the web uses separate protocols to describe web page syntax and web page transfer. Protocol designers make the distinction clear:

As a convention, the word Transfer *in the title of an application-layer protocol means that the protocol specifies the data transfer aspect of communication.*

4.4 Web Protocols

The *World Wide Web* is one of the most widely used services in the Internet. Because the Web is complex, many protocol standards have been devised to specify various aspects and details. Figure 4.2 lists the three key standards.

Standard	Purpose
HyperText Markup Language (HTML)	A representation standard used to specify the contents and layout of a web page
Uniform Resource Locator (URL)	A representation standard that specifies the format and meaning of web page identifiers
HyperText Transfer Protocol (HTTP)	A transfer protocol that specifies how a browser interacts with a web server to transfer data

Figure 4.2 Three key standards that the World Wide Web service uses.

4.5 Document Representation With HTML

The *HyperText Markup Language (HTML)* is a representation standard that specifies the syntax for a web page. HTML has the following general characteristics:

- Uses a textual representation
- Describes pages that contain multimedia
- Follows a declarative rather than procedural paradigm
- Provides markup specifications instead of formatting
- Permits a hyperlink to be embedded in an arbitrary object
- Allows a document to include metadata

Although an HTML document consists of a text file, the language allows a programmer to specify an arbitrarily complex web page that contains graphics, audio and video, as well as text. In fact, to be accurate, the designers should have used *hypermedia* in the name instead of *hypertext* because HTML allows an arbitrary object, such as an image, to contain a link to another web page (sometimes called a *hyperlink*).

HTML is classified as *declarative* because the language only allows one to specify what is to be done, not how to do it. HTML is classified as a *markup language* because it only gives general guidelines for display and does not include detailed formatting instructions. For example, HTML allows a page to specify the level of importance of a heading, but HTML does not require the author to specify the exact font, typeface, point size, or spacing for the heading†. In essence, a browser chooses all display details. The use of a markup language is important because it allows a browser to adapt the page to the underlying display hardware. For example, a page can be formatted for a high resolution or low resolution display, a large screen or a small hand-held device such as an iPhone or PDA.

To summarize:

> *HyperText Markup Language is a representation standard for web pages. To permit a page to be displayed on an arbitrary device, HTML gives general guidelines for display and allows a browser to choose details.*

To specify markup, HTML uses *tags* embedded in the document. Tags, which consist of a term bracketed by *less-than* and *greater-than* symbols, provide structure for the document as well as formatting hints. Tags control all display; white space (i.e., extra lines and blank characters) can be inserted at any point in the HTML document without any effect on the formatted version that a browser displays.

For example, an HTML document starts with the tag <HTML>, and ends with the tag </HTML>. The pair of tags <HEAD> and </HEAD> bracket the head, while the pair of

---

†HTML extensions have been created that do allow the specification of an exact font, typeface, point size, and formatting.

tags <BODY> and </BODY> bracket the body. In the head, the tags <TITLE> and </TI-TLE> bracket the text that forms the document title. Figure 4.3 illustrates the general form of an HTML document†.

```
<HTML>

   <HEAD>
       <TITLE>
                 text that forms the document title
       </TITLE>
   </HEAD>

   <BODY>
      body of the document appears here
   </BODY>

</HTML>
```

Figure 4.3 The general form of an HTML document.

HTML uses the *IMG* tag to encode a reference to an external image. For example, the tag:

```
<IMG SRC="house_icon.gif">
```

specifies that file *house_icon.gif* contains an image that the browser should insert in the document. Additional parameters can be specified in an IMG tag to specify the alignment of the figure with surrounding text. For example, Figure 4.4 illustrates the output for the following HTML, which aligns text with the middle of the figure:

```
Here is an icon of a house. <IMG SRC="house_icon.gif" ALIGN=middle>
```

A browser positions the image vertically so the text aligns with the middle of the image.

Here is an icon of a house.

Figure 4.4 Illustration of figure alignment in HTML.

---

†HTML does not distinguish between uppercase and lowercase letters in tags; uppercase is used in examples for emphasis.

4.6 Uniform Resource Locators And Hyperlinks

The Web uses a syntactic form known as a *Uniform Resource Locator* (*URL*) to specify a web page. The general form of a URL is:

protocol :// computer_name : port / document_name ? parameters

where *protocol* is the name of the protocol used to access the document, *computer_name* is the domain name of the computer on which the document resides, *:port* is an optional protocol port number at which the server is listening, *document_name* is the optional name of the document on the specified computer, and *%parameters* give optional parameters for the page.

For example, the URL

http://www.netbook.cs.purdue.edu/toc/toc01.htm

specifies protocol *http*, a computer named *www.netbook.cs.purdue.edu*, and a file named *toc/toc01.htm*.

Typical URLs that a user enters omit many of the parts. For example, the URL:

www.netbook.cs.purdue.edu

omits the protocol (http is assumed), the port (80 is assumed), the document name (index.html is assumed), and parameters (none are assumed).

A URL contains the information a browser needs to retrieve a page. The browser uses the separator characters colon, slash, and percent, to divide the URL into four components: a protocol, a computer name, a document name, and parameters. The browser uses the computer name and protocol port to form a connection to the server on which the page resides, and uses the document name and parameters to request a specific page.

In HTML, an *anchor* tag uses URLs to provide a hyperlink capability (i.e., the ability to link from one web document to another). The following example shows an HTML source document with an anchor surrounding the name *Prentice Hall*:

```
This book is published by
<A HREF="http://www.prenhall.com">
Prentice Hall, </A> one of
the larger publishers of Computer Science textbooks.
```

The anchor references the URL *http://www.prenhall.com*. When displayed on a screen, the HTML input produces:

This book is published by <u>Prentice Hall,</u> one of the larger
publishers of Computer Science textbooks.

4.7 Web Document Transfer With HTTP

The *HyperText Transfer Protocol* (*HTTP*) is the primary transfer protocol that a browser uses to interact with a web server. In terms of the client-server model, a browser is a client that extracts a server name from a URL and contacts the server. Most URLs contain an explicit protocol reference of *http://*, or omit the protocol altogether, in which case HTTP is assumed.

HTTP can be characterized as follows:

- Uses textual control messages
- Transfers binary data files
- Can download or upload data
- Incorporates caching

Once it establishes a connection, a browser sends an HTTP *request* to the server. Figure 4.5 lists the four major request types:

Request	Description
GET	Requests a document; server responds by sending status information followed by a copy of the document
HEAD	Requests status information; server responds by sending status information, but does not send a copy of the document
POST	Sends data to a server; the server appends the data to a specified item (e.g., a message is appended to a list)
PUT	Sends data to a server; the server uses the data to completely replace the specified item (i.e., overwrites the previous data)

Figure 4.5 The four major HTTP request types.

The most common form of interaction begins when a browser requests a page from the server. The browser sends a *GET* request over the connection, and the server responds by sending a header, a blank line, and the requested document. In HTTP, a request and a header used in a response each consist of textual information. For example, a *GET* request has the following form:

GET /item versionCRLF

where *item* gives the URL for the item being requested, *version* specifies a version of the protocol (usually HTTP/1.0 or HTTP/1.1), and *CRLF* denotes two ASCII characters, *carriage return* and *linefeed*, that are used to signify the end of a line of text.

Version information is important in HTTP because it allows the protocol to change and yet remain backward compatible. For example, when a browser that uses version 1.0 of the protocol interacts with a server that uses a higher version, the server reverts to the older version of the protocol and formulates a response accordingly. To summarize:

> *When using HTTP, a browser sends version information which allows a server to choose the highest version of the protocol that they both understand.*

The first line of a response header contains a status code that tells the browser whether the server handled the request. If the request was incorrectly formed or the requested item was not available, the status code pinpoints the problem. For example, a server returns the well-known status code *404* if the requested item cannot be found. When it honors a request, a server returns status code *200*; additional lines of the header give further information about the item such as its length, when it was last modified, and the content type. Figure 4.6 shows the general format of lines in a basic response header.

HTTP/1.0 *status_code status_string CRLF*
Server: *server_identification CRLF*
Last-Modified: *date_document_was_changed CRLF*
Content-Length: *datasize CRLF*
Content-Type: *document_type CRLF*
CRLF

Figure 4.6 General format of lines in a basic response header.

Field *status_code* is a numeric value represented as a character string of decimal digits that denotes a status, and *status_string* is a corresponding explanation for a human to read. Figure 4.7 lists examples of commonly used status codes and strings. Field *server_identification* contains a descriptive string that gives a human-readable description of the server, possibly including the server's domain name. The *datasize* field in the *Content-Length* header specifies the size of the data item that follows, measured in bytes. The *document_type* field contains a string that informs the browser about the document contents. The string contains two items separated by a slash: the type of the document and its representation. For example, when a server returns an HTML document, the *document_type* is *text/html*, and when the server returns a jpeg file, the type is *image/jpeg*.

Status Code	Corresponding Status String
200	OK
400	Bad Request
404	Not Found

Figure 4.7 Examples of status codes used in HTTP.

Figure 4.8 shows sample output from an Apache web server. The item being re-quested is a text file containing sixteen characters (i.e., the text *This is a test.* plus a *NEWLINE* character). Although the GET request specifies HTTP version 1.0, the server runs version 1.1. The server returns nine lines of header, a blank line, and the contents of the file.

```
HTTP/1.1 200 OK
Date: Sat, 15 Mar 2008 07:35:25 GMT
Server: Apache/1.3.37 (Unix)
Last-Modified: Tue,  1 Jan 2008 12:03:37 GMT
ETag: "78595-81-3883bbe9"
Accept-Ranges: bytes
Content-Length: 16
Connection: close
Content-Type: text/plain

This is a test.
```

Figure 4.8 Sample HTTP response from an Apache web server.

4.8 Caching In Browsers

Caching provides an important optimization for web access because users tend to visit the same web sites repeatedly. Much of the content at a given site consists of large images that use the *Graphics Image Format* (*GIF*) or *Joint Photographic Experts Group* (*JPEG*) standards. Such images often contain backgrounds or banners that do not change frequently. The key idea is:

> *A browser can reduce download times significantly by saving a copy of each image in a cache on the user's disk and using the cached copy.*

A question arises: what happens if the document on the web server changes after a browser stores a copy in its cache? That is, how can a browser tell whether its cached copy is *stale*? The response in Figure 4.8 contains one clue: the *Last-Modified* header. Whenever a browser obtains a document from a web server, the header specifies the last time the document was changed. A browser saves the Last-Modified date information along with the cached copy. Before it uses a document from the local cache, a browser makes a *HEAD* request to the server and compares the *Last-Modified* date of the server's copy to the *Last-Modified* date on the cached copy. If the cached version is stale, the browser downloads the new version. Algorithm 4.1 summarizes caching.

Algorithm 4.1

Given:
    A URL for an item on a web page
Obtain:
    A copy of the page
Method:
    if (item is not in the local cache) {
            Issue GET request and place a copy in the cache;
    } else {
        Issue HEAD request to the server;
        if (cached item is up-to-date) {
            use cached item;
        } else {
            Issue GET request and place a copy in the cache;
        }
    }

Algorithm 4.1 Caching in a browser used to reduce download times.

The algorithm omits several minor details. For example, HTTP allows a web site to include a *No-cache* header that specifies a given item should not be cached. In addition, browsers do not cache small items because the time to download the item with a GET request is approximately the same as the time to make a HEAD request and keeping many small items in a cache can increase cache lookup times.

4.9 Browser Architecture

Because it provides general services and supports a graphical interface, a browser is complex. Of course, a browser must understand HTTP, but a browser also provides support for other protocols. In particular, because a URL can specify a protocol, a browser must contain client code for each of the protocols used. For each service, the browser must know how to interact with a server and how to interpret responses. For example, a browser must know how to access the FTP service discussed in the next section. Figure 4.9 illustrates components that a browser includes.

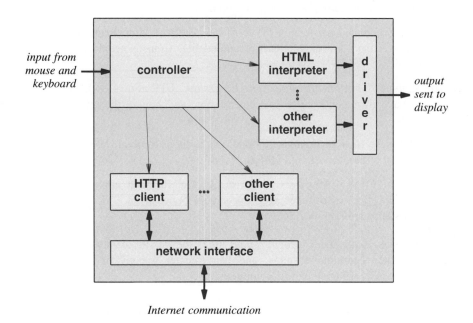

Figure 4.9 Architecture of a browser that can access multiple services.

4.10 File Transfer Protocol (FTP)

A *file* is the fundamental storage abstraction. Because a file can hold an arbitrary object (e.g., a document, spreadsheet, computer program, graphic image, or data), a facility that sends a copy of a file from one computer to another provides a powerful mechanism for the exchange of data. We use the term *file transfer* for such a service.

File transfer across the Internet is complicated because computers are heterogeneous, which means that each computer system defines file representations, type information, naming, and file access mechanisms. On some computer systems, the extension *.jpg* is used for a JPEG image, and on others, the extension is *.jpeg*. On some systems, each line in a text file is terminated by a single *LINEFEED* character, while other systems require *CARRIAGE RETURN* followed by *LINEFEED*. Some systems use slash (/) as a separator in file names, and others use a backslash (\). Furthermore, an operating system may define a set of user accounts that are each given the right to access certain files. However, the account information differs among computers, so user *X* on one computer is not the same as user *X* on another.

The most widely-deployed file transfer service in the Internet uses the *File Transfer Protocol* (*FTP*). FTP can be characteristized as:

- *Arbitrary File Contents.* FTP can transfer any type of data, including documents, images, music, or stored video.

- *Bidirectional Transfer.* FTP can be used to download files (transfer from server to client) or upload files (transfer from server to client).

- *Support For Authentication And Ownership.* FTP allows each file to have ownership and access restrictions, and honors the restrictions.

- *Ability To Browse Folders.* FTP allows a client to obtain the contents of a directory (i.e., a folder).

- *Textual Control Messages.* Like many other Internet application services, the control messages exchanged between an FTP client and server are sent as ASCII text.

- *Accommodates Heterogeneity.* FTP hides the details of individual computer operating systems, and can transfer a copy of a file between an arbitrary pair of computers.

Because few users launch an FTP application, the protocol is usually invisible. However, FTP is invoked automatically by a browser when a user requests a file *download*.

4.11 FTP Communication Paradigm

One of the most interesting aspects of FTP arises from the way a client and server interact. Overall, the approach seems straightforward: a client establishes a connection to an FTP server and sends a series of requests to which the server responds. Unlike HTTP, an FTP server does not send responses over the same connection on which the client sends requests. Instead, the original connection the client creates, called a *control connection*, is reserved for commands. Each time the server needs to download or upload a file, the server opens a new connection. To distinguish them from the control connection, the connections used to transfer files are called *data connections*.

Surprisingly, FTP inverts the client-server relationship for data connections. That is, when opening a data connection, the client acts like a server (i.e., waits for the data connection) and the server acts like a client (i.e., initiates the data connection). After it has been used for one transfer, the data connection is closed. If the client sends another request, the server opens a new data connection. Figure 4.10 illustrates the interaction.

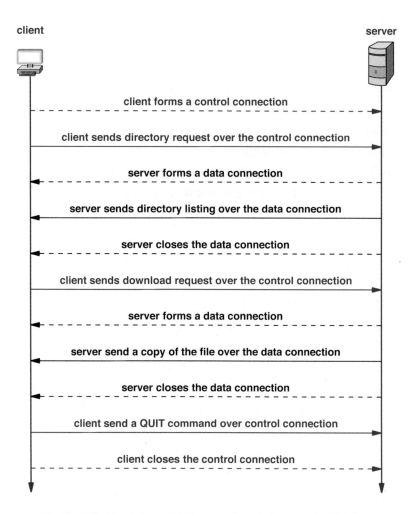

Figure 4.10 Illustration of FTP connections during a typical session.

The figure omits several important details. For example, after creating the control connection, a client must log into the server. FTP provides a *USER* command that the client sends to provide a login name, and a *PASS* command that the client sends to provide a password. The server sends a numeric status response over the control connection to let the client know whether the login was successful. A client can only send other commands after a login is successful†.

Another important detail concerns the protocol port number to be used for a data connection. What protocol port number should a server specify when connecting to the client? The FTP protocol provides an interesting answer: before making a request to the server, a client allocates a protocol port on its local operating system and sends the port number to the server. That is, the client binds to the port to await a connection, and then transmits a *PORT* command over the control connection to inform the server about the port number being used. Algorithm 4.2 summarizes the steps.

Algorithm 4.2

Given:
  An FTP control connection
Achieve:
  Transmission of a data item over an FTP data connection
Method:

  Client sends request for a specific file over control connection;
  Server receives request;
  Client allocates a local protocol port, call it X;
  Client binds to port X and prepares to accept a connection;
  Client sends "PORT X" to server over control connection;
  Server receives PORT command and request for data item;
  Client waits for a data connection at port X and accepts;
  Server creates a data connection to port X on client's computer;
  Server sends the requested file over the data connection;
  Server closes the data connection;

Algorithm 4.2 Steps an FTP client and server take to use a data connection.

The transmission of port information between a pair of applications may seem innocuous, but it is not, and the technique does not work well in all situations. In particular, transmission of a protocol port number will fail if one of the two endpoints lies behind a Network Address Translation (NAT) device, such as a wireless router used in a residence or small office. Chapter 23 explains that FTP is an exception — to support FTP, a NAT device recognizes an FTP control connection, inspects the contents of the connection, and rewrites the values in a PORT command.

---

†When accessing public files, a client uses *anonymous login*, which consists of user name *anonymous* and password *guest*.

4.12 Electronic Mail

Although services such as instant messaging have become popular, email remains one of the most widely used Internet applications. Because it was conceived before personal computers and hand-held PDAs were available, email was designed to allow a user on one computer to send a message directly to a user on another computer. Figure 4.11 illustrates the architecture, and Algorithm 4.3 lists the steps taken.

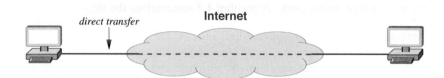

Figure 4.11 The original email configuration with direct transfer from a sender's computer directly to a recipient's computer.

Algorithm 4.3

Given:
  Email communication from one user to another.
Provide:
  Transmission of a message to the intended recipient.
Method:
  User invokes interface application and generates an email
      message for user *x @ destination.com*;
  User's email interface program queues message for transfer;
  Mail transfer program on user's computer examines the
      outgoing mail queue, and finds message;
  Mail transfer program opens connection to *destination.com*;
  Mail transfer program uses SMTP to transfer the message;
  Mail transfer program closes connection;
  Mail server on *destination.com* receives message and places
      a copy in user x's mailbox;
  User x on *destination.com* runs mail interface program, which
      displays the user's mailbox, including the new message;

Algorithm 4.3 Steps taken to send email in the original paradigm.

As the algorithm indicates, even early email software was divided into two conceptually separate pieces:

- An email interface application
- A mail transfer program

A user invokes the *email interface application* directly. The interface provides mechanisms that allow a user to compose and edit outgoing messages as well as read and process incoming email. The email interface application does not act as a client or server, and does not transfer messages to other users. Instead, the interface application reads messages from the user's *mailbox* (i.e., a file on the user's computer) and deposits outgoing messages in an *outgoing mail queue* (typically a folder on the user's disk). Separate programs known as a *mail transfer program* and a *mail server* handle transfer. The mail transfer program acts as a client to send a message to the mail server on the destination computer; the mail server accepts incoming messages and deposits each in the appropriate user's mailbox.

The specifications used for Internet email can be divided into three broad categories as Figure 4.12 lists.

Type	Description
Transfer	A protocol used to move a copy of an email message from one computer to another
Access	A protocol that allows a user to access their mailbox and to view or send email messages
Representation	A protocol that specifies the format of an email message when stored on disk

Figure 4.12 The three types of protocols used with email.

4.13 The Simple Mail Transfer Protocol (SMTP)

The *Simple Mail Transfer Protocol* (*SMTP*) is the standard protocol that a mail transfer program uses to transfer a mail message across the Internet to a server. SMTP can be characterized as:

- Follows a stream paradigm
- Uses textual control messages
- Only transfers text messages
- Allows a sender to specify recipients' names and check each name
- Sends one copy of a given message

The most unexpected aspect of SMTP arises from its restriction to textual content. A later section explains the MIME standard that allows email to include attachments such as graphic images or binary files, but the underlying SMTP mechanism is restricted to text.

The second aspect of SMTP focuses on its ability to send a single message to multiple recipients on a given computer. The protocol allows a client to list users one-at-a-time and then send a single copy of a message for all users on the list. That is, a client sends a message "I have a mail message for user A," and the server either replies "OK" or "No such user here". In fact, each SMTP server message starts with a numeric code; so replies are of the form "250 OK" or "550 No such user here". Figure 4.13 gives an example SMTP session that occurs when a mail message is transferred from user *John_Q_Smith* on computer *example.edu* to two users on computer *somewhere.com*

```
Server:     220 somewhere.com Simple Mail Transfer Service Ready

Client:     HELO example.edu
Server::    250 OK

Client:     MAIL FROM:<John_Q_Smith@example.edu>
Server:     250 OK

Client:     RCPT TO:<Mathew_Doe@somewhere.com>
Server:     550 No such user here

Client:     RCPT TO:<Paul_Jones@somewhere.com>
Server:     250 OK

Client:     DATA
Server:     354 Start mail input; end with <CR><LF>.<CR><LF>
Client:     ...sends body of mail message, which can contain
Client:     ...arbitrarily many lines of text
Client:     <CR><LF>.<CR><LF>
Server:     250 OK

Client:     QUIT
Server:     221 somewhere.com closing transmission channel
```

Figure 4.13 *An example SMTP session.*

In the figure, each line is labeled *Client:* or *Server:* to indicate whether the server or the client sends the line; the protocol does not include the labels. The *HELO* command allows the client to authenticate itself by sending its domain name. Finally, the notation *<CR><LF>* denotes a carriage return followed by a linefeed (i.e., an end-of-line). Thus, the body of an email message is terminated by a line that consists of a period with no other text or spacing.

The term *Simple* in the name implies that SMTP is simplified. Because a predecessor to SMTP was incredibly complex, the designers eliminated unnecessary features
and concentrated on the basics.

4.14 ISPs, Mail Servers, And Mail Access

As the Internet expanded to include consumers, a new paradigm arose for email.
Because most users leave their computer running continuously and do not know how to
configure and manage an email server, ISPs began offering email services. In essence,
an ISP runs an email server and provides a mailbox for each subscriber. Instead of
traditional email software, each ISP provides interface software that allows a user to access their mailbox. Figure 4.14 illustrates the arrangement.

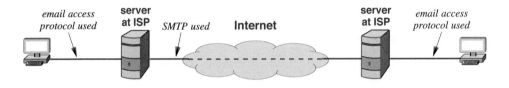

Figure 4.14 An email configuration where an ISP runs an email server and
provides a user access to a mailbox.

Email access follows one of two forms:

- A special-purpose email interface application
- A web browser that accesses an email web page

The web browser approach is straightforward: an ISP provides a special web page
that displays messages from a user's mailbox. Thus, a user launches a standard web
browser and accesses the ISP. The web page asks the user for a login ID and password,
which the web server uses to identify the user's mailbox. The web server retrieves messages from the mailbox, and displays the messages as a web page. The chief advantage
of using a web page for email arises from the ability to read email from any computer
— a user does not need to run a special mail interface application.

The advantage of using a special mail application lies in the ability to download an
entire mailbox onto a local computer. Downloading is particularly important for mobile
users who have a laptop. When the laptop is connected to the Internet, a user can run
an email program that downloads an entire mailbox onto the laptop. The user can then
process email when the laptop is disconnected from the Internet (e.g., while on an air-
plane). Once Internet connectivity is regained, software on the laptop communicates
with the server at the ISP to upload email the user has created and download any new
email that may have arrived in the user's mailbox.

4.15 Mail Access Protocols (POP, IMAP)

Protocols have been created that provide email *access*. An access protocol is distinct from a transfer protocol because access only involves a single user interacting with a single mailbox, whereas transfer protocols allow a user to send mail to other users. Access protocols have the following characteristics:

- Provide access to a user's mailbox
- Permit a user to view headers, download, delete, or send individual messages
- Client runs on user's personal computer
- Server runs on a computer that stores user's mailbox

The ability to view a list of messages without downloading the message contents is especially useful in cases where the link between a user and a mail server is slow. For example, a user browsing on a cell phone may look at headers and delete spam without waiting to download the message contents.

A variety of mechanisms have been proposed for email access. Some ISPs provide free email access software to their subscribers. In addition, two standard email access protocols have been created. Figure 4.15 lists the standard protocol names.

Acronym	Expansion
POP3	Post Office Protocol version 3
IMAP	Internet Mail Access Protocol

Figure 4.15 The two standard email access protocols.

Although they offer the same basic services, the two protocols differ in many details. In particular, each provides its own authentication mechanism that a user follows to identify themselves. Authentication is needed to insure that a user does not access another user's mailbox.

4.16 Email Representation Standards (RFC2822, MIME)

Two important email representation standards exist:

- RFC2822 Mail Message Format
- Multi-purpose Internet Mail Extensions (MIME)

RFC2822 Mail Message Format. The mail message format standard takes its name from the IETF standards document *Request For Comments 2822.* The format is straightforward: a mail message is represented as a text file and consists of a *header* section, a blank line, and a *body.* Header lines each have the form:

Keyword: information

where the set of keywords is defined to include *From:, To:, Subject:, Cc:,* and so on. In addition, header lines that start with uppercase X can be added without affecting mail processing. Thus, an email message can include a random header line such as:

X-Worst-TV-Shows: any reality show

Multi-purpose Internet Mail Extensions (MIME). Recall that SMTP only supports text messages. The MIME standard extends the functionality of email to allow the transfer of non-text data in a message. MIME specifies how a binary file can be encoded into printable characters, included in a message, and decoded by the receiver.

Although it introduced a *Base64* encoding standard that has become popular, MIME does not restrict encoding to a specific form. Instead, MIME permits a sender and receiver to choose an encoding that is convenient. To specify the use of an encoding, the sender includes additional lines in the header of the message. Furthermore, MIME allows a sender to divide a message into several parts and to specify an encoding for each part independently. Thus, with MIME, a user can send a plain text message and attach a graphic image, a spreadsheet, and an audio clip, each with their own encoding. The receiving email system can decide how to process the attachments (e.g., save a copy on disk or display a copy).

In fact, MIME adds two lines to an email header: one to declare that MIME has been used to create the message and another to specify how MIME information is included in the body. For example, the header lines:

MIME-Version: 1.0
Content-Type: Multipart/Mixed; Boundary=Mime_separator

specify that the message was composed using version *1.0* of MIME, and that a line containing *Mime_separator* will appear in the body before each part of the message. When MIME is used to send a standard text message, the second line becomes:

Content-Type: text/plain

MIME is backward compatible with email systems that do not understand the MIME standard or encoding. Of course, such systems have no way of extracting non-text attachments — they treat the body as a single block of text. To summarize:

> *The MIME standard inserts extra header lines to allow non-text attachments to be sent within an email message. An attachment is encoded as printable letters, and a separator line appears before each attachment.*

4.17 Domain Name System (DNS)

The *Domain Name System* (*DNS*) provides a service that maps human-readable symbolic names to computer addresses. Browsers, mail software, and most other Internet applications use the DNS. The system provides an interesting example of client-server interaction because the mapping is not performed by a single server. Instead, the naming information is distributed among a large set of servers located at sites across the Internet. Whenever an application program needs to translate a name, the application becomes a client of the naming system. The client sends a request message to a name server, which finds the corresponding address and sends a reply message. If it cannot answer a request, a name server temporarily becomes the client of another name server, until a server is found that can answer the request.

Syntactically, each name consists of a sequence of alpha-numeric segments separated by periods. For example, a computer in the Computer Science Department at Purdue University has the domain name:

mordred.cs.purdue.edu

and a computer at Cisco, Incorporated has the domain name:

anakin.cisco.com

Domain names are hierarchical, with the most significant part of the name on the right. The left-most segment of a name (*mordred* and *anakin* in the examples) is the name of an individual computer. Other segments in a domain name identify the group that owns the name. For example, the segment *purdue* gives the name of a university, and *cisco* gives the name of a company. DNS does not specify the number of segments in a name. Instead, each organization can choose how many segments to use for computers inside the organization and what the segments represent.

The Domain Name System does specify values for the most significant segment, which is called a *top-level domain* (*TLD*). Top-level domains are controlled by the *Internet Corporation for Assigned Names and Numbers* (*ICANN*), which designates one or more *domain registrars* to administer a given top-level domain and approve specific names. Some TLDs are *generic*, which means they are generally available. Other TLDs are restricted to specific groups or government agencies. Figure 4.16 lists example top-level DNS domains.

Domain Name	Assigned To
aero	Air transport industry
arpa	Infrastructure domain
asia	For or about Asia
biz	Businesses
com	Commercial organizations
coop	Cooperative associations
edu	Educational institutions
gov	United States Government
info	Information
int	International treaty organizations
jobs	Human resource managers
mil	United States military
mobi	Mobile content providers
museum	Museums
name	Individuals
net	Major network support centers
org	Non-commercial organizations
pro	Credentialed professionals
travel	Travel and tourism
country code	A sovereign nation

Figure 4.16 Example top-level domains and the group to which each is assigned.

An organization applies for a name under one of the existing top-level domains. For example, most U.S. corporations choose to register under the *com* domain. Thus, a corporation named *Foobar* might request to be assigned domain *foobar* under the top-level domain *com*. Once the request is approved, Foobar Corporation will be assigned the domain:

foobar.com

Once the name has been assigned another organization named Foobar can apply for *foobar.biz* or *foobar.org*, but not *foobar.com*. Furthermore, once *foobar.com* has been assigned, the Foobar Corporation can choose how many additional levels to add and the meaning of each. Thus, if Foobar has locations on the East and West coast, one might find names such as:

computer1.east-coast.foobar.com

or Foobar may choose a relatively flat naming hierarchy with all computers identified by name and the company's domain name:

computer1.foobar.com

In addition to the familiar organizational structure, the DNS allows organizations to use a geographic registration. For example, the Corporation For National Research Initiatives registered the domain:

cnri.reston.va.us

because the corporation is located in the town of Reston, Virginia in the United States. Thus, names of computers at the corporation end in *.us* instead of *.com.*

Some foreign countries have adopted a combination of geographic and organizational domain names. For example, universities in the United Kingdom register under the domain:

ac.uk

where *ac* is an abbreviation for *academic*, and *uk* is the official country code for the United Kingdom.

4.18 Domain Names That Begin With www

Many organizations assign domain names that reflect the service a computer provides. For example, a computer that runs a server for the File Transfer Protocol might be named:

ftp.foobar.com

Similarly, a computer that runs a web server, might be named:

www.foobar.com

Such names are mnemonic, but are not required. In particular, the use of *www* to name computers that run a web server is merely a convention — an arbitrary computer can run a web server, even if the computer's domain name does not contain *www*. Furthermore, a computer that has a domain name beginning with *www* is not required to run a web server. The point is:

Using the first label in a domain name to denote a service (e.g., www) is merely a convention to help humans.

4.19 The DNS Hierarchy And Server Model

One of the main features of the Domain Name System is autonomy — the system is designed to allow each organization to assign names to computers or to change those names without informing a central authority. To achieve autonomy, each organization is permitted to operate DNS servers for its part of the hierarchy. Thus, Purdue University operates a server for names ending in *purdue.edu*, and IBM Corporation operates a server for names ending in *ibm.com*. Each DNS server contains information that links the server to other domain name servers up and down the hierarchy. Furthermore, a given server can be *replicated*, such that multiple physical copies of the server exist. Replication is especially useful for heavily used servers, such as the *root servers* that provide information about top-level domains. In such cases, administrators must guarantee that all copies are coordinated so they provide exactly the same information.

Each organization is free to choose the details of its servers. For example, a small organization that only has a few computers can contract with an ISP to run a DNS server. A large organization that runs its own server can choose to place all names for the organization in a single physical server, or can choose to divide its names among multiple servers. For example, Figure 4.17 illustrates how the hypothetical Foobar Corporation might choose to structure servers if the corporation had a candy division and a soap division.

4.20 Name Resolution

The translation of a domain name into an address is called *name resolution*, and the name is said to be *resolved* to an address. Software to perform the translation is known as a *name resolver* (or simply *resolver*). In the socket API, for example, the resolver is invoked by calling function *gethostbyname*. The resolver becomes a client, contacts a DNS server, and returns an answer to the caller.

Each resolver is configured with the address of one or more *local* domain name servers†. The resolver forms a *DNS request* message, sends the message to the local server, and waits for the server to send a *DNS reply* message that contains the answer. A resolver can choose to use either the stream or message paradigm when communicating with a DNS server; most resolvers are configured to use a message paradigm because it imposes less overhead for a small request.

As an example of name resolution, consider the server hierarchy that Figure 4.17a illustrates, and assume a computer in the soap division generates a request for name *chocolate.candy.foobar.com*. The resolver will be configured to send the request to the local DNS server (i.e., the server for foobar.com). Although it cannot answer the request, the server knows to contact the server for *candy.foobar.com*, which can generate an answer.

---

†The significance of contacting a local server first will become apparent when we discuss caching.

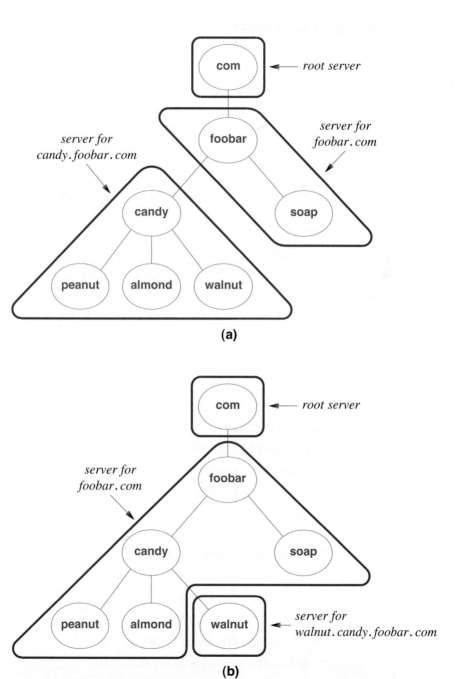

Figure 4.17 A hypothetical DNS hierarchy and two possible assignments of names to servers.

4.21 Caching In DNS Servers

The *locality of reference* principle that forms the basis for caching applies to the Domain Name System in two ways:

- Spatial: A user tends to look up the names of local computers more often than the names of remote computers
- Temporal: A user tends to look up the same set of domain names repeatedly

We have already seen how DNS exploits spatial locality: a name resolver contacts a local server first. To exploit temporal locality, a DNS server caches all lookups. Algorithm 4.4 summarizes the process.

Algorithm 4.4

Given:

　　A request message from a DNS name resolver

Provide:

　　A response message that contains the address

Method:

　　Extract the name, N, from the request

　　if (server is an authority for N) {

　　　　Form and send a response to the requester;

　　else if (answer for N is in the cache) {

　　　　Form and send a response to the requester;

　　else {　/* Need to look up an answer */

　　　　if (authority server for N is known) {

　　　　　　Send request to authority server;

　　　　} else {

　　　　　　Send request to root server;

　　　　}

　　　　Receive response and place in cache;

　　　　Form and send a response to the requester;

　　}

Algorithm 4.4 Steps a DNS server takes to resolve a name.

According to the algorithm, when a request arrives for a name outside the set for which the server is an authority, further client-server interaction results. The server temporarily becomes a client of another name server. When the other server returns an answer, the original server caches the answer and sends a copy of the answer back to the resolver from which the request arrived. Thus, in addition to knowing the address of all servers down the hierarchy, each DNS server must know the address of a root server.

The fundamental question in all caching relates to the length of time items should be cached — if an item is cached too long, the item will become *stale*. DNS solves the problem by arranging for an authoritative server to specify a cache timeout for each item. Thus, when a local server looks up a name, the response consists of a *Resource Record* that specifies a cache timeout as well as an answer. Whenever a server caches an answer, the server honors the timeout specified in the Resource Record. The point is:

> *Because each DNS Resource Record generated by an authoritative server specifies a cache timeout, items can be removed from a DNS cache when they become stale.*

DNS caching does not stop with servers: a resolver can cache items as well. In fact, the resolver software in most computer systems caches the answers from DNS lookups, which means that successive requests for the same name do not need to use the network because the resolver can satisfy the request from the cache on the local disk.

4.22 Types Of DNS Entries

Each entry in a DNS database consists of three items: a domain name, a record type, and a value. The record type specifies how the value is to be interpreted (e.g., that the value is an IP address). More important, a query sent to a DNS server specifies both a domain name and a type; the server only returns a binding that matches the type of the query.

The principal type maps a domain name to an IP address. DNS classifies such bindings as type *A*, and type *A* lookup is used by applications such as *FTP*, *ping*, or a browser. DNS supports several other types, including type *MX* that specifies a *Mail eXchanger*. When it looks up the name in an email address, SMTP uses type *MX*. The answer that the server returns matches the requested type. Thus, an email system will receive an answer that matches type *MX*. The important point is:

> *Each entry in a DNS server has a type. When a resolver looks up a name, the resolver specifies the type that is desired, and the DNS server returns only entries that match the specified type.*

The DNS type system can produce unexpected results because the address returned can depend on the type. For example, a corporation may decide to use the name *corporation.com* for both web and email services. With the DNS, it is possible for the corporation to divide the workload between separate computers by mapping type *A* lookups to one computer and type MX lookups to another. The disadvantage of such a scheme is that it seems counterintuitive to humans — it may be possible to send email to *corporation.com* even if it is not possible to access the web server or ping the computer.

4.23 Aliases And CNAME Resource Records

The DNS offers a *CNAME* type that is analogous to a symbolic link in a file system — the entry provides an alias for another DNS entry. To understand how aliases can be useful, suppose Foobar Corporation has two computers named *hobbes.foobar.com* and *calvin.foobar.com*. Further suppose that Foobar decides to run a web server on computer *hobbes*, and wants to follow the convention of using the name *www* for the computer that runs the organization's web server. Although the organization could choose to rename computer *hobbes*, a much easier solution exists: the organization can create a *CNAME* entry for *www.foobar.com* that points to *hobbes*. Whenever a resolver sends a request for *www.foobar.com*, the server returns the address of computer *hobbes*.

The use of aliases is especially convenient because it permits an organization to change the computer used for a particular service without changing the names or addresses of the computers. For example, Foobar Corporation can move its web service from computer *hobbes* to computer *calvin* by moving the server and changing the *CNAME* record in the DNS server — the two computers retain their original names and IP addresses. The use of aliases also allows an organization to associate multiple aliases with a single computer. Thus, Foobar corporation can run an FTP server and a web server on the same computer, and can create CNAME records:

www.foobar.com

ftp.foobar.com

4.24 Abbreviations And The DNS

The DNS does not incorporate abbreviations — a server only responds to a full name. However, most resolvers can be configured with a set of suffixes that allow a user to abbreviate names. For example, each resolver at Foobar Corporation might be programmed to look up a name twice: once with no change and once with the suffix *foobar.com* appended. If a user enters a full domain name, the local server will return the address, and processing will proceed. If a user enters an abbreviated name, the resolver will first try to resolve the name and will receive an error because no such name exists. The resolver will then try appending a suffix and looking up the resulting name. Because a resolver runs on a user's personal computer, the approach allows each user to choose the order in which suffixes are tried.

Of course, allowing each user to configure their resolver to handle abbreviations has a disadvantage: the name a given user enters can differ from the name another user enters. Thus, if the users communicate names to one another (e.g., by sending a domain name in an email message), each must be careful to specify full names and not abbreviations.

4.25 Internationalized Domain Names

Because it uses the ASCII character set, the DNS cannot store names in alphabets that are not represented in ASCII. In particular, languages such as Russian, Greek, Chinese, and Japanese each contain characters for which no ASCII representation exists. Many European languages use diacritical marks that cannot be represented in ASCII.

For years, the IETF debated modifications and extensions of the DNS to accommodate international domain names. After considering many proposals, the IETF chose an approach known as *Internationalizing Domain Names in Applications* (*IDNA*). Instead of modifying the underlying DNS, IDNA uses ASCII to store all names. That is, when given a domain name that contains a non-ASCII character, IDNA translates the name into a sequence of ASCII characters, and stores the result in the DNS. When a user looks up the name, the same translation is applied to convert the name into an ASCII string and the resulting ASCII string is placed in a DNS query. In essence, IDNA relies on applications to translate between the international character set that a user sees and the internal ASCII form used in the DNS.

The rules for translating international domain names are complex and use *Unicode*†. In essence, the translation is applied to each label in the domain name, and results in labels of the form:

$$xn\text{-}\text{-}\alpha\text{-}\beta$$

where *xn--* is a reserved four-character string that indicates the label is an international name, α is the subset of characters from the original label that can be represented in ASCII, and β is a string of additional ASCII characters that tell an IDNA application how to insert non-ASCII characters into α to form the printable version of the label.

The latest versions of the widely-used browsers, Firefox and Internet Explorer, can accept and display non-ASCII domain names because they each implement IDNA. If an application does not implement IDNA, the output may appear strange to a user. That is, when an application that does not implement IDNA displays an international domain name, the user will see the internal form illustrated above, including the initial string *xn--* and the subsequent parts α and β.

---

†The translation algorithm used to encode non-ASCII labels is known as the *Puny* algorithm, and the resulting string is known as *Punycode*.

To summarize:

> *The IDNA standard for international domain names encodes each la-*
> *bel as an ASCII string, and relies on applications to translate between*
> *the character set a user expects and the encoded version stored in the*
> *DNS.*

4.26 Extensible Representations (XML)

The traditional application protocols covered in this chapter each employ a fixed representation. That is, the application protocol specifies an exact set of messages that a client and server can exchange as well as the exact form of data that accompanies the message. The chief disadvantage of a fixed approach arises from the difficulty involved in making changes. For example, because email standards restrict message content to text, a major change was needed to add MIME extensions.

The alternative to a fixed representation is an extensible system that allows a sender to specify the format of data. One standard for extensible representation has become widely accepted: the *Extensible Markup Language (XML)*. XML resembles HTML in the sense that both languages embed tags into a text document. Unlike HTML, the tags in XML are not specified a priori and do not correspond to formatting commands. Instead, XML describes the structure of data and provides names for each field. Tags in XML are well-balanced — each occurrence of a tag *<X>* must be followed by an occurrence of *</X>*. Furthermore, because XML does not assign any meaning to tags, tag names can be created as needed. In particular, tag names can be selected to make data easy to parse or access. For example, if two companies agree to exchange corporate telephone directories, they can define an XML format that has data items such as an employee's name, phone number, and office. The companies can choose to further divide a name into a last name and a first name. Figure 4.18 contains an example.

```
<ADDRESS>
    <NAME>
        <FIRST>  John     </FIRST>
        <LAST>   Public   </LAST>
    </NAME>
    <OFFICE> Room 320      </OFFICE>
    <PHONE>  765-555-1234 </PHONE>
</ADDRESS>
```

Figure 4.18 An example of XML for a corporate phone book.

4.27 Summary

Application-layer protocols, required for standardized services, define data representation and data transfer aspects of communication. Representation protocols used with the World Wide Web include HyperText Markup Language (HTML) and the URL standard. The web transfer protocol, which is known as the HyperText Transfer Protocol (HTTP), specifies how a browser communicates with a web server to download or upload contents. To speed downloads, a browser caches page content and uses an HTTP *HEAD* command to request status information about the page. If the cached version remains current, the browser uses the cached version; otherwise, the browser issues a *GET* request to download a fresh copy.

HTTP uses textual messages. Each response from a server begins with a header that describes the response. Lines in the header begin with a numeric value, represented as ASCII digits, that tells the status (e.g., whether a request is in error). Data that follows the header can contain arbitrary binary values.

The File Transfer Protocol (FTP) is frequently used for file download. FTP requires a client to log into the server's system; FTP supports a login of *anonymous* and password *guest* for public file access. The most interesting aspect of FTP arises from its unusual use of connections. A client establishes a control connection that is used to send a series of commands. Whenever a server needs to send data (e.g., a file download or the listing of a directory), the server acts as a client and the client acts as a server. That is, the server initiates a new data connection to the client. Once a single file has been sent, the data connection is closed.

Three types of application-layer protocols are used with electronic mail: transfer, representation, and access. The Simple Mail Transfer Protocol serves as the key transfer standard; SMTP can only transfer a textual message. There are two representation standards for email: RFC 2822 defines the mail message format to be a header and body separated by a blank line. The Multi-purpose Internet Mail Extensions (MIME) standard defines a mechanism to send binary files as attachments to an email message. MIME inserts extra header lines that tell the receiver how to interpret the message. MIME requires a sender to encode a file as printable text.

Email access protocols, such as POP3 and IMAP, permit a user to access a mailbox. Access has become popular because a subscriber can allow an ISP to run an email server and maintain the user's mailbox.

The Domain Name System (DNS) provides automated mapping from human-readable names to computer addresses. DNS consists of many servers that each control one part of the namespace. Servers are arranged in a hierarchy, and a server knows the locations of servers in the hierarchy.

The DNS uses caching to maintain efficiency; when an authoritative server provides an answer, each server that transfers the answer also places a copy in its cache. To prevent cached copies from becoming stale, the authority for a name specifies how long the name can be cached.

EXERCISES

4.1   What does a browser cache, and why is caching used?

4.2   What are the characteristics of SMTP?

4.3   True or false: a multi-national company can choose to divide its domain name hierarchy in such a way that the company has a domain name server in Europe, one in Asia, and one in North America.

4.4   How does XML allow an application to specify fields such as a name and address?

4.5   What details does an application protocol specify?

4.6   Does the IDNA standard require changes in DNS servers? in DNS clients? Explain.

4.7   What are the four HTTP request types, and when is each used?

4.8   What are the two main email access protocols?

4.9   Where is an email access protocol used?

4.10 Why is a protocol for a standardized service documented independent of an implementation?

4.11 Search the web to find out about iterative DNS lookup. Under what circumstances is iterative lookup used?

4.12 Can a browser use transfer protocols other than HTTP? Explain.

4.13 Describe the steps a browser takes to determine whether to use an item from its cache.

4.14 How does an FTP server know the port number to use for a data connection?

4.15 What are the two key aspects of application protocols, and what does each include?

4.16 What is the overall purpose of the Domain Name System?

4.17 Why was MIME invented?

4.18 Give examples of web protocols that illustrate each of the two aspects of an application protocol.

4.19 Can SMTP transfer an email message that contains a period on a line by itself? Why or why not?

4.20 True or false: a web server must have a domain name that begins with www. Explain.

4.21 True or false: a DNS server can return a different IP address for a given name, depending on whether the lookup specifies email or web service. Explain.

4.22 Summarize the characteristics of HTML.

4.23 When does a domain name server send a request to an authoritative server and when does it answer the request without sending to the authoritative server?

4.24 What are the four parts of a URL, and what punctuation is used to separate the parts?

4.25 How does a browser know whether an HTTP request is syntactically incorrect or whether the referenced item does not exist?

4.26 When a user requests an FTP directory listing, how many TCP connections are formed? Explain.

4.27 List the three types of protocols used with email, and describe each.

4.28 True or false: when a user runs an FTP application, the application acts as both a client and server. Explain your answer.

4.29 Assuming ISO has assigned *N* country codes, how many top-level domains exist?

4.30 According to the original email paradigm, could a user receive email if the user's computer did not run an email server? Explain.

PART II

Data Communications

The basics of media, encoding, transmission, modulation, multiplexing, connections, and remote access

Chapters

Chapter Contents

5

Overview Of Data Communications

5.1 Introduction

The first part of the text discusses network programming and reviews Internet applications. The chapter on socket programming explains the API that operating systems provide to application software, and shows that a programmer can create applications that use the Internet without understanding the underlying mechanisms. In the remainder of the text, we will learn about the complex protocols and technologies that support communication, and see that understanding the complexity can help programmers write better code.

This part of the text explores the transmission of information across physical media, such as wires, optical fibers, and radio waves. We will see that although the details vary, basic ideas about information and communication apply to all forms of transmission. We will understand that data communications provides conceptual and analytical tools that offer a unified explanation of how communication systems operate. More important, data communications tells us what transfers are theoretically possible as well as how the reality of the physical world limits practical transmission systems.

This chapter provides an overview of data communications and explains how the conceptual pieces form a complete communication system. Successive chapters each explain one concept in detail.

5.2 The Essence Of Data Communications

What does data communications entail? As Figure 5.1 illustrates, the subject is an interesting combination of ideas and approaches from three disciplines.

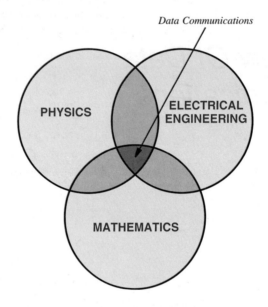

Figure 5.1 The subject of data communications lies at the intersection of Physics, Mathematics, and Electrical Engineering.

Because it involves the transmission of information over physical media, data communications touches on physics. The subject draws on ideas about electric current, light, and other forms of electro-magnetic radiation. Because information is digitized and digital data is transmitted, data communications uses mathematics and includes various forms of analysis. Finally, because the ultimate goal is to develop practical ways to design and build transmission systems, data communications focuses on developing techniques that electrical engineers can use. The point is:

> *Although it includes concepts from physics and mathematics, data communications does not merely offer abstract theories. Instead, data communications provides a foundation that is used to construct practical communication systems.*

5.3 Motivation And Scope Of The Subject

Three main ideas provide much of the motivation for data communications and help define the scope.

- The sources of information can be of arbitrary types
- Transmission uses a physical system
- Multiple sources of information can share the underlying medium

The first point is especially relevant considering the popularity of multimedia applications: information is not restricted to bits that have been stored in a computer. Instead, information can also be derived from the physical world, including audio and video. Thus, it is important to understand the possible sources and forms of information and the ways that one form can be transformed into another.

The second point suggests that we must use natural phenomena, such as electricity and electromagnetic radiation, to transmit information. Thus, it is important to understand the types of media that are available and the properties of each. Furthermore, we must understand how physical phenomena can be used to transmit information over each medium, and the relationship between data communications and the underlying transmission. Finally, we must understand the limits of physical systems, the problems that can arise during transmission, and techniques that can be used to detect or solve the problems.

The third point suggests that sharing is fundamental. Indeed, we will see that sharing plays a fundamental role in most computer networks. That is, a network usually permits multiple pairs of communicating entities to communicate over a given physical medium. Thus, it is important to understand the possible ways underlying facilities can be shared, the advantages and disadvantages of each, and the resulting modes of communication.

5.4 The Conceptual Pieces Of A Communication System

To understand data communications, imagine a working communication system that accommodates multiple sources of information, and allows each source to send to a separate destination. It may seem that communication in such a system is straightforward. Each source needs a mechanism to gather the information, prepare the information for transmission, and transmit the information across the shared physical medium. Similarly, a mechanism is needed that extracts the information for the destination and delivers the information. Figure 5.2 illustrates the simplistic view.

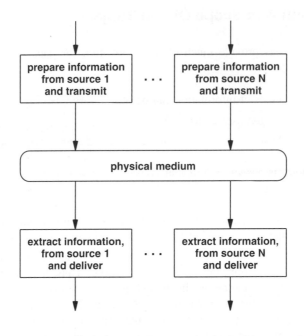

Figure 5.2 A simplistic view of data communications with a set of sources sending to a set of destinations across a shared medium.

In practice, data communications is much more complex than the simplistic diagram in Figure 5.2 suggests. Because information can arrive from many types of sources, the techniques used to handle sources vary. Before it can be sent, information must be digitized, and extra data must be added to protect against errors. If privacy is a concern, the information may need to be encrypted. To send multiple streams of information across a shared communication mechanism, the information from each source must be identified, and data from all the sources must be intermixed for transmission. Thus, a mechanism is needed to identify each source, and guarantee that the information from one source is not inadvertently confused with information from another source.

To explain the major aspects of data communications, engineers have derived a conceptual framework that shows how each subtopic fits into a communication system. The idea is that each item in the framework can be studied independently, and once all pieces have been examined, the entire subject will be understood. Figure 5.3 illustrates the framework, and shows how the conceptual aspects fit into the overall organization of a communication system.

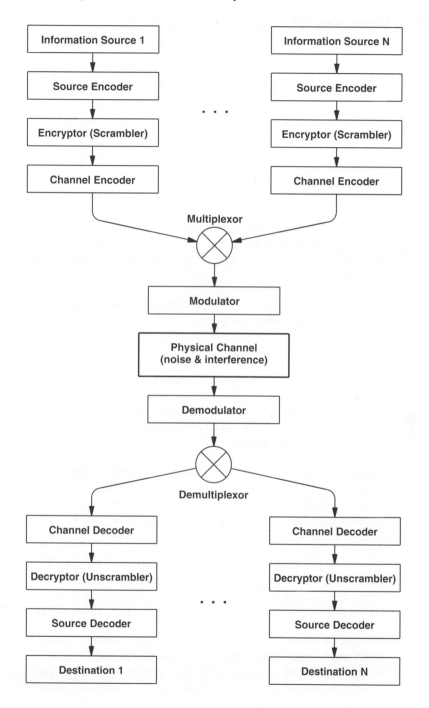

Figure 5.3 A conceptual framework for a data communications system. Multiple sources send to multiple destinations through an underlying physical channel.

5.5 The Subtopics Of Data Communications

Each of the boxes in Figure 5.3 corresponds to one subtopic of data communications. The following paragraphs explain the terminology. Successive chapters each examine one of the conceptual subtopics.

- *Information Sources.* The source of information can be either analog or digital. Important concepts include characteristics of signals, such as amplitude, frequency, and phase, and classification as either periodic or aperiodic. In addition, the subtopic focuses on the conversion between analog and digital representations of information.

- *Source Encoder and Decoder.* Once information has been digitized, digital representations can be transformed and converted. Important concepts include data compression and consequences for communications.

- *Encryptor and Decryptor.* To protect information and keep it private, the information can be encrypted (i.e., scrambled) before transmission and decrypted upon reception. Important concepts include cryptographic techniques and algorithms.

- *Channel Encoder and Decoder.* Channel coding is used to detect and correct transmission errors. Important topics include methods to detect and limit errors, and practical techniques like parity checking, checksums, and cyclic redundancy codes that are employed in computer networks.

- *Multiplexor and Demultiplexor.* Multiplexing refers to the way information from multiple sources is combined for transmission across a shared medium. Important concepts include techniques for simultaneous sharing as well techniques that allow sources to take turns when using the medium.

- *Modulator and Demodulator.* Modulation refers to the way electromagnetic radiation is used to send information. Concepts include both analog and digital modulation schemes, and devices known as modems that perform the modulation and demodulation.

- *Physical Channel and Transmission.* The subtopic includes transmission media and transmission modes. Important concepts include bandwidth, electrical noise and interference, and channel capacity, as well as transmission modes, such as serial and parallel.

5.6 Summary

Because it deals with transmission across physical media and digital information, data communications draws on physics and mathematics. The focus is on techniques that allow Electrical Engineers to design practical communication mechanisms.

To simplify understanding, engineers have devised a conceptual framework for data communications systems. The framework divides the entire subject into a set of subtopics. Each of the successive chapters in this part of the text discuss one of the subtopics.

EXERCISES

5.1   What are the conceptual pieces of a data communications system?

5.2   Which piece of a data communications system prevents transmission errors from corrupting data?

5.3   What three disciplines are involved in data communications?

5.4   What are the motivations for data communications?

5.5   Which piece of a data communications system handles analog input?

Chapter Contents

6

Information Sources And Signals

6.1 Introduction

The previous chapter begins the study of data communications, the foundation of all networking. The chapter introduces the topic, gives a conceptual framework for data communications, identifies the important aspects, and explains how the aspects fit together. The chapter also gives a brief description of each conceptual piece.

This chapter begins an exploration of data communications in more detail. The chapter examines the topics of information sources and the characteristics of the signals that carry information. Successive chapters continue the exploration of data communications by explaining additional aspects of the subject.

6.2 Information Sources

Recall that a communication system accepts input from one or more *sources* and delivers the information from a given source to a specified *destination*. For a network, such as the global Internet, the source and destination of information are a pair of application programs that generate and consume data. However, data communications theory concentrates on low-level communications systems, and applies to arbitrary sources of information. For example, in addition to conventional computer peripherals such as keyboards and mice, information sources can include microphones, sensors, and measuring devices, such as thermometers and scales. Similarly, destinations can include audio output devices such as earphones and loud speakers as well as devices such as LEDs that emit light. The point is:

> *Throughout the study of data communications, it is important to remember that the source of information can be arbitrary and includes devices other than computers.*

6.3 Analog And Digital Signals

Data communications deals with two types of information: analog and digital. An analog signal is characterized by a continuous mathematical function — when the input changes from one value to the next, it does so by moving through all possible intermediate values. In contrast, a digital signal has a fixed set of valid levels, and each change consists of an instantaneous move from one valid level to another. Figure 6.1 illustrates the concept by showing examples of how the signals from an analog source and a digital source vary over time. In the figure, the analog signal might result if one measured the output of a microphone, and the digital signal might result if one measured the output of a computer keyboard.

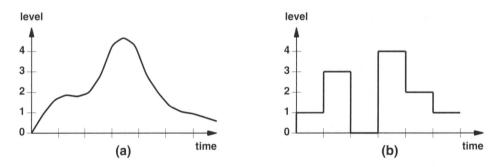

Figure 6.1 Illustration of (a) an analog signal, and (b) a digital signal.

6.4 Periodic And Aperiodic Signals

Signals are broadly classified as *periodic* or *aperiodic* (sometimes called *nonperiodic*), depending on whether they repeat. For example, the analog signal in Figure 6.1a is aperiodic over the time interval shown because the signal does not repeat. Figure 6.2 illustrates a signal that is periodic (i.e., repeating).

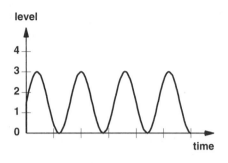

Figure 6.2 A periodic signal repeats.

6.5 Sine Waves And Signal Characteristics

We will see that much of the analysis in data communications involves the use of sinusoidal trigonometric functions, especially *sine*, which is usually abbreviated *sin*. Sine waves are especially important in information sources because natural phenomena produce sine waves. For example, when a microphone picks up an audible tone, the output is a sine wave. Similarly, electromagnetic radiation can be represented as a sine wave. We will specifically be interested in sine waves that correspond to a signal that oscillates in time, such as the wave that Figure 6.2 illustrates. The point is:

> *Sine waves are fundamental to input processing because many natural phenomena produce a signal that corresponds to a sine wave as a function of time.*

There are four important characteristics of signals that relate to sine waves:

- Frequency: the number of oscillations per unit time (usually seconds)
- Amplitude: the difference between the maximum and minimum signal heights
- Phase: how far the start of the sine wave is shifted from a reference time
- Wavelength: the length of a cycle as a signal propagates across a medium

Wavelength is determined by the speed with which a signal propagates (i.e., is a function of the underlying medium). The other three characteristics can be expressed mathematically. Amplitude is easiest to understand. Recall that $sin(\omega t)$ produces values between -1 to $+1$, and has an amplitude of *1*. Thus, if the value is multiplied by A, the amplitude of the resulting wave is A. Mathematically, the phase is an offset added to t that shifts the sine wave to the right or left along the x-axis. Thus, $sin(\omega t + \phi)$ has a phase of ϕ. The frequency of a signal is measured in the number of sine wave cycles per second, *Hertz*. A complete sine wave requires 2π radians. Therefore, if t is a time in seconds and $\omega = 2\pi$, $sin(\omega t)$ has a frequency of 1 Hertz. Figure 6.3 illustrates the three mathematical characteristics.

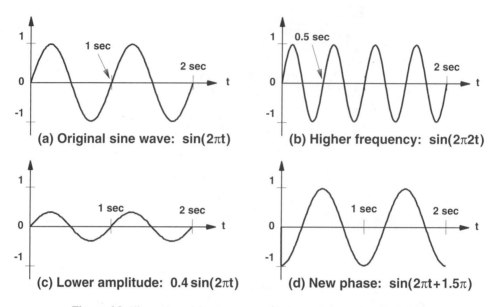

Figure 6.3 Illustration of frequency, amplitude, and phase characteristics.

The frequency can be calculated as the inverse of the time required for one cycle, which is known as the *period*. The example sine wave in Figure 6.3a has a period $T = 1$ seconds, and a frequency of $1/T$ or 1 Hertz. The example in Figure 6.3b has a period of $T = 0.5$ seconds, so its frequency is 2 Hertz; both are considered extremely *low* frequencies. Typical communication systems use *high* frequencies, often measured in millions of cycles per second. To clarify high frequencies, engineers express time in fractions of a second or express frequency in units such as *megahertz*. Figure 6.4 lists time scales and common prefixes used with frequency.

Time Unit	Value	Frequency Unit	Value
Seconds (s)	10^0 seconds	Hertz (Hz)	10^0 Hz
Milliseconds (ms)	10^{-3} seconds	Kilohertz (KHz)	10^3 Hz
Microseconds (μs)	10^{-6} seconds	Megahertz (MHz)	10^6 Hz
Nanoseconds (ns)	10^{-9} seconds	Gigahertz (GHz)	10^9 Hz
Picoseconds (ps)	10^{-12} seconds	Terahertz (THz)	10^{12} Hz

Figure 6.4 Prefixes and abbreviations for units of time and frequency.

6.6 Composite Signals

Signals like the ones illustrated in Figure 6.3 are classified as *simple* because they consist of a single sine wave that cannot be decomposed further. In practice, most signals are classified as *composite* because the signal can be decomposed into a set of simple sine waves. For example, Figure 6.5 illustrates a composite signal formed by adding two simple sine waves.

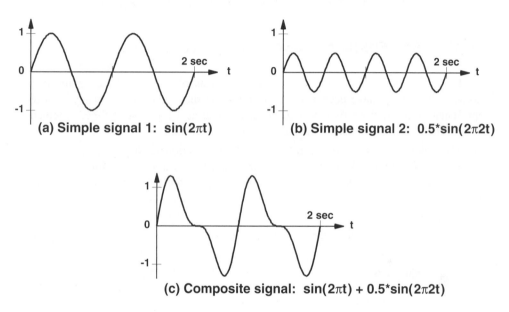

(a) Simple signal 1: sin(2πt)

(b) Simple signal 2: 0.5*sin(2π2t)

(c) Composite signal: sin(2πt) + 0.5*sin(2π2t)

Figure 6.5 Illustration of a composite signal formed from two simple signals.

6.7 The Importance Of Composite Signals And Sine Functions

Why does data communications seem obsessed with sine functions and composite signals? When we discuss modulation and demodulation, we will understand one of the primary reasons: the signals that result from modulation are usually composite signals. For now, it is only important to understand the motivation:

- Modulation usually forms a composite signal.
- A mathematician named Fourier discovered that it is possible to decompose a composite signal into its constituent parts, a set of sine functions, each with a frequency, amplitude, and phase.

The analysis by Fourier shows that if the composite signal is periodic, the constituent parts will also be periodic. Thus, we will see that most data communications systems use composite signals to carry information: a composite signal is created at the sending end, and the receiver decomposes the signal into the original simple components. The point is:

A mathematical method discovered by Fourier allows a receiver to decompose a composite signal into constituent parts.

6.8 Time And Frequency Domain Representations

Because they are fundamental, composite signals have been studied extensively, and several methods have been invented to represent them. We have already seen one representation in previous figures: a graph of a signal as a function of time. Engineers say that such a graph represents the signal in the *time domain*.

The chief alternative to a time domain representation is known as a *frequency domain* representation. A frequency domain graph shows a set of simple sine waves that constitute a composite function. The y-axis gives the amplitude, and the x-axis gives the frequency. Thus, the function $A \sin(2\pi t)$ is represented by a single line of height A that is positioned at x=t. For example, the frequency domain graph in Figure 6.6 represents a composite from Figure 6.5c†.

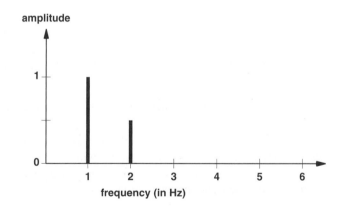

Figure 6.6 Representation of $\sin(2\pi t)$ and $0.5\sin(2\pi 2t)$ in the frequency domain.

The figure shows a set of simple periodic signals. A frequency domain representation can also be used with nonperiodic signals, but aperiodic representation is not essential to an understanding of the subject.

---

†Frequency domain diagrams used with real data communications systems have an x-axis that extends to thousands or millions of Hertz.

One of the advantages of the frequency domain representation arises from its compactness. Compared to a time domain representation, a frequency domain representation is both small and easy to read because each sine wave occupies a single point along the x-axis. The advantage becomes clear when a composite signal contains many simple signals.

6.9 Bandwidth Of An Analog Signal

Almost everyone has heard of "network bandwidth", and understands that a network with high bandwidth is desirable. We will discuss the definition of network bandwidth later. For now, we will explore a related concept, *analog bandwidth*.

We define the bandwidth of an analog signal to be the difference between the highest and lowest frequencies of the constituent parts (i.e., the highest and lowest frequencies obtained by Fourier analysis). In the trivial example of Figure 6.5c, Fourier analysis produces signals of 1 and 2 Hertz, which means the bandwidth is the difference, or 1 Hertz. An advantage of a frequency domain plot becomes clear when one computes bandwidth because the highest and lowest frequencies are obvious. For example, the plot in Figure 6.6 makes it clear that the bandwidth is 1.

Figure 6.7 shows a frequency domain plot with frequencies measured in Kilohertz (KHz). Such frequencies are in the range audible to a human ear. In the figure, the bandwidth is the difference between the highest and lowest frequency (5 KHz − 1 KHz = 4 KHz).

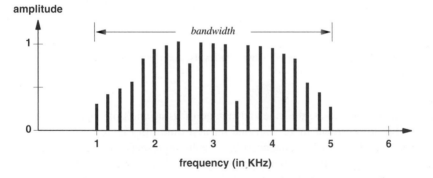

Figure 6.7 A frequency domain plot of an analog signal with a bandwidth of 4 KHz.

To summarize:

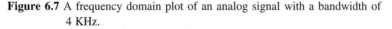

The bandwidth *of an analog signal is the difference between the highest and lowest frequency of its components. If the signal is plotted in the frequency domain, the bandwidth is trivial to compute.*

6.10 Digital Signals And Signal Levels

We said in addition to being represented by an analog signal, information can also be represented by a *digital* signal. We further defined a signal to be digital if a fixed set of valid levels has been chosen and at any time, the signal is at one of the valid levels. Some systems use voltage to represent digital values by making a positive voltage correspond to a logical one, and zero voltage correspond to a logical zero. For example, +5 volts can be used for a logical one and 0 volts for a logical zero.

If only two levels of voltage are used, each level corresponds to one data bit (0 or 1). However, some physical transmission mechanisms can support more than two signal levels. When multiple digital levels are available, each level can represent multiple bits. For example, consider a system that uses four levels of voltage: -5 volts, -2 volts, +2 volts, and +5 volts. Each level can correspond to two bits of data as Figure 6.8 illustrates.

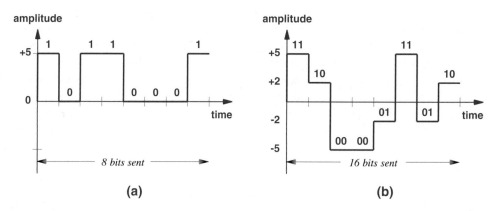

Figure 6.8 (a) A digital signal using two levels, and (b) a digital signal using four levels.

As the figure illustrates, the chief advantage of using multiple signal levels arises from the ability to represent more than one bit at a time. In Figure 6.8b, for example, -5 volts represents the two-bit sequence *00*, -2 volts represents *01*, +2 volts represents *10*, and +5 volts represents *11*. Because multiple levels of signal are used, each time slot can transfer two bits, which means that the four-level representation in Figure 6.8b sends twice as many bits per unit time as the two-level representation in Figure 6.8a.

The relationship between the number of levels required and the number of bits to be sent is straightforward. There must be a signal level for each possible combination of bits. Because 2^n combinations are possible with n bits, a communication system must use 2^n levels to represent n bits. To summarize:

> *A communication system that uses two signal levels can only send one bit at a given time; a system that supports 2^n signal levels can send n bits at a time.*

It may seem that voltage is an arbitrary quantity, and that one could achieve arbitrary numbers of levels by dividing voltage into arbitrarily small increments. Mathematically, one could create a million levels between 0 and 1 volts merely by using 0.0000001 volts for one level, 0.0000002 for the next level, and so on. Unfortunately, practical electronic systems cannot distinguish between signals that differ by arbitrarily small amounts. Thus, practical systems are restricted to a few signal levels.

6.11 Baud And Bits Per Second

How much data can be sent in a given time? The answer depends on two aspects of the communication system. As we have seen, the rate at which data can be sent depends on the number of signal levels. A second factor is also important: the amount of time the system remains at a given level before moving to the next. For example, the diagram in Figure 6.8a shows time along the x-axis, and the time is divided into eight segments, with one bit being sent during each segment. If the communication system is modified to use half as much time for a given bit, twice as many bits will be sent in the same amount of time. The point is:

> *An alternative method of increasing the amount of data that can be transferred in a given time consists of decreasing the amount of time that the system leaves a signal at a given level.*

As with signal levels, the hardware in a practical system places limits on how short the time can be — if the signal does not remain at a given level long enough, the receiving hardware will fail to detect it. Interestingly, the accepted measure of a communication system does not specify a length of time. Instead, engineers measure the inverse: how many times the signal can change per second, which is defined as the *baud*. For example, if a system requires the signal to remain at a given level for .001 seconds, we say that the system operates at 1000 baud.

The key idea is that both baud and the number of signal levels control the bit rate. If a system with two signal levels operates at 1000 baud, the system can transfer exactly 1000 bits per second. However, if a system that operates at 1000 baud has four signal levels, the system can transfer 2000 bits per second (because four signal levels can represent two bits). Equation 6.1 expresses the relationship between baud, signal levels, and bit rate.

$$ bits\ per\ second\ =\ baud\ \times\ \left\lfloor \log_2(levels\ ) \right\rfloor \qquad (6.1) $$

6.12 Converting A Digital Signal To Analog

How can a digital signal be converted into an equivalent analog signal? Recall that according to Fourier, an arbitrary curve can be represented as a composite of sine waves, where each sine wave in the set has a specific amplitude, frequency, and phase. Because it applies to any curve, Fourier's theorem also applies to a digital signal. From an engineering perspective, Fourier's result is impractical for digital signals because accurate representation of a digital signal requires an infinite set of sine waves.

Engineers adopt a compromise: conversion of a signal from digital to analog is *approximate*. That is, engineers build equipment to generate analog waves that closely approximate the digital signal. Approximation involves building a composite signal from only a few sine waves. By choosing sine waves that are the correct multiples of the digital signal frequency, as few as three can be used. The exact details are beyond the scope of this text, but Figure 6.9 illustrates the approximation by showing (a) a digital signal and approximations with (b) a single sine wave, (c) a composite of the original sine wave plus a sine wave of 3 times the frequency, and (d) a composite of the wave in (c) plus one more sine wave at 5 times the original frequency.

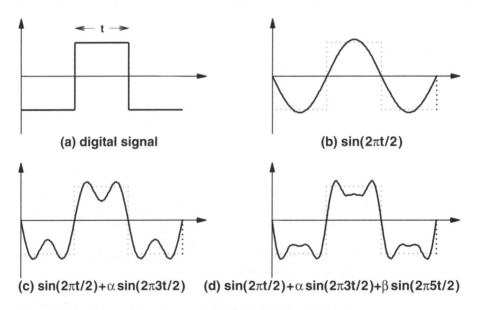

Figure 6.9 Approximation of a digital signal with sine waves.

6.13 The Bandwidth Of A Digital Signal

What is the bandwidth of a digital signal? Recall that the bandwidth of a signal is the difference between the highest and lowest frequency waves that constitute the signal. Thus, one way to calculate the bandwidth consists of applying Fourier analysis to find the constituent sine waves and then examining the frequencies.

Mathematically, when Fourier analysis is applied to a square wave, such as the digital signal illustrated in Figure 6.9a, the analysis produces an infinite set of sine waves. Furthermore, frequencies in the set continue to infinity. Thus, when plotted in the frequency domain, the set continues along the x-axis to infinity. The important consequence is:

> *According to the definition of bandwidth, a digital signal has infinite bandwidth because Fourier analysis of a digital signal produces an infinite set of sine waves with frequencies that grow to infinity.*

6.14 Synchronization And Agreement About Signals

Our examples leave out many of the subtle details involved in creating a viable communication system. For example, to guarantee that the sender and receiver agree on the amount of time allocated to each element of a signal, the electronics at both ends of a physical medium must have circuitry to measure time precisely. That is, if one end transmits a signal with 10^9 elements per second, the other end must expect exactly 10^9 elements per second. At slow speeds, making both ends agree is trivial. However, building electronic systems that agree at the high speeds used in modern networks is extremely difficult.

A more fundamental problem arises from the way data is represented in signals. The problem concerns *synchronization* of the sender and receiver. For example, suppose a receiver misses the first bit that arrives, and starts interpreting data starting at the second bit. Or consider what happens if a receiver expects data to arrive at a faster rate than the sender transmits the data. Figure 6.10 illustrates how a mismatch in interpretation can produce errors. In the figure, both the sender and receiver start and end at the same point in the signal, but because the receiver allocates slightly less time per bit, the receiver misinterprets the signal as containing more bits than were sent.

In practice, synchronization errors can be extremely subtle. For example, suppose a receiver's hardware has a timing error of 1 in 10^{-8}. The error might not show up until ten million bits are transmitted in a sequence. Nevertheless, because high-speed communication systems transfer gigabits per second, such small errors can surface quickly and become significant.

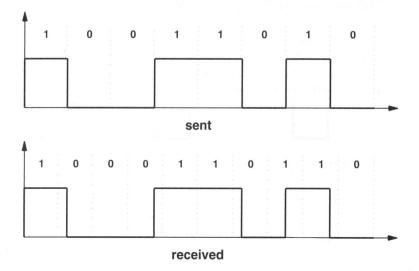

sent

received

Figure 6.10 Illustration of a synchronization error in which the receiver allows slightly less time per bit than the sender.

6.15 Line Coding

Several techniques have been invented that can help avoid synchronization errors. In general, there are two broad approaches. In one approach, before it transmits data, the sender transmits a known pattern of bits, typically a set of alternating 0s and 1s, that allows the receiver to synchronize. In the other approach, data is represented by the signal in such a way that there can be no confusion about the meaning. We use the term *line coding* to describe the way data is encoded in a signal.

As an example of line coding that eliminates ambiguity, consider how one can use a transmission mechanism that supports three discrete signal levels. To guarantee synchronization, reserve one of the signal levels to start each bit. For example, if the three possible levels correspond to -5, 0, and +5 volts, reserve -5 to start each bit. Logical 0 can be represented by the sequence -5 0, and logical 1 can be represented by the sequence -5 +5. If we specify that no other combinations are valid, the occurrence of -5 volts always starts a bit, and a receiver can use an occurrence of -5 volts to correctly synchronize with the sender. Figure 6.11 illustrates the representation.

Of course, using multiple signal elements to represent a single bit means fewer bits can be transmitted per unit time. Thus, designers prefer schemes that transmit multiple bits per signal element, such as the one that Figure 6.8b illustrates.

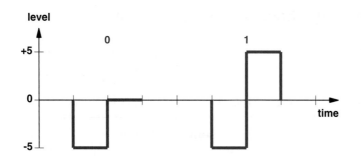

Figure 6.11 Example of two signal elements used to represent each bit.

Figure 6.12 lists the names of line coding techniques in common use, and groups them into related categories. Although the details are beyond the scope of this text, it is sufficient to know that the choice depends on the specific needs of a given communication system.

Category	Scheme	Synchronization
Unipolar	NRZ	No, if many 0s or 1s are repeated
	NRZ-L	No, if many 0s or 1s are repeated
	NRZ-I	No, if many 0s or 1s are repeated
	Biphase	Yes
Bipolar	AMI	No, if many 0s are repeated
Multilevel	2B1Q	No, if many double bits are repeated
	8B6T	Yes
	4D-PAM5	Yes
Multiline	MLT-3	No, if many 0s are repeated

Figure 6.12 Names of line coding techniques in common use.

The point is:

A variety of line coding techniques are available that differ in how they handle synchronization as well as other properties such as the bandwidth used.

6.16 Manchester Encoding Used In Computer Networks

In addition to the list in Figure 6.12, one particular standard for line coding is especially important for computer networks: the *Manchester Encoding* used with Ethernet†.

To understand Manchester Encoding, it is important to know that detecting a transition in signal level is easier than measuring the signal level. The fact, which arises from the way hardware works, explains why the Manchester Encoding uses transitions rather than levels to define bits. That is, instead of specifying that 1 corresponds to a level (e.g., +5 volts), Manchester Encoding specifies that a 1 corresponds to a transition from 0 volts to a positive voltage level. Correspondingly, a 0 corresponds to a transition from a positive voltage level to zero. Furthermore, the transitions occur in the "middle" of the time slot allocated to a bit, which allows the signal to return to the previous level in case the data contains two repeated 0s or two repeated 1s. Figure 6.13a illustrates the concept.

A variation known as a *Differential Manchester Encoding* (also called a *Conditional DePhase Encoding*) uses relative transitions rather than absolute. That is, the representation of a bit depends on the previous bit. Each bit time slot contains one or two transitions. A transition *always* occurs in the middle of the bit time. The logical value of the bit is represented by the presence or absence of a transition at the beginning of a bit time: logical 0 is represented by a transition, and logical 1 is represented by no transition. Figure 6.13b illustrates Differential Manchester Encoding. Perhaps the most important property of differential encoding arises from a practical consideration: the encoding works correctly even if the two wires carrying the signal are accidentally reversed.

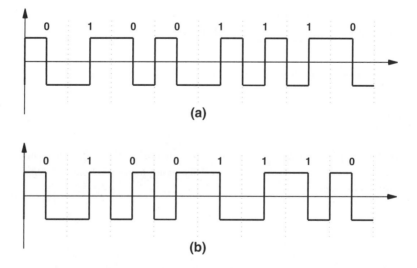

(a)

(b)

Figure 6.13 (a) Manchester and (b) Differential Manchester Encodings; each assumes the previous bit ended with a low signal level.

---

†Chapter 15 discusses Ethernet.

6.17 Converting An Analog Signal To Digital

Many sources of information are analog, which means they must be converted to digital form for further processing (e.g., before they can be encrypted). There are two basic approaches:

- Pulse code modulation
- Delta modulation

Pulse code modulation (PCM†) refers to a technique where the level of an analog signal is measured repeatedly at fixed time intervals and converted to digital form. Figure 6.14 illustrates the steps.

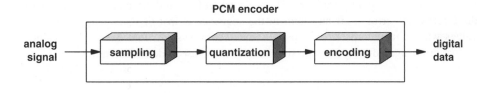

Figure 6.14 The three steps used in pulse code modulation.

Each measurement is known as a *sample*, which explains why the first stage is known as *sampling*. After it has been recorded, a sample is *quantized* by converting it into a small integer value which is then *encoded* into a specific format. The quantized value is not a measure of voltage or any other property of the signal. Instead, the range of the signal from the minimum to maximum levels is divided into a set of slots, typically a power of 2. Figure 6.15 illustrates the concept by showing a signal quantized into eight slots.

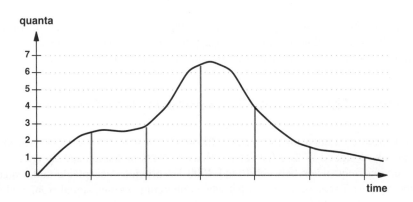

Figure 6.15 An illustration of the sampling and quantization used in pulse code modulation.

---

†The acronym PCM is ambiguous because it can refer to the general idea or to a specific form of pulse code modulation used by the telephone system. A later section discusses the latter.

In the figure, the six samples are represented by vertical gray lines. Each sample is quantized by choosing the closest quantum interval. For example, the third sample, taken near the peak of the curve is assigned a quantized value of 6.

In practice, slight variations in sampling have been invented. For example, to avoid inaccuracy caused by a brief spike or a dip in the signal, averaging can be used. That is, instead of relying on a single measurement for each sample, three measurements can be taken close together and an arithmetic mean can be computed.

The chief alternative to pulse code modulation is known as *delta modulation*. Delta modulation also takes samples. However, instead of sending a quantization for each sample, delta modulation sends one quantization value followed by a string of values that give the difference between the previous value and the current value. The idea is that transmitting differences requires fewer bits than transmitting full values, especially if the signal does not vary rapidly. The main tradeoff with delta modulation arises from the effect of an error — if any item in the sequence is lost or damaged, all successive values will be misinterpreted. Thus, communication systems that expect data values to be lost or changed during transmission usually use pulse code modulation (PCM).

6.18 The Nyquist Theorem And Sampling Rate

Whether pulse code or delta modulation is used, the analog signal must be sampled. How frequently should an analog signal be sampled? Taking too few samples (known as *undersampling*) means that the digital values only give a crude approximation of the original signal. Taking too many samples (known as *oversampling*) means that more digital data will be generated, which uses extra bandwidth.

A mathematician named Nyquist discovered the answer to the question of how much sampling is required:

$$sampling \ rate \ = \ 2 \times f_{max} \qquad\qquad (6.2)$$

where f_{max} is the highest frequency in the composite signal. The result, which is known as the *Nyquist Theorem* provides a practical solution to the problem: sample a signal at least twice as fast as the highest frequency that must be preserved.

6.19 Nyquist Theorem And Telephone System Transmission

As a specific example of the Nyquist theorem, consider the telephone system that was originally designed to transfer voice. Measurements of human speech have shown that preserving frequencies between 0 and 4000 Hz provides acceptable audio quality. Thus, the Nyquist Theorem specifies that when converting a voice signal from analog to digital, the signal should be sampled at a rate of 8000 samples per second.

To further provide reasonable quality reproduction, the PCM standard used by the phone system quantifies each sample into an 8 bit value. That is, the range of input is divided into 256 possible levels so that each sample has a value between 0 and 255. As a consequence, the rate at which digital data is generated for a single telephone call is:

$$\textit{digitized voice call} \;=\; 8000 \frac{\textit{samples}}{\textit{second}} \;\times\; 8 \frac{\textit{bits}}{\textit{sample}} \;=\; 64,000 \frac{\textit{bits}}{\textit{second}} \qquad (6.3)$$

As we will see in later chapters, the telephone system uses the rate of 64,000 bits per second (64 Kbps) as the basis for digital communication. We will further see that the Internet uses digital telephone circuits to span long distances.

6.20 Encoding And Data Compression

We use the term *data compression* to refer to a technique that reduces the number of bits required to represent data. Data compression is especially relevant to a communication system because reducing the number of bits used to represent data reduces the time required for transmission. That is, a communication system can be optimized by compressing data before transmission.

Chapter 29 considers compression in multimedia applications. At this point, we only need to understand the basic definitions of two types of compression:

- Lossy — some information is lost during compression
- Lossless — all information is retained in the compressed version.

Lossy compression is generally used with data that a human consumes, such as an image, a segment of video, or an audio file. The key idea is that the compression only needs to preserve details to the level of human perception. That is, a change is acceptable if humans cannot detect the change. We will see that well-known compression schemes such as JPEG (used for images) or MPEG-3 (abbreviated MP3 and used for audio recordings) employ lossy compression.

Lossless compression preserves the original data without any change. Thus, lossless compression can be used for documents or in any situation where data must be preserved exactly. When used for communication, a sender compresses the data before transmission and the receiver decompresses the result. Because the compression is lossless, arbitrary data can be compressed by a sender and decompressed by a receiver to recover an exact copy of the original.

Most lossless compression uses a *dictionary* approach. Compression finds strings that are repeated in the data, and forms a *dictionary* of the strings. To compress the data, each occurrence of a string is replaced by a reference to the dictionary. The sender must transmit the dictionary along with the compressed data. If the data contains strings that are repeated many times, the combination of the dictionary plus the compressed data is smaller than the original data.

6.21 Summary

An information source can deliver analog or digital data. An analog signal has the property of being aperiodic or periodic; a periodic signal has properties of amplitude, frequency, and phase. Fourier discovered that an arbitrary curve can be formed from a sum of sine waves; a single sine wave is classified as simple, and a signal that can be decomposed into multiple sine waves is classified as composite.

Engineers use two main representations of composite signals. A time domain representation shows how the signal varies over time. A frequency domain representation shows the amplitude and frequency of each component in the signal. The bandwidth, which is the difference between the highest and lowest frequencies in a signal is especially clear on a frequency domain graph.

The baud rate of a signal is the number of times the signal can change per second. A digital signal that uses multiple signal levels can represent more than one bit per change, making the effective transmission rate the number of levels times the baud rate. Although it has infinite bandwidth, a digital signal can be approximated with three sine waves.

Various line coding techniques exist. The Manchester Encoding, used with Ethernet networks, is especially important. Rather than using absolute signal levels to represent bits, the Manchester Encoding uses transitions in signal level. The Differential Manchester Encoding uses relative transitions, and has the property that it works even if the two wires are reversed.

Pulse code modulation and delta modulation are used to convert an analog signal to digital. The PCM scheme used by the telephone system employs 8-bit quantization and takes 8,000 samples per second, which results in a rate of 64 Kbps.

Compression is lossy or lossless. Lossy compression is most appropriate for images, audio, or video that will be viewed by humans because loss can be controlled to keep changes below the threshold of human perception. Lossless compression is most appropriate for documents or data that must be preserved exactly.

EXERCISES

6.1   When shown a graph of a sine wave, what is the quickest way to determine whether the phase is zero?

6.2   Give three examples of information sources other than computers.

6.3   Why are sine waves fundamental to data communications?

6.4   Why is an analog signal used to approximate a digital signal?

6.5   Describe the difference between lossy and lossless compressions, and tell when each might be used.

6.6   If the maximum frequency audible to a human ear is 20,000 Hz, at what rate must the analog signal from a microphone be sampled when converting it to digital?

6.7   What does Fourier analysis of a composite wave produce?

6.8   What is the analog bandwidth of a signal?

6.9   Name a common household device that emits an aperiodic signal.

6.10 On a frequency domain graph, what does the y-axis represent?

6.11 Why do some coding techniques use multiple signal elements to represent a single bit?

6.12 Is bandwidth easier to compute from a time domain or frequency domain representation? Why?

6.13 What time elapses between samples for the PCM encoding used in the telephone system?

6.14 Suppose an engineer increases the number of possible signal levels from two to four. How many more bits can be sent in the same amount of time? Explain.

6.15 State and describe the four fundamental characteristics of a sine wave.

6.16 What is the bandwidth of a digital signal? Explain.

6.17 What aspect of a signal does the Manchester Encoding use to represent a bit?

6.18 When converting an analog signal to digital, what step follows sampling?

6.19 When is a wave classified as *simple*?

6.20 What is the definition of *baud*?

6.21 What is a synchronization error?

6.22 What is the chief advantage of a Differential Manchester Encoding?

Chapter Contents

7

Transmission Media

7.1 Introduction

Chapter 5 provides an overview of data communications. The previous chapter considers the topic of information sources. The chapter examines analog and digital information, and explains encodings.

This chapter continues the discussion of data communications by considering transmission media, including wired, wireless, and optical media. The chapter gives a taxonomy of media types, introduces basic concepts of electromagnetic propagation, and explains how shielding can reduce or prevent interference and noise. Finally, the chapter explains the concept of capacity. Successive chapters continue the discussion of data communications.

7.2 Guided And Unguided Transmission

How should transmission media be divided into classes. There are two broad approaches:

- By type of path: communication can follow an exact path such as a wire, or can have no specific path, such as a radio transmission.

- By form of energy: electrical energy is used on wires, radio transmission is used for wireless, and light is used for optical fiber.

We use the terms *guided* and *unguided* transmission to distinguish between physical media such as copper wiring or optical fibers that provide a specific path and a radio transmission that travels in all directions through free space. Informally, engineers use the terms *wired* and *wireless*. Note that the informality can be somewhat confusing because one is likely to hear the term *wired* even when the physical medium is an optical fiber.

7.3 A Taxonomy By Forms Of Energy

Figure 7.1 illustrates how physical media can be classified according to the form of energy used to transmit data. Successive sections describe each of the media types.

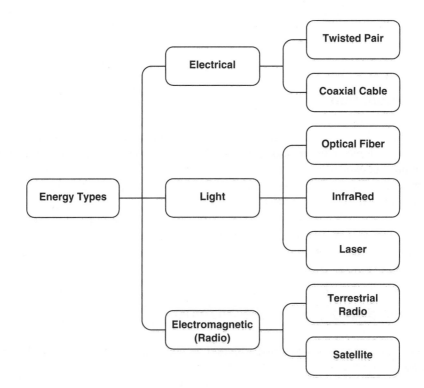

Figure 7.1 A taxonomy of media types according to the form of energy used.

Like most taxonomies, the categories are not perfect, and exceptions exist. For example, a space station in orbit around the earth might employ non-terrestrial communication that does not involve a satellite. Nevertheless, our taxonomy covers most communications.

7.4 Background Radiation And Electrical Noise

Recall from basic physics that electrical current flows along a complete circuit. Thus, all transmissions of electrical energy need two wires to form a circuit — a wire to the receiver and a wire back to the sender. The simplest form of wiring consists of a cable that contains two copper wires. Each wire is wrapped in a plastic coating, which insulates the wires electrically. The outer coating on the cable holds related wires together to make it easier for humans who connect equipment.

Computer networks use an alternative form of wiring. To understand why, one must know three facts.

1. Random electromagnetic radiation, called *noise*, permeates the environment. In fact, communication systems generate minor amounts of electrical noise as a side-effect of normal operation.

2. When it hits metal, electromagnetic radiation induces a small signal, which means that random noise can interfere with signals used for communication.

3. Because it absorbs radiation, metal acts as a *shield*. Thus, placing enough metal between a source of noise and a communication medium can prevent noise from interfering with communication.

The first two facts outline a fundamental problem inherent in communication media that use electrical or radio energy. The problem is especially severe near a source that emits random radiation. For example, florescent light bulbs and electric motors both emit radiation, especially powerful motors such as those used to operate elevators, air conditioners, and refrigerators. Surprisingly, smaller devices such as paper shredders or electric power tools can also emit enough radiation to interfere with communication. The point is:

The random electromagnetic radiation generated by devices such as electric motors can interfere with communication that uses radio transmission or electrical energy sent over wires.

7.5 Twisted Pair Copper Wiring

The third fact in the previous section explains the wiring used with communication systems. There are three forms of wiring that help reduce interference from electrical noise.

- Unshielded Twisted Pair (UTP)
- Coaxial Cable
- Shielded Twisted Pair (STP)

The first form, which known as *twisted pair* wiring or *unshielded twisted pair* wiring†, is used extensively in communications. As the name implies, twisted pair wiring consists of two wires that are twisted together. Of course, each wire has a plastic coating that insulates the two wires and prevents electrical current from flowing between them.

Surprisingly, twisting two wires makes them less susceptible to electrical noise than leaving them parallel. Figure 7.2 illustrates why.

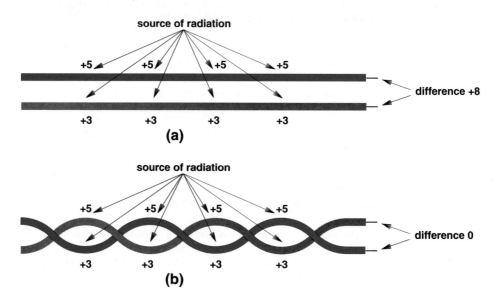

Figure 7.2 Unwanted electromagnetic radiation affecting (a) two parallel wires, and (b) twisted pair wiring.

As the figure shows, when two wires are in parallel, there is a high probability that one of them is closer to the source of electromagnetic radiation than the other. In fact, one wire tends to act as a shield that absorbs some of the electromagnetic radiation. Thus, because it is hidden behind the first wire, the second wire receives less energy. In the figure, a total of 32 units of radiation strikes each of the two cases. In Figure 7.2a, the top wire absorbs 20 units, and the bottom wire absorbs 12, producing a difference of 8. In Figure 7.2b, each of the two wires is on top one-half of the time, which means each wire absorbs the same amount of radiation.

Why does equal absorption matter? The answer is that if interference induces exactly the same amount of electrical energy in each wire, no extra current will flow. Thus, the original signal will not be disturbed. The point is:

---

†A later section explains the term *shielded.*

> *To reduce the interference caused by random electromagnetic radiation, communication systems use twisted pair wiring rather than parallel wires.*

7.6 Shielding: Coaxial Cable And Shielded Twisted Pair

Although it is immune to most background radiation, twisted pair wiring does not solve all problems. Twisted pair tends to have problems with:

- Especially strong electrical noise
- Close physical proximity to the source of noise
- High frequencies used for communication

If the intensity is high (e.g., in a factory that uses electric arc welding equipment) or communication cables run close to the source of electrical noise, even twisted pair may not be sufficient. Thus, if a twisted pair runs above the ceiling in an office building on top of a florescent light fixture, interference may result. Furthermore, it is difficult to build equipment that can distinguish between valid high frequency signals and noise, which means that even a small amount of noise can cause interference when high frequencies are used.

To handle situations where twisted pair is insufficient, forms of wiring are available that have extra metal shielding. The most familiar form is the wiring used for cable television. Known as *coaxial cable (coax)*, the wiring has a thick metal shield formed from braided wires that completely surround a center wire that carries the signal. Figure 7.3 illustrates the concept.

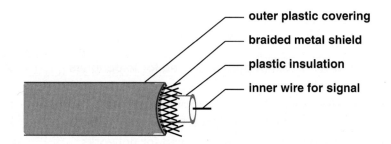

outer plastic covering
braided metal shield
plastic insulation
inner wire for signal

Figure 7.3 Illustration of coaxial cable with a shield surrounding the signal wire.

The shield in a coaxial cable forms a flexible cylinder around the inner wire that provides a barrier to electromagnetic radiation from any direction. The barrier also prevents signals on the inner wire from radiating electromagnetic energy that could affect other wires. Consequently, a coaxial cable can be placed adjacent to sources of electrical noise and other cables, and can be used for high frequencies. The point is:

> *The heavy shielding and symmetry makes coaxial cable immune to noise, capable of carrying high frequencies, and prevents signals on the cable from emitting noise to surrounding cables.*

Using braided wire instead of a solid metal shield keeps coaxial cable flexible, but the heavy shield does make coaxial cable less flexible than twisted pair wiring. Variations of shielding have been invented that provide a compromise: the cable is more flexible, but has slightly less immunity to electrical noise. One popular variation is known as *shielded twisted pair* (*STP*). The cable has a thinner, more flexible metal shield surrounding one or more twisted pairs of wires. In most versions of STP cable, the shield consists of metal foil, similar to the aluminum foil used in a kitchen. STP cable has the advantages of being more flexible than a coaxial cable and less susceptible to electrical interference than *unshielded twisted pair* (*UTP*).

7.7 Categories Of Twisted Pair Cable

The telephone companies originally specified standards for twisted pair wiring used in the telephone network. More recently, three standards organizations worked together to create standards for twisted pair cables used in computer networks. The *American National Standards Institute* (*ANSI*), the *Telecommunications Industry Association* (*TIA*), and the *Electronic Industries Alliance* (*EIA*) created a list of wiring categories, with strict specifications for each. Figure 7.4 summarizes the main categories.

Category	Description	Data Rate (in Mbps)
CAT 1	Unshielded twisted pair used for telephones	< 0.1
CAT 2	Unshielded twisted pair used for T1 data	2
CAT 3	Improved CAT2 used for computer networks	10
CAT 4	Improved CAT3 used for Token Ring networks	20
CAT 5	Unshielded twisted pair used for networks	100
CAT 5E	Extended CAT5 for more noise immunity	125
CAT 6	Unshielded twisted pair tested for 200 Mbps	200
CAT 7	Shielded twisted pair with a foil shield around the entire cable plus a shield around each twisted pair	600

Figure 7.4 Twisted pair wiring categories and a description of each.

7.8 Media Using Light Energy And Optical Fibers

According to the taxonomy in Figure 7.1, three forms of media use light energy to carry information:

- Optical fibers
- InfraRed transmission
- Point-to-point lasers

The most important type of media that uses light is an *optical fiber*. Each fiber consists of a thin strand of glass or transparent plastic encased in a plastic cover. A typical optical fiber is used for communication in a single direction — one end of the fiber connects to a laser or LED used to transmit light, and the other end of the fiber connects to a photosensitive device used to detect incoming light. To provide two-way communication, two fibers are used, one to carry information in each direction. Thus, optical fibers are usually collected into a cable by wrapping a plastic cover around them; a cable has at least two fibers, and a cable used between large sites with multiple network devices may contain many fibers.

Although it cannot be bent at a right angle, an optical fiber is flexible enough to form into a circle with diameter less than two inches without breaking. The question arises, why does light travel around a bend in the fiber? The answer comes from physics: when light encounters the boundary between two substances, its behavior depends on the density of the two substances and the angle at which the light strikes the boundary. For a given pair of substances, there exists a *critical angle*, θ, measured with respect to a line that is perpendicular to the boundary. If the angle of incidence is exactly equal to the critical angle, light travels along the boundary. When the angle is less than θ degrees, light crosses the boundary and is *refracted*, and when the angle is greater than θ degrees, light is reflected as if the boundary were a mirror. Figure 7.5 illustrates the concept.

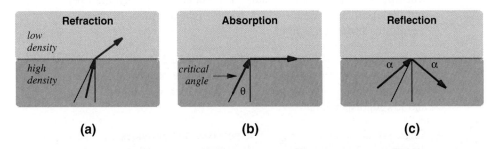

Figure 7.5 Behavior of light at a density boundary when the angle of incidence is (a) less than the critical angle θ, (b) equal to the critical angle, and (c) greater than the critical angle.

Figure 7.5c explains why light stays inside an optical fiber — a substance called *cladding* is bonded to the fiber to form a boundary. As it travels along, light is reflected off the boundary.

Unfortunately, reflection in an optical fiber is not perfect. Reflection absorbs a small amount of energy. Furthermore, if a photon takes a zig-zag path that reflects from the walls of the fiber many times, the photon will travel a slightly longer distance than a photon that takes a straight path. The result is that a pulse of light sent at one end of a fiber emerges with less energy and is *dispersed* (i.e., stretched) over time, as Figure 7.6 illustrates.

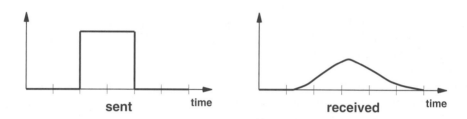

Figure 7.6 A light pulse as sent and received over an optical fiber.

7.9 Types Of Fiber And Light Transmission

Although it is not a problem for optical fibers used to connect a computer to a nearby device, dispersion becomes a serious problem for long optical fibers, such as those used between two cites or under the Atlantic Ocean. Consequently, three forms of optical fibers have been invented that provide a choice between performance and cost:

- *Multimode, Step Index* fiber is the least expensive, and is used when performance is unimportant. The boundary between the fiber and the cladding is abrupt which causes light to reflect frequently. Therefore, dispersion is high.

- *Multimode, Graded Index* fiber is slightly more expensive than the step index fiber. However, it has the advantage of making the density of the fiber increase near the edge, which reduces reflection and lowers dispersion.

- *Single Mode* fiber is the most expensive, and provides the least dispersion. The fiber has a smaller diameter and other properties that help reduce reflection. Single mode is used for long distances and higher bit rates.

Single mode fiber and the equipment used at each end are designed to focus light. As a result, a pulse of light can travel thousands of kilometers without becoming dispersed. Minimal dispersion helps increase the rate at which bits can be sent because a pulse corresponding to one bit does not disperse into the pulse that corresponds to a successive bit.

How is light sent and received on a fiber? The key is that the devices used for transmission must match the fiber. The available mechanisms include:

- Transmission: Light Emitting Diode (LED) or Injection Laser Diode (ILD)
- Reception: photo-sensitive cell or photodiode

In general, LEDs and photo-sensitive cells are used for short distances and slower bit rates common with multimode fiber; single mode fiber, used over long distance with high bit rates, generally requires ILDs and photodiodes.

7.10 Optical Fiber Compared To Copper Wiring

Optical fiber has several properties that make it more desirable than copper wiring. Optical fiber is immune to electrical noise, has higher bandwidth, and light traveling across a fiber does not attenuate as much as electrical signals traveling across copper. However, copper wiring is less expensive. Furthermore, because the ends of an optical fiber must be polished before they can be used, installation of copper wiring does not require as much special equipment or expertise as optical fiber. Finally, because they are stronger, copper wires are less likely to break if accidentally pulled or bent. Figure 7.7 summarizes the advantages of each media type.

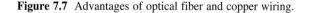

Optical Fiber
• Immune to electrical noise
• Less signal attenuation
• Higher bandwidth
Copper
• Lower overall cost
• Less expertise/equipment needed
• Less easily broken

Figure 7.7 Advantages of optical fiber and copper wiring.

7.11 InfraRed Communication Technologies

InfraRed (*IR*) communication technologies use the same type of energy as a typical television remote control: a form of electromagnetic radiation that behaves like visible light but falls outside the range that is visible to a human eye. Like visible light, infrared disperses quickly. Infrared signals can reflect from a smooth, hard surface, but an opaque object as thin as a sheet of paper can block the signal, as does moisture in the atmosphere.

The point is:

> *Infrared communication technologies are best suited for use indoors in situations where the path between sender and receiver is short and free from obstruction.*

The most commonly used infrared technology is intended to connect a computer to a nearby peripheral, such as a printer. An interface on the computer and an interface on the printer each send an infrared signal that covers an arc of approximately $30°$. Provided the two devices are aligned, each can receive the other's signal. The wireless aspect of infrared is especially attractive for laptop computers because a user can move around a room and still have access to a printer. Figure 7.8 lists the three commonly used infrared technologies along with the data rate that each supports.

Name	Expansion	Speed
IrDA-SIR	Slow-speed InfraRed	0.115 Mbps
IrDA-MIR	Medium-speed InfraRed	1.150 Mbps
IrDA-FIR	Fast-speed InfraRed	4.000 Mbps

Figure 7.8 Three common infrared technologies and the data rate of each.

7.12 Point-To-Point Laser Communication

Because they connect a pair of devices with a beam that follows the line-of-sight, the infrared technologies described above can be classified as providing *point-to-point* communication. In addition to infrared, other point-to-point communication technologies exist. One form of point-to-point communication uses a beam of coherent light produced by a *laser*.

Like infrared, laser communication follows line-of-sight, and requires a clear, unobstructed path between the communicating sites. Unlike an infrared transmitter, however, a laser beam does not cover a broad area. Instead, the beam is only a few centimeters wide. Consequently, the sending and receiving equipment must be aligned precisely to insure that the sender's beam hits the sensor in the receiver's equipment. In a typical communication system, two-way communication is needed. Thus, each side must have both a transmitter and receiver, and both transmitters must be aligned carefully. Because alignment is critical, point-to-point laser equipment is usually mounted permanently.

Laser beams have the advantage of being suitable for use outdoors, and can span greater distances than infrared. As a result, laser technology is especially useful in cities to transmit from building to building. For example, imagine a large corporation with offices in two adjacent buildings. A corporation is not permitted to string wires across streets between buildings. However, a corporation can purchase laser communication equipment and permanently mount the equipment, either on the sides of the two buildings or on the roofs. Once the equipment has been purchased and installed, the operating costs are relatively low.

To summarize:

> *Laser technology can be used to create a point-to-point communication system. Because a laser emits a narrow beam of light, the transmitter and receiver must be aligned precisely; typical installations affix the equipment to a permanent structure such as the roof of a building.*

7.13 Electromagnetic (Radio) Communication

Recall that the term *unguided* is used to characterize communication technologies that can propagate energy without requiring a medium such as a wire or optical fiber. The most common form of unguided communication mechanisms consists of *wireless* networking technologies that use electromagnetic energy in the *Radio Frequency* (*RF*) range. RF transmission has a distinct advantage over light because RF energy can traverse long distances and penetrate objects such as the walls of a building.

The exact properties of electromagnetic energy depend on the frequency. We use the term *spectrum* to refer to the range of possible frequencies; governments around the world allocate frequencies for specific purposes. In the U.S., the *Federal Communications Commission* sets rules for how frequencies are allocated, and sets limits on the amount of power that communication equipment can emit at each frequency. Figure 7.9 shows the overall electromagnetic spectrum and general characteristics of each piece. As the figure shows, one part of the spectrum corresponds to infrared light described above. The spectrum used for RF communications spans frequencies from approximately 3 KHz to 300 GHz, and includes frequencies allocated to radio and television broadcast as well as satellite and microwave communications.

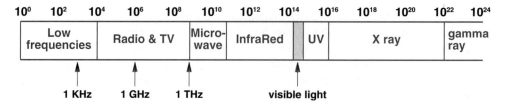

Figure 7.9 Major pieces of the electromagnetic spectrum with frequency in Hz shown on a log scale.

7.14 Signal Propagation

Chapter 6 explains that the amount of information an electromagnetic wave can represent depends on the wave's frequency. The frequency of an electromagnetic wave also determines how the wave *propagates*. Figure 7.10 describes the three broad types of propagation.

Classification	Range	Type Of Propagation
Low Frequency	< 2 Mbps	Wave follows earth's curvature, but can be blocked by unlevel terrain
Medium Frequency	2 to 30 Mbps	Wave can reflect from layers of the atmosphere, especially the ionosphere
High Frequency	> 30 Mbps	Wave travels in a direct line, and will be blocked by obstructions

Figure 7.10 Electromagnetic wave propagation at various frequencies.

According to the figure, the lowest frequencies of electromagnetic radiation follow the earth's surface, which means that if the terrain is relatively flat, it will be possible to place a receiver beyond the horizon from a transmitter. With medium frequencies, a transmitter and receiver can be farther apart because the signal can bounce off the ionosphere to travel between them. Finally, the highest frequencies of radio transmission behave like light — the signal propagates in a straight line from the transmitter to the receiver, and the path must be free from obstructions. The point is:

> *The frequencies used for wireless networking technologies cannot be chosen arbitrarily because governments control the use of spectrum and each frequency has characteristics such as wave propagation, power requirements, and susceptibility to noise.*

Wireless technologies are classified into two broad categories as follows:

- *Terrestrial.* Communication uses equipment such as radio or microwave transmitters that is relatively close to the earth's surface. Typical locations for antennas or other equipment include the tops of hills, man-made towers, and tall buildings.
- *Nonterrestrial.* Some of the equipment used in communication is outside the earth's atmosphere (e.g., a satellite in orbit around the earth).

Chapter 16 presents specific wireless technologies, and describes the characteristics of each. For now, it is sufficient to understand that the frequency and amount of power used can affect the speed at which data can be sent, the maximum distance over which communication can occur, and characteristics such as whether the signal can penetrate solid objects.

7.15 Types Of Satellites

The laws of physics (specifically *Kepler's Law*) govern the motion of an object, such as a satellite, that orbits the earth. In particular, the period (i.e., time required for a complete orbit) depends on the distance from the earth. Consequently, communication satellites are classified into three broad categories, depending on their distance from the earth. Figure 7.11 lists the categories, and describes each.

Orbit Type	Description
Low Earth Orbit (LEO)	Has the advantage of low delay, but the disadvantage that from an observer's point of view on the earth, the satellite appears to move across the sky
Medium Earth Orbit (MEO)	An elliptical (rather than circular) orbit primarily used to provide communication at the North and South Poles
Geostationary Earth Orbit (GEO)	Has the advantage that the satellite remains at a fixed position with respect to a location on the earth's surface, but the disadvantage of being farther away

Figure 7.11 The three basic categories of communication satellites.

7.16 GEO Communication Satellites

As Figure 7.11 explains, the main tradeoff in communication satellites is between height and period. The chief advantage of a satellite in *Geostationary Earth Orbit* (*GEO*) arises because the orbital period is exactly the same as the rate at which the earth rotates. If positioned above the equator, a GEO satellite remains in exactly the same location over the earth's surface at all times. A stationary satellite position means that once a *ground station* has been aligned with the satellite, the equipment never needs to move. Figure 7.12 illustrates the concept.

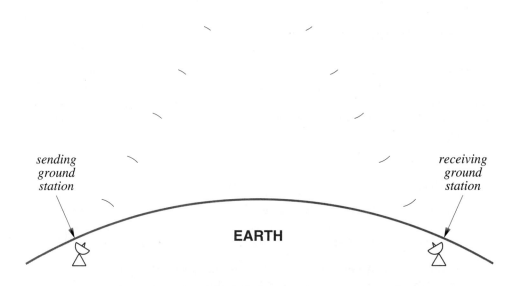

Figure 7.12 A GEO satellite and ground stations permanently aligned.

Unfortunately, the distance required for a geostationary orbit is 35,785 kilometers or 22,236 miles, which is approximately one tenth the distance to the moon. To understand what such a distance means for communication, consider a radio wave traveling to a GEO satellite and back. At the speed of light, 3×10^8 meters per second, the trip takes:

$$\frac{2 \times 35.8 \times 10^6 \, meters}{3 \times 10^8 \, meters/sec} = 0.238 \; sec \qquad (7.1)$$

Although it may seem unimportant, a delay of approximately 0.2 seconds can be significant for some applications. In a telephone call or a video teleconference, a human can notice a 0.2 second delay. For electronic transactions such as a stock exchange offering a limited set of bonds, delaying an offer by 0.2 seconds may mean the difference between a successful and unsuccessful offer. To summarize:

> *Even at the speed of light, a signal takes more than 0.2 seconds to travel from a ground station to a GEO satellite and back to another ground station.*

7.17 GEO Coverage Of The Earth

How many GEO communication satellites are possible? Interestingly, there is a limited amount of "space" available in the geosynchronous orbit above the equator because communication satellites using a given frequency must be separated from one another to avoid interference. The minimum separation depends on the power of the transmitters, but may require an angular separation of between *4* and *8* degrees. Thus, without further refinements, the entire *360*-degree circle above the equator can only hold *45* to *90* satellites.

What is the minimum number of satellites needed to cover the earth? Three. To see why, consider Figure 7.13, which illustrates the earth with three GEO satellites positioned around the equator with 120° separation. The figure illustrates how the signals from the three satellites cover the circumference. In the figure, the size of the earth and the distance of the satellites are drawn to scale.

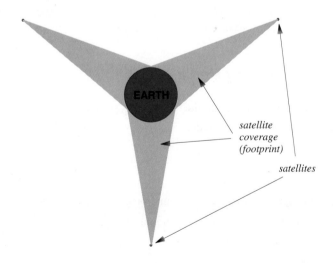

Figure 7.13 The signals from three GEO satellites are sufficient to cover the earth.

7.18 Low Earth Orbit (LEO) Satellites And Clusters

For communication, the primary alternative to GEO is known as *Low Earth Orbit* (*LEO*), which is defined as altitudes up to 2000 Kilometers. As a practical matter, a satellite must be placed above the fringe of the atmosphere to avoid the drag produced by encountering gases. Thus, LEO satellites are typically placed at altitudes of 500 Kilometers or higher. LEO offers the advantage of short delays (typically 1 to 4 milliseconds), but the disadvantage that the orbit of a satellite does not match the rotation of the earth. Thus, from an observer's point of view on the earth, an LEO satellite appears to move across the sky, which means a ground station must have an antenna that can rotate to track the satellite. Tracking is difficult because satellites move rapidly. The lowest altitude LEO satellites orbit the earth in approximately 90 minutes; higher LEO satellites require several hours.

The general technique used with LEO satellites is known as *clustering* or *array deployment*. A large group of LEO satellites are designed to work together. In addition to communicating with ground stations, a satellite in the group can also communicate with other satellites in the group. Members of the group stay in communication, and agree to forward messages, as needed. For example, consider what happens when a user in Europe sends a message to a user in North America. A ground station in Europe transmits the message to the satellite currently overhead. The cluster of satellites communicate to forward the message to the satellite in the cluster that is currently over a ground station in North America. Finally, the satellite currently over North America transmits the message to a ground station. To summarize:

> *A cluster of LEO satellites work together to forward messages. Members of the cluster must know which satellite is currently over a given area of the earth, and forward messages to the appropriate member for transmission to a ground station.*

7.19 Tradeoffs Among Media Types

The choice of medium is complex, and involves the evaluation of multiple factors. Items that must be considered include:

- Cost: materials, installation, operation, and maintenance
- Data rate: number of bits per second that can be sent
- Delay: time required for signal propagation or processing
- Affect on signal: attenuation and distortion
- Environment: susceptibility to interference and electrical noise
- Security: susceptibility to eavesdropping

7.20 Measuring Transmission Media

We have already mentioned the two most important measures of performance used to assess a transmission medium:

- *Propagation delay*: the time required for a signal to traverse the medium

- *Channel capacity*: the maximum data rate that the medium can support

Chapter 6 explains that in the 1920s, a researcher named Nyquist discovered a fundamental relationship between the bandwidth of a transmission system and its capacity to transfer data. Known as *Nyquist Theorem*, the relationship provides a theoretical bound on the maximum rate at which data can be sent without considering the effect of noise. If a transmission system uses K possible signal levels and has an analog bandwidth B, Nyquist's Theorem states that the maximum data rate in bits per second, D, is:

$$D = 2 B \log_2 K \tag{7.2}$$

7.21 The Effect Of Noise On Communication

Nyquist's Theorem provides an absolute maximum that cannot be achieved in practice. In particular, engineers have observed that a real communication system is subject to small amounts of electrical *noise* and that such noise makes it impossible to achieve the theoretical maximum transmission rate. In 1948, Claude Shannon extended Nyquist's work to specify the maximum data rate that could be achieved over a transmission system that experiences noise. The result, called *Shannon's Theorem*†, can be stated as:

$$C = B \log_2(1 + S/N) \tag{7.3}$$

where C is the effective limit on the channel capacity in bits per second, B is the hardware bandwidth, and S/N is the *signal-to-noise ratio*, the ratio of the average signal power divided by the average noise power.

As an example of Shannon's Theorem, consider a transmission medium that has a bandwidth of 1 KHz, an average signal power of 70 units, and an average noise power of 10 units. The channel capacity is:

$$C = 10^3 \times \log_2(1 + 7) = 10^3 \times 3 = 3,000 \; bits \; per \; second$$

---

†The result is also called the *Shannon-Hartley Law*.

The signal-to-noise ratio is often given in *decibels* (abbreviated *dB*), where a decibel is defined as a measure of the difference between two power levels. Figure 7.14 illustrates the measurement.

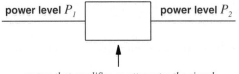

system that amplifies or attenuates the signal

Figure 7.14 Power levels measured on either side of a system.

Once two power levels have been measured, the difference is expressed in decibels, defined as follows:

$$dB \;=\; 10 \log_{10}\left[\frac{P_2}{P_1}\right] \tag{7.4}$$

Using dB as a measure may seem usual, but has two interesting advantages. First, a negative dB value means that the signal has been *attenuated* (i.e., reduced), and a positive dB value means the signal has been *amplified*. Second, if a communication system has multiple parts arranged in a sequence, the decibel measures of the parts can be summed to produce a measure of the overall system.

The voice telephone system has a signal-to-noise ratio of approximately 30 dB and an analog bandwidth of approximately 3000 Hz. To convert signal-to-noise ratio dB into a simple fraction, divide by 10 and use the result as a power of 10 (i.e. $30/10=3$, and $10^3=1000$, so the signal-to-noise ratio is 1000). Shannon's Theorem can be applied to determine the maximum number of bits per second that can be transmitted across the telephone network:

$$C \;=\; 3000 \times \log_2(1 \;+\; 1000)$$

or approximately 30,000 bps. Engineers recognize this as a fundamental limit — faster transmission speeds will only be possible if the signal-to-noise ratio can be improved.

7.22 The Significance Of Channel Capacity

The theorems of Nyquist and Shannon described above have consequences for engineers who design data communication networks. Nyquist's work has provided an incentive to explore complex ways to encode bits on signals:

Nyquist's Theorem encourages engineers to explore ways to encode bits on a signal because a clever encoding allows more bits to be transmitted per unit time.

In some sense, Shannon's Theorem is more fundamental because it represents an absolute limit derived from the laws of physics. Much of the noise on a transmission line, for example, can be attributed to background radiation in the universe left over from the Big Bang. Thus,

Shannon's Theorem informs engineers that no amount of clever encoding can overcome the laws of physics that place a fundamental limit on the number of bits per second that can be transmitted in a real communication system.

7.23 Summary

A variety of transmission media exists that can be classified as guided / unguided or divided according to the form of energy used (electrical, light, or radio transmission). Electrical energy is used over wires. To protect against electrical interference, copper wiring can consist of twisted pairs or can be wrapped in a shield.

Light energy can be used over optical fiber or for point-to-point communication using infrared or lasers. Because it reflects from the boundary between the fiber and cladding, light stays in an optical fiber provided the angle of incidence is greater than the critical angle. As it passes along a fiber, a pulse of light disperses; dispersion is greatest in multimode fiber and least in single mode fiber. Single mode fiber is more expensive.

Wireless communication uses electromagnetic energy. The frequency used determines both the bandwidth and the propagation behavior; low frequencies follow the earth's surface, higher frequencies reflect from the ionosphere, and the highest frequencies behave like visible light by requiring a direct, unobstructed path from the transmitter to the receiver.

The chief nonterrestrial communication technology relies on satellites. The orbit of a GEO satellite matches the earth's rotation, but the high altitude incurs a delay measured in tenths of seconds. LEO satellites have low delay, and move across the sky quickly; clusters are used to relay messages.

Nyquist's Theorem gives a theoretical limit on the channel capacity of transmission media when no noise is present; Shannon's Theorem specifies the channel capacity in realistic situations where noise is present. The signal-to-noise ratio, a term in Shannon's Theorem, is often measured in decibels.

EXERCISES

7.1   List the three forms of optical fiber, and give the general properties of each.

7.2   If a telephone system can be created with a signal-to-noise ratio of 40 dB and an analog bandwidth of 3000 Hz, how many bits per second could be transmitted?

7.3   What is the difference between guided and unguided transmission?

7.4   What are the three energy types used when classifying physical media according to energy used?

7.5   What is dispersion?

7.6   What is propagation delay?

7.7   What is the approximate conical angle that can be used with InfraRed technology?

7.8   If a system has an input power level of 9000, and an output power level of 3000, what is the difference when expressed in dB?

7.9   What happens when noise encounters a metal object?

7.10 Draw a diagram that illustrates the cross section of a coaxial cable.

7.11 Explain how twisted pair cable reduces the effect of noise.

7.12 If you are installing computer network wiring in a new house, what category of twisted pair cable would you choose? Why?

7.13 Can laser communication be used from a moving vehicle? Explain.

7.14 If two signal levels are used, what is the data rate that can be sent over a coaxial cable that has an analog bandwidth of 6.2 MHz?

7.15 What is the chief disadvantage of optical fiber as opposed to copper wiring?

7.16 What light sources and sensors are used with optical fibers?

7.17 What are the two broad categories of wireless communications?

7.18 If messages are sent from Europe to the United States using a GEO satellite, how long will it take for a message to be sent and a reply to be received?

7.19 List the three types of communications satellites, and give the characteristics of each.

7.20 How many GEO satellites are needed to reach all populated areas on the earth?

7.21 If a system has an average power level of 100, an average noise level of 33.33, and a bandwidth of 100 MHz, what is the effective limit on channel capacity?

7.22 What is the relationship between bandwidth, signal levels, and data rate?

7.23 What three types of wiring are used to reduce interference form noise?

7.24 Explain why light does not leave an optical fiber when the fiber is bent into an arc.

7.25 Why might low-frequency electromagnetic radiation be used for communications? Explain.

Chapter Contents

8

Reliability And Channel Coding

8.1 Introduction

Chapters in this part of the text each present one aspect of data communications, the foundation for all computer networking. The previous chapter discusses transmission media, and points out the problem of electromagnetic noise. This chapter continues the discussion by examining errors that can occur during transmission and techniques that can be used to control errors.

The concepts presented here are fundamental to computer networking, and are used in communication protocols at many layers of the stack. In particular, the approaches to error control and techniques appear throughout the Internet protocols discussed in the fourth part of the text.

8.2 The Three Main Sources Of Transmission Errors

All data communications systems are susceptible to errors. Some of the problems are inherent in the physics of the universe, and some result either from devices that fail or from equipment that does not meet the engineering standards. Extensive testing can eliminate many of the problems that arise from poor engineering, and careful monitoring can identify equipment that fails. However, small errors that occur during transmission are more difficult to detect than complete failures, and much of computer networking focuses on ways to control and recover from such errors. There are three main categories of transmission errors:

- *Interference.* As Chapter 7 explains, electromagnetic radiation emitted from devices such as electric motors and background cosmic radiation cause noise that can disturb radio transmissions and signals traveling across wires.

- *Distortion.* All physical systems distort signals. As a pulse travels along an optical fiber, the pulse disperses. Wires have properties of capacitance and inductance that block signals at some frequencies while admitting signals at other frequencies. Simply placing a wire near a large metal object can change the set of frequencies that can pass through the wire. Similarly, metal objects can block some frequencies of radio waves, while passing others.

- *Attenuation.* As a signal passes across a medium, the signal becomes weaker. Engineers say that the signal has been *attenuated*. Thus, signals on wires or optical fibers become weaker over long distances, just as a radio signal becomes weaker with distance.

Shannon's Theorem suggests one way to reduce errors: increase the signal-to-noise ratio (either by increasing the signal or lowering noise). Even though mechanisms like shielded wiring can help lower noise, a physical transmission system is always susceptible to errors, and it may not be possible to change the signal-to-noise ratio.

Although they cannot be eliminated completely, many transmission errors can be detected. In some cases, errors can be corrected automatically. We will see that error detection adds overhead. Thus, all error handling is a tradeoff in which a system designer must decide whether a given error is likely to occur, and if so, what the consequences will be (e.g., a single bit error in a bank transfer can make a difference of over a million dollars, but one bit in an image is less important). The point is:

> *Although transmission errors are inevitable, error detection mechanisms add overhead. Therefore, a designer must choose exactly which error detection and compensation mechanisms will be used.*

8.3 Effect Of Transmission Errors On Data

Instead of examining physics and the exact cause of transmission errors, data communications focuses on the effect of errors on data. Figure 8.1 lists the three principal ways transmission errors affect data.

Although any transmission error can cause each of the possible data errors, the figure points out that an underlying transmission error often manifests itself as a specific data error. For example, extremely short duration interference, called a *spike*, is often the cause of a single bit error. Longer duration interference or distortion can produce burst errors. Sometimes a signal is neither clearly 1 nor clearly 0, but falls in an ambiguous region, which is known as an *erasure*.

Type Of Error	Description
Single Bit Error	A single bit in a block of bits is changed and all other bits in the block are unchanged (often results from very short-duration interference)
Burst Error	Multiple bits in a block of bits are changed (often results from longer-duration interference)
Erasure (Ambiguity)	The signal that arrives at a receiver is ambiguous (does not clearly correspond to either a logical 1 or a logical 0 (can result from distortion or interference)

Figure 8.1 The three types of data errors in a data communications system.

For a burst error, the *burst size*, or *length*, is defined as the number of bits from the start of the corruption to the end of the corruption. Figure 8.2 illustrates the definition.

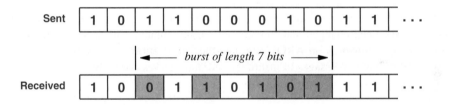

Figure 8.2 Illustration of a burst error with changed bits marked in gray.

8.4 Two Strategies For Handling Channel Errors

A variety of mathematical techniques have been developed that overcome data errors and increase reliability. Known collectively as *channel coding*, the techniques can be divided into two broad categories:

- Forward Error Correction (FEC) mechanisms
- Automatic Repeat reQuest (ARQ) mechanisms

The basic idea of forward error correction is straightforward: add additional information to data that allows a receiver to verify that data arrives correctly and to correct errors, if possible. Figure 8.3 illustrates the conceptual organization of a forward error correction mechanism.

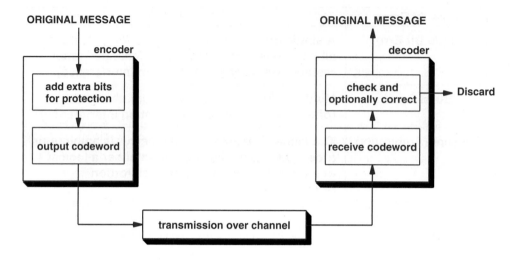

Figure 8.3 The conceptual organization of a forward error correction mechanism.

Basic *error detection mechanisms* allow a receiver to detect when an error has occurred; forward error correction mechanisms allow a receiver to determine exactly which bits have been changed and to compute correct values. The second approach to channel coding, known as an ARQ†, requires the cooperation of a sender — a sender and receiver exchange messages to insure that all data arrives correctly.

8.5 Block And Convolutional Error Codes

The two types of forward error correction techniques satisfy separate needs:

- *Block Error Codes*. A block code divides the data to be sent into a set of blocks, and attaches extra information known as *redundancy* to each block. The encoding for a given block of bits depends only on the bits themselves, not on bits that were sent earlier. Block error codes are *memoryless* in the sense that the encoding mechanism does not carry state information from one block of data to the next.

- *Convolutional Error Codes*. A convolutional code treats data as a series of bits, and computes a code over a continuous series. Thus, the code computed for a set of bits depends on the current input and some of the previous bits in the stream. Convolutional codes are said to be codes with *memory*.

---

†Section 8.15 introduces ARQ.

When implemented in software, convolutional error codes usually require more computation than block error codes. However, convolutional codes often have a higher probability of detecting problems.

8.6 An Example Block Error Code: Single Parity Checking

To understand how additional information can be used to detect errors, consider a *single parity checking (SPC)* mechanism. One form of SPC defines a block to be an 8-bit unit of data (i.e., a single *byte*). On the sending side, an encoder adds an extra bit, called a *parity bit* to each byte before transmission; a receiver removes the parity bit and uses it to check whether bits in the byte are correct.

Before parity can be used, the sender and receiver must be configured for either *even parity* or *odd parity*. When using even parity, the sender chooses a parity bit of 0 if the byte has an even number of 1 bits, and 1 if the byte has an odd number of 1 bits. The way to remember the definition is: even or odd parity specifies whether the 9 bits sent across a channel have an even or odd number of 1 bits. Figure 8.4 lists examples of data bytes and the value of the parity bit that is sent when using even or odd parity.

To summarize:

> *Single parity checking (SPC) is a basic form of channel coding in which a sender adds an extra bit to each byte to make an even (or odd) number of 1 bits and a receiver verifies that the incoming data has the correct number of 1 bits.*

Original Data	Even Parity	Odd Parity
0 0 0 0 0 0 0 0	0	1
0 1 0 1 1 0 1 1	1	0
0 1 0 1 0 1 0 1	0	1
1 1 1 1 1 1 1 1	0	1
1 0 0 0 0 0 0 0	1	0
0 1 0 0 1 0 0 1	1	0

Figure 8.4 Data bytes and the corresponding value of a single parity bit when using even parity or odd parity.

Single parity checking is a weak form of channel coding that can detect errors, but cannot correct them. Furthermore, parity mechanisms can only handle errors where an odd number of bits are changed. If one of the nine bits (including the parity bit) is changed during transmission, the receiver will declare that the incoming byte is invalid.

However, if a burst error occurs in which two, four, six, or eight bits change value, the receiver will incorrectly classify the incoming byte as valid.

8.7 The Mathematics Of Block Error Codes And (n,k) Notation

Observe that forward error correction takes as input a set of messages and inserts additional bits to produce an encoded version. Mathematically, we define the set of all possible messages to be a set of *datawords*, and define the set of all possible encoded versions to be a set of *codewords*. If a dataword contains k bits and r additional bits are added to form a codeword, we say that the result is an

(n, k) encoding scheme

where $n = k + r$. The key to successful error detection lies in choosing a subset of the 2^n possible combinations that are valid codewords. The valid subset is known as a *codebook*.

As an example, consider single parity checking. The set of datawords consists of any possible combination of 8-bits. Thus, $k = 8$ and there are 2^8 or 256 possible data words. The data sent consists of $n = 9$ bits, so there are 2^9 or 512 possibilities. However, only half of the 512 values form valid codewords.

Think of the set of all possible n-bit values and the valid subset that forms the codebook. If an error occurs during transmission, one or more of the bits in a codeword will be changed, which will either produce another valid codeword or an invalid combination. For example, in the single parity scheme discussed above, a change to a single bit of a valid codeword produces an invalid combination, but changing two bits produces another valid codeword. Obviously, we desire an encoding where an error produces an invalid combination. To generalize:

An ideal channel coding scheme is one where any change to bits in a valid codeword produces an invalid combination.

8.8 Hamming Distance: A Measure Of A Code's Strength

No channel coding scheme is ideal — changing enough bits will always transform to a valid codeword. Thus, for a practical scheme, the question becomes, "what is the minimum number of bits of a valid codeword that must be changed to produce another valid codeword?"

To answer the question, engineers use a measure known as the *Hamming distance*, named after a theorist at Bell Laboratories who was a pioneer in the field of information theory and channel coding. Given two strings of n bits each, the Hamming distance is defined as the number of differences (i.e., the number of bits that must be changed to transform one bit string to the other). Figure 8.5 illustrates the definition.

d(000,001) = 1	d(000,101) = 2
d(101,100) = 1	d(001,010) = 2
d(110,001) = 3	d(111,000) = 3

Figure 8.5 Examples of Hamming distance for various pairs of 3-bit strings.

One way to compute the Hamming distance consists of taking the *exclusive or* (*xor*) between two strings and counting the number of 1 bits in the answer. For example, consider the Hamming distance between strings 110 and 011. The *xor* of the two strings is:

$$1\ 1\ 0\quad \oplus \quad 0\ 1\ 1\quad =\quad 1\ 0\ 1$$

which contains two 1 bits. Therefore, the Hamming distance between 011 and 101 is 2.

8.9 The Hamming Distance Among Strings In A Codebook

Recall that we are interested in whether errors can transform a valid codeword into another valid codeword. To measure such transformations, we compute the Hamming distance between all pairs of codewords in a given codebook. As a trivial example, consider odd parity applied to 2-bit data words. Figure 8.6 lists the four possible datawords, the four possible codewords that result from appending a parity bit, and the Hamming distances for pairs of codewords.

Dataword	Codeword
0 0	0 0 1
0 1	0 1 0
1 0	1 0 0
1 1	1 1 1

d(001,010) = 2	d(010,100) = 2
d(001,100) = 2	d(010,111) = 2
d(001,111) = 2	d(100,111) = 2

(a)   (b)

Figure 8.6 (a) The datawords and codewords for a single parity encoding of 2-bit data strings, and (b) the Hamming distance for all pairs of codewords.

An entire set of codewords is known as a *codebook*. We use d_{min} to denote the *minimum Hamming distance* among pairs in a codebook. The concept gives a precise answer to the question of how many bit errors can cause a transformation from one valid codeword into another valid code word. In the single parity example of Figure 8.6, the set consists of the Hamming distance between each pair of codewords, and $d_{min} = 2$. The definition means that there is at least one valid codeword that can be transformed into another valid codeword if two bit errors occur during transmission. The point is:

> *To find the minimum number of bit changes that can transform a valid codeword into another valid codeword, compute the minimum Hamming distance between all pairs in the codebook.*

8.10 The Tradeoff Between Error Detection And Overhead

For a set of codewords, a large value of d_{min} is desirable because the code is immune to more bit errors — if fewer than d_{min} bits are changed, the code can detect that error(s) occurred. Equation 8.1 specifies the relationship between d_{min} and e, the maximum number of bit errors that can be detected:

$$e = d_{min} - 1$$

$$(8.1)$$

The choice of error code is a tradeoff — although it detects more errors, a code with a higher value of d_{min} sends more redundant information than an error code with a lower value of d_{min}. To measure the amount of overhead, engineers define a *code rate* that gives the ratio of a dataword size to the codeword size. Equation 8.2 defines the code rate, R, for an (n, k) error coding scheme.

$$R = \frac{k}{n}$$

$$(8.2)$$

8.11 Error Correction With Row And Column (RAC) Parity

We have seen how a channel coding scheme can detect errors. To understand how a code can be used to correct errors, consider an example. Assume a dataword consists of $k = 12$ bits. Instead of thinking of the bits as a single string, imagine arranging them into an array of three rows and four columns, with a parity bit added for each row and for each column. Figure 8.7 illustrates the arrangement, which is known as a *Row And Column (RAC)* code. The example RAC encoding has $n = 20$, which means that it is a $(20, 12)$ encoding.

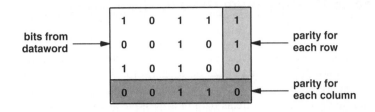

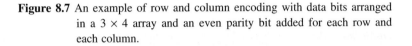

Figure 8.7 An example of row and column encoding with data bits arranged in a 3 × 4 array and an even parity bit added for each row and each column.

To see how error correction works, assume that one of the data bits in Figure 8.7 is changed during transmission. When the receiver arranges the bits into an array and parity bits are recalculated, two of the calculations will disagree with the parity bits received, as Figure 8.8 illustrates.

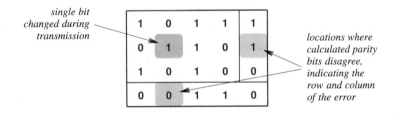

Figure 8.8 Illustration of how a single-bit error can be corrected using a row and column encoding.

As the figure illustrates, a single bit error will cause two calculated parity bits to disagree with the parity bit received. The two disagreements correspond to the row and column of the error. A receiver uses the calculated parity bits to determine exactly which data bit is in error, and then corrects the data bit. Thus, an RAC can correct any error that changes a single data bit.

What happens to an RAC code if an error changes more than one bit in a given block? RAC can only correct single-bit errors. In cases where two or three bits are changed, however, an RAC encoding will be able to detect an odd number of errors.

To summarize:

> *A Row And Column (RAC) encoding allows a receiver to correct any single bit error and to detect errors in which two or three bits are changed.*

8.12 The 16-Bit Checksum Used In The Internet

A particular channel coding scheme plays a key role in the Internet. Known as the *Internet checksum*, the code consists of a 16-bit 1s complement checksum. The Internet checksum does not impose a fixed size on a dataword. Instead, the algorithm allows a message to be arbitrarily long, and computes a checksum over the entire message. In essence, the Internet checksum treats data in a message as a series of 16-bit integers, as Figure 8.9 illustrates.

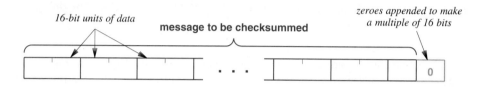

Figure 8.9 The Internet checksum divides data into 16-bit units, appending zeroes if the data is not an exact multiple of 16 bits.

To compute a checksum, a sender adds the numeric values of the 16-bit integers, and transmits the result. To validate the message, a receiver performs the same computation. Algorithm 8.1 gives the details of the computation.

Algorithm 8.1

Given:

    A message, M, of arbitrary length

Compute:

    A 16-bit 1s complement checksum, C, using 32-bit arithmetic

Method:

    Pad M with zero bits to make an exact multiple of 16 bits

    Set a 32-bit checksum integer, C, to 0;

    for (each 16-bit group in M) {

        Treat the 16 bits as an integer and add to C;

    }

    Extract the high-order 16 bits of C and add them to C;

    The inverse of the low-order 16 bits of C is the checksum;

    If the checksum is zero, substitute the all 1s form of zero.

Algorithm 8.1 The 16-bit checksum algorithm used in the Internet protocols.

The key to understanding the algorithm is to realize that the checksum is computed in 1s complement arithmetic instead of the 2s complement arithmetic found on most computers, and uses 16 bit integers instead of 32 or 64 bit integers. Thus, the algorithm is written to use 32-bit 2s complement arithmetic to perform a 1s complement computation. During the *for* loop, the addition may overflow. Thus, following the loop, the algorithm adds the overflow (the high-order bits) back into the sum.

Why is a checksum computed as the arithmetic inverse of the sum instead of the sum? The answer is efficiency: a receiver can apply the same checksum algorithm as the sender, but can include the checksum itself. Because it contains the arithmetic inverse of the total, adding the checksum to the total will produce zero. Thus, a receiver includes the checksum in the computation, and then tests to see if the resulting sum is zero.

A final detail of 1s complement arithmetic arises in the last step of the algorithm. Ones complement arithmetic has two forms of zero: all zeroes and all ones. The Internet checksum uses the all-ones form to indicate that a checksum was computed and the value of the checksum is zero; the Internet protocols use the all-zeroes form to indicate that no checksum was computed.

8.13 Cyclic Redundancy Codes (CRCs)

A form of channel coding known as a *Cyclic Redundancy Code (CRC)* is used in high-speed data networks. CRC codes have three key properties that make them important, as Figure 8.10 summarizes.

Arbitrary Length Message	As with a checksum, the size of a dataword is not fixed, which means a CRC can be applied to an arbitrary length message
Excellent Error Detection	Because the value computed depends on the sequence of bits in a message, a CRC provides excellent error detection capability
Fast Hardware Implementation	Despite its sophisticated mathematical basis, a CRC computation can be carried out extremely fast by hardware

Figure 8.10 The three key aspects of a CRC that make it important in data networking.

The term *cyclic* is derived from a property of the codewords: a circular shift of the bits of any codeword produces another codeword. Figure 8.11 illustrates a $(7, 4)$ cyclic redundancy code that was introduced by Hamming.

Dataword	Codeword	Dataword	Codeword
0000	0000 000	1000	1000 101
0001	0001 011	1001	1001 110
0010	0010 110	1010	1010 011
0011	0011 101	1011	1011 000
0100	0100 111	1100	1100 010
0101	0101 100	1101	1101 001
0110	0110 001	1110	1110 100
0111	0111 010	1111	1111 111

Figure 8.11 An example $(7, 4)$ cyclic redundancy code.

CRC codes have been studied extensively, and a variety of mathematical explanations and computational techniques have been produced. The descriptions seem so disparate that it is difficult to understand how they can all refer to the same concept. Principal views include:

- *Mathematicians* explain a CRC computation as the remainder from a division of two polynomials with binary coefficients, one representing the message and another representing a fixed divisor.

- *Theoretical Computer Scientists* explain a CRC computation as the remainder from a division of two binary numbers, one representing the message and the other representing a fixed divisor.

- *Cryptographers* explain a CRC computation as a mathematical operation in a Galois field of order 2, written GF(2).

- *Computer programmers* explain a CRC computation as an algorithm that iterates through a message and uses table lookup to obtain an additive value for each step.

- *Hardware architects* explain a CRC computation as a small hardware pipeline unit that takes as input a sequence of bits from a message and produces a CRC without using division or iteration.

As an example of the views above, consider the division of binary numbers under the assumption of no carries. Figure 8.12 illustrates the division of 1010, which represents a message, by a constant chosen for a specific CRC, 1011.

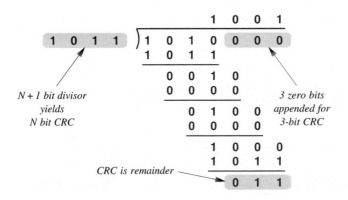

Figure 8.12 Illustration of a CRC computation viewed as the remainder of a binary division with no carries.

To understand how mathematicians can view the above as a polynomial division, think of each bit in a binary number as the coefficient of a term in a polynomial. For example, we can think of the divisor in Figure 8.12, *1011*, as coefficients in the following polynomial:

$$1 \times x^3 + 0 \times x^2 + 1 \times x^1 + 1 \times x^0 = x^3 + x + 1$$

Similarly, the dividend in Figure 8.12, *1010000*, represents the polynomial:

$$x^6 + x^4$$

We use the term *generator polynomial* to describe a polynomial that corresponds to a divisor. The selection of a generator polynomial is key to creating a CRC with good error detection properties. Therefore, much mathematical analysis has been conducted on generator polynomials. We know, for example, that an ideal polynomial is irreducible (i.e., can only be divided evenly by itself and 1) and that a polynomial with more than one non-zero coefficient can detect all single-bit errors.

8.14 An Efficient Hardware Implementation Of CRC

The hardware needed to compute a CRC is surprisingly straightforward. CRC hardware is arranged as a shift register with *exclusive or* (*xor*) gates between some of the bits. The shift register operates once per input bit. At each stage, the register either accepts the bit from the previous stage or performs an *xor* operation of the bit and accepts the result. When the entire input has been shifted into the register, the value in the register is the CRC.

Figure 8.13 illustrates the hardware needed for the 3-bit CRC computation from Figure 8.12. Because an *xor* operation and *shift* can each be performed at high speed, the arrangement can be used for high-speed computer networks.

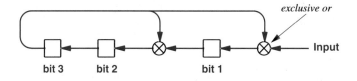

Figure 8.13 A hardware unit to compute a 3-bit CRC for $x^3 + x^1 + 1$.

8.15 Automatic Repeat reQuest (ARQ) Mechanisms

Recall that an ARQ approach to error correct requires a sender and receiver to communicate metainformation. That is, whenever one side sends a message to another, the receiving side sends a short *acknowledgement* message back. For example, if *A* sends a message to *B*, *B* sends an acknowledgement back to *A*. Once it receives an acknowledgement, *A* knows that the message arrived correctly. If no acknowledgement is received after *T* time units, *A* assumes the message was lost and *retransmits* a copy.

ARQ is especially useful in cases where the underlying system provides error detection, but not error correction. For example, many computer networks use a CRC to detect transmission errors. In such cases, an ARQ scheme can be added to guarantee delivery — if a transmission error occurs, the receiver discards the message, and the sender retransmits another copy.

Chapter 26 will discuss the details of an Internet protocol that uses the ARQ approach. In addition to showing how the timeout-and-retransmission paradigm works in practice, the chapter explains how the sender and receiver identify the data being acknowledged, and discusses how long a sender waits before retransmitting.

8.16 Summary

Physical transmission systems are susceptible to interference, distortion, and attenuation, all of which can cause errors. Transmission errors can result in single-bit errors or burst errors, and erasures can occur whenever a received signal is ambiguous (i.e., neither clearly 1 nor clearly 0). To control errors, data communications systems employ a forward error correction mechanism or use an automatic repeat request (ARQ) technique.

Forward error correction arranges for a sender to add redundant bits to the data and encode the result before transmission across a channel, and arranges for a receiver to decode and check incoming data. A coding scheme is (n, k) if a dataword contains k bits and a codeword contains n bits.

One measure of an encoding assesses the chance that an error will change a valid codeword into another valid codeword. The minimum Hamming distance provides a precise measure.

Simplistic block codes, such as a single parity bit added to each byte, can detect an odd number of bit errors, but cannot detect an even number of bit changes. A Row And Column (RAC) code can correct single-bit errors, detect up to three errors in a block, and can detect any error in which an odd number of bits are changed.

The 16-bit checksum used in the Internet can be used with an arbitrary size message. The checksum algorithm divides a message into 16-bit blocks, and computes the arithmetic inverse of the 1s-complement sum of the blocks; the overflow is added back into the checksum.

Cyclic redundancy codes (CRCs) are used in high-speed data networks because a CRC accepts a message of arbitrary length, provides extremely good error detection, and has an efficient hardware implementation. CRC techniques have a mathematical basis, and have been studied extensively. A CRC computation can be viewed as computing the remainder of a binary division, computing the remainder of a polynomial division, or an operation using Galois field theory. The hardware to perform a CRC computation uses a shift register and *exclusive or* operations.

EXERCISES

8.1   List and explain the three main sources of transmission errors.

8.2   How do transmission errors effect data?

8.3   What does an ideal channel coding scheme achieve?

8.4   What are the characteristics of a CRC?

8.5   Define the concept of *Hamming distance*.

8.6   List and explain the function of the two hardware building blocks used to implement CRC computation.

8.7 How does one compute the minimum number of bit changes that can transform a valid code-word into another valid codeword?

8.8 Compute the Hamming distance for the following pairs: (0000,0001), (0101,0001), (1111,1001), and (0001,1110).

8.9 In a burst error, how is burst length measured?

8.10 Give an example of a block error code used with character data.

8.11 What is a codeword, and how is it used in forward error correction?

8.12 Explain the concept of *code rate*. Is a high code rate or low code rate desirable?

8.13 Generate a RAC parity matrix for a (20, 12) coding of the dataword *100011011111*.

8.14 Show the division of 10010101010 by 10101.

8.15 Express the two values in the previous exercise as polynomials.

8.16 Write a computer program that implements the (7,4) cyclic redundancy code in Figure 8.11.

8.17 Write a computer program that computes a 16-bit Internet checksum.

8.18 What can a RAC scheme achieve that a single parity bit scheme cannot?

Chapter Contents

9

Transmission Modes

9.1 Introduction

Chapters in this part of the text cover fundamental concepts that underlie data communications. This chapter continues the discussion by focusing on the ways data is transmitted. The chapter introduces common terminology, explains the advantages and disadvantages of parallelism, and discusses the important concepts of synchronous and asynchronous communication. Later chapters show how the ideas presented here are used in networks throughout the Internet.

9.2 A Taxonomy Of Transmission Modes

We use the term *transmission mode* to refer to the manner in which data is sent over the underlying medium. Transmission modes can be divided into two fundamental categories:

- Serial — one bit is sent at a time
- Parallel — multiple bits are sent at the same time

As we will see, serial transmission is further categorized according to timing of transmissions. Figure 9.1 gives an overall taxonomy of the transmission modes discussed in the chapter.

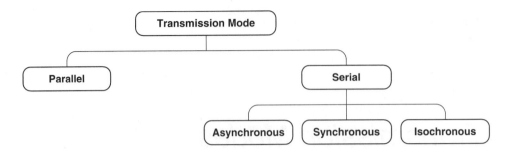

Figure 9.1 A taxonomy of transmission modes.

9.3 Parallel Transmission

The term *parallel transmission* refers to a transmission mechanism that transfers multiple data bits at the same time over separate media. In general, parallel transmission is used with a wired medium that uses multiple, independent wires. Furthermore, the signals on all wires are synchronized so that a bit travels across each of the wires at precisely the same time. Figure 9.2 illustrates the concept, and shows why engineers use the term *parallel* to characterize the wiring.

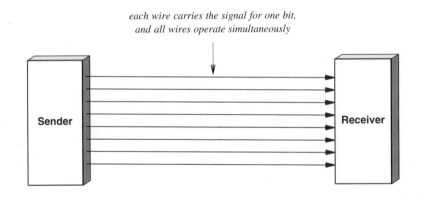

Figure 9.2 Illustration of parallel transmission that uses 8 wires to send 8 bits at the same time.

The figure omits two important details. First, in addition to the parallel wires that each carry data, a parallel interface usually contains other wires that allow the sender and receiver to coordinate. Second, to make installation and troubleshooting easy, the wires for a parallel transmission system are placed in a single physical cable. Thus, one expects to see a single, large cable connecting a sender and receiver rather than a set of independent physical wires.

A parallel mode of transmission has two chief advantages:

- *High speed.* Because it can send N bits at the same time, a parallel interface can operate N times faster than an equivalent serial interface.

- *Match to underlying hardware.* Internally, computer and communication hardware uses parallel circuitry. Thus, a parallel interface matches the internal hardware well.

9.4 Serial Transmission

The alternative to parallel transmission, known as *serial transmission*, sends one bit at a time. With the emphasis on speed, it may seem that anyone designing a data communications system would choose parallel transmission. However, most communication systems use serial mode. There are two main reasons. First, serial networks can be extended over long distances at much less cost because fewer physical wires are needed and intermediate electronic components are less expensive. Second, using only one physical wire means that there is never a timing problem caused by one wire being slightly longer than another (a difference of millimeters can be significant in a high-speed communication system).

To use serial transmission, the sender and receiver must contain a small amount of hardware that converts data from the parallel form used in the device to the serial form used on the wire. Figure 9.3 illustrates the configuration.

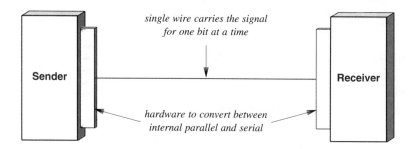

single wire carries the signal for one bit at a time

hardware to convert between internal parallel and serial

Figure 9.3 Illustration of a serial transmission mode.

The hardware needed to convert data between an internal parallel form and a serial form can be straightforward or complex, depending on the type of serial communication mechanism. In the simplest case, a single chip that is known as a *Universal Asynchronous Receiver And Transmitter* (*UART*) performs the conversion. A related chip, *Universal Synchronous-Asynchronous Receiver And Transmitter* (*USART*) handles conversion for synchronous networks.

9.5 Transmission Order: Bits And Bytes

The serial transmission mode introduces an interesting question: when sending bits, which bit should be sent across the medium first? For example, consider an integer. Should a sender transmit the *Most Significant Bit* (*MSB*) or the *Least Significant Bit* (*LSB*) first?

Engineers use the term *little-endian* to describe a system that sends the LSB first, and the term *big-endian* to describe a system that sends the MSB first. Either form can be used, but the sender and receiver must agree.

Interestingly, the order in which bits are transmitted does not settle the entire question of transmission order. Data in a computer is divided into bytes, and each byte is further divided into bits (typically 8 bits per byte). Thus, it is possible to choose a byte order and a bit order independently. For example, Ethernet technology specifies that data is sent byte big-endian and bit little-endian. Figure 9.4 illustrates the order in which Ethernet sends bits from a 32-bit quantity.

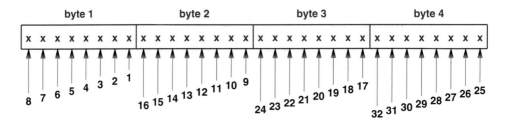

Figure 9.4 Illustration of byte big-endian, bit little-endian order in which the least-significant bit of the most-significant byte is sent first.

9.6 Timing Of Serial Transmission

Serial transmission mechanisms can be divided into three broad categories, depending on how transmissions are spaced in time:

- *Asynchronous* transmission can occur at any time, with an arbitrary delay between the transmission of two data items.

- *Synchronous* transmission occurs continuously with no gap between the transmission of two data items.

- *Isochronous* transmission occurs at regular intervals with a fixed gap between the transmission of two data items.

9.7 Asynchronous Transmission

A transmission system is classified as *asynchronous* if the system allows the physical medium to be idle for an arbitrary time between two transmissions. The asynchronous style of communication is well-suited to applications that generate data at random (e.g., a user typing on a keyboard or a user that clicks on a link to obtain a web page, reads for awhile, and then clicks on a link to obtain another page).

The disadvantage of asynchrony arises from the lack of coordination between sender and receiver — while the medium is idle, a receiver cannot know how long the medium will remain idle before more data arrives. Thus, asynchronous technologies usually arrange for a sender to transmit a few extra bits before each data item to inform the receiver that a data transfer is starting. The extra bits allow the receiver's hardware to synchronize with the incoming signal. In some asynchronous systems, the extra bits are known as a *preamble*; in others, the extra bits are known as *start bits*. To summarize:

> *Because it permits a sender to remain idle an arbitrarily long time between transmissions, an asynchronous transmission mechanism sends extra information before each transmission that allows a receiver to synchronize with the signal.*

9.8 RS-232 Asynchronous Character Transmission

As an example of asynchronous communication, consider the transfer of characters across copper wires between a computer and a device such as a keyboard. An asynchronous communication technology standardized by the *Electronic Industries Alliance* (*EIA*) has become the most widely accepted for character communication. Known as *RS-232-C*, and commonly abbreviated *RS-232*†, the EIA standard specifies the details of the physical connection (e.g., the connection must be less than 50 feet long), electrical details (e.g., the voltage ranges from -15 volts to +15 volts), and the line coding (e.g., negative voltage corresponds to logical 1 and positive voltage corresponds to logical 0).

Because it is designed for use with devices such as keyboards, the RS-232 standard specifies that each data item represents one character. The hardware can be configured to control the exact number of bits per second and to send seven-bit or eight-bit characters. Although a sender can delay arbitrarily long before sending a character, once transmission begin, a sender transmits all bits of the character one after another with no delay between them. When it finishes transmission, the sender leaves the wire with a negative voltage (corresponding to logical *1*) until another character is ready for transmission.

How does a receiver know where a new character starts? RS-232 specifies that a sender transmit an extra *0* bit (called a *start bit*) before transmitting the bits of a character. Furthermore, RS-232 specifies that a sender must leave the line idle between char-

---

†Although the later RS-449 standard provides slightly more functionality, most engineers still use the original name.

acters for at least the time required to send one bit. Thus, one can think of a phantom *1* bit appended to each character. In RS-232 terminology, the phantom bit is called a *stop bit*. Figure 9.5 illustrates how voltage varies when a start bit, eight bits of a character, and a stop bit are sent.

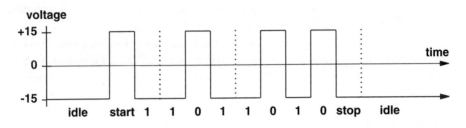

Figure 9.5 Illustration of voltage during transmission of an 8-bit character when using RS-232.

To summarize:

> *The RS-232 standard used for asynchronous, serial communication over short distances precedes each character with a start bit, sends each bit of the character, and follows each character with an idle period at least one bit long (stop bit).*

9.9 Synchronous Transmission

The chief alternative to asynchronous transmission is known as *synchronous transmission*. At the lowest level, a synchronous mechanism transmits bits of data continually, with no idle time between bits. That is, after transmitting the final bit of one data byte, the sender transmits a bit of the next data byte.

The chief advantage of a synchronous mechanism arises because the sender and receiver constantly remain synchronized, which means less synchronization overhead. To understand the overhead compare the transmission of 8-bit characters on an asynchronous system as illustrated in Figure 9.5 and a synchronous transmission system as illustrated in Figure 9.6. Each character sent using RS-232 requires an extra start bit and stop bit, meaning that each 8-bit character requires a minimum of 10 bit times, even if no idle time is inserted. On a synchronous system, each character is sent without start or stop bits.

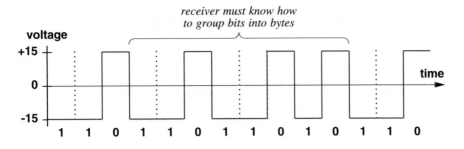

Figure 9.6 Illustration of synchronous transmission where the first bit of a byte immediately follows the last bit of the previous byte.

The point is:

> *When compared to synchronous transmission an asynchronous RS-232 mechanism has 25% overhead per character.*

9.10 Bytes, Blocks, And Frames

If the underlying synchronous mechanism must send bits continually, what happens if a sender does not have data ready to send at all times? The answer lies in a technique known as *framing*: an interface is added to a synchronous mechanism that accepts and delivers a *block* of bytes known as a *frame*. To insure that the sender and receiver stay synchronized, a frame starts with a special sequence of bits. Furthermore, most synchronous systems include a special *idle sequence* (or *idle byte*) that is transmitted when the sender has no data to send. Figure 9.7 illustrates the concept.

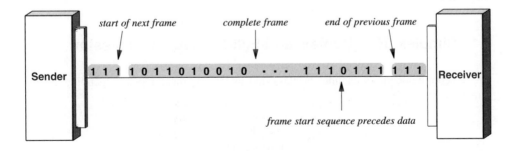

Figure 9.7 Illustration of framing on a synchronous transmission system.

The consequence of framing can be summarized:

> *Although the underlying mechanism transmits bits continuously, the use of an idle sequence and framing permits a synchronous transmission mechanism to provide a byte-oriented interface and to allow idle gaps between blocks of data.*

9.11 Isochronous Transmission

The third type of serial transmission system does not provide a new underlying mechanism. Instead, it can be viewed as an important way to use synchronous transmission. Known as *isochronous transmission*†, the system is designed to provide steady bit flow for multimedia applications that contain voice or video. Delivering such data at a steady rate is essential because variations in delay, which are known as *jitter*, can disrupt reception (i.e., cause pops or clicks in audio or make video freeze for a short time).

Instead of using the presence of data to drive transmission, an isochronous network is designed to accept and send data at a fixed rate, R. In fact, the interface to the network is such that data *must* be handed to the network for transmission at exactly R bits per second. For example, an isochronous mechanism designed to transfer voice operates at a rate of 64,000 bits per second. A sender must generate digitized audio continuously, and a receiver must be able to accept and play the stream.

An underlying network can use framing and may choose to transmit extra information along with data. However, to be isochronous, a system must be designed so the sender and receiver see a continuous stream of data, with no extra delays at the start of a frame. Thus, an isochronous network that provides a data rate of R bits per second usually has an underlying synchronous mechanism that operates at slightly more than R bits per second.

9.12 Simplex, Half-Duplex, and Full-Duplex Transmission

A communications channel is classified as one of three types, depending on the direction of transfer:

- Simplex
- Full-Duplex
- Half-Duplex

Simplex. A *simplex* mechanism is the easiest to understand. As the name implies, a simplex mechanism can only transfer data in a single direction. For example, a single

---

†Isochronous is pronounced *eye-sock'-run-us.*

optical fiber acts as a simplex transmission mechanism because the fiber has a transmitting device (i.e., an LED or laser) at one end and a receiving device (i.e., a photosensitive receptor) at the other. Simplex transmission is analogous to broadcast radio or television. Figure 9.8a illustrates simplex communication.

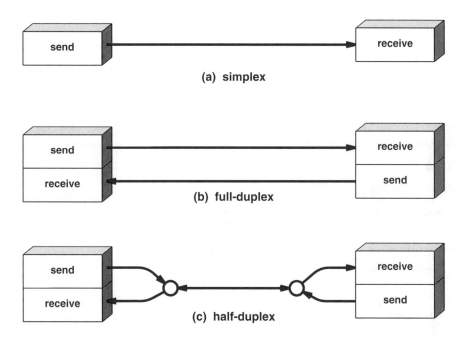

Figure 9.8 Illustration of the three modes of operation.

Full-Duplex. A *full-duplex* mechanism is also straightforward: the underlying system allows transmission in two directions simultaneously. Typically a full-duplex mechanism consists of two *simplex* mechanisms, one carrying information in each direction, as Figure 9.8b illustrates. For example, a pair of optical fibers can be used to provide full-duplex communication by running the two in parallel and arranging to send data in opposite directions. Full duplex communication is analogous to a voice telephone conversation in which a participant can speak even if they are able to hear background music at the other end.

Half-Duplex. A *half-duplex* mechanism involves a shared transmission medium. The shared medium can be used for communication in each direction, but the communication cannot proceed simultaneously. Thus, half-duplex communication is analogous to using walkie-talkies where only one side can transmit at a time. An additional mechanism is needed at each end of a half-duplex communication that coordinates transmission to insure that only one side transmits at a given time. Figure 9.8c illustrates half-duplex communication.

9.13 DCE and DTE Equipment

The terms *Data Communications Equipment* (*DCE*) and *Data Terminal Equipment* (*DTE*) were originally created by AT&T to distinguish between the communications equipment owned by the phone company and the *terminal* equipment owned by a subscriber.

The terminology persists: if a business leases a data circuit from a phone company, the phone company installs DCE equipment at the business, and the business purchases DTE equipment that attaches to the phone company's equipment.

From an academic point of view, the important concept behind the DCE-DTE distinction is not ownership of the equipment. Instead, it lies in the ability to define an arbitrary interface for a user. For example, if the underlying network uses synchronous transmission, the DCE equipment can provide either a synchronous or isochronous interface to the user's equipment. Figure 9.9 illustrates the conceptual organization†.

Figure 9.9 Illustration of Data Communications Equipment and Data Terminal Equipment providing a communication service between two locations.

Several standards exist that specify a possible interface between DCE and DTE. For example, the RS-232 standard described in this chapter and the RS-449 standard proposed as a replacement can each be used. In addition, a standard known as *X.21* is available.

9.14 Summary

Communication systems use parallel or serial transmission. A parallel system has multiple wires, and at any time, each wire carries the signal for one bit. Thus, a parallel transmission system with K wires can send K bits at the same time. Although parallel communication offers higher speed, most communication systems use lower-cost serial mechanisms that send one bit at a time.

---

†Note: the terms DCE and DTE are also used to distinguish between two types of connectors, even if the equipment is not owned by a phone company (e.g., the connector on a PC and the connector on an external modem).

Serial communication requires a sender and receiver to agree on timing and the order in which bits are sent. Transmission order refers to whether the most-significant or least-significant bit is sent first and whether the most-significant or least-significant byte is sent first.

The three types of timing are: asynchronous, in which transmission can occur at any time and the communication system can remain idle between transmissions, synchronous, in which bits are transmitted continually and data is grouped into frames, and isochronous, in which transmission occurs at regular intervals with no extra delay at frame boundaries.

A communication system can be simplex, full-duplex, or half-duplex. A simplex mechanism sends data in a single direction. A full-duplex mechanism transfers data in two directions simultaneously, and a half-duplex mechanism allows two-way transfer, but only allows a transfer in one direction at a given time.

The distinction between Data Communications Equipment and Data Terminal Equipment was originally devised to denote whether a provider or a subscriber owned equipment. The key concept arises from the ability to define an interface for a user that offers a different service than the underlying communication system.

EXERCISES

9.1 What are the advantages of parallel transmission? What is the chief disadvantage?

9.2 Describe the difference between serial and parallel transmission.

9.3 When using a synchronous transmission scheme, what happens when a sender does not have data to send?

9.4 What is the chief characteristic of asynchronous transmission?

9.5 Which type (or types) of serial transmission is appropriate for video transmission? For a keyboard connection to a computer?

9.6 Use the Web to find the definition of the DCE and DTE pinouts used on a DB-25 connector. Hint: pins 2 and 3 are transmit or receive. On a DCE type connector, does pin 2 transmit or receive?

9.7 Is a modem classified as DTE or DCE?

9.8 When transmitting a 32-bit 2's complement integer in big-endian order, when is the sign bit transmitted?

9.9 What is a start bit, and with which type of serial transmission is a start bit used?

9.10 When two humans hold a conversation, do they use simplex, half-duplex, or full-duplex transmission?

Chapter Contents

10

Modulation And Modems

10.1 Introduction

Chapters in this part of the text each cover one aspect of data communications. Previous chapters discuss information sources, explain how a signal can represent information, and describe forms of energy used with various transmission media.

This chapter continues the discussion of data communications by focusing on the use of high-frequency signals to carry information. The chapter discusses how information is used to change a high-frequency electromagnetic wave, explains why the technique is important, and describes how analog and digital inputs are used. Later chapters extend the discussion by explaining how the technique can be used to devise a communication system that transfers multiple, independent streams of data over a shared transmission medium simultaneously.

10.2 Carriers, Frequency, And Propagation

Many long-distance communication systems use a continuously oscillating electromagnetic wave called a *carrier*. The system makes small changes to the carrier that represent information being sent. To understand why carriers are important, recall from Chapter 7 that the frequency of electromagnetic energy determines how the energy propagates. One motivation for the use of carriers arises from the desire to select a frequency that will propagate well, independent of the rate that data is being sent.

10.3 Analog Modulation Schemes

We use the term *modulation* to refer to changes made in a carrier according to the information being sent. Conceptually, modulation takes two inputs, a carrier and a signal, and generates a modulated carrier as output, as Figure 10.1 illustrates.

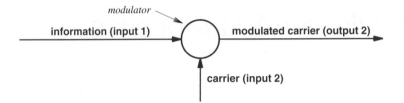

Figure 10.1 The concept of modulation with two inputs.

In essence, a sender must change one of the fundamental characteristics of the wave. Thus, there are three primary techniques that modulate an electromagnetic carrier according to a signal:

- Amplitude modulation

- Frequency modulation

- Phase shift modulation

The first two methods of modulation are the most familiar and have been used extensively. Indeed, they did not originate with computer networks — they were devised and used for broadcast radio, and are also used for broadcast television.

10.4 Amplitude Modulation

A technique known as *amplitude modulation* varies the amplitude of a carrier in proportion to the information being sent (i.e., according to a signal). The carrier continues oscillating at a fixed frequency, but the amplitude of the wave varies. Figure 10.2 illustrates an unmodulated carrier wave, an analog information signal, and the resulting amplitude modulated carrier.

Amplitude modulation is easy to understand because only the amplitude (i.e., magnitude) of the sine wave is modified. Furthermore, a time-domain graph of a modulated carrier has a shape similar to the signal that was used. For example, if one imagines an *envelope* consisting of a curve that connects the peaks of the sine wave in Figure 10.2c, the resulting curve has the same shape as the signal in Figure 10.2b.

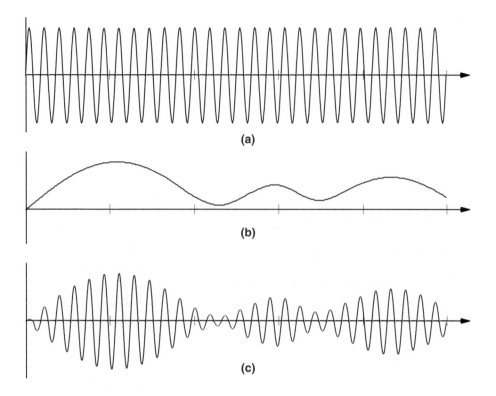

Figure 10.2 Illustration of (a) an unmodulated carrier wave, (b) an analog information signal, and (c) an amplitude modulated carrier.

10.5 Frequency Modulation

An alternative to amplitude modulation is known as *frequency modulation*. When
frequency modulation is employed, the amplitude of the carrier remains fixed, but the
frequency changes according to the signal: when the signal is stronger, the carrier frequency increases slightly, and when the signal is weaker, the carrier frequency decreases
slightly. Figure 10.3 illustrates a carrier wave modulated with frequency modulation according to the signal in Figure 10.2b.

As the figure shows, frequency modulation is more difficult to visualize because
slight changes in frequency are not as clearly visible. However, one can notice that the
modulated wave has higher frequencies when the signal used for modulation is stronger.

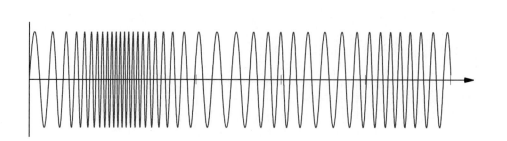

Figure 10.3 Illustration of a carrier wave with frequency modulation according to the signal in Figure 10.2b.

10.6 Phase Shift Modulation

The third property of a sine wave is its *phase*, the offset from a reference time at which the sine wave begins. It is possible to use changes in phase to represent a signal. We use the term *phase shift* to characterize such changes.

Although modulating phase is possible in theory, the technique is seldom used with an analog signal. To understand why, observe that if phase changes after cycle k, the next sine wave will start slightly later than the time at which cycle k completes. A slight delay resembles a change in frequency. Thus, for analog input, phase shift modulation can be thought of as a special form of frequency modulation. We will see, however, that phase shifts are important when a digital signal is used to modulate a carrier.

10.7 Amplitude Modulation And Shannon's Theorem

The illustration in Figure 10.2c shows the amplitude varying from a maximum to almost zero. Although it is easy for a human to understand, the figure is slightly misleading: in practice, modulation only changes the amplitude of a carrier slightly, depending on a constant known as the *modulation index*.

To understand why practical systems do not allow for a modulated signal to approach zero, consider Shannon's Theorem. Assuming the amount of noise is constant, the signal-to-noise ratio will approach zero as the signal approaches zero. Thus, keeping the carrier wave near maximum insures that the signal-to-noise ratio remains as large as possible, which permits the transfer of more bits per second.

10.8 Modulation, Digital Input, And Shift Keying

The description of modulation above shows how an analog information signal is used to modulate a carrier. The question arises, "how can digital input be used?" The answer lies in straightforward modifications of the modulation schemes described above: instead of modulation that is proportional to a continuous signal, digital schemes use discrete values. Furthermore, to distinguish between analog and digital modulation, we use the term *shift keying* rather than modulation.

In essence, shift keying operates similar to analog modulation. Instead of a continuum of possible values, digital shift keying has a fixed set. For example, amplitude modulation allows the amplitude of a carrier to vary by arbitrarily small amounts in response to a change in the signal being used. In contrast, amplitude shift keying uses a fixed set of possible amplitudes. In the simplest case, a full amplitude can correspond to a logical 1 and a significantly smaller amplitude can correspond to a logical 0. Similarly, frequency shift keying uses two basic frequencies. Figure 10.4 illustrates a carrier wave, a digital input signal, and the resulting waveforms for *Amplitude Shift Keying (ASK)* and *Frequency Shift Keying (FSK)*.

10.9 Phase Shift Keying

Although amplitude and frequency changes work well for audio, both require at least one cycle of a carrier wave to send a single bit unless a special encoding scheme is used (e.g., unless positive and negative parts of the signal are changed independently). The Nyquist Theorem described in Chapter 6 suggests that the number of bits sent per unit time can be increased if the encoding scheme permits multiple bits to be encoded in a single cycle of the carrier. Thus, data communications systems often use techniques that can send more bits. In particular, *phase shift keying* changes the phase of the carrier wave abruptly to encode data. Each such change is called a *phase shift*. After a phase shift, the carrier continues to oscillate, but it immediately jumps to a new point in the sine wave cycle. Figure 10.5 illustrates how a phase shift affects a sine wave.

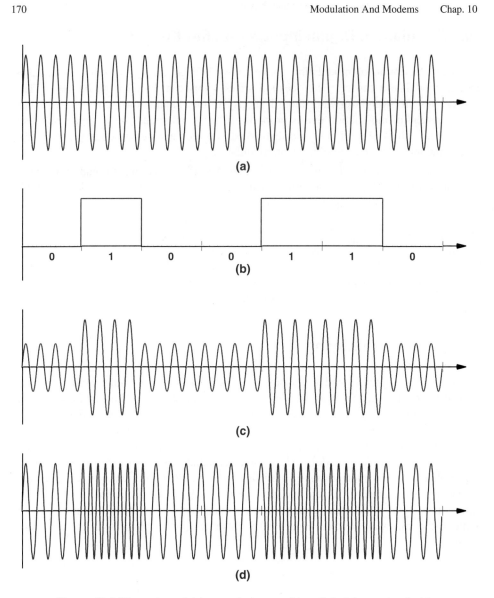

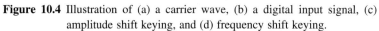

Figure 10.4 Illustration of (a) a carrier wave, (b) a digital input signal, (c) amplitude shift keying, and (d) frequency shift keying.

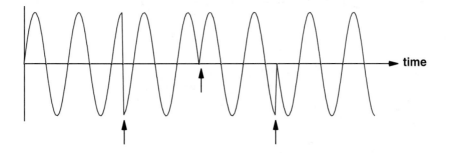

Figure 10.5 An illustration of phase shift modulation with arrows indicating
times at which the carrier abruptly jumps to a new point in the
sine wave cycle.

A phase shift is measured by the angle of the change. For example, the leftmost
shift in Figure 10.5 changes the angle by $\pi / 2$ radians or $180°$. The second phase
change in the figure also corresponds to a $180°$ shift. The third phase change
corresponds to a shift of $-90°$ (which is equivalent to $270°$).

10.10 Phase Shift And A Constellation Diagram

How can data be encoded using phase shifts? In the simplest case, a sender and
receiver can agree on the number of bits per second, and can use no phase shift to
denote logical 0, and the presence of a phase shift to denote a logical 1. For example, a
system might use a $180°$ phase shift. A *constellation diagram* is used to express the
exact assignment of data bits to specific phase changes. Figure 10.6 illustrates the concept.

Hardware can do more than detect the presence of a phase shift — a receiver can
measure the amount a carrier shifted during a phase change. Thus, it is possible to devise a communication system that recognizes a set of phase shifts, and use each particular
phase shift to represent specific values of data. Usually, systems are designed to use a
power of two possible shifts, which means a sender can use bits of data to select among
the shifts.

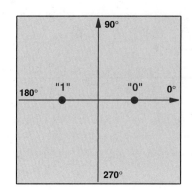

Figure 10.6 A constellation diagram that shows logical 0 as a 0° phase shift
and logical 1 as a 180° phase shift.

Figure 10.7 shows the constellation diagram for a system that uses four possible
phase shifts (i.e., 2^2). At each stage of transmission, a sender uses two bits of data to
select among the four possible shift values.

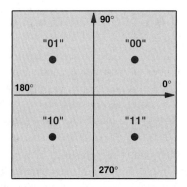

Figure 10.7 A constellation diagram for a system that uses four possible
phase shifts that each represent two data bits.

To summarize:

*The chief advantage of mechanisms like phase shift keying arises from
the ability to represent more than one data bit at a given change. A
constellation diagram shows the assignment of data bits to phase
changes.*

Many variations of phase shift keying exist. For example, a phase shift mechanism such as the one illustrated in Figure 10.6 that permits a sender to transfer one bit at a time is classified as a *Binary Phase Shift Keying (BPSK)* mechanism. The notation *2-PSK* is used to denote the two possible values. Similarly, the variation illustrated in Figure 10.7 is known as a *4-PSK* mechanism.

In theory, it is possible to increase the data rate by increasing the range of phase shifts. Thus, a 16-PSK mechanism can send twice as many bits per second as a 4-PSK mechanism. In practice, however, noise and distortion limit the ability of hardware to distinguish among minor differences in phase shifts. The point is:

> *Although many variations of phase shift keying exist, noise and distortion limit the ability of practical systems to distinguish among arbitrarily small differences in phase changes.*

10.11 Quadrature Amplitude Modulation

If hardware is incapable of detecting arbitrary phase changes, how can the data rate be increased further? The answer lies in a combination of modulation techniques that change two characteristics of a carrier at the same time. The most sophisticated technology combines amplitude modulation and phase shift keying. Known as *Quadrature Amplitude Modulation†* (*QAM*), the approach uses both change in phase and change in amplitude to represent values.

To represent QAM on a constellation diagram, we use distance from the origin as a measure of amplitude. For example, Figure 10.8 shows the constellation diagram for a variant known as *16QAM* with dark gray areas indicating the amplitudes.

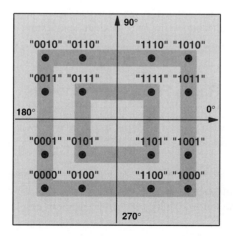

Figure 10.8 A constellation diagram for 16QAM in which distance from the origin reflects amplitude.

---

†The literature often uses the term *quadrature amplitude modulation* rather than *quadrature amplitude shift keying*.

10.12 Modem Hardware For Modulation And Demodulation

A hardware mechanism that accepts a sequence of data bits and applies modulation to a carrier wave according to the bits is called a *modulator*; a hardware mechanism that accepts a modulated carrier wave and recreates the sequence of data bits that was used to modulate the carrier is called a *demodulator*. Thus, transmission of data requires a modulator at one end of the transmission medium and a demodulator at the other. In practice, most communication systems are full duplex communication, which means each location needs both a modulator, which is used to send data, and a demodulator, which is used to receive data. To keep cost low and make the pair of devices easy to install and operate, manufacturers combine modulation and demodulation mechanisms into a single device called a *modem* (*mo*dulator and *dem*odulator). Figure 10.9 illustrates how a pair of modems use a 4-wire connection to communicate.

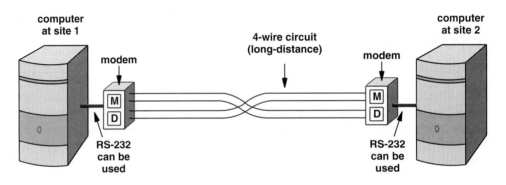

Figure 10.9 Illustration of two modems that use a 4-wire connection.

As the figure indicates, modems are designed to provide communication over long distances. A 4-wire circuit connecting two modems can extend inside a building, across a corporate campus between buildings, or between cities†.

10.13 Optical And Radio Frequency Modems

In addition to dedicated wires, modems are also used with other media, including RF transmission and optical fibers. For example, a pair of *Radio Frequency* (*RF*) modems can be used to send data via radio, and a pair of *optical modems* can be used to send data across a pair of optical fibers. Although such modems use entirely different media than modems that operate over dedicated wires, the principle remains the same: at the sending end, a modem modulates a carrier; at the receiving end, data is extracted from the modulated carrier.

---

†A circuit that crosses pubic property must be leased from a service provider, usually a telephone company.

10.14 Dialup Modems

Another interesting application of modems involves the voice telephone system. Instead of using an electrical signal as a carrier, a *dialup modem* uses an audio tone. As with conventional modems, the carrier is modulated at the sending end and demodulated at the receiving end. Thus, besides the ability to place and receive telephone calls, the chief difference between dialup and conventional modems arises from the lower bandwidth of audible tones.

When dialup modems were first designed, the approach made complete sense — a dialup modem converted data into a modulated analog carrier because the telephone system transported analog signals. Ironically, the interior of a modern telephone system is digital. Thus, on the sending side, a dialup modem uses data to modulate an audible carrier, which is transmitted to the phone system. The phone system digitizes the incoming audio, transports a digital form internally, and converts the digitized version back to analog audio for delivery. The receiving modem demodulates the analog carrier, and extracts the original digital data. Figure 10.10 illustrates the ironic use of analog and digital signals by dialup modems.

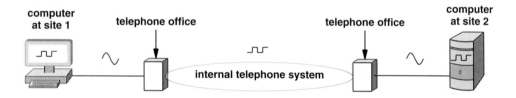

Figure 10.10 Illustration of digital and analog signals (denoted by a square wave and a sine wave) that occur when a dialup modem is used to send data from one computer to another.

As the figure indicates, a dialup modem is usually embedded in a computer. We use the term *internal modem* to denote an embedded device, and the term *external modem* to denote a separate physical device.

10.15 QAM Applied To Dialup

Quadrature Amplitude Modulation is also used with dialup modems as a way to maximize the rate at which data can be sent. To understand why, consider Figure 10.11, which shows the bandwidth available on a dialup connection. As the figure illustrates, most telephone connections transfer frequencies between 300 and 3000 Hz, but a given connection may not handle the extremes well. Thus, to guarantee better reproduction and lower noise, dialup modems use frequencies between 600 and 3000 Hz, which means the available bandwidth is 2400 Hz. A QAM scheme can increase the data rate dramatically.

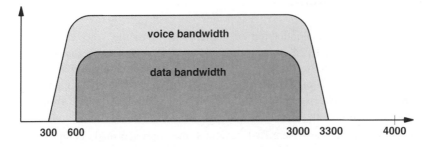

Figure 10.11 Illustration of the voice and data bandwidth on a dialup tele-
         phone connection.

10.16 V.32 and V.32bis Dialup Modems

As an example of dialup modems that use QAM, consider the *V.32* and *V.32bis*
standards. Figure 10.12 illustrates the QAM constellation for a V.32 modem that uses
32 combinations of amplitude shift and phase shift to achieve a data rate of 9600 bps in
each direction.

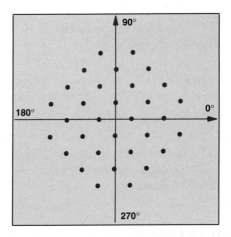

Figure 10.12 Illustration of the QAM constellation for a V.32 dialup modem.

A V.32bis modem uses 128 combinations of phase shift and amplitude shift to
achieve a data rate of 14,400 bps in each direction. Figure 10.13 illustrates the constellation. Sophisticated signal analysis is needed to detect the minor change that occurs
from a point in the constellation to a neighboring point.

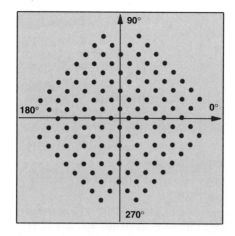

Figure 10.13 Illustration of the QAM constellation for a V.32bis dialup modem.

10.17 Summary

Long distance communication systems use a modulated carrier wave to transfer information. A carrier is modulated by changing the amplitude, frequency, or phase. Amplitude and frequency modulation are the most common forms used with an analog input.

When a digital signal is used as input, modulation is known as shift keying. As with analog modulation, shift keying changes a carrier. However, only a fixed set of possibilities are allowed. A constellation diagram is used to represent the possibilities for phase shift keying. If the system permits a power of two possibilities, multiple input bits can be used to select a possibility at each point in time. Quadrature Amplitude Modulation combines amplitude shift keying and phase shift keying to produce more possibilities.

A modem is a hardware device that includes circuitry to perform both modulation and demodulation; a pair of modems is used for full-duplex communication. Optical, RF, and dialup modems also exist. Because bandwidth is limited, dialup modems use Quadrature Amplitude Modulation schemes. A V.32 modem uses 32 possible combinations of phase shifts and amplitude changes; a V.32bis modem uses 128 possible combinations.

EXERCISES

10.1   Search the Web and find a constellation diagram for 32QAM. How many points are defined
in each quadrant?

10.2   List the three basic types of analog modulation.

10.3   In phase shift keying, is it possible to have a phase shift of 90°? Of 270°? Of 360°? Draw an
example to explain your answer.

10.4   When using amplitude modulation, does it make sense for a 1 Hz carrier to be modulated by
a 2 Hz sine wave? Why or why not?

10.5   Using Shannon's Theorem, explain why practical amplitude modulation systems keep the
carrier near maximum strength.

10.6   Assuming a signal-to-noise ration of 30 dB, what is the maximum data rate that can be
achieved for the dialup bandwidth illustrated in Figure 10.11?

10.7   What is the difference between shift keying and modulation?

10.8   Figure 10.9 shows a full-duplex configuration with four wires, two of which are used to
transmit in each direction. Argue that it should be possible to use three wires instead.

10.9   In the previous question, why are four wires preferable?

Chapter Contents

11

Multiplexing And Demultiplexing (Channelization)

11.1 Introduction

Chapters in this part of the text cover the fundamentals of data communications. The previous chapter discusses the concept of modulation, and explains how a carrier wave can be modulated to carry analog or digital information.

This chapter continues the discussion of data communications by introducing multiplexing. The chapter describes the motivation, and defines basic types of multiplexing that are used throughout computer networks and the Internet. The chapter also explains how modulated carriers provide the basis for many multiplexing mechanisms.

11.2 The Concept Of Multiplexing

We use the term *multiplexing* to refer to the combination of information streams from multiple sources for transmission over a shared medium, and *multiplexor* to denote a mechanism that implements the combination. Similarly, we use the term *demultiplexing* to refer to the separation of a combination back into separate information streams, and *demultiplexor* to refer to a mechanism that implements separation. Multiplexing and demultiplexing are not restricted to hardware or to individual bit streams — the idea of combining and separating communication forms a fundamental basis used in many parts of computer networking. Figure 11.1 illustrates the concept.

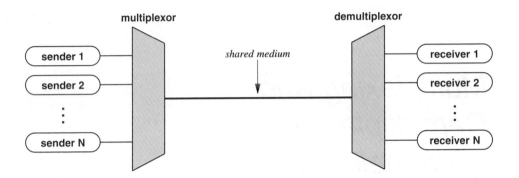

Figure 11.1 The concept of multiplexing in which independent pairs of senders and receivers share a transmission medium.

In the figure, each sender communicates with a single receiver. Although they carry on independent communication, all pairs share a single transmission medium. The multiplexor combines information from the senders for transmission in such a way that the demultiplexor can separate the information for receivers.

11.3 The Basic Types Of Multiplexing

There are four basic approaches to multiplexing that each have a set of variations and implementations.

- Frequency Division Multiplexing
- Wavelength Division Multiplexing
- Time Division Multiplexing
- Code Division Multiplexing

Time and frequency division multiplexing are widely used. Wavelength division multiplexing is a form of frequency division multiplexing used for optical fiber. Code division multiplexing is a mathematical approach used in cell phone mechanisms.

11.4 Frequency Division Multiplexing (FDM)

Frequency Division Multiplexing (FDM) is easy to understand because it forms the basis for broadcast radio. The underlying principle arises from the physics of transmission: a set of radio stations can transmit electromagnetic signals simultaneously without interference provided they each use a separate *channel* (i.e., carrier frequency). Data communications systems apply the same principle by simultaneously sending multiple carrier waves over a single copper wire or using wavelength division multiplexing to send multiple frequencies of light over an optical fiber. At the receiving end, a demultiplexor applies a set of filters that each extract a small range of frequencies near one of the carrier frequencies. Figure 11.2 illustrates the organization.

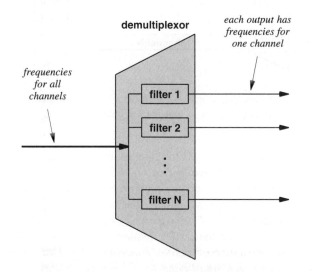

Figure 11.2 Illustration of the basic FDM demultiplexing where a set of filters each selects the frequencies for one channel and suppresses other frequencies.

A key idea is that the filters used in FDM only examine frequencies. If a sender and receiver pair are assigned a particular carrier frequency, the FDM mechanism will separate the frequency from others without otherwise modifying the signal. Thus, any of the modulation techniques discussed in Chapter 10 can be used with any carrier.

The point is:

Because carrier waves on separate frequencies do not interfere, frequency division multiplexing provides each sender and receiver pair with a private communication channel over which any modulation scheme can be used.

The most significant advantage of FDM arises from the simultaneous use of a transmission medium by multiple pairs of communicating entities. We imagine FDM as providing each pair with a private transmission path as if the pair had a separate physical transmission medium. Figure 11.3 illustrates the concept.

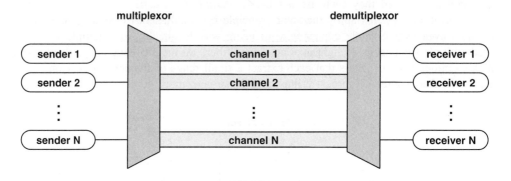

Figure 11.3 The conceptual view of Frequency Division Multiplexing (FDM) as providing a set of independent channels.

Of course, any practical FDM system imposes limits on the set of frequencies that can be used for channels. If the frequencies of two channels are arbitrarily close, interference can occur. Furthermore, demultiplexing hardware that receives a combined signal must be able to divide the signal into separate carriers. For broadcast radio in the U.S., the *Federal Communications Commission* (*FCC*) regulates stations to insure that adequate *spacing* occurs between the carrier frequencies. For data communications systems, designers follow the same approach by choosing a set of carrier frequencies with a gap between them known as a *guard band*.

As an example of channel allocation, consider the assignment in Figure 11.4 that allocates 200 KHz to each of 6 channels with a guard band of 20 KHz between each.

Channel	Frequencies Used
1	100 KHz - 300 KHz
2	320 KHz - 520 KHz
3	540 KHz - 740 KHz
4	760 KHz - 960 KHz
5	980 KHz - 1180 KHz
6	1200 KHz - 1400 KHz

Figure 11.4 An example assignment of frequencies to channels with a guard band between adjacent channels.

When plotted in the frequency domain, the guard band is clearly visible. Figure 11.5 contains the plot for the assignment in Figure 11.4.

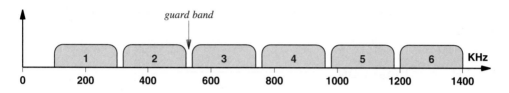

Figure 11.5 A frequency domain plot of the channel allocation from Figure 11.4 with a guard band visible between channels.

11.5 Using A Range Of Frequencies Per Channel

If a carrier uses a single frequency, why does the example allocate blocks of frequencies? To understand the motivation, consider general characteristics of FDM:

- Long-lived. FDM predates modern data communications — the idea of dividing the electromagnetic spectrum into channels arose in early experiments with radio.

- Widely used. FDM is used in broadcast radio and television, cable television, and the AMPS cellular telephone system.

- Analog. FDM multiplexing and demultiplexing hardware accepts and delivers analog signals. Even if a carrier has been modulated to contain digital information, FDM hardware treats the carrier as an analog wave.

- Versatile. Because it filters on ranges of frequency without examining other aspects of signals, FDM is versatile.

The analog characteristic has the disadvantage of making frequency division multiplexing susceptible to noise and distortion†, but the advantage of providing flexibility. In particular, most FDM systems assign each sender and receiver pair a range of frequencies and the ability to choose how the frequencies can be used. There are two primary ways that systems use a range of frequencies.

- Increase the data rate
- Increase immunity to interference

To increase the overall data rate, a sender divides the frequency range of the channel into K carriers, and sends $1/K$ of the data over each carrier. In essence, a sender performs frequency division multiplexing within the channel that has been allocated. Some systems use the term *subchannel allocation* to refer to the subdivision.

---

†Data communications systems that use FDM often require coaxial cable to provide more immunity to noise.

To increase immunity to interference, a sender uses a technique known as *spread spectrum*. Various forms of spread spectrum can be used, but the basic idea is to divide the range of the channel into K carriers, transmit the same data over multiple channels, and allow a receiver to use a copy of the data that arrives with fewest errors. The scheme works extremely well in cases where noise is likely to interfere with some frequencies at a given time.

11.6 Hierarchical FDM

Some of the flexibility in FDM arises from the ability of hardware to shift frequencies. If a set of incoming signals all use the frequency range between 0 and 4 KHz, multiplexing hardware can leave the first stage as is, map the second onto the range 4 KHz to 8 KHz, map the third onto the range 8 KHz to 12 KHz, and so on. The technique forms the basis for a hierarchy of FDM multiplexors that each map their inputs to a larger, continuous band of frequencies. Figure 11.6 illustrates the concept of *hierarchical FDM†*.

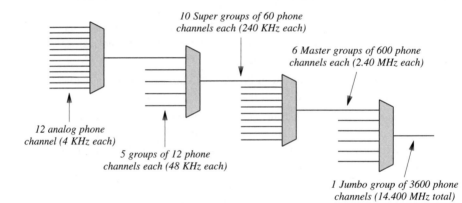

Figure 11.6 Illustration of the FDM hierarchy used in the telephone system.

As the figure illustrates, the basic input consists of a set of twelve analog telephone signals, which each occupy frequencies 0 through 4 KHz. At the first stage, the signals are multiplexed into a single signal known as a *group* that uses the frequency range of 0 through 48 KHz. At the next stage, five groups are multiplexed into a single *super-group* that uses frequencies 0 through 240 KHz, and so on. At the final stage, 3600 telephone signals have been multiplexed into a single signal. To summarize:

> *It is possible to build a hierarchy of frequency division multiplexing in which each stage accepts as inputs the outputs from the previous stage.*

---

†In practice, additional bandwidth is needed to carry framing bits.

11.7 Wavelength Division Multiplexing (WDM)

The term *Wavelength Division Multiplexing (WDM)* refers to the application of frequency division multiplexing to optical fiber†. The inputs and outputs of such multiplexing are wavelengths of light, denoted by the Greek letter λ, and informally called *colors*. To understand how multiplexing and demultiplexing can work with light, recall from basic physics that when white light passes through a prism, colors of the spectrum are spread out. A prism operates in the reverse mode as well: if a set of colored light beams are each directed into a prism at the correct angle, the prism will combine the beams to form a single beam of white light. Finally, recall that what humans perceive as a color is in fact a range of wavelengths of light.

Prisms form the basis of optical multiplexing and demultiplexing. A multiplexor accepts beams of light of various wavelengths and uses a prism to combine them into a single beam; a demultiplexor uses a prism to separate the wavelengths. Figure 11.7 illustrates the concept.

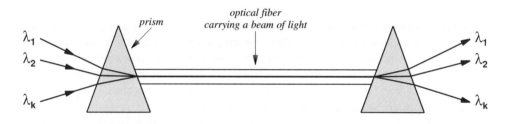

Figure 11.7 Illustration of prisms used to combine and separate wavelengths of light in wavelength division multiplexing technologies.

The point is:

> *When frequency division multiplexing is applied to optical fiber, prisms are used to combine or separate individual wavelengths of light, and the result is known as wavelength division multiplexing.*

11.8 Time Division Multiplexing (TDM)

The chief alternative to FDM is known as *Time Division Multiplexing (TDM)*. TDM is less esoteric than FDM and does not rely on special properties of electromagnetic energy. Instead, multiplexing in time simply means transmitting an item from one source, then transmitting an item from another source, and so on. Figure 11.8 illustrates the concept.

---

†Some sources use the term *Dense Wavelength Division Multiplexing (DWDM)* to emphasize that many wavelengths of light can be employed.

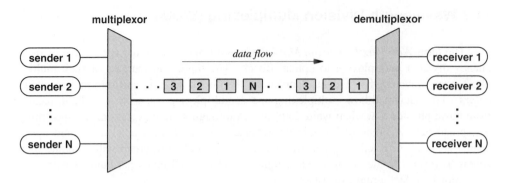

Figure 11.8 Illustration of the Time Division Multiplexing (TDM) concept
with items from multiple sources sent over a shared medium.

11.9 Synchronous TDM

Time division multiplexing is a broad concept that appears in many forms and is
widely used throughout the Internet. Thus, the diagram in Figure 11.8 is merely a conceptual view, and the details may vary. For example, the figure shows items being sent
in a *round-robin* fashion (i.e., an item from sender 1 followed by an item from sender 2,
etc). Although some TDM systems use round-robin order, other do not.

A second detail in Figure 11.8 does not apply to all types of TDM. Namely, the
figure shows a slight gap between items. Recall from Chapter 9 that no gap occurs
between bits if a communication system uses synchronous transmission. When TDM is
applied to synchronous networks, no gap occurs between items. The result is known as
Synchronous Time Division Multiplexing. A synchronous TDM system uses round-
robin order to select items. Figure 11.9 illustrates how synchronous TDM works for a
system of four senders.

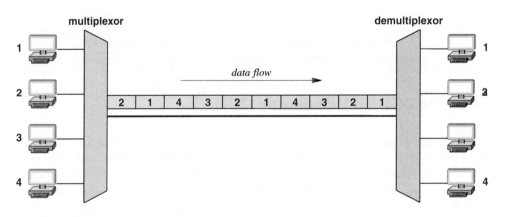

Figure 11.9 Illustration of a Synchronous Time Division Multiplexing system
with four senders.

11.10 Framing Used In The Telephone System Version Of TDM

Telephone systems use synchronous TDM to multiplex digital streams from multiple phone calls over a single medium. In fact, telephone companies use the acronym TDM to refer to the specific form of TDM used to multiplex digital telephone calls.

The phone system standards for TDM include an interesting technique to insure that a demultiplexor stays synchronized with the multiplexor. To understand why synchronization is needed, observe that a synchronous TDM system sends one slot after another without any indication of the output to which a given slot occurs. Because a demultiplexor cannot tell where a slot begins, a slight difference in the clocks used to time bits can cause a demultiplexor to misinterpret the bit stream.

To prevent misinterpretation, the version of TDM used in the phone system includes an extra *framing channel* as input. Instead of taking a complete slot, framing inserts a single bit in the stream on each round. Along with other channels, a demultiplexor extracts data from the framing channel and checks for alternating 0 and 1 bits. The idea is that if an error causes a demultiplexor to lose a bit, it is highly likely that the framing check will detect the error and allow the transmission to be restarted. Figure 11.10 illustrates the use of framing bits.

To summarize:

> *The synchronous TDM mechanism used for digital telephone calls includes a framing bit at the beginning of each round. The framing sequence of alternating 1s and 0s insures that a demultiplexor either remains synchronized or detects the error.*

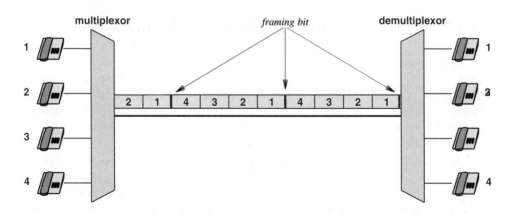

Figure 11.10 Illustration of the synchronous TDM system used by the telephone system in which a framing bit precedes each round of slots.

11.11 Hierarchical TDM

Like FDM, TDM can be arranged in a hierarchy. The difference is that each successive stage of a TDM hierarchy uses N times the bit rate, whereas each successive stage of an FDM hierarchy uses N times the frequencies. Additional framing bits are added to the data, which means that the bit rate of each successive layer of hierarchy is slightly greater than the aggregate voice traffic. Compare the example TDM hierarchy in Figure 11.11 with the FDM example in Figure 11.6.

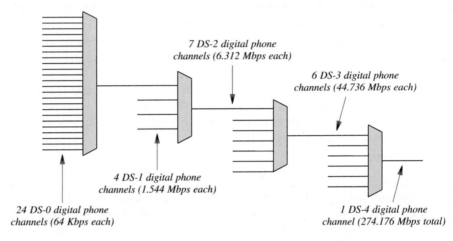

Figure 11.11 Illustration of the TDM hierarchy used in the telephone system.

11.12 The Problem With Synchronous TDM: Unfilled Slots

Synchronous TDM works well if each source produces data at a uniform, fixed rate equal to $1/N$ of the capacity of the shared medium. For example, if a source corresponds to a digital telephone call, the data will arrive at a uniform rate of 64 Kbps. As Chapter 9 points out, however, many sources generate data in bursts, with idle time between bursts, which does not work well with a synchronous TDM system. To understand why, consider the example in Figure 11.12.

In the figure, sources on the left produce data items at random. Thus, the synchronous multiplexor leaves a slot unfilled if the corresponding source has not produced an item by the time the slot must be sent. In practice, of course, a slot cannot be empty because the underlying system must continue to transmit data. Thus, the slot is assigned a value (such as zero), and an extra bit is set to indicate that the value is invalid.

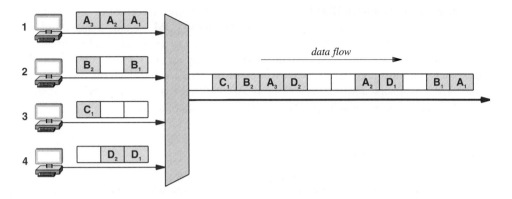

Figure 11.12 Illustration of a synchronous TDM system leaving slots unfilled when a source does not have a data item ready in time.

11.13 Statistical TDM

How can a multiplexing system make better use of a shared medium? One technique to increase the overall data rate is known as *statistical time division multiplexing* or *statistical multiplexing*†. The terminology is awkward, but the technique is straightforward: select items for transmission in a round-robin fashion, but instead of leaving a slot unfilled, skip any source that does not have data ready. By eliminating unused slots, statistical TDM takes less time to send the same amount of data. For example, Figure 11.13 illustrates how a statistical TDM system sends the data from Figure 11.12 in only 8 slots instead of 12.

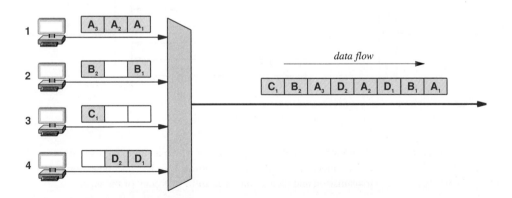

Figure 11.13 Illustration that shows how statistical multiplexing avoids unfilled slots and takes less time to send data.

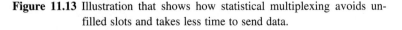

†Some literature uses the term *asynchronous time division multiplexing*.

Although it avoids unfilled slots, statistical multiplexing incurs extra overhead. To see why, consider demultiplexing. In a synchronous TDM system a demultiplexor knows that every N^{th} slot corresponds to a given receiver. In a statistical multiplexing system, the data in a given slot can correspond to any receiver. Thus, in addition to data, each slot must contain the identification of the receiver to which the data is being sent. Later chapters discuss identification mechanisms that are used with statistical multiplexing in packet switching networks and the Internet.

11.14 Inverse Multiplexing

An interesting twist on multiplexing arises in cases where the only connection between two points consists of multiple transmission media, but no single medium has a bit rate that is sufficient. At the core of the Internet, for example, service providers need higher bit rates than are available. To solve the problem, multiplexing is used in reverse: spread a high-speed digital input over multiple lower-speed circuits for transmission and combine the results at the receiving end. Figure 11.14 illustrates the concept.

In practice, an inverse multiplexor cannot be constructed merely by connecting the pieces of a conventional multiplexor backward. Instead, hardware must be designed so that the sender and receiver agree on how data arriving from the input will be distributed over the lower-speed connections. More important, to insure that all data is delivered in the same order as it arrived, the system must be engineered to handle cases where one or more of the lower-speed connections has longer latency than others. Despite its complexity, inverse multiplexing is widely used in the Internet.

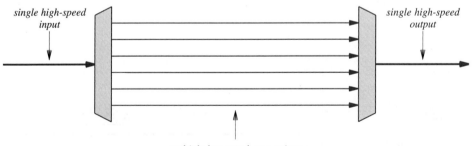

Figure 11.14 Illustration of inverse multiplexing in which a single high-speed digital input is distributed over lower-speed connections for transmission and then recombined to form a copy of the input.

11.15 Code Division Multiplexing

A final form of multiplexing used in parts of the cellular telephone system and for some satellite communication is known as *Code Division Multiplexing (CDM)*. The specific version of CDM used in cell phones is known as *Code Division Multi-Access (CDMA)*.

Unlike FDM and TDM, CDM does not rely on physical properties, such as frequency or time. Instead, CDM relies on an interesting mathematical idea: values from orthogonal vector spaces can be combined and separated without interference. The particular form used in the telephone network is easiest to understand. Each sender is assigned a unique binary code C_i that is known as a *chip sequence*. Chip sequences are selected to be orthogonal vectors (i.e., the dot product of any two chip sequences is zero). At any point in time, each sender has a value to transmit, V_i. The senders each multiply $C_i \times V_i$, and transmit the results. In essence, the senders transmit at the same time, and the values are added together. To extract value V_i, a receiver multiplies the sum by C_i.

To clarify the concept, consider an example. To keep the example easy to understand, we will use a chip sequence that is only two bits long and data values that are four bits long. We think of the chip sequence as a vector. Figure 11.15 lists the values.

Sender	Chip Sequence	Data Value
A	1 0	1 0 1 0
B	1 1	0 1 1 0

Figure 11.15 Example values for use with code division multiplexing.

The first step consists of converting the binary values into vectors that use -1 to represent 0:

$$C_1 = (1, -1) \qquad V_1 = (1, -1, 1, -1) \qquad\qquad C_2 = (1, 1) \qquad V_2 = (-1, 1, 1, -1)$$

Multiplying $C_1 \times V_1$ and $C_2 \times V_2$ produces:

$$((1, -1), (-1, 1), (1, -1), (-1, 1)) \qquad\qquad ((-1, -1), (1, 1), (1, 1), (-1, -1))$$

If we think of the resulting values as a sequence of signal strengths to be transmitted at the same time, the resulting signal will be the sum of the two signals:

1	- 1	- 1	1	1	- 1	- 1	1
+ - 1	- 1	1	1	1	1	- 1	- 1
0	- 2	0	2	2	0	- 2	0

A receiver treats the sequence as a vector, computes the product of the vector and the chip sequence, treats the result as a sequence, and converts the result to binary by interpreting positive values as binary 1 and negative values as binary 0. Thus, receiver number 1 computes:

$$(1, -1) \cdot ((0, -2), (0, 2), (2, 0), (-2, 0))$$

to get:

$$((0 + 2), (0 - 2), (2 + 0), (-2 + 0))$$

Interpreting the result as a sequence produces:

$$2 \quad -2 \quad 2 \quad -2$$

which becomes the binary value:

$$1 \quad 0 \quad 1 \quad 0$$

Note that 1010 is the correct value of V_1. Meanwhile, receiver 2 will extract V_2 from the same transmission.

It may seem that CDM offers little real advantage over TDM. In fact, CDM is somewhat inefficient because a large chip sequence is required, even if only a few senders transmit during a given interval. Thus, if the utilization is low, statistical TDM works better than CDM.

The advantages of CDM arise from its ability to scale and because it offers lower delay in a highly utilized network. To see why low delay is important, consider a statistical TDM system. Once a sender transmits, a TDM multiplexor allows $N-1$ other senders to transmit before giving the first sender another turn. Thus, if all senders are active, the potential delay between successive transmissions from a given sender can be high. In a CDM system, however, a sender can transmit at the same time as other senders, which means the delay is lower. CDM is especially attractive for a telephone service because low delay between transmissions is essential to delivering high-quality voice. To summarize:

CDM incurs lower delay than statistical TDM when a network is highly utilized.

11.16 Summary

Multiplexing is a fundamental concept in data communications. A multiplexing mechanism allows pairs of senders and receivers to communicate over a shared medium. A multiplexor sends inputs from many senders over a shared medium, and a demultiplexor separates and delivers the items.

There are four basic approaches to multiplexing: frequency division, time division, wavelength division, and code division. Frequency Division Multiplexing (FDM) permits simultaneous communication over multiple channels, each of which corresponds to a separate frequency of electromagnetic radiation. Wavelength Division Multiplexing (WDM) is a form of frequency division multiplexing that sends frequencies of light, called wavelengths, over an optical fiber.

Time Division Multiplexing (TDM) sends one item at a time over the shared medium. A Synchronous TDM system transmits items with no idle time between them, usually using round-robin selection. A statistical TDM system avoids empty slots by skipping any sender that does not have an item ready to send during its turn.

Code Division Multiplexing (CDM) uses a mathematical combination of codes that permits multiple senders to transmit at the same time without interference. The chief advantages of CDM arise from the ability to scale with low delay.

EXERCISES

11.1   In a hierarchical FDM system, explain how a high-capacity channel is divided into sub-channels.

11.2   Suppose N users compete using a statistical TDM system, and suppose the underlying physical transport can send K bits per second. What is the minimum and maximum data rate that an individual user can experience?

11.3   Give an example of multiplexing in a non-electronic communication system.

11.4   How does FDM use electromagnetic radiation?

11.5   In a hierarchical TDM system, at what bit rate does the output of a given level need to operate? (Express the answer in terms of the number and bit rate of inputs.)

11.6   Is a TDM system required to use round-robin service?

11.7   What are the four basic types of multiplexing?

11.8   Explain how a range of frequencies can be used to increase data rate.

11.9   What is a guard band?

11.10 Suppose an OC-12 circuit is twenty percent the cost of an OC-48 circuit. What multiplexing technology can an ISP use to lower the cost of sending data at the OC-48 rate. Explain.

11.11 Of the four basic multiplexing techniques, is CDM always the best? Explain.

11.12 An FDM system may assign each channel a range of frequencies. Using a range is essential when which type of modulation is used for each carrier?

11.13 What is the key mechanism used to combine or separate wavelengths of light in a WDM system?

11.14 Explain why framing and synchronization are important in a TDM system.

11.15 Search the Web to find the length of a chip sequence used in CDMA phone systems.

Chapter Contents

12

Access And Interconnection Technologies

12.1 Introduction

Previous chapters each examine one of the fundamental aspects of data communications. The previous chapter discusses multiplexing and the concept of a multiplexing hierarchy. The chapter describes the time and frequency division multiplexing schemes that phone companies use for digital telephony.

This chapter concludes the discussion of data communications by examining two facilities used in the Internet. First, the chapter discusses access technologies, such as dialup, DSL, and cable modems, that are used to connect individual residences and businesses to the Internet. Second, the chapter considers high-capacity digital circuits used in the core of the Internet. The chapter expands the discussion of the telephone system multiplexing hierarchy, and gives examples of circuits that common carriers offer to businesses and Internet Service Providers. The discussion focuses on the data communications aspects of the technologies by considering multiplexing and data rates.

12.2 Internet Access Technology: Upstream And Downstream

Internet access technology refers to a data communications system that connects an Internet *subscriber* (typically a private residence or business) to an *Internet Service Provider* (*ISP*), such as a telephone company or cable company. To understand how access technology is designed, one must know that most Internet users follow an *asymmetric* pattern. A typical residential subscriber receives more data from the Internet than they send. For example, to view a web page, a browser sends a URL that comprises a few bytes. In response, a web server sends content that may consist of thousands of bytes of text or an image that can comprise tens of thousands of bytes. A business that runs a web server may have the opposite traffic pattern — the business sends more data than it receives. The point is:

> *Because a typical residential subscriber receives much more informa-*
> *tion than the subscriber sends, Internet access technologies are*
> *designed to transfer more data in one direction than the other.*

The networking industry uses the term *downstream* to refer to data traveling from a service provider in the Internet to a subscriber, and *upstream* to refer to data traveling from a subscriber to a service provider. Figure 12.1 illustrates the definitions.

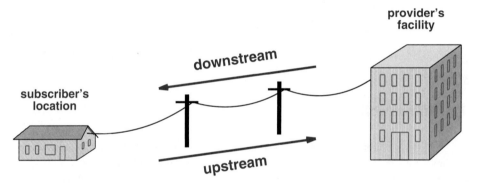

Figure 12.1 Definition of upstream and downstream directions as used in access technologies.

12.3 Narrowband And Broadband Access Technologies

A variety of technologies are used to provide Internet access. They can be divided into two broad categories based on the data rate they provide:

- Narrowband
- Broadband

Although Chapter 6 explains the difference between the bandwidth of a transmission medium and the data rate, the terminology used for access networks does not observe the distinction. Instead, the networking industry generally uses the term *network bandwidth* to refer to data rate. Thus, the terms *narrowband* and *broadband* reflect industry practice.

12.3.1 Narrowband Technologies

Narrowband generally refers to technologies that deliver data at up to 128 Kbps. For example, the maximum data rate that can be achieved over a dialup connection with the most sophisticated modem technology and the least noisy phone lines is 56 Kbps. Thus, dialup is classified as a narrowband technology. Similarly, analog circuits that use modems, slower-speed digital circuits, and some of the data services offered by telephone companies (e.g., ISDN) are narrowband. Figure 12.2 summarizes the main narrowband access technologies.

Narrowband
Dialup telephone connections
Leased circuit using modems
Fractional T1 data circuits
ISDN and other telco data services

Figure 12.2 The main narrowband technologies used for Internet access.

12.3.2 Broadband Technologies

The term *broadband* generally refers to technologies that offer high data rates, but the exact boundary between broadband and narrowband is blurry. Many professionals suggest that broadband technologies deliver more than 1 Mbps. However, providers such as telephone companies use the term *broadband* when they advertise a service that offers a higher rate than dialup. Thus, phone companies sometimes claim that ISDN service, which provides 128 Kbps, is broadband. Figure 12.3 summarizes the main broadband access technologies.

Broadband
DSL technologies
Cable modem technologies
Wireless access technologies
Data circuits at T1 speed or higher

Figure 12.3 The main broadband Internet access technologies.

12.4 The Local Loop And ISDN

The term *local subscriber line* or *local loop* describes the physical connection between a telephone company *Central Office (CO)* and a subscriber's location. To understand how a local loop can be used, it is important to think of the local loop as independent from the rest of the phone system. Although the overall phone system is engineered to provide each dialup call with 4 KHz of bandwidth, the local loop portion consists of twisted pair and often has much higher bandwidth. In particular, the local loop for a subscriber close to a CO may be able to handle frequencies above 1 MHz.

As data networking became important, telephone companies explored ways to use the local loop to provide higher-speed data communication. One of the first phone company efforts to provide large-scale digital services to subscribers is offered under the name *Integrated Services Digital Network (ISDN)*. From a subscriber's point of view, ISDN offers three separate digital channels, designated *B*, *B*, and *D* (usually written *2B + D*). The two *B* channels, which each operate at a speed of 64 Kbps, are intended to carry digitized voice, data, or compressed video; the *D* channel, which operates at 16 Kbps, is used as a control channel. In general, a subscriber uses the *D* channel to request services which are then supplied over the *B* channels (e.g., a phone call that uses digital voice). Both of the *B* channels can be combined or *bonded* to produce a single channel with an effective data rate of 128 Kbps. When ISDN was first proposed, 128 Kbps seemed much faster than dialup modems. Newer local loop technologies provide higher data rates at lower cost, relegating ISDN to a few special cases.

12.5 Digital Subscriber Line (DSL) Technologies

Digital Subscriber Line (DSL) is one of the main technologies used to provide high-speed data communication services over a local loop. Figure 12.4 lists DSL variants. Because the names differ only in the first word, the set is collectively referred to by the acronym *xDSL*.

Name	Expansion	General Use
ADSL	Asymmetric DSL	Residential customers
ADSL2	Asymmetric DSL version 2	Approximately three times faster
SDSL	Symmetric DSL	Businesses that export data
HDSL	High bit rate DSL	Businesses up to 3 miles away
VDSL	Very-high bit rate DSL	Proposed version for 52-Mbps

Figure 12.4 Main variants of DSL that are collectively known as xDSL.

ADSL is the most widely deployed variant, and the one that most residential customers use. ADSL uses frequency division multiplexing to divide the bandwidth of the local loop into three regions. One of the regions corresponds to traditional analog phone service, which is known in the industry as *Plain Old Telephone Service* (*POTS*), and two regions provide data communication. The point is:

> *Because it uses frequency division multiplexing, ADSL and traditional analog phone service (POTS) can use the same wires simultaneously.*

Figure 12.5 illustrates how ADSL divides bandwidth.

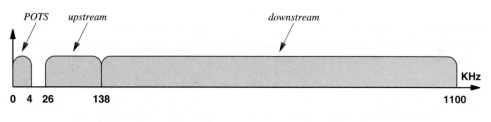

Figure 12.5 An illustration of how ADSL divides the available bandwidth of the local loop.

In the figure, the x-axis is not linear. If it were, the 4 KHz region reserved for POTS would not be visible, nor would the 22 KHz guard band between POTS and the upstream region.

12.6 Local Loop Characteristics And Adaptation

ADSL technology is complex because no two local loops have identical electrical characteristics. Instead, the ability to carry signals depends on the distance, the diameter of the wiring used, and the level of electrical interference. For example, consider two subscribers who live in different parts of a town. If the telephone line leading to the first subscriber passes near a commercial radio station, the station's signal will cause interference at the frequency the station uses. If the second subscriber does not live near the same radio station, the frequency the radio station uses may work well for data on that subscriber's line. However, the second subscriber can experience interference on another frequency. Thus, the ADSL designers could not pick a particular set of carrier frequencies or modulation techniques that would work well in all local loops.

To accommodate differences in local loop characteristics, ADSL is *adaptive*. That is, when a pair of ADSL modems are powered on, they probe the line between them to find its characteristics, and then agree to communicate using techniques that are optimal for the line. In particular, ADSL uses a scheme known as *Discrete Multi Tone modula-*

tion (DMT) that combines frequency division multiplexing and inverse multiplexing techniques.

Frequency division multiplexing in DMT is implemented by dividing the bandwidth into *286* separate frequencies called *subchannels†*, with *255* subchannels allocated for downstream data transmission and *31* allocated for upstream data transmission. Two of the upstream channels are reserved for control information. Conceptually, there is a separate "modem" running on each subchannel, which has its own modulated carrier. Carriers are spaced at 4.1325 KHz intervals to keep the signals from interfering with one another. Furthermore, to guarantee that its transmissions do not interfere with analog phone signals, ADSL avoids using the bandwidth below 26 KHz. When ADSL starts, both ends probe the available frequencies to determine which frequencies work well and which experience interference. In addition to selecting frequencies, the two ends assess the signal quality at each frequency, and use the quality to select a modulation scheme. If a particular frequency has a high signal-to-noise ratio, ADSL selects a modulation scheme that encodes many bits per baud; if the quality on a given frequency is low, ADSL selects a modulation scheme that encodes fewer bits per baud. We can summarize:

> *Because the electrical characteristics of local loops vary, ADSL uses an adaptive technology in which a pair of modems probe many frequencies on the line between them, and select frequencies and modulation techniques that yield optimal results on that line.*

12.7 The Data Rate Of ADSL

How fast can ADSL operate? ADSL can achieve a downstream rate of 8.448 Mbps on short local loops, and an upstream rate of 640 Kbps. Because the mandatory network control channel requires 64 Kbps, the effective upstream rate for user data is 576 Kbps. Under the best conditions, ADSL2 can download at close to 20 Mbps.

From a user's point of view, adaptation has an interesting property: ADSL does not guarantee a data rate. Instead, ADSL can only guarantee to do as well as line conditions allow its techniques to operate. Subscribers who live farther from a Central Office or whose local loop passes near sources of interference experience lower data rates than subscribers who live near the Central Office and whose local loop does not pass near sources of interference. Thus, the downstream rate varies from 32 Kbps to 8.448 Mbps, and the upstream rate varies from 32 to 640 Kbps.

It is important to understand that the ADSL data rate only applies to the local loop connection between a subscriber and the telephone Central Office. Many other factors affect the overall data rates that a user experiences. For example, when a user contacts a web server, the effective data rate can be limited by: the speed or current load on the server, the access technology used to connect the server's site to the Internet, or intermediate networks between the user's CO and the provider that handles the server.

---

†The term *subchannel* arises because some DSL variants divide bandwidth into 1.544 Mbps "channels" that each correspond to a T1 circuit as described later in the chapter.

12.8 ADSL Installation And Splitters

Although traditional analog phones operate at frequencies below 4 KHz, lifting a receiver can generate noise that interferes with DSL signals. To provide complete isolation, ADSL uses an FDM device known as a *splitter* that divides the bandwidth by passing low frequencies to one output and high frequencies to another. Interestingly, a splitter is *passive*, which means that it does not require power. A splitter is usually installed at the location where the local loop enters a residence or business. One side of the splitter connects to the POTS wiring and the other side connects to an ADSL modem. Figure 12.6 illustrates the connection.

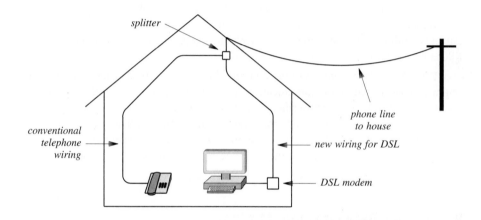

Figure 12.6 Illustration of a splitter and the wiring used with ADSL.

An interesting variation of ADSL wiring has become popular. Sometimes called *DSL lite*, the alternative approach does not require a splitter to be installed on the incoming phone line. Instead, existing house wiring is used for DSL, and a splitter must be installed between each telephone and the house wiring. The advantage of the alternative approach is that a subscriber can install DSL by plugging a splitter into a wall jack and plugging a telephone into the splitter.

12.9 Cable Modem Technologies

Although technologies like ADSL provide data rates that are much higher than originally thought possible, telephone local loop wiring has inherent limitations. The chief problem lies in the electrical characteristics of twisted pair wiring. The lack of shielding makes the wiring susceptible to interference that substantially degrades performance for some subscribers. As demand for higher bit rates increased, alternative wiring schemes have become important. Consequently, a variety of wireless and wired technologies have been developed for use in the local loop.

An alternative access technology that stands out as particularly attractive uses the wiring already in place for *cable television†*. The medium used in cable systems is coaxial cable, which has high bandwidth and is less susceptible to electromagnetic interference than twisted pair. Furthermore, cable television systems use frequency division multiplexing (FDM) to deliver many channels of entertainment simultaneously.

One might assume that with many channels available, a cable provider could use a separate channel to deliver digital information to each subscriber. That is, configure a pair of *cable modems*, one in the CATV center and the other at a subscriber's site, to use a given channel (i.e., carrier frequency) for communication, and multiplex the channel onto the cable along with television signals.

Despite the large bandwidth available in CATV systems, the bandwidth is insufficient to handle a frequency division multiplexing scheme that extends a channel to each user. To understand why, observe that in a dense metropolitan area, a single cable supplier can have millions of subscribers. As a result, using a separate channel per subscriber does not scale.

To solve the problem, cable systems combine FDM and statistical multiplexing by allocating a channel for digital communication for a set of subscribers (typically, everyone in a neighborhood). Each subscriber is assigned a unique *address*, and each message sent over the channel contains the address to which it has been sent. A subscriber's modem listens to the assigned frequency, but before accepting a message, the modem verifies that the address in the message matches the address assigned to the subscriber.

12.10 The Data Rate Of Cable Modems

How fast can a cable modem operate? In theory, a cable system can support data rates of 52 Mbps downstream and 512 Kbps upstream. In practice, the rate can be much less. First, the data rate of a cable modem only pertains to communication between the local cable office and the subscriber's site. Second, the bandwidth is shared among a set of N subscribers, where the size of the set is controlled by the cable provider. From a subscriber's point of view, sharing the bandwidth with other subscribers can be a disadvantage because the effective data rate available to each individual subscriber varies over time. In the worst case, if N subscribers share a single frequency, the amount of capacity available to an individual subscriber will be $1/N$.

12.11 Cable Modem Installation

Because cable systems use FDM, cable modem installation is straightforward. Unlike xDSL technologies that requires the use of splitters, cable modems attach to the cable wiring directly. The FDM hardware in existing cable boxes and in cable modems

---

†Cable television, formally known as *Community Antenna TeleVision* (*CATV*), uses FDM to deliver broadcast television signals to subscribers over coaxial cable. CATV is not available in all countries.

guarantees that data and entertainment channels will not interfere with one another. The point is:

> *Because cable systems use frequency division multiplexing, a cable modem can be attached directly to existing cable wiring without the need for a splitter.*

12.12 Hybrid Fiber Coax

One of the most promising ideas for technologies that provide high-speed data communications is known by the general name of *Hybrid Fiber Coax* (*HFC*). As the name implies, a Hybrid Fiber Coax system uses a combination of optical fibers and coaxial cables, with fiber used for the central facilities and coax used for connections to individual subscribers. In essence, an HFC system is hierarchical. It uses fiber optics for the portions of the network that require the highest bandwidth, and uses coax for parts that can tolerate lower data rates. To implement such a system, a provider places devices in each neighborhood that can convert between optical and coaxial cable. Each device connects back to the provider over an optical fiber, and connects to houses in the neighborhood via coaxial cable. Figure 12.7 illustrates the architecture.

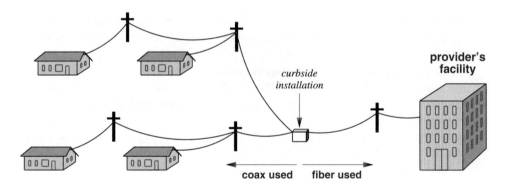

Figure 12.7 Illustration of a Hybrid Fiber Coax access system.

The cable industry uses the term *trunk* to refer to the high-capacity connections between the cable office and each neighborhood area, and the term *feeder circuit* to refer to the connection to an individual subscriber. Trunk connections can be up to *15* miles long; feeder circuits are usually less than a mile.

12.13 Access Technologies That Employ Optical Fiber

Cable companies have proposed a variety of technologies that either employ optical fiber in a hybrid system or deploy optical fiber all the way to each subscriber. Figure 12.8 summarizes names of key technologies.

Name	Expansion
FTTC	Fiber To The Curb
FTTB	Fiber To The Building
FTTH	Fiber To The Home
FTTP	Fiber To The Premises

Figure 12.8 Names of additional access technologies that use optical fiber.

Fiber To The Curb (FTTC). As the name implies, FTTC is similar to HFC because it uses optical fiber for high capacity trunks. The idea is to run optical fiber close to the end subscriber, and then use copper for the feeder circuits. FTTC differs from HFC because it uses two media in each feeder circuit to allow the cable system to provide an additional service, such as voice. The technology is being deployed in some areas, especially in the U.S. and Canada.

Fiber To The Building (FTTB). A fundamental question concerns the bandwidth that will be needed by businesses, and whether access technologies using copper (even coaxial cable) will suffice. FTTB is a technology that will use optical fiber to allow high upstream data rates.

Fiber To The Home (FTTH). A counterpart of FTTB, FTTH is an access technology that uses optical fiber to deliver higher downstream data rates to residential subscribers. Although FTTH also provides higher upstream data rates, the emphasis is on many channels of entertainment and video.

Fiber To The Premises (FTTP). A generic term, FTTP, encompasses both FTTB and FTTH.

12.14 Head-End And Tail-End Modem Terminology

An access technology requires a pair of modems, with one at the subscriber's site and one at the provider's site. The industry uses the term *head-end modem* to refer to a modem used at the central office, and the term *tail-end modem* to refer to a modem used at the subscriber's location.

Head-end modems are not individual devices. Instead, a large set of modems is built as a unit that can be configured, monitored, and controlled together. A set of head-end modems used by a cable provider is known as a *Cable Modem Termination*

System (*CMTS*). A set of industry standards known as the *Data Over Cable System Interface Specifications* (*DOCSIS*) specifies both the format of data that can be sent as well as the messages that are used to request services (e.g., *pay-per-view* movies).

12.15 Wireless Access Technologies

Although technologies such as ADSL or HFC can deliver digital services to most subscribers, they do not handle all circumstances. The primary problems arise in rural areas. For example, imagine a farm or remote village many miles from the nearest city. The twisted pair wiring used to deliver telephone service to such locations exceeds the maximum distance for technologies like ADSL. In addition, rural areas are least likely to have cable television service.

Even in suburban areas, technologies like ADSL may have technical restrictions on the type of line they can use. For example, it may be impossible to use high frequencies on telephone lines that contain *loading coils*, *bridge taps*, or *repeaters*. Thus, even in areas where a local loop technology works for most subscribers, it may not work on all lines.

To handle special cases, a variety of wireless access technologies have been explored. Figure 12.9 lists a few examples, and Chapter 16 discusses several technologies.

Technology	Description
3G services	Third generation cellular telephone services for data (e.g., EVDO)
WIMAX	Wireless access technology up to 155 Mbps using radio frequencies
Satellite	Various commercial vendors offer data services over satellite

Figure 12.9 Examples of wireless access technologies.

12.16 High-Capacity Connections At The Internet Core

Networking professionals say that access technologies handle the *last mile problem*, where the last mile is defined as the connection to a typical residential subscriber or a small business. An access technology provides sufficient capacity for a residential subscriber or a small business (industry uses the term *Small Office Home Office* or *SOHO*). Connections to large businesses or connections among providers require substantially more bandwidth. To differentiate such connections from those found at the edge of the Internet, professionals use the term *core* and refer to high-speed technologies as *core technologies*.

To understand the data rates needed for the core, consider a provider that has 5,000 customers. Assume the provider uses an access technology that can provide up to 2 Mbps per customer. Consider what happens if all subscribers attempt to download data at the same time. Figure 12.10 shows the aggregate traffic from the Internet to the provider.

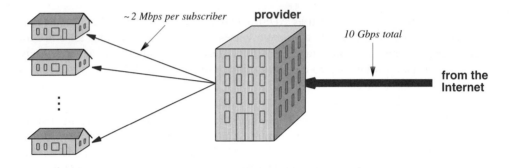

Figure 12.10 Aggregate traffic from the Internet to a provider assuming the provider has 5,000 customers each downloading 2 Mbps.

The question arises: what technology can a provider use to move data a long distance at a rate of 10 Gbps? The answer lies in a *point-to-point digital circuit* leased from a telephone company. Although originally designed to be used internally in the phone system, high-capacity digital circuits are available for a monthly fee, and can be used to transfer data. Because telephone companies have the authority to install wiring that crosses municipal streets, a circuit can extend between two buildings, across a city, or from a location in one city to a location in another. The fee charged depends on the data rate of the circuit and the distance spanned. To summarize:

> *Digital circuits leased from common carriers form the fundamental building blocks for long-distance data communications. The cost depends on the circuit capacity and distance.*

12.17 Circuit Termination, DSU/CSU, and NIU

To use a leased digital circuit, one must agree to follow the rules of the telephone system, including adhering to the standards that were designed for transmitting digitized voice. It may seem that following standards for digitized information would be trivial because computers are digital as well. However, because the computer industry and the telephone industry developed independently, the standards for telephone system digital circuits differ from those used in the computer industry. Thus, a special piece of hardware is needed to interface a computer to a digital circuit provided by a telephone company. Known as a *Data Service Unit/Channel Service Unit* (*DSU/CSU*) the device contains two functional parts, usually combined into a single chassis. The CSU portion of the DSU/CSU device handles line termination and diagnostics. For example, a CSU contains diagnostic circuitry that can test whether the line has been disconnected. A CSU also contains a *loopback* test facility that allows the CSU to transmit a copy of all data that arrives across the circuit back to the sender without further processing.

A CSU provides a service that computer engineers find surprising — it prohibits excessive consecutive *1* bits. The need to prevent excessive *1*s arises from the electrical signals used. In particular, because the telephone company originally designed their digital circuits to work over copper cables, engineers were concerned that having too many contiguous *1* bits would mean excessive current on the cable. To prevent problems, a CSU can either use an encoding that guarantees a balance (e.g., a differential encoding) or a technique known as *bit stuffing*.

The DSU portion of a DSU/CSU handles the data. It translates data between the digital format used on the carrier's circuit and the digital format required by the customer's computer equipment. The interface standard used on the computer side depends on the rate that the circuit operates. If the data rate is less than 56 Kbps, the computer can use RS-232. For rates above 56 Kbps, the computer must use interface hardware that supports higher speeds (e.g., hardware that uses the *RS-449* or *V.35* standards).

The phone company provides one additional piece of equipment, known as a *Network Interface Unit* (*NIU†*), that forms a boundary between equipment owned by the telephone company and equipment provided by the subscriber. The telephone company refers to the boundary as the *demarc*.

> *A digital circuit needs a device known as a DSU/CSU at each end. The DSU/CSU translates between the digital representation used by phone companies and the digital representation used by the computer industry.*

12.18 Telephone Standards For Digital Circuits

A digital circuit leased from a telephone company follows the same digital transmission standards that the phone company uses to transport digital phone calls. In the U.S., standards for digital telephone circuits were given names that consist of the letter *T* followed by a number. Engineers refer to them collectively as the *T-series standards*. One of the most popular is known as T1; many small businesses use a T1 circuit to carry data.

Unfortunately, T-standards are not universal. Japan adopted a modified version of the T-series standards, and Europe chose a slightly different scheme. European standards can be distinguished because they use the letter *E*. Figure 12.11 lists the data rates of several digital circuit standards.

---

†Although the term *Smartjack* is sometimes used as a synonym for NIU, Smartjack refers to a specific type of NIU manufactured by Westell Corporation.

Name	Bit Rate	Voice Circuits	Location
basic rate	0.064 Mbps	1	
T1	1.544 Mbps	24	North America
T2	6.312 Mbps	96	North America
T3	44.736 Mbps	672	North America
E1	2.048 Mbps	30	Europe
E2	8.448 Mbps	120	Europe
E3	34.368 Mbps	480	Europe

Figure 12.11 Examples of digital circuits and their capacity.

12.19 DS Terminology And Data Rates

Recall from Chapter 11 that the telephone companies use a multiplexing hierarchy that combines multiple voice calls into a single digital circuit. Thus, the data rates of T standards have been chosen so they can each handle a multiple of voice calls. The important thing to note is that the capacity of circuits does not increase linearly with their numbers. For example, the T3 standard defines a circuit with much more than three times the capacity of T1. Finally, it should be noted that phone companies do lease circuits with lower capacity than those listed in the figure; they are known as *fractional T1* circuits.

To be technically precise, one must distinguish between the T-standards, which define the underlying carrier system, and the standards that specify how to multiplex multiple phone calls onto a single connection. The latter are known as *Digital Signal Level standards* or *DS standards*. The names are written as the letters *DS* followed by a number, analogous to the T-standards. For example, DS1 denotes a service that can multiplex 24 phone calls onto a single circuit, and T1 denotes a specific standard that does so. Because DS1 defines the effective data rate, it is technically more accurate to say, "a circuit running at DS1 speed" than to refer to "T1 speed." In practice, few engineers bother to distinguish between T1 and DS1. Thus, one is likely to hear someone refer to "T1-speed".

12.20 Highest Capacity Circuits (STS Standards)

Telephone companies use the term *trunk* to denote a high-capacity circuit, and have created a series of standards for digital trunk circuits. Known as the *Synchronous Transport Signal (STS)* standards, they specify the details of high-speed connections. Figure 12.12 summarizes the data rates associated with various STS standards. All data rates in the table are given in Mbps, making it easy to compare. It should be noted that data rates for STS-24 and above are greater than 1 Gbps.

Copper Name	Optical Name	Bit Rate	Voice Circuits
STS-1	OC-1	51.840 Mbps	810
STS-3	OC-3	155.520 Mbps	2430
STS-12	OC-12	622.080 Mbps	9720
STS-24	OC-24	1,244.160 Mbps	19440
STS-48	OC-48	2,488.320 Mbps	38880
STS-192	OC-192	9,953.280 Mbps	155520

Figure 12.12 Data rates of digital circuits according to the STS hierarchy of standards.

12.21 Optical Carrier Standards

In addition to STS standards, the phone company defines an equivalent set of *Optical Carrier (OC)* standards. Figure 12.12 gives the names for optical standards as well as for copper standards. To be precise, one should observe a distinction between the STS and OC terminology: the STS standards refer to the electrical signals used in the digital circuit interface (i.e., over copper), while the OC standards refer to the optical signals that propagate across the fiber. As with other network terminology, few professionals make the distinction. Thus, one often hears networking professionals use the term *OC-3* to refer to a digital circuit that operates at 155 Mbps, independent of whether the circuit uses copper or optical fiber.

12.22 The C Suffix

The Synchronous Transport Signal and Optical Carrier terminology described above has one additional feature not shown in Figure 12.12: an optional suffix of the letter *C*, which stands for *concatenated*. The presence of the suffix denotes a circuit with no inverse multiplexing. That is, an OC-3 circuit can consist of three OC-1 circuits operating at 51.840 Mbps each, or it can consist of a single OC-3C (STS-3C) circuit that operates at 155.520 Mbps.

Is a single circuit operating at full speed better than multiple circuits operating at lower rates? The answer depends on how the circuit is being used. In general, having a single circuit operating at full capacity provides more flexibility and eliminates the need for inverse multiplexing equipment. More to the point, data networks are unlike voice networks. In a voice system, high-capacity circuits are used as a way of aggregating smaller voice streams. In a data network, however, there is a single stream of data traffic. Thus, if given a choice, most network designers prefer an OC-3C circuit over an OC-3 circuit.

12.23 Synchronous Optical NETwork (SONET)

In addition to the STS and OC standards described above, the phone companies defined a broad set of standards for digital transmission. In North America, the standards are known by the term *Synchronous Optical NETwork* (*SONET*), while in Europe they are known as the *Synchronous Digital Hierarchy* (*SDH*). SONET specifies details such as how data is framed, how lower-capacity circuits are multiplexed into a high-capacity circuit, and how synchronous clock information is sent along with data. Because carriers use SONET extensively, when someone leases an STS-1 circuit, the carrier is likely to require them to use SONET encoding on the circuit. For example, Figure 12.13 shows the SONET frame format used on an STS-1 circuit.

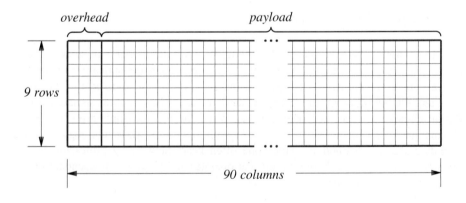

Figure 12.13 Illustration of a SONET frame when used over an STS-1 circuit.

Each frame is 810 octets long. According to SONET terminology, octets in the frame are divided into 9 "rows", with 90 "columns" in each row. Interestingly, the size of a SONET frame depends on the bit rate of the underlying circuit. When used on an STS-3 circuit, however, each SONET frame holds 2430 octets. How do the numbers arise? To understand the difference, recall that digital telephony takes 8,000 PCM samples per second, which means that a sample is taken every 125 μ seconds. SONET uses the time to define frame size. At the STS-1 transmission rate of 51.840 Mbps, exactly 6480 bits are transferred in 125 μ seconds, which means that a frame consists of 810 8-bit octets. Similarly, at the STS-3 rate, 2430 octets can be transmitted in 125 μ seconds. The chief advantage of making the frame size depend on the bit rate of the circuit is that it makes synchronous multiplexing trivial — retaining synchronization while combining three STS-1 SONET streams into one STS-3 SONET stream is straightforward.

Although most data networks use SONET as an encoding scheme on a single point-to-point circuit, the standard provides more possibilities. In particular, it is possible to build a high-capacity counter rotating ring network using SONET technology that handles single-point failures. Each station on the ring uses a device known as an *add/drop mux*. In addition to passing received data around the ring, the add/drop mux can be configured to accept additional data from a local circuit and add it to frames passing across the ring or to extract data and deliver it to a local computer. If the ring is broken, the hardware detects the loss of framing information and uses the counter rotating ring to reconnect. To summarize:

> *Although the SONET standard defines a technology that can be used to build a high-capacity ring network with multiple data circuits multiplexed across the fibers that constitute the ring, most data networks only use SONET to define framing and encoding on a leased circuit.*

12.24 Summary

Access technologies provide Internet connections to individual residences or small businesses. A variety of access technologies exist, including dialup telephone connections, wireless (using radio frequency or satellite), and wired. Two current access technologies are Digital Subscriber Line (DSL) and cable modems. DSL uses FDM techniques to allow digital communication and a traditional analog voice call to proceed simultaneously on the local loop between a telephone company Central Office and a subscriber. Cable modem service uses FDM to multiplex digital communication over the same coaxial cable system used to carry entertainment channels. When using cable modem technology, cable modems in each neighborhood employ statistical multiplexing to share a single data communications channel.

Technologies like Hybrid Fiber Coax (HFC) and Fiber To The Curb (FTTC) use optical fibers to distribute data to each neighborhood and use coaxial cable to reach an individual subscriber. Future technologies have been proposed that will use optical fiber to deliver higher data rates to each individual residence.

Although they suffice for individual residences and small businesses, access technologies do not provide sufficient capacity for use in the core of the Internet. To achieve the highest data rates over long distances, service providers and large businesses lease point-to-point circuits from common carriers. Digital circuits use time division multiplexing standards (T-standards in North America or E-standards in Europe). High-speed circuits are defined using the Synchronous Transport Signal (North America) or Synchronous Digital Hierarchy (Europe). A parallel set of Optical Carrier standards exists for use with optical fiber; many professionals use the OC standard names, independent of whether the circuit uses fiber or copper.

A telephone company standard known as SONET defines framing for use on a digital circuit. The size of a SONET frame depends on the bit rate of the circuit; one frame always takes 125 μ seconds to send. In addition to its use on point-to-point circuits, SONET can be configured into a ring, which allows hardware to determine if the ring is broken and automatically reconfigure around the malfunction.

EXERCISES

12.1 If a customer intends to transmit more data than they receive, which forms of DSL would be appropriate?

12.2 Why would a service provider choose Hybrid Fiber Coax instead of Fiber To The Premises?

12.3 Why did the designers of the Synchronous Digital Hierarchy choose unusual values for data rates instead of exact powers of ten?

12.4 Two neighbors, who live on the same street, both use ADSL service, but measurements show that one subscriber can download at approximately 1.5 Mbps and the other can download at 2.0 Mbps. Explain.

12.5 What is an *access technology*?

12.6 Explain how the size of a SONET frame is computed.

12.7 Give examples of narrowband and broadband access technologies.

12.8 What is the advantage of WiMAX access technology compared to satellite? What is the advantage of satellite?

12.9 Why do service providers distinguish between upstream and downstream communication?

12.10 Telephone companies once promoted ISDN as a high-speed access technology. Why has use of ISDN declined?

12.11 If you had a choice between DSL and cable modem, which would provide the highest potential data rate?

12.12 If someone shows you a copper cable and claims that it is an "OC-12 circuit", what error have they made? What is the correct name they should have used?

12.13 If you lease a T1 circuit, what equipment will be installed between the circuit and a computer at your site?

12.14 What type of multiplexing does ADSL use?

12.15   Use the Web to find the approximate size of a movie on DVD. How long does it take to download a movie over a T1 line? Over a T3 line? (Ignore overhead.)

12.16   Why is a splitter used with DSL?

12.17   Where is a head-end modem located? A tail-end modem?

PART III

Packet Switching and Network Technologies

An overview of packet switching and packet technologies that use wired and wireless media

Chapters

Chapter Contents

13

Local Area Networks: Packets, Frames, And Topologies

13.1 Introduction

The first part of the text covers Internet applications and network programming. The second part explores topics in data communications. Each chapter covers a fundamental concept, such as multiplexing, that forms the basis for all of computer networking.

This chapter begins the part of the text that examines packet switching and computer network technologies. After a brief overview, the chapter explains the IEEE standards model, and concentrates on the concepts of hardware addressing and frame identification.

Later chapters in this part expand the discussion by considering the use of packets in Wide Area Networks. In addition, later chapters cover a variety of wired and wireless networking technologies that accept and deliver packets.

13.2 Circuit Switching

The term *circuit switching* refers to a communication mechanism that establishes a path between a sender and receiver with guaranteed isolation from paths used by other pairs of senders and receivers. Circuit switching is usually associated with telephone technology because a telephone system provides a dedicated connection between two telephones. In fact, the term originated with early dialup telephone networks that used electromechanical switching devices to form a physical circuit. Figure 13.1 illustrates how communication proceeds over a circuit-switched network.

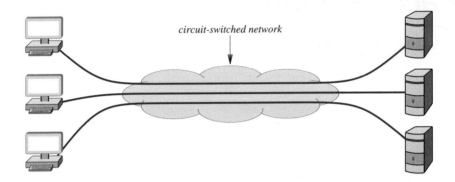

Figure 13.1 A circuit-switched network that provides a direct connection between each pair of communicating entities.

Currently, circuit switching networks use electronic devices to establish circuits. Furthermore, instead of having each circuit correspond to a physical path, multiple circuits are multiplexed over shared media, and the result is known as a *virtual circuit*. Thus, the distinction between circuit switching and other forms of networking does not arise from the existence of separate physical paths. Instead, three general properties define a circuit switched paradigm:

- Point-to-point communication
- Separate steps for circuit creation, use, and termination
- Performance equivalent to an isolated physical path

The first property means that a circuit is formed between exactly two endpoints, and the second property distinguishes circuits that are *switched* (i.e., established when needed) from circuits that are *permanent* (i.e., always remain in place ready for use). Switched circuits use a three-step process analogous to placing a phone call. In the first step, a circuit is established. In the second, the two parties use the circuit to communicate, and in the third, the two parties terminate use.

The third property provides a crucial distinction between circuit switched networks and other types. Circuit switching means that the communication between two parties is not affected in any way by communication among other parties, even if all communication is multiplexed over a common medium. In particular, circuit switching must provide the illusion of an isolated path for each pair of communicating entities. Thus, techniques such as frequency division multiplexing or synchronous time division multiplexing must be used to multiplex circuits over a shared medium.

The point is:

Circuit switching provides the illusion of an isolated physical path between a pair of communicating entities; a path is created when needed, and discontinued after use.

13.3 Packet Switching

The main alternative to circuit switching, *packet switching*, forms the basis for the Internet. A packet switching system uses statistical multiplexing in which communication from multiple sources competes for the use of shared media. Figure 13.2 illustrates the concept.

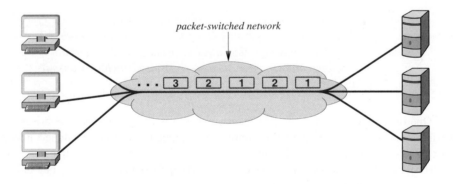

Figure 13.2 A packet-switched network sending one packet at a time across a shared medium.

The chief difference between packet switching and other forms of statistical multiplexing arises because a packet switching system requires a sender to divide each message into blocks of data that are known as *packets*. The size of a packet varies; each packet switching technology defines a maximum packet size†.

---

†Packets are not large: a common maximum packet size is 1500 bytes.

Three general properties define a packet switched paradigm:

- Arbitrary, asynchronous communication
- No set-up required before communication begins
- Performance varies due to statistical multiplexing among packets

The first property means that packet switching can allow a sender to communicate with one recipient or multiple recipients, and a given recipient can receive messages from one sender or multiple senders. Furthermore, communication can occur at any time, and a sender can delay arbitrarily long between successive communications. The second property means that, unlike a circuit switched system, a packet switched system remains ready to deliver a packet to any destination at any time. Thus, a sender does not need to perform initialization before communicating, and does not need to notify the underlying system when communication terminates.

The third property means that multiplexing occurs among packets rather than among bits or bytes. That is, once a sender gains access to the underlying channel, the sender transmits an entire packet, and then allows other senders to transmit a packet. When no other senders are ready to transmit a packet, a single sender can transmit repeatedly. However, if N senders each have a packet to send, a given sender will transmit approximately $1/N$ of all packets.

To summarize:

> *Packet switching, which forms the basis of the Internet, is a form of statistical multiplexing that permits many-to-many communication. A sender must divide a message into a set of packets; after transmitting a packet, a sender allows other senders to transmit before transmitting a successive packet.*

One of the chief advantages of packet switching is the lower cost that arises from sharing. To provide communication among N computers, a circuit-switched network must have a connection for each computer plus at least $N/2$ independent paths. With packet switching, a network must have a connection for each computer, but only requires one path that is shared.

13.4 Local And Wide Area Packet Networks

Packet switching technologies are commonly classified according to the distance they span. The least expensive networks use technologies that span a short distance (e.g., inside a single building), and the most expensive span long distances (e.g., across several cities). Figure 13.3 summarizes the terminology used.

Name	Expansion	Description
LAN	Local Area Network	Least expensive; spans a single room or a single building
MAN	Metropolitan Area Network	Medium expense; spans a major city or a metroplex
WAN	Wide Area Network	Most expensive; spans sites in multiple cities

Figure 13.3 The three categories of packet switched networks.

In practice, few MAN technologies have been created, and MAN networks have not been commercially successful. Consequently, networking professionals tend to group MAN technologies into the WAN category, and use only the terms LAN and WAN.

13.5 Standards For Packet Format And Identification

Because packet switching systems rely on sharing, each packet sent across such a network must contain the identification of the intended recipient. Furthermore, to insure that no ambiguity arises, all senders must agree on the exact details of how to identify a recipient and where to place the identification in a packet. Standards organizations create protocol documents that specify all details. The most widely used set of standards for LANs has been created by the *Institute for Electrical and Electronic Engineers (IEEE)*.

In 1980, IEEE organized the *Project 802 LAN/MAN Standards Committee* to produce standards for networking. To understand IEEE standards, it is important to know that the organization is composed of engineers who focus on the lower two layers of the protocol stack. In fact, if one reads the IEEE documents, it may seem that all other aspects of networking are unimportant. However, other standards organizations exist, and each emphasizes particular layers of the stack. Figure 13.4 gives a humorous illustration of a protocol as viewed by various standards organizations.

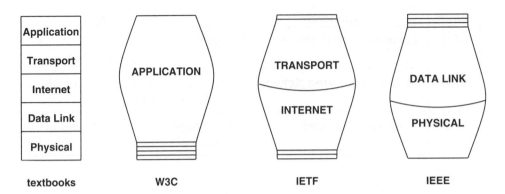

Figure 13.4 A humorous illustration of a protocol stack as depicted by various standards organizations.

Thus, one should not conclude that the standards from a particular organization are comprehensive or that the quantity of standards publications is proportional to the importance of a particular layer. To summarize:

> *Each standards organization focuses on particular layers of the protocol stack. IEEE standards focus on specification for the lowest two layers of the stack and LAN technologies.*

13.6 IEEE 802 Model And Standards

To help characterize standards, IEEE divides Layer 2 of the protocol stack into two conceptual *sublayers*, as Figure 13.5 illustrates.

Sub-Layer	Expansion	Purpose
LLC	Logical Link Control	Addressing and demultiplexing
MAC	Media Access Control	Access to shared media

Figure 13.5 The conceptual division of Layer 2 into sublayers according to the IEEE model.

The *Logical Link Control* (*LLC*) sublayer specifies addressing and the use of addresses for demultiplexing as described later in the chapter. The *Media Access Control* (*MAC*) sublayer specifies how multiple computers share the underlying medium.

Rather than use textual names to identify the group of people who work on a standard or the final standard document, IEEE assigns a multi-part identifier of the form *XXX.YYY.ZZZ*. The numeric value *XXX* denotes the category of the standard, and the suffix *YYY* denotes a subcategory. If a subcategory is large enough, a third level can be added to distinguish among specific standards. For example, LAN specifications have been assigned the category 802. Thus, each working group that devises a LAN standard is assigned an ID such as 802.1, 802.2, and so on. Note that neither the value 802 nor the individual suffixes convey any technical meaning — they merely identify standards. Figure 13.6 lists examples of IEEE assignments.

As the figure shows, IEEE has created many working groups that are each intended to standardize one type of network technology. A group, which consists of representatives from the industrial and academic communities, meets regularly to discuss approaches and devise standards. IEEE allows a working group to remain active provided the group makes progress and the technology is still deemed important. If a working group decides that the technology under investigation is no longer relevant, the group can decide to disband. For example, a better technology might be discovered that makes further standardization pointless. Alternatively, another standards organization might produce a standard first, making an IEEE effort redundant. Thus, Figure 13.6 includes topics that were once important, but have been disbanded.

ID	Topic
802.1	Higher layer LAN protocols
802.2	Logical link control
802.3	Ethernet
802.4	Token bus (disbanded)
802.5	Token Ring
802.6	Metropolitan Area Networks (disbanded)
802.7	Broadband LAN using Coaxial Cable (disbanded)
802.9	Integrated Services LAN (disbanded)
802.10	Interoperable LAN Security (disbanded)
802.11	Wireless LAN (Wi-Fi)
802.12	Demand priority
802.13	Category 6 - 10Gb LAN
802.14	Cable modems (disbanded)

802.15	Wireless PAN
	   802.15.1 (Bluetooth)
	   802.15.4 (ZigBee)

802.16	Broadband Wireless Access 802.16e (Mobile) Broadband Wireless
802.17	Resilient packet ring
802.18	Radio Regulatory TAG
802.19	Coexistence TAG
802.20	Mobile Broadband Wireless Access
802.21	Media Independent Handoff
802.22	Wireless Regional Area Network

Figure 13.6 Examples of the identifiers IEEE has assigned to various LAN standards.

13.7 Point-To-Point And Multi-Access Networks

Recall that the term *point-to-point* refers to a communication mechanism that connects exactly two communicating entities. LAN technologies allow multiple computers to share a medium in such a way that any computer on the LAN can communicate with any other. To describe such arrangements, we use the term *multi-access* and say that a LAN is a *multi-access network*.

In general, LAN technologies provide direct connection among communicating entities. Professionals say that LANs connect *computers*, with the understanding that a device such as a printer can also connect to a multi-access LAN.

13.8 LAN Topologies

Because many LAN technologies have been invented, it is important to know how specific technologies are similar and how they differ. To help understand similarities, each network is classified into a category according to its *topology* or general shape. This section describes four basic topologies that are used to construct LANs; a later chapter discusses specific technologies. Figure 13.7 illustrates the topologies.

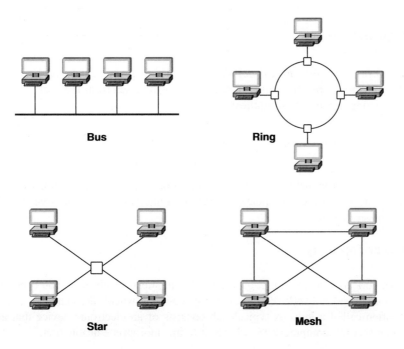

Figure 13.7 Four network topologies used with LANs.

13.8.1 Bus Topology

A network that uses a *bus topology* usually consists of a single cable to which computers attach†. Any computer attached to a bus can send a signal down the cable, and all computers receive the signal. Because all computers attach directly to the cable, any computer can send data to any other computer. Of course, the computers attached to a bus network must coordinate to ensure that only one computer sends a signal at any time.

13.8.2 Ring Topology

A network that uses a *ring topology* arranges for computers to be connected in a closed loop — a cable connects the first computer to a second computer, another cable connects the second computer to a third, and so on, until a cable connects the final computer back to the first. Some technologies that use a ring topology require a computer to connect to a small device that forms the ring. The advantage of using a separate device lies in the ability of the ring to continue operation even if some of the computers are disconnected. The name *ring* arises because one can imagine the computers and the cables connecting them arranged in a circle as Figure 13.7 illustrates. In practice, the cables in a ring network do not form a circle. Instead, they run along hallways or rise vertically from one floor of a building to another.

13.8.3 Mesh Topology

A network that uses a *mesh topology* provides a direct connection between each pair of computers. The chief disadvantage of a mesh arises from the cost: a mesh network connecting *n* computers requires:

$$connections\ in\ a\ mesh\ network\ =\ \frac{n\,!}{(n-2)!\ 2!}\ =\ \frac{n^2 - n}{2} \qquad (13.1)$$

The important point is that the number of connections needed for a mesh network grows faster than the number of computers. Because connections are expensive, few LANs employ a mesh topology.

13.8.4 Star Topology

A network uses a *star topology* when all computers attach to a central point. Because a star-shaped network resembles the spokes of a wheel, the center of a star network is often called a *hub*. A typical hub consists of an electronic device that accepts data from a sending computer and delivers it to the appropriate destination.

In practice, star networks seldom have a symmetric shape in which the hub is located an equal distance from all computers. Instead, a hub often resides in a location

---

†In practice, the ends of a bus network must be terminated to prevent electrical signals from reflecting back along the bus.

separate from the computers attached to it. For example, computers can reside in individual offices, while the hub resides in a location accessible to an organization's networking staff.

13.8.5 The Reason For Multiple Topologies

Each topology has advantages and disadvantages. A ring topology makes it easy for computers to coordinate access and to detect whether the network is operating correctly. However, an entire ring network is disabled if one of the cables is cut. A star topology helps protect the network from damage to a single cable because each cable connects only one machine. A bus requires fewer wires than a star, but has the same disadvantage as a ring: a network is disabled if someone accidentally cuts the main cable. Later chapters that describe specific network technologies provide additional details about differences. For now, it is sufficient to understand:

> *Networks are classified into broad categories according to their general shape. Although a mesh topology is possible, the primary topologies used with LANs are star, ring, and bus; each has advantages and disadvantages.*

13.9 Packet Identification, Demultiplexing, MAC Addresses

In addition to standards that specify the details of various LAN technologies, IEEE has created a standard for *addressing*. To understand addressing, consider packets traversing a shared medium as Figure 13.2 illustrates†. In the simplest case, each packet that travels across the shared medium is intended for a specific recipient, and only the intended recipient should process the packet. In packet switching systems, demultiplexing uses an identifier known as an *address*. Each computer is assigned a unique address, and each packet contains the address of the intended recipient.

In the IEEE addressing scheme, each address consists of 48 bits. IEEE uses the term *Media Access Control address* (*MAC address*). Because 48-bit addresses originated with Ethernet technology, networking professionals often use the term *Ethernet address*. To guarantee that each address is unique, IEEE allocates an address for each piece of network interface hardware. Thus, if a consumer purchases a *Network Interface Card* (*NIC*) for their PC, the NIC contains a unique IEEE address assigned when the device was manufactured.

Rather than assign individual addresses, IEEE assigns a block of addresses to each equipment vendor, and allows the vendor to assign a unique value to each device they manufacture. Thus, a 48-bit address is divided into a 3-byte *Organizationally Unique ID* (*OUI*) that identifies the equipment vendor and a 3-byte block that identifies a particular *Network Interface Controller* (*NIC*). Figure 13.8 illustrates the division.

---

†Figure 13.2 can be found on page 223.

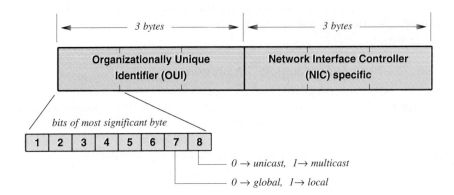

Figure 13.8 The division of a 48-bit IEEE MAC address.

Interestingly, the two low-order bits of the most significant byte of the OUI are assigned a special meaning as the figure indicates. The least significant bit of the most significant byte is a *multicast* bit that specifies whether the address is *unicast* (0) or *multicast* (1), and the next bit specifies whether the OUI is globally unique (0) or locally assigned (1). The next section explains multicast. Globally unique addresses are assigned by the IEEE; locally assigned addresses are available for experimental work or for organizations that desire to create their own address space.

13.10 Unicast, Broadcast, And Multicast Addresses

The IEEE addressing scheme supports three types of addresses that correspond to three types of packet delivery. Figure 13.9 provides a summary.

Address Type	Meaning And Packet Delivery
unicast	Uniquely identifies a single computer, and specifies that only the identified computer should receive a copy of the packet
broadcast	Corresponds to all computers, and specifies that each computer on the network should receive a copy of the packet
multicast	Identifies a subset of the computers on a given network, and specifies that each computer in the subset should receive a copy of the packet

Figure 13.9 The three types of MAC addresses and the corresponding meanings.

It may seem odd that the IEEE address format reserves a bit to distinguish between unicast and multicast, but does not provide a way to designate a broadcast address. The standard specifies that a *broadcast address* consists of 48 bits that are all 1s. Thus, a broadcast address has the multicast bit set. Conceptually, broadcast can be viewed as a special form of multicast. That is, each multicast address corresponds to a group of computers, and the broadcast address corresponds to a group that includes all computers on the network.

13.11 Broadcast, Multicast, And Efficient Multi-Point Delivery

Broadcast and multicast addresses are especially useful in LANs because they permit efficient delivery to many computers. To understand the efficiency, recall that a LAN transmits packets over a shared medium. In a typical LAN, each computer on the LAN monitors the shared medium, extracts a copy of each packet, and then examines the address in the packet to determine whether the packet should be processed or ignored. Algorithm 13.1 gives the algorithm a computer uses to process packets.

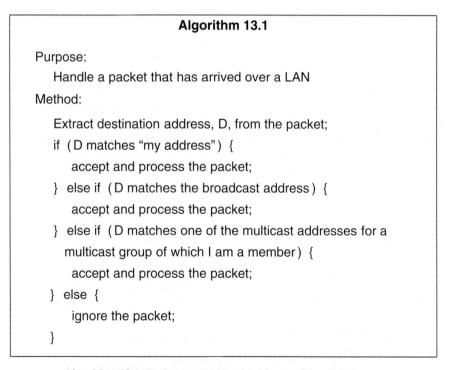

Algorithm 13.1

Purpose:
    Handle a packet that has arrived over a LAN
Method:
    Extract destination address, D, from the packet;
    if (D matches "my address") {
        accept and process the packet;
    } else if (D matches the broadcast address) {
        accept and process the packet;
    } else if (D matches one of the multicast addresses for a
        multicast group of which I am a member) {
        accept and process the packet;
    } else {
        ignore the packet;
    }

Algorithm 13.1 Packet processing algorithm used in a LAN.

From the algorithm, the efficiency should be clear. In the case of broadcast or multicast, a single copy of the packet is transmitted over the shared medium and all computers receive and process the copy. For example, consider broadcasting. Instead of *N* separate transmissions that each send an individual copy of a packet to a single computer, a sender transmits one copy of the packet that contains the broadcast address and all computers receive a copy.

13.12 Frames And Framing

Chapter 9 introduces the concept of framing in the context of synchronous communication systems as a mechanism that allows a receiver to know where a message begins and ends. In a more general sense, we use the term *framing* to refer to the structure added to a sequence of bits or bytes that allows a sender and receiver to agree on the exact format of the message. In a packet-switched network, each *frame* corresponds to a packet. A frame consists of two conceptual parts:

- Header that contains metadata, such as an address
- Payload that contains the data being sent

A frame *header* contains information used to process the frame. In particular, a header usually contains an address that specifies the intended recipient. The *payload* area contains the message being sent, and is usually much larger than the frame header. In most network technologies, the message is *opaque* in the sense that the network only examines the frame header. Thus, the payload can contain an arbitrary sequence of bytes that are only meaningful to the sender and receiver.

A frame is usually arranged so the header is transmitted before the payload, which allows a receiver to begin processing the frame as the bits arrive. Some technologies delineate each frame by sending a short prelude before the frame and a short postlude after the frame. Figure 13.10 illustrates the concept.

Figure 13.10 Typical structure of a frame in a packet-switched network.

To understand how framing works, consider an example using bytes. That is, suppose a data communication mechanism can transfer an arbitrary 8-bit byte from a sender to a receiver, and imagine that the mechanism is used to send packets. Assume that a packet header consists of 6 bytes and the payload consists of an arbitrary number of bytes. We will use a single byte to mark the start of a frame, and a single byte to mark the end of a frame. In the ASCII character set, the *Start Of Header (SOH)* character marks the beginning of a frame, and the *End Of Transmission (EOT)* character marks the end of a frame. Figure 13.11 illustrates the format.

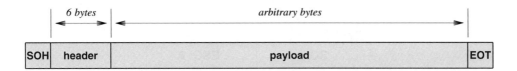

Figure 13.11 An example frame format that uses SOH and EOT characters to delineate a frame.

The example format appears to have unnecessary overhead. To understand why, consider what happens when a sender transmits two frames with no delay between them. At the end of the first frame, the sender transmits EOT, and then with no delay, the sender transmits SOH to start the second frame. In such circumstances, only one character is needed to separate two blocks of data — a framing scheme that delimits both the beginning and end of each frame appears to send an extra, unnecessary character between frames.

The advantage of sending a character at the end of a frame becomes clear when one considers that packet transmission is asynchronous and that errors can occur. For asynchronous communication, using an EOT to mark the end of a frame allows a receiver to process the frame without waiting for the start of a successive frame. In the case of an error, using SOH and EOT to bracket the frame helps with recovery and synchronization — if a sender crashes during transmission of a frame, a receiver will be able to determine that a partial frame arrived.

13.13 Byte And Bit Stuffing

In the ASCII character set, SOH has hexadecimal value 201 and EOT has the hexadecimal value 204. The question arises: what happens if the payload of a frame includes one or more bytes with value 201 or 204? The answer lies in a technique known as *byte stuffing* that allows transmission of arbitrary data without confusion.

In general, to distinguish between data and control information, such as frame delimiters, a sender changes the data to replace each control byte with a sequence and the receiver replaces the sequence with the original value. As a result, a frame can transfer arbitrary data and the underlying system never confuses data with control information. The technique is known as *byte stuffing*; the terms *data stuffing* and *character stuffing* are sometimes used. A related technique used with systems that transfer a bit stream is known as *bit stuffing*.

As an example of byte stuffing, consider a frame as illustrated in Figure 13.11. Because SOH and EOT are used to delimit the frame, those two bytes must not appear in the payload. Byte stuffing solves the problem by reserving a third character to mark occurrences of reserved characters in the data. For example, suppose the ASCII character ESC (hexadecimal value 1B) has been selected as the third character. When any of the three special characters occur in the data, the sender replaces the character with a two-character sequence. Figure 13.12 lists one possible mapping.

Byte In Payload	Sequence Sent
SOH	ESC A
EOT	ESC B
ESC	ESC C

Figure 13.12 An example of byte stuffing that maps each special character into a 2-character sequence.

As the figure specifies, the sender replaces each occurrence of SOH by the two characters ESC and A, each occurrence of EOT by the characters ESC and B, and each occurrence of ESC by the two characters ESC and C. A receiver reverses the mapping by looking for ESC followed by one of A, B, or C and replacing the 2-character combination with the appropriate single character. Figure 13.13 shows an example payload and the same payload after byte stuffing has occurred. Note that once byte stuffing has been performed, neither SOH nor EOT appears anywhere in the payload.

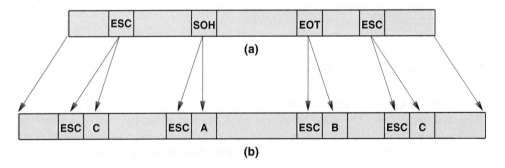

Figure 13.13 Illustration of (a) original data, and (b) a version after byte-stuffing has been performed.

13.14 Summary

Data networks can be classified as using circuit-switching or packet-switching. Packet switching, which forms the basis of the Internet, is a form of statistical multiplexing in which senders divide messages into small packets. Packet switched network technologies are classified as Local Area Networks (LANs), Wide Area Networks (WANs), and Metropolitan Area Networks (MANs); LANs and WANs are the most popular.

An organization named IEEE has created standards for data networking. IEEE standards primarily specify details for LANs, and focus on the first two layers of the protocol stack.

Four basic shapes or topologies are used to characterize LANs: bus, star, ring, and mesh. Mesh topologies are seldom used because they are expensive.

Each packet sent across a LAN contains a MAC address that identifies the intended recipient. The IEEE standard for MAC addresses specifies a 48-bit value divided into two fields: one that identifies the organization that assigns the address and another that gives a unique value for the particular piece of hardware to which the address is assigned. An address can specify unicast (a single computer), broadcast (all computers on a given LAN), or multicast (a subset of computers on a LAN).

The term *frame* is used to specify the format of a packet on a particular network. A frame consists of two conceptual parts: a header that contains meta-information and a payload area that contains the data being sent. For a network that transmits characters, a frame can be formed by using one byte value to indicate the beginning of the frame and another to indicate the end of the frame.

Byte (bit) stuffing techniques permit bytes (sequences of bits) to be reserved for use in marking the start and end of a frame. To insure that a payload does not contain reserved bytes (bit strings), a sender replaces occurrences of reserved values before transmission, and a receiver reverses the change to obtain the original data.

EXERCISES

13.1   What is circuit switching, and what are its chief characteristics?

13.2   What are the characteristics of LANs, MANs, and WANs?

13.3   Name the two sublayers of Layer 2 protocols defined by IEEE, and give the purpose of each.

13.4   In a circuit-switched network, can multiple circuits share a single optical fiber? Explain.

13.5   Give a definition of the term *frame*.

13.6   What is a point-to-point network?

13.7 Write a pair of computer programs, one that accepts a data file as input and produces a byte stuffed version of the file according to the mapping in Figure 13.12, and another that removes byte stuffing. Show that your programs interoperate with those written by others.

13.8 Can the wires of a ring network be arranged in a straight line (e.g., down a hallway)? Explain.

13.9 What are the four basic LAN topologies?

13.10 In a packet switching system, how does a sender transfer a large file?

13.11 If someone wanted to broadcast a copy of a video presentation, is a circuit switching system or a packet switching preferable? Why?

13.12 Define unicast, multicast, and broadcast addresses. Explain the meaning of each.

13.13 Why is byte stuffing needed?

13.14 Given an IEEE MAC address, how can one tell if the address refers to unicast?

13.15 How does a computer attached to a shared LAN decide whether to accept a packet?

13.16 What term is used to describe the metadata that accompanies a packet?

13.17 In a mesh network, how many connections are required among 20 computers?

Chapter Contents

14

The IEEE MAC Sub-Layer

14.1 Introduction

Chapters in this part of the text cover data communication networks that use packet switching. The previous chapter introduces the concept of packet switching and defines the two basic types of packet switched networks: WANs and LANs. The chapter also introduces the IEEE model for standards, and explains that IEEE divides Layer 2 into two sublayers.

This chapter continues the discussion by examining the IEEE's MAC sublayer. The chapter explains multi-access protocols, and considers both static and dynamic channel allocation. Later chapters in this part discuss specific networking technologies that use the access mechanisms explained here.

14.2 A Taxonomy Of Mechanisms For Multi-Access

How do multiple, independent computers coordinate access to a shared medium? There are three broad approaches: they can use a modified form of a multiplexing technique, they can engage in a distributed algorithm for controlled access, or they can use a random access strategy. Figure 14.1 illustrates the taxonomy, including specific forms of each approach.

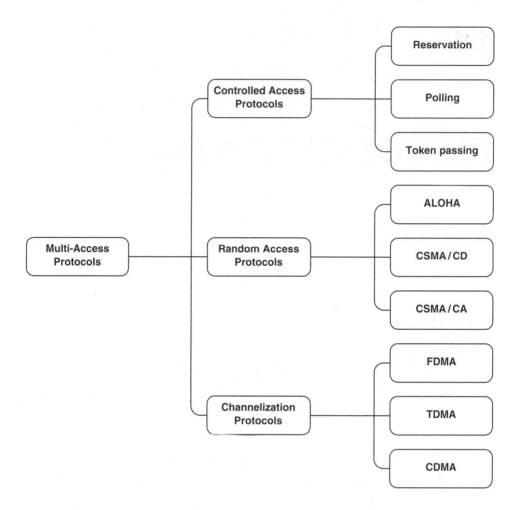

Figure 14.1 A taxonomy of protocols that control access to a shared medium.

14.3 Static And Dynamic Channel Allocation

We use the term *channelization* to refer to a mapping between a given communication and a channel in the underlying transmission system. Channelization is related to the multiplexing techniques that Chapter 11 discusses. For example, consider a frequency division multiplexing (FDM) mechanism. Most FDM systems assign each pair of communicating entities a unique carrier frequency. That is, each pair is assigned a unique channel. Furthermore, the mapping between a pair of entities and a carrier frequency does not change. In such situations, we describe the mapping between communicating entities and a channel as *1-to-1* and *static*.

Static channel allocation works well for situations where the set of communicating entities is known in advance and does not change. In many networks, however, the set of entities using the network varies over time. For example, consider cellular telephones in a city. Users move, and they can turn a cell phone on and off at any time. Thus, the set of cell phones that are operating in the range of a given cell tower varies constantly. In such situations, a *dynamic channel allocation* scheme is needed — a mapping can be established when a new station (e.g., cell phone) appears, and the mapping can be removed when the station disappears.

To summarize:

> *Static channel allocation suffices when the set of communicating entities is known in advance and does not change; most networks require a form of dynamic channel allocation.*

14.4 Channelization Protocols

Channelization protocols extend the multiplexing techniques covered in Chapter 11. Figure 14.2 lists the main channelization techniques.

Protocol	Expansion
FDMA	Frequency Division Multi-Access
TDMA	Time Division Multi-Access
CDMA	Code Division Multi-Access

Figure 14.2 The three main types of channelization.

14.4.1 FDMA

As the figure shows, channelization techniques employ frequency, time, and code division multiplexing. For example, *Frequency Division Multiple Access (FDMA)* extends frequency division multiplexing. In essence, the extension consists of a mechanism that allows independent stations to choose carrier frequencies that will not conflict with the carriers used by other stations. How does FDMA assign carriers? In some systems, a central controller provides a dynamic assignment. Whenever a new station appears, the station uses a reserved control channel to communicate with the controller. The station makes a request, the controller chooses a frequency that is currently unused, and the controller informs the station. After the initial exchange, the station uses the assigned carrier frequency (i.e., the assigned channel) for all communication.

14.4.2 TDMA

The extension to time division multiplexing, known as *Time Division Multi-Access* is analogous to the extension for frequency division multiplexing. In the simplest case, each active participant is assigned a sequence number from 1 to N, and stations transmit in order 1, 2, 3, ... N. As with FDMA, some TDMA systems offer dynamic allocation — a station is assigned a time slot when the station first appears on the network.

14.4.3 CDMA

Code-division multiplexing allows multiple stations to transmit at the same time by encoding each transmission mathematically. *Code Division Multi-Access* (*CDMA*), explained in Chapter 11, constitutes the primary application of code division multiplexing.

14.5 Controlled Access Protocols

Controlled access protocols provide a distributed version of statistical multiplexing. Figure 14.3 lists the three principal forms:

Type	Description
Polling	Centralized controller repeatedly polls stations and allows each to transmit one packet
Reservation	Stations submit a request for the next round of data transmission
Token Passing	Stations circulate a token; each time it receives the token, a station transmits one packet

Figure 14.3 The main types of controlled access protocols.

14.5.1 Polling

A network that employs *polling* uses a centralized controller, which cycles through stations on the network and gives each an opportunity to transmit a packet. Algorithm 14.1 gives the steps a controller follows. The selection step is significant because it means a controller can choose which station to poll at a given time. There are two general polling policies:

- Round robin order
- Priority order

Round-robin means each station has an equal opportunity to transmit packets. Priority order means some stations will have more opportunity to send. For example, priority order might be used to assign an IP telephone higher priority than a personal computer.

Algorithm 14.1

Purpose:

   Control transmission of packets through polling

Method:

   Controller repeats forever {

      Select a station, S, and send a polling message to S;

      Wait for S to respond by sending a packet or passing;

   }

Algorithm 14.1 Controlled access through polling.

14.5.2 Reservation

A *reservation* system, often used with satellite transmission, employs a two-step process in which each round of packet transmissions is planned in advance. Typically, reservation systems have a central controller that follows Algorithm 14.2.

Algorithm 14.2

Purpose:

   Control transmission of packets through reservation

Method:

   Controller repeats forever {

      Form a list of stations that have a packet to send;

      Allow stations on the list to transmit;

   }

Algorithm 14.2 Controlled access through reservation.

In the first step, each potential sender specifies whether they have a packet to send during the next round and the controller transmits a list of the stations that will be transmitting. In the second step, stations use the list to know when they should

transmit. Variations exist where a controller uses an alternate channel to gather reserva-
tions for the next round while the current round of transmissions proceeds over the main
channel.

14.5.3 Token Passing

Token passing has been used in several LAN technologies, and is most often associated with ring topologies†. To understand token passing, imagine a set of computers
connected in a ring, and imagine that at any instant, exactly one of the computers has
received a special control message called a *token*. To control access, each computer follows Algorithm 14.3

Algorithm 14.3

Purpose:

    Control transmission of packets through token passing

Method:

    Each computer on the network repeats {

        Wait for the token to arrive;

        Transmit a packet if one is waiting to be sent;

        Send the token to the next station;

    }

Algorithm 14.3 Controlled access through token passing.

In a token passing system, when no station has any packets to send, the token cir-
culates among all stations continuously. For a ring topology, the order of circulation is
defined by the ring. That is, if a ring is arranged to send messages in a clockwise
fashion, the *next station* mentioned in the algorithm refers to the next physical station in
a clockwise order. When token passing is applied to other topologies (e.g., a bus), each
station is assigned a position in a logical sequence, and the token is passed according to
the assigned sequence.

14.6 Random Access Protocols

Many networks, especially LANs, do not employ a controlled access mechanism.
Instead, a set of computers attached to a shared medium attempt to access the medium
without coordination. The term *random* is used because access only occurs when a
given station has a packet to send and randomization is employed to prevent all computers on a LAN from attempting to use the medium at the same time. The descriptions of

---

†Although older LANs used token passing ring technology, popularity has decreased, and few token passing networks remain.

specific methods below will clarify the use of randomization. Figure 14.4 lists the three random access methods that are discussed.

Type	Description
ALOHA	**Historic protocol used in an early radio network in Hawaii; popular in textbooks and easy to analyze, but not used in real networks**
CSMA/CD	**Carrier Sense Multi-Access with Collision Detection The basis for Ethernet, and the most widely used random access protocol**
CSMA/CA	**Carrier Sense Multi-Access with Collision Avoidance The basis for Wi-Fi wireless networks**

Figure 14.4 Three random access protocols.

14.6.1 ALOHA

An early network in Hawaii, known as *ALOHAnet*, pioneered the concept of random access. Although the network is no longer used, the ideas have been extended. The network consisted of a single powerful transmitter in a central geographic location surrounded by a set of stations that each corresponded to a computer. Each station had a transmitter capable of reaching the central transmitter (but not powerful enough to reach all the other stations). ALOHAnet used two carrier frequencies: one at 413.475 MHz for *outbound* broadcast traffic sent by the central transmitter to all stations, and another at 407.305 MHz for *inbound* traffic sent by stations to the central transmitter.

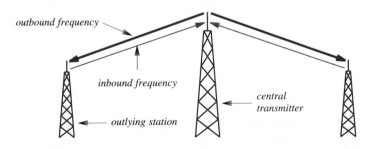

Figure 14.5 Illustration of outbound and inbound frequencies in ALOHAnet.

The ALOHA protocol is straightforward: when a station has a packet to send, it transmits the packet on the inbound frequency. The central transmitter repeats the transmission on the outbound frequency (which all stations can receive). To insure that transmission is successful, a sending station listens to the outbound channel. If a copy of its packet arrives, the sending station moves to the next packet; if no copy arrives, the sending station waits a short time and tries again.

Why might a packet fail to arrive? The answer is interference — if two stations simultaneously attempt to transmit on the inbound frequency, the signals will interfere and the two transmissions will be garbled. We use the term *collision*, and say that the two transmitted packets *collide* in the medium. The protocol handles a collision by requiring a sender to *retransmit* each lost packet. The idea is common, and appears in many network protocols.

The amount of time to wait before retransmission must be chosen carefully. Otherwise, two stations will each wait exactly the same amount of time before resending, and will interfere with one another again. Thus, if randomization is added (i.e., each station chooses a random delay), the probability of interfering is much lower. Analysis shows that when ALOHAnet became busy, many collisions occurred. Even with randomization, collisions lowered the successful data transfer in ALOHAnet to about 18% of channel capacity (i.e., the utilization of the channel was 18%).

14.6.2 CSMA/CD

In 1973, researchers at Xerox PARC created an extremely successful network technology that used a random access protocol. In 1978, a standard (informally called the *DIX standard*) was created by Digital Equipment Corporation, Intel, and Xerox. Known as *Ethernet*, the original Ethernet technology consisted of a single long cable to which computers attach†. The cable served as a shared medium — instead of broadcasting radio frequency transmissions through the atmosphere, Ethernet transmitted signals down a cable. Furthermore, instead of using two frequencies and a central transmitter, Ethernet allows all communication to proceed across the shared cable. Despite their differences, Ethernet and ALOHAnet had to solve the same basic problem: if two stations attempt to transmit at the same time, the signals interfere and a collision occurs.

Ethernet offered three innovations in the way collisions are handled:

- Carrier sense
- Collision detection
- Binary exponential backoff

Carrier Sense. Instead of allowing a station to transmit whenever a packet becomes ready, Ethernet requires each station to monitor the cable to detect whether another transmission is already in progress. The mechanism, which is known as *carrier*

---

†The next chapter considers modern Ethernet wiring.

sense, prevents the most obvious collision problems, and substantially improves network utilization.

Collision Detection. Although carrier sense is used, a collision can occur if two stations wait for a transmission to stop, find the cable idle, and both start transmitting. A small part of the problem is that even at the speed of light, some time is required for a signal to travel down the cable. Thus, a station at one end of the cable cannot know instantly when a station at the other end begins to transmit.

To handle collisions, each station monitors the cable during transmission. If the signal on the cable differs from the signal that the station is sending, it means that a collision has occurred. The technique is known as *collision detection*. When a collision is detected, the sending station aborts transmission.

Many details complicate Ethernet transmission. For example, following a collision, transmission does not abort until enough bits have been sent to guarantee that the collided signals reach all stations. Furthermore, following a transmission, stations must wait for an *interpacket gap* (9.6 μsec for a 10 Mbps Ethernet) to insure that all stations sense an idle network and have a chance to transmit. Such details illustrate how carefully the technology was designed.

Binary Exponential Backoff. Ethernet does more than merely detect collisions — it also recovers from them. After a collision occurs, a computer must wait for the cable to become idle again before transmitting a frame. As with ALOHAnet, randomization is used to avoid having multiple stations transmit simultaneously as soon as the cable is idle. That is, the standard specifies a maximum delay, *d*, and requires each station to choose a random delay less than *d* after a collision occurs. In most cases, when two stations each choose a random value, the station that chooses the smallest delay will proceed to send a packet and the network will return to normal operation.

In the case where two or more computers happen to choose nearly the same amount of delay, they will both begin to transmit at nearly the same time, producing a second collision. To avoid a sequence of collisions, Ethernet requires each computer to double the range from which a delay is chosen after each collision. A computer chooses a random delay from *0* to *d* after one collision, a random delay between *0* and *2d* after a second collision, between *0* and *4d* after a third, and so on. After a few collisions, the range from which a random value is chosen becomes large. Thus, some computer will choose a random delay shorter than the others, and will transmit without a collision.

Doubling the range of the random delay after each collision is known as *binary exponential backoff*. In essence, exponential backoff means that an Ethernet can recover quickly after a collision because each computer agrees to wait longer times between attempts when the cable becomes busy. Even in the unlikely event that two or more computers choose delays that are approximately equal, exponential backoff guarantees that contention for the cable will be reduced after a few collisions.

The combination of techniques described above is known by the name *Carrier Sense Multi-Access with Collision Detection. (CSMA/CD)*. Algorithm 14.4 summarizes CSMA/CD.

Algorithm 14.4

Purpose:

    Use CSMA/CD to send a packet

Method:

    Wait for a packet to be ready;

    Wait for the medium to be idle (carrier sense);

    Delay for the interpacket gap;

    Set variable x to the standard backoff range, d ;

    Attempt to transmit the packet (collision detection);

    While   (a collision occurred during previous transmission)   {

        Choose q to be a random delay between 0 and x ;

        Delay for q microseconds;

        Double x in case needed for the next round;

        Attempt to retransmit the packet (collision detection);

    }

Algorithm 14.4 Packet transmission using CSMA/CD.

14.6.3 CSMA/CA

Although it works well on a cable, CSMA/CD does not work as well in wireless LANs because a transmitter used in a wireless LAN has a limited range, δ. That is, a receiver that is more than δ away from the transmitter will not receive a signal, and will not be able to detect a carrier. To see why limits cause problems for CSMA/CD, consider three computers with wireless LAN hardware positioned as Figure 14.6 illustrates.

Figure 14.6 Three computers with wireless LAN hardware at maximal distance.

In the figure, computer 1 can communicate with computer 2, but cannot receive the signal from computer 3. Thus, if computer 3 is transmitting a packet to computer 2, computer 1's carrier sense mechanism will not detect the transmission. Similarly, if computers 1 and 3 simultaneously transmit, only computer 2 will detect a collision. The problem is sometimes called the *hidden station problem* because some stations are not visible to others.

To ensure that all stations share the transmission media correctly, wireless LANs use a modified access protocol known as *Carrier Sense Multiple Access With Collision Avoidance (CSMA/CA)*. Instead of depending on all other computers to receive all transmissions, the CSMA/CA used with wireless LANs triggers a brief transmission from the intended receiver before transmitting a packet. The idea is that if both the sender and receiver transmit a message, all computers within range of either will know a packet transmission is beginning. Figure 14.7 illustrates the sequence.

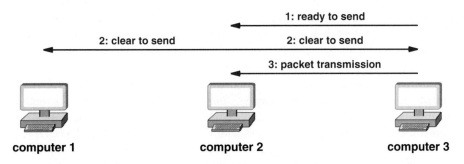

Figure 14.7 A sequence of messages sent when computer 3 transmits a packet to computer 2.

In the figure, computer 3 sends a short message to announce that it is ready to transmit a packet to computer 2, and computer 2 responds by sending a short message announcing that it is ready to receive the packet. All computers in range of computer 3 receive the initial announcement, and all computers in the range of computer 2 receive the response. As a result, even though it cannot receive the signal or sense a carrier, computer 1 knows that a packet transmission is taking place.

Collisions of control messages can occur when using CSMA/CA, but they can be handled easily. In the figure, for example, if computers 1 and 3 each attempt to transmit a packet to computer 2 at exactly the same time, their control messages will collide. Computer 2 will detect the collision, and will not reply. When a collision occurs, the sending stations apply random backoff before resending the control messages. Because control messages are much shorter than a packet, the probability of a second collision is low. Eventually, one of the two control messages arrives intact, and computer 2 transmits a response.

We can summarize:

> *Because computers on a wireless LAN can span distances greater than a signal can propagate, wireless LANs use CSMA/CA in which the sending and receiving computers each send a control message before packet transmission occurs.*

14.7 Summary

The IEEE MAC layer contains protocols that control access to a shared medium. Channelization protocols consist of extensions to time, frequency, and code division multiplexing; the extensions are known as Frequency, Time, and Code Division Multi-Access. Static or dynamic channel allocation is possible.

Controlled access protocols allow independent stations to engage in statistical multiplexing. Polling uses a central controller that repeatedly checks whether stations are ready to send a packet. A reservation system, often used with satellites, requires stations to declare whether they are ready for the next round of transmission. Token passing, often used with a ring topology, passes a control message among stations; a station can transmit a packet when it receives the token.

Random access protocols allow stations to contend for access. The historic ALOHA protocol used two frequencies, one for inbound and one for outbound transmissions; if a station did not receive a copy of its packet, the station retransmitted. Ethernet uses Carrier Sense Multi-Access with Collision Detection (CSMA/CD) to permit access to a shared cable. In addition to preventing a station from transmitting while another transmission is in progress, the protocol uses binary exponential backoff to recover from collisions.

Because some stations are hidden from others, wireless LANs use Carrier Sense Multi-Access with Collision Avoidance (CSMA/CA). Before transmission of a packet from one computer to another, each of the two computers sends a short control message, which allows all computers in range of the two to know that a transmission is about to occur.

EXERCISES

14.1   Explain the three basic approaches used to arbitrate access to a shared medium.

14.2   Why is CSMA/CA needed in a wireless network?

14.3   Explain polling and the two general polling policies.

14.4   In the Aloha protocol, what happens if two stations attempt simultaneous transmission on the inbound frequency, and how is the problem handled?

14.5   What is binary exponential backoff?

14.6   Give an example of a network that uses dynamic channel allocation.

14.7   List the three main types of channelization and the characteristics of each.

14.8   In a reservation system, how does a controller form a list of stations that will transmit in a given round?

14.9   Expand the acronym CSMA/CD, and explain each part.

14.10   Why does CSMA/CD use a random delay? (Hint: think of many identical computers on a network.)

14.11   What is a token, and how are tokens used to control network access?

Chapter Contents

15

Wired LAN Technology
(Ethernet And 802.3)

15.1 Introduction

Chapters in this part of the text describe packet switching networking technologies. Chapter 13 presents the IEEE 802 model used in LANs and the division of Layer 2 into Logical Link and MAC sublayers. The chapters also discusses the 48-bit addressing scheme that forms a significant part of the Logical Link sublayer. Chapter 13 focuses on the MAC sublayer, and considers protocols for medium access, including CSMA / CD.

This chapter continues the discussion of Local Area Networks by focusing on wired LAN technologies. The chapter shows how concepts from previous chapters form the basis of Ethernet, the wired LAN technology that has proceeded to dominate all others.

15.2 The Venerable Ethernet

Recall from Chapter 14 that Ethernet is a LAN technology originally invented at Xerox PARC and later standardized by Digital Equipment Corporation, Intel, and Xerox. Ethernet has survived for thirty years. Although the hardware devices, cabling, and media used with Ethernet have changed dramatically, many of the fundamentals remain constant. One of the most interesting aspects of Ethernet evolution concerns the way newer versions of Ethernet remain backward compatible — a new version can sense an older form and automatically adapt to accommodate the older technology.

15.3 Ethernet Frame Format

The term *frame format* refers to the way a packet is organized, including details such as the size and meaning of individual fields. The main reason that older versions of Ethernet have remained compatible with newer versions arises from the frame format, which has remained constant since the DIX standard was created in the 1970s. Figure 15.1 illustrates the basic format and the details of the frame header.

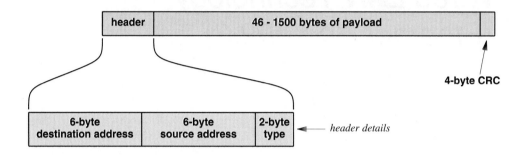

Figure 15.1 Illustration of the Ethernet frame format and header details.

As the figure shows, an Ethernet frame consists of a fixed-length header, a variable-length payload, and a fixed-length Cyclic Redundancy Check†. The header contains three fields: a 48-bit *destination address* field that gives the address of the intended recipient, a 48-bit *source address* field that contains the address of the computer that sent the frame, and a 16-bit *type* field.

15.4 Ethernet Type Field And Demultiplexing

The type field in an Ethernet frame provides multiplexing and demultiplexing that allows a given computer to have multiple protocols operating simultaneously. For example, later chapters explain that the protocols used on the Internet send IP datagrams and ARP messages over Ethernet. Each is assigned a unique Ethernet type (hexadecimal 0800 for IP datagrams and hexadecimal 0806 for ARP messages). When transmitting a datagram in an Ethernet frame, the sender assigns a type 0800. When a frame arrives at its destination, the receiver examines the type field, and uses the value to determine which software module should process the frame. Figure 15.2 illustrates the demultiplexing.

---

†When an Ethernet frame is sent over a network, bits are encoded using the Manchester encoding described in Chapter 6 and the frame may be preceded by a 64-bit preamble of alternating 1s and 0s.

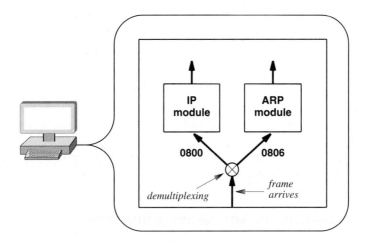

Figure 15.2 Illustration of using the frame type field for demultiplexing.

15.5 IEEE's Version Of Ethernet (802.3)

Interestingly, in 1983 IEEE developed a standard for Ethernet and attempted to redefine the Ethernet frame format†. The IEEE working group that produced the standard is numbered 802.3, and to distinguish the IEEE standard from others, professionals often refer to it as *802.3 Ethernet*.

The major difference between conventional Ethernet and 802.3 Ethernet arises from the interpretation of the type field. The 802.3 standard interprets the original type field as a *packet length*, and adds an extra 8-byte header that contains the packet type. The extra header is known as a *Logical Link Control/Sub-Network Attachment Point (LLC/SNAP)* header; most professionals simply call it a *SNAP header*. Figure 15.3 illustrates the format.

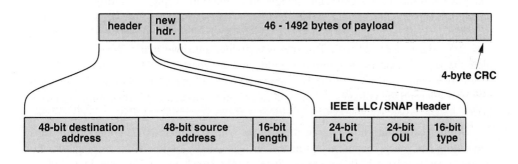

Figure 15.3 The IEEE 802.3 frame format with an LLC/SNAP header.

---

†The IEEE version has not enjoyed much success — most installations still use the original frame format.

As the figure shows, the overall frame size in 802.3 Ethernet remains the same as conventional Ethernet: 1514 bytes. Therefore, IEEE reduced the maximum payload from 1500 bytes to 1492 bytes. We can think of a SNAP header occupying the first 8 bytes of the payload area.

To keep the two versions of Ethernet compatible, a convention is used:

> *If bytes 13-14 of an Ethernet frame contain a numeric value less than 1500, the field is interpreted as a packet length and the 802.3 standard applies; otherwise, the field is interpreted as a type field and the original Ethernet standard applies.*

15.6 LAN Connections And Network Interface Cards

In terms of computer architecture, a LAN appears to be an I/O device, and connects to the computer in the same manner as a disk or video device. That is, a *Network Interface Card*† (*NIC*) plugs into the computer's bus. Logically, a NIC handles address recognition, CRC computation, and frame recognition (e.g., a NIC checks the destination address on a frame, and ignores frames not destined for the computer). In addition, a NIC connects to a network, and handles details of data communication (i.e., sending and receiving frames). Physically, a NIC consists of a circuit board with a plug on one side that matches the computer's bus and a connector on the other side that accepts a plug appropriate for a given LAN. Most computers come with a NIC already installed. However, the NIC is independent from the rest of the computer, and a user can choose to replace the NIC without making other changes.

15.7 Ethernet Evolution And Thicknet Wiring

Since the original version in the 1970s, Ethernet has undergone several major changes, with the most significant changes in media and wiring. The original Ethernet wiring scheme was informally called *thick wire Ethernet* or *Thicknet* because the communication medium consisted of a heavy coaxial cable; the formal term for the wiring is *10Base5*. Hardware used with Thicknet was divided into two major parts. A NIC handled the digital aspects of communication, and a separate electronic device called a *transceiver* connected to the Ethernet cable and handled carrier detection, conversion of bits into appropriate voltages for transmission, and conversion of incoming signals to bits.

A physical cable known as an *Attachment Unit Interface* (*AUI*) connected a transceiver to a NIC in a computer. A transceiver was usually remote from a computer. For example, in an office building, transceivers might attach to an Ethernet in a hallway ceiling. Figure 15.4 illustrates how the original Thicknet wiring used an AUI cable to connect a computer to a transceiver.

---

†Formally, the device is a *Network Interface Controller*.

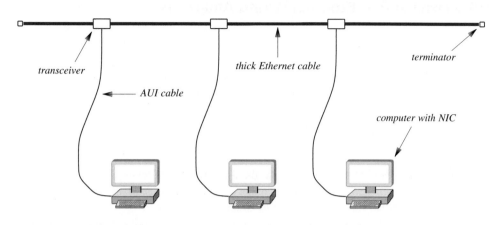

Figure 15.4 Illustration of the original Thicknet Ethernet wiring.

15.8 Thinnet Ethernet Wiring

A second generation of Ethernet wiring was devised that uses a thinner, coaxial cable that was more flexible than Thicknet. Formally named *10Base2* and informally known as *Thinwire Ethernet* or *Thinnet*, the wiring scheme differed dramatically from Thicknet. Instead of using AUI connections between a computer and a transceiver, Thinnet integrates a transceiver directly on the Network Interface Card, and runs a coaxial cable from one computer to another. Figure 15.5 illustrates Thinnet wiring.

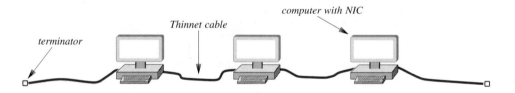

Figure 15.5 Illustration of the second generation Ethernet wiring known as Thinnet.

Thinnet had advantages and disadvantages. The primary advantages were lower overall cost and ease of installation. No external transceivers were needed, and Thinnet cable could be installed in a convenient path (e.g., across a tabletop between computers, under the floor, or in a conduit). The chief disadvantage arose because the entire network was vulnerable — if a user unplugged a segment of the network to relocate wires or move a computer, the entire network would stop working.

15.9 Twisted Pair Ethernet Wiring And Hubs

A third generation of Ethernet wiring made a dramatic shift in two ways:

- In place of coaxial cable, the third generation uses a central electronic device separate from the computers attached to the network.
- Instead of heavy, shielded cabling, the third generation uses twisted pair wiring.

Because it does not use coaxial cable, the third-generation technology is informally known as *twisted pair Ethernet*, and has replaced other versions. Thus, when someone now refers to Ethernet, they are referring to twisted pair Ethernet.

For the original version of twisted pair Ethernet, the electronic device that served as the central interconnection was known as a *hub*. Hubs were available in a variety of sizes, with the cost proportional to size. A small hub had four or eight *ports* that each connected to a computer or other device (e.g., a printer). Larger hubs accommodated hundreds of connections. Figure 15.6 illustrates the wiring scheme.

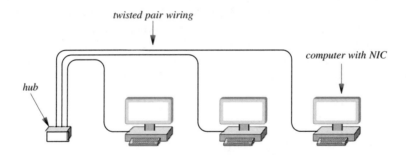

Figure 15.6 Illustration of the third generation Ethernet using twisted pair wiring.

Electronic components in a hub emulate a physical cable, making the entire system operate like a conventional Ethernet. For example, a computer attached to a hub uses CSMA/CD to access the network, receives a copy of each frame, and uses the address in a frame to determine whether to process or ignore the frame. Furthermore, twisted pair Ethernet retains the same frame format as the previous versions. In fact, software on a computer cannot distinguish between thick Ethernet, thin Ethernet, and twisted pair Ethernet — the network interface on a computer handles the details and hides any differences. The point is:

> *Twisted pair Ethernet wiring uses an electronic device known as a hub in place of a shared cable.*

15.10 Physical And Logical Ethernet Topology

Recall that LANs are classified according to their topology (i.e., overall shape). Figure 13.7 summarizes the major topologies†. The question arises, "what is the topology of Ethernet?". Surprisingly, the answer is complex.

Clearly, the original Thicknet version of Ethernet followed a bus topology. Indeed, the original Ethernet is often cited as a classic example of bus topology. It may appear that twisted pair Ethernet follows a star topology. In fact, the term *hub* arose to clarify the concept of a central interconnection point. However, because a hub emulates a physical cable, the system appears to perform as if computers attach to a cable. In fact, professionals joked that a hub really provided a:

"bus in a box"

To understand Ethernet topology, we must distinguish between *logical* and *physical* topologies. Logically, twisted pair Ethernet employs a bus topology. Physically, however, twisted pair Ethernet forms a star-shaped topology. The point is:

> *Distinguishing between logical and physical topologies allows us to understand that twisted pair Ethernet uses a star physical topology, but logically acts like a bus.*

15.11 Wiring In An Office Building

The styles of wiring used for LANs make little difference in a machine room or laboratory. When used in an office building, however, the type of wiring makes a major difference in terms of the type and number of wires needed, the distance spanned, and the cost. The three versions of Ethernet wiring illustrate the three principal forms that LANs use. Figure 15.7 depicts wiring on a floor of an office building.

In the figure, note that twisted pair Ethernet requires many individual cables to go between offices and a central point, which is known as a *wiring closet*. Thus, twisted pair Ethernet requires careful labeling of cables.

---

†Figure 13.7 can be found on page 229.

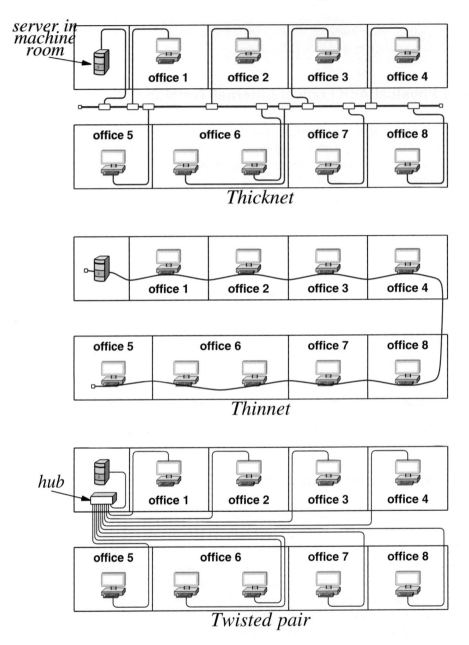

Figure 15.7 Illustration of various LAN wiring schemes that have been used in an office building.

15.12 Variants Of Twisted Pair Ethernet And Speeds

Since twisted pair Ethernet first emerged, significant improvements have been made in the quality and shielding available in twisted pair cables. As a result, the data rate used on twisted pair Ethernet has increased. Figure 15.8 summarizes the three types of twisted pair Ethernet and the cable used with each.

Designation	Name	Data Rate	Cable Used
10BaseT	Twisted Pair Ethernet	10 Mbps	Category 5
100BaseT	Fast Ethernet	100 Mbps	Category 5E
1000BaseT	Gigabit Ethernet	1 Gbps	Category 6

Figure 15.8 Three types of twisted pair Ethernet, their data rates, and the cable used with each.

As the figure shows, the first version of twisted pair Ethernet was given the formal designation *10BaseT*, where the value 10 designates that the speed is 10 Mbps. A later version that was introduced under the name *Fast Ethernet* ran at 100 Mbps, and was given the formal designation *100BaseT*. A third version, called *Gigabit Ethernet*, operates at 1 Gbps (i.e., 1000 Mbps). Professionals often abbreviate the name as *Gig-E*. Chapter 17 explains that higher-speed Ethernet technologies use an electronic device known as a *switch* rather than a hub. Furthermore, to remain backward compatible, standards for the higher-speed versions specify that interfaces should automatically sense the speed at which a connection can operate, and slow down to accommodate older devices. Thus, if one plugs an Ethernet cable between an old device that uses 10BaseT and a new device that uses 1000BaseT, the new device will *autosense* the discrepancy and slow down to 10 Mbps.

15.13 Twisted Pair Connectors And Cables

Twisted pair Ethernet uses *RJ45* connectors, which are larger versions of the RJ11 connectors used to connect telephones. An RJ45 connector can only be plugged into a socket one way, and a physical piece holds the connector in place. Thus, connectors cannot be plugged in incorrectly, and once inserted, the connectors do not fall out.

Cables can be purchased in various lengths with an RJ45 connector mounted on each end, which means that most users do not need to create a cable. However, confusion arises because there are two type of cables: *straight* and *crossed*. A crossed cable, which is used to connect two switches, connects a pin on one end to a different pin on the other end. A straight cable, used between a computer and a switch, connects each pin of the RJ45 attached to one end of the cable directly to the corresponding pin on the RJ45 at the other end. Thus, pin 1 connects to pin 1, and so on. Although the most sophisticated interface hardware can detect an incorrect cable and adapt, most hardware will not function correctly if a crossed cable is used when a straight cable is required.

To help technicians make the correct connections, individual wires in a Category 5 or Category 6 cable are coated with colored plastic. Figure 15.9 lists the color codes used with a straight cable†.

RJ45 Pin	Color Of Wire Used	Function
1	white-green	TX_D1+
2	green	TX_D1-
3	white-orange	RX_D2+
4	blue	BI_D3+
5	white-blue	BI_D3-
6	orange	RX_D2-
7	white-brown	BI_D4+
8	brown	BI_D4-

Figure 15.9 List of color codes used with an RJ45 connector.

15.14 Summary

Ethernet technology, first invented in the 1970s, has become the de facto standard for wired Local Area Networks. An Ethernet frame begins with a 14-byte header that contains a 48-bit destination address, 8-bit source address, and 16-bit type field. Although IEEE standard 802.3 attempted to define a new frame format with an additional 8-byte header, the IEEE version is seldom used.

The Ethernet type field is used for demultiplexing after a frame arrives at its destination. When creating a frame, a sender specifies the type; a recipient uses the type to determine which module should process the frame.

Although the Ethernet frame format has remained unchanged since the first standard, the cables used for Ethernet and the wiring scheme have changed dramatically. There have been three major versions of Ethernet wiring. Thicknet used a large coaxial

---

†Abbreviations in the figure label each pin as being used to *Transmit*, *Receive*, or for *Bi-directional* communication on each of four possible data paths.

cable with transceivers separate from computers. Thinnet used a flexible coaxial cable that ran from computer to computer, and the network interface in each computer contained a transceiver. Twisted Pair Ethernet replaces the coaxial cable with an electronic device called a *hub* or *switch*, and uses twisted pair wiring between a computer and a hub. The resulting system has a physical star topology and a logical bus topology.

Like earlier versions of Ethernet, the first Twisted Pair technology operated at 10 Mbps, and was designated 10BaseT. A version formally named 100BaseT operates at 100 Mbps, and is known commercially as *Fast Ethernet*. A third version, called *Gigabit Ethernet* or *Gig-E*, operates at 1000 Mbps, which is equivalent to 1 Gbps. Hardware for higher-speed Ethernet automatically senses when a low-speed device is connected, and reduces the speed accordingly.

EXERCISES

15.1   What is an Ethernet hub, and what wiring is used with a hub?

15.2   How large is the maximum Ethernet frame, including the CRC?

15.3   What category of twisted pair wiring is needed for a 10 Mbps network?100 Mbps? 1000 Mbps?

15.4   How can a receiver tell whether an Ethernet frame uses the 802.3 standard?

15.5   How did a computer attach to a Thicknet Ethernet?

15.6   How were computers attached to a Thinnet Ethernet?

15.7   Which style of Ethernet wiring requires more physical wires in an office building?

15.8   How is the type field in the Ethernet header used?

15.9   Look up switches and hubs on the Web. If you were offered a switch or hub that operated at the same bit rate for the same price, which would you choose? Why?

15.10   In an 802.3 Ethernet frame, what is the maximum payload size?

15.11   When it is used, where is an LLC/SNAP header placed?

15.12   Give an example of a network with differing physical and logical topologies.

Chapter Contents

16

Wireless Networking Technologies

16.1 Introduction

This part of the text focuses on networking technologies and their use in packet switching systems. Chapters introduce packet switching and give the IEEE model. The previous chapter explains wired technologies used in Local Area Networks.

This chapter describes wireless technologies. The chapter explains that a myriad of wireless technologies have been proposed, that wireless communication is used across a wide range of distances, and that many commercial systems exist. Thus, unlike the situation in wired networking where a single technology dominates, wireless networking appears to have multiple technologies, many with similar characteristics.

16.2 A Taxonomy Of Wireless Networks

Wireless communication applies across a wide range of network types and sizes. Part of the motivation for variety arises from government regulations that make specific ranges of the electromagnetic spectrum available for communication. A license is required to operate transmission equipment in some parts of the spectrum, and other parts of the spectrum are unlicensed. Many wireless technologies have been created, and new variants appear continually. Wireless technologies can be classified broadly according to network type, as the taxonomy in Figure 16.1 illustrates.

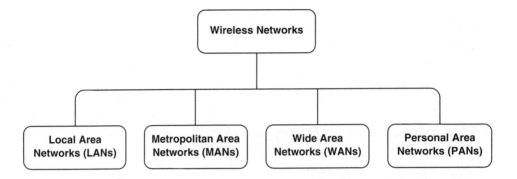

Figure 16.1 A taxonomy of wireless networking technologies.

16.3 Personal Area Networks (PANs)

In addition to the three network types described in Chapter 13 (LANs, MANs, and WANs), wireless networking includes *Personal Area Networks* (*PANs*). A PAN technology provides communication over a short distance, and is intended for use with devices that are owned and operated by a single user. For example, a PAN can provide communication between a wireless headset and a cell phone. PAN technologies are also used between a computer and a nearby wireless mouse or keyboard.

PAN technologies can be grouped into three broad categories. Figure 16.2 lists the categories, and gives a brief description of each; later sections explain PAN communication in more detail, and list PAN standards.

Type	Purpose
Bluetooth	Communication over a short distance between a small peripheral device such as a headset or mouse and a system such as a cell phone or a computer
InfraRed	Line-of-sight communication between a small device, often a hand-held controller, and a nearby system such as a computer or entertainment center
ISM wireless	Communication using frequencies set aside for Industrial Scientific and Medical devices, an environment where electromagnetic interference may be present

Figure 16.2 Three basic types of wireless Personal Area Network technologies.

16.4 ISM Wireless Bands Used By LANs And PANs

Governments have reserved three areas of the electromagnetic spectrum for use by *Industrial, Scientific,* and *Medical* groups. Known as *ISM wireless,* the frequencies are not licensed to specific carriers, are broadly available for products, and are used for LANs and PANs. Figure 16.3 illustrates the ISM frequency ranges.

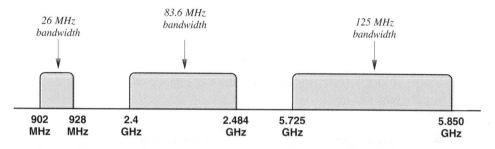

Figure 16.3 Blocks of frequencies that constitute the ISM bands and the bandwidth of each.

16.5 Wireless LAN Technologies And Wi-Fi

A variety of wireless LAN technologies exist that use various frequencies, modulation techniques, and data rates. IEEE provides most of the standards, which are categorized as *IEEE 802.11.* In 1999, a group of vendors who build wireless equipment formed the Wi-Fi Alliance, a non-profit organization that tests and certifies wireless equipment using the 802.11 standards. Because the alliance has received extensive marketing, most consumers associate wireless LANs with the term *Wi-Fi†*. Figure 16.4 lists the key IEEE standards that fall under the Wi-Fi Alliance.

IEEE Standard	Frequency Band	Data Rate	Modulation Technique	Multiplexing Technique
original 802.11	2.4 GHz	1 or 2 Mbps	FSK	DSSS
	2.4 GHz	1 or 2 Mbps	FSK	FHSS
	InfraRed	1 or 2 Mbps	PPM	–none–
802.11a	5.725 GHz	6 to 54 Mbps	PSK or QAM	OFDM
802.11b	2.4 GHz	5.5 and 11 Mbps	PSK	DSSS
802.11g	2.4 GHz	22 and 54 Mbps	various	OFDM

Figure 16.4 Key wireless standards certified by the Wi-Fi Alliance.

---

†Although the phrase *wireless fidelity* originally appeared in its advertising, the alliance has dropped the phrase and does not provide an explanation for the name.

16.6 Spread Spectrum Techniques

Chapter 11 introduces the term *spread spectrum*, and explains that spread spectrum transmission uses multiple frequencies to send data. That is, the sender spreads data across multiple frequencies, and the receiver combines the information obtained from multiple frequencies to reproduce the original data.

In general, spread spectrum can be used to achieve one of the following two goals:

- Increase overall performance
- Make transmission more immune to noise

The table in Figure 16.5 summarizes the three key multiplexing techniques used in Wi-Fi wireless networks.

Name	Expansion	Description
DSSS	Direct Sequence Spread Spectrum	Similar to CDMA where a sender multiplies the outgoing data by a sequence to form multiple frequencies and the receiver multiplies by the same sequence to decode
FHSS	Frequency Hopping Spread Spectrum	A sender uses a sequence of frequencies to transmit data, and a receiver uses the same sequence of frequencies to extract data
OFDM	Orthogonal Frequency Division Multiplexing	A frequency division multiplexing scheme where the transmission band is divided into many carriers in such a way that the carriers do not interfere

Figure 16.5 The major multiplexing techniques used with Wi-Fi.

Each technique has advantages. OFDM offers the greatest flexibility. DSSS has good performance, and FHSS makes a transmission more immune to noise. Thus, when a wireless technology is defined, the designers choose an appropriate multiplexing technique. For example, two versions of the original 802.11 standard were created to accommodate DSSS and FHSS. To summarize:

Spread spectrum techniques can help wireless LANs function in noisy environments.

16.7 Other Wireless LAN Standards

IEEE has created many wireless networking standards that handle various types of communication. Each standard specifies a frequency range, the modulation and multiplexing to be used, and a data rate. Figure 16.6 lists the major standards that have been created or proposed, and gives a brief description of each.

Standard	Purpose
802.11e	Improved quality of service, such as a guarantee of low jitter
802.11h	Like 802.11a, but adds control of spectrum and power (primarily intended for use in Europe)
802.11i	Enhanced security, including Advanced Encryption Standard; the full version is known as WPA2
802.11k	Will provide radio resource management, including transmission power
802.11n	Data rate over 100 Mbps to handle multimedia (video) applications (may be 500 Mbps)
802.11p	Dedicated Short-Range Communication (DSRC) among vehicles on a highway and vehicle-to-roadside
802.11r	Improved ability to roam among access points without losing connectivity
802.11s	Proposed for a mesh network in which a set of nodes automatically form a network and pass packets

Figure 16.6 Major 802.11 standards and the purpose of each.

In 2007, IEEE "rolled up" many of the existing 802.11 standards into a single document known as *802.11-2007*. The document describes basics, and has an appendix for each variant.

The point is:

Many variants of 802.11 have been created or proposed; each offers some advantage.

16.8 Wireless LAN Architecture

The three building blocks of a wireless LAN are: *access points*, which are informally called *base stations*, an interconnection mechanism, such as a switch or router used to connect access points, and a set of wireless *hosts*, also called wireless *nodes* or wireless *stations*. In principle, two types of wireless LANs are possible:

- Ad hoc — wireless hosts communicate among themselves without a base station

- Infrastructure — a wireless host only communicates with an access point, and the access point relays all packets

In practice few ad hoc networks exist. Instead, an organization or service provider deploys a set of access points, and each wireless host communicates through one of the access points. For example, a private company or a university might deploy access points throughout its buildings. Figure 16.7 illustrates the architecture.

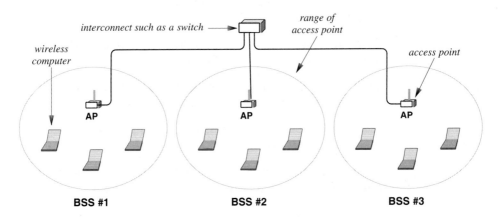

Figure 16.7 Illustration of an infrastructure architecture for a wireless LAN.

The wired connections that extend to access points usually consist of twisted pair Ethernet. The set of computers within range of a given access point is known as a *Basic Service Set (BSS)*†. In the figure, three Basic Service Sets exist, one for each access point.

To summarize:

> *Most wireless LANs use an infrastructure architecture in which a wireless computer communicates through an access point (base station).*

---

†Analogous to the cellular telephone system, the region reached by a given access point is informally called a *cell*.

16.9 Overlap, Association, And 802.11 Frame Format

In practice, many details complicate an infrastructure architecture. On one hand, if a pair of access points are too far apart, a *dead zone* will exist between them (i.e., a physical location with no wireless connectivity). On the other hand, if a pair of access points is too close together, an overlap will exist in which a wireless host can reach both access points. Furthermore, most wireless LANs connect to the Internet. Thus, the interconnect mechanism usually has an additional wired connection to an Internet router. Figure 16.8 illustrates the architecture.

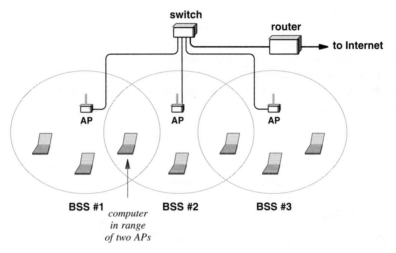

Figure 16.8 Illustration of an infrastructure with overlapping regions.

To handle overlap, 802.11 networks require a wireless host to *associate* with a single access point. That is, a wireless host sends frames to a particular access point, which forwards the frames across the network. Figure 16.9 illustrates the 802.11 frame format, and shows that when used with an infrastructure architecture, the frame carries the MAC address of an access point as well as the address of an Internet router.

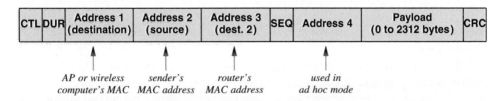

Figure 16.9 The frame format used with an 802.11 wireless LAN.

16.10 Coordination Among Access Points

An interesting question arises: to what extent do access points need to coordinate? Many early access point designs were complex. The access points coordinated to provide seamless mobility similar to the cellular phone system. That is, the access points communicated among themselves to insure smooth handoff as a wireless computer moved from the region of one access point to the region of another. For example, some designs measured signal strength, and attempted to move a wireless node to a new access point when the signal received at the new access point exceeded the signal strength at the existing access point.

As an alternative, some vendors began to offer lower cost, less complex access points that do not coordinate. The vendors argue that signal strength does not provide a valid measure of mobility, that a mobile computer can handle changing from one access point to another, and that the wired infrastructure connecting access points has sufficient capacity to allow more centralized coordination. A less complex access point design is especially appropriate in situations where an installation consists of a single access point.

To summarize:

Two basic approaches exist: complex access points coordinate to insure smooth handoff or lower cost access points operate independently and rely on wireless computers to change their association from one access point to another.

16.11 Contention And Contention-Free Access

The original 802.11 standard defined two general approaches for channel access. They can be characterized as:

- Point Coordinated Function (PCF) for contention-free service
- Distributed Coordinated Function (DCF) for contention-based service

Point-coordinated service means that an access point controls stations in the Basic Service Set (BSS) to insure that transmissions do not interfere with one another. For example, an access point can assign each station a separate frequency. In practice, PCF is never used.

The distributed coordinated function arranges for each station in a BSS to run a random access protocol. Recall from Chapter 14 that wireless networks can experience a *hidden station problem*, where two stations can communicate but a third station can only receive the signal from one of them. Also recall that to solve the problem, 802.11 networks use *Carrier Sense Multi-Access with Collision Avoidance (CSMA/CA)* which requires a pair to exchange *Ready To Send* (*RTS*) and *Clear To Send* (*CTS*) messages before transmitting a packet. The 802.11 standard includes several details that Chapter 14 omits. For example, the standard defines three timing parameters as follows:

- SIFS — Short Inter-Frame Space of 10 μsec
- DIFS — Distributed Inter-Frame Space of 50 μsec
- Slot Time of 20 μsec

Intuitively, the SIFS parameter defines how long a receiving station waits before sending an ACK or other response; the DIFS parameter, which is equal to SIFS plus two Slot Times, defines how long a channel must be idle before a station can attempt transmission. Figure 16.10 illustrates how the parameters are used in a packet transmission.

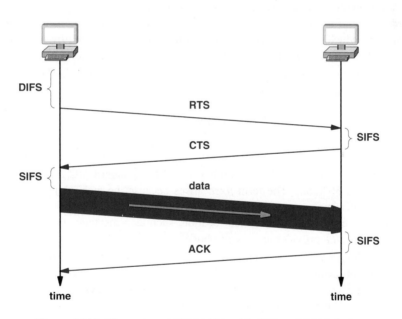

Figure 16.10 Illustration of CSMA/CA with SIFS and DIFS timing.

The point is:

> *The CSMA/CA technique used in Wi-Fi networks includes timing parameters that specify how long a station waits before sending an initial packet and how long a station waits before sending a reply.*

Physical separation among stations and electrical noise makes it difficult to distinguish between weak signals, interference, and collisions. Therefore, Wi-Fi networks do not employ collision detection. That is, the hardware does not attempt to sense interference during a transmission. Instead, a sender waits for an acknowledgement (*ACK*) message. If no ACK arrives, the sender assumes the transmission was lost, and employs a *backoff* strategy similar to the strategy used for wired Ethernet. In practice, 802.11 networks that have few users and do not experience electrical interference seldom need retransmission. However, other 802.11 networks experience frequent packet loss and depend on retransmission.

16.12 Wireless MAN Technology and WiMax

In general, MAN technologies have not been commercially successful. One wireless MAN technology stands out as having the potential for success. The technology is standardized by IEEE under the category *802.16*. A group of companies coined the term *WiMAX*, which is interpreted to mean *World-wide Interoperability for Microwave Access*, and formed the *WiMAX Forum* to promote use of the technology.

Two main versions of WiMAX are being developed that differ in their overall approach. The two are commonly referred to as:

- Fixed WiMAX
- Mobile WiMAX

Fixed WiMAX refers to systems built using IEEE standard *802.16-2004*, which is informally called *802.16d*. The term *fixed* arises because the technology does not provide for handoff among access points. Thus, it is designed to provide connections between a service provider and a fixed location, such as a residence or office building, rather than between a provider and a cell phone.

Mobile WiMAX refers to systems built according to standard *802.16e-2005*, which is informally abbreviated *802.16e*. As the term *mobile* implies, the technology offers handoff among access points, which means a mobile WiMAX system can be used with portable devices such as laptop computers or cell phones.

WiMAX offers broadband communication that can be used in a variety of ways. Some service providers plan to use WiMAX as an Internet access technology that spans the last mile. Others see the potential of WiMAX to provide a general-purpose interconnection among physical sites, especially in a city. Another type of interconnection is known as *backhaul* — the connection between a service provider's central network facility and remote locations, such as cell towers. Figure 16.11 lists a few of the proposed uses.

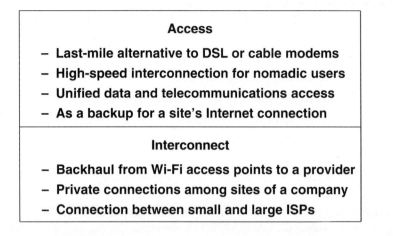

Figure 16.11 Potential uses of WiMAX technology.

In general, deployments of WiMAX used for backhaul will have the highest data rates, and will use frequencies that require a clear *Line-Of-Sight* (*LOS*) between two communicating entities. LOS stations are typically mounted on towers or on tops of buildings. Although deployments used for Internet access may used fixed or mobile WiMAX, such deployments usually use frequencies that do not require LOS. Thus, they are classified as *Non-Line-Of-Sight* (*NLOS*). Figure 16.12 illustrates the two deployments.

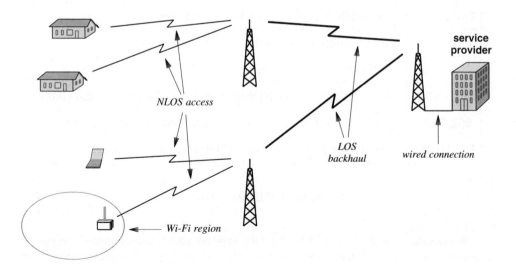

Figure 16.12 Illustration of WiMAX used for access and backhaul.

The key features of WiMAX can be summarized as follows:

- Uses licensed spectrum (i.e., offered by carriers)
- Each cell can cover a radius of 3 to 10 Km
- Uses scalable orthogonal FDM
- Guarantees quality of services (for voice or video)
- Can transport 70 Mbps in each direction at short distances
- Provides 10 Mbps over a long distance (10 Km)

To summarize:

> *WiMAX is a wireless LAN technology that can be used for backhaul, fixed, or mobile access; deployments for access do not require a clear line-of-sight.*

16.13 PAN Technologies And Standards

IEEE has assigned the number 802.15 to PAN standards. Several task groups and industry consortia have been formed for each of the key PAN technologies. Figure 16.13 lists the major PAN standards.

Standard	Purpose
802.15.1a	Bluetooth technology (1 Mbps; 2.4 GHz)
802.15.2	Coexistence among PANs (noninterference)
802.15.3	High rate PAN (55 Mbps; 2.4 GHz)
802.15.3a	Ultra Wideband (UWB) high rate PAN (110 Mbps; 2.4 GHz)
802.15.4	Zigbee technology – low data rate PAN for remote control
802.15.4a	Alternative low data rate PAN that uses low power

Figure 16.13 IEEE PAN standards.

Bluetooth. The IEEE 802.15.1a standard evolved after vendors created *Bluetooth* technology as a short-distance wireless connection technology. The characteristics of Bluetooth technology are:

- Wireless replacement for cables (e.g., headphones or mouse)
- Uses 2.4 GHz frequency band
- Short distance (up to 5 meters, with variations that extend the range to 10 or 50 meters)
- Device is *master* or *slave*
- Master grants permission to slave
- Data rate is up to 721 Kbps

Ultra Wideband (UWB). The idea behind UWB communication is that spreading data across many frequencies requires less power to reach the same distance. The key characteristics of UWB are:

- Uses wide spectrum of frequencies
- Consumes very low power
- Short distance (2 to 10 meters)
- Signal permeates obstacles such as walls
- Data rate of 110 at 10 meters, and up to 500 Mbps at 2 meters
- IEEE unable to resolve disputes and form a single standard

Zigbee. The Zigbee standard (802.15.4) arose from a desire to standardize wireless remote control technology, especially for industrial equipment. Because remote control units only send short commands, high data rates are not required. The chief characteristics of Zigbee are:

- Wireless standard for remote control, not data
- Target is industry as well as home automation
- Three frequency bands used (868 MHz, 915 MHz, and 2.4 GHz)
- Data rate of 20, 40, or 250 Kbps, depending on frequency band
- Low power consumption
- Three levels of security being defined

16.14 Other Short-Distance Communication Technologies

Although not normally grouped with wireless PANs, two other wireless technologies provide communication over short distances. InfraRED technologies provide control and low-speed data communications, and RFID technologies are used with sensors.

InfraRED. InfraRED technology is often used in remote controls, and may be used as a cable replacement (e.g., for a wireless mouse). The *Infrared Data Association*

(*IrDA*) has produced a set of standards that are widely accepted. The chief characteristics of the IrDA technology are:

- Family of standards for various speeds and purposes
- Practical systems have range of one to several meters
- Directional transmission with a cone covering $30°$
- Data rates between 2.4 Kbps (control) and 16 Mbps (data)
- Generally low power consumption with very-low power versions
- Signal may reflect from surfaces, but cannot penetrate solid objects

Radio Frequency Identification (*RFID*). The RFID technology uses an interesting form of wireless communication to create a mechanism whereby a small *tag* contains identification information that a receiver can "pull" from the tag.

- Over 140 RFID standards exist for a variety of applications
- Passive RFIDs draw power from the signal sent by the reader
- Active RFIDs contain a battery, which may last up to 10 years
- Limited distance, although active RFIDs extend farther than passive
- Can use frequencies from less than 100 MHz to 868-954 MHz
- Used for inventory control, sensors, passports, and other applications

16.15 Wireless WAN Technologies

Wireless WAN technologies can be divided into two categories:

- Cellular communication systems
- Satellite communication systems

16.15.1 Cellular Communication Systems

Cellular systems were originally designed to provide voice services to mobile customers. Therefore, the system was designed to interconnect cells to the public telephone network. Increasingly, cellular systems are being used to provide data services and Internet connectivity.

In terms of architecture, each cell contains a tower, and a group of (usually adjacent) cells is connected to a *Mobile Switching Center*. The center tracks a mobile user, and manages handoff as the user passes from one cell to another. Figure 16.14 illustrates how cells might be arranged along a highway.

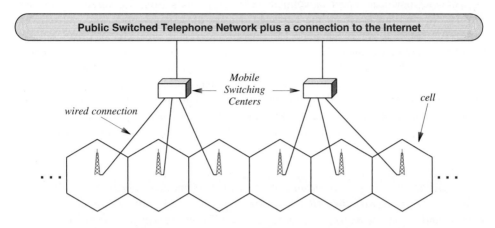

Figure 16.14 Illustration of the cellular architecture.

When a user moves between two cells that connect to the same Mobile Switching Center, the switching center handles the change. When a user passes from one geographic region to another, two Mobile Switching Centers are involved in the handoff.

In theory, perfect cellular coverage occurs if each cell forms a hexagon because the cells can be arranged in a honeycomb. In practice, cellular coverage is imperfect. Most cell towers use *omnidirectional* antennas that transmit in a circular pattern. However, obstructions and electrical interference can attenuate a signal or cause an irregular pattern. As a result, in some cases, cells overlap and in others, gaps exist with no coverage. Figure 16.15 illustrates ideal and realistic coverage.

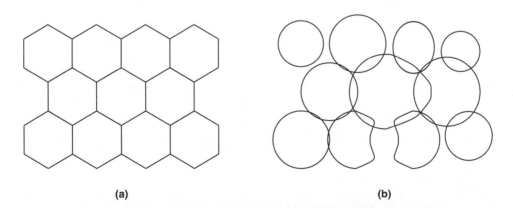

Figure 16.15 Illustration of (a) an idealized cellular coverage, and (b) a realistic version with overlaps and gaps.

Another practical aspect of cellular technology arises from the variability of cell density. In rural areas where the expected density of cell phones is low, cell size is large — a single tower is adequate for a large geographic area. In an urban setting, however, many cell phones are concentrated in a given area. For example, consider a city block in a large metropolitan area. In addition to pedestrians and people riding in vehicles, such an area can contain office or apartment buildings with many occupants. To handle more cell phones, designers break a region into many cells. Thus, unlike the idealized structure in Figure 16.15a which has a single cell size, a practical deployment uses various size cells, with smaller cells used to cover metropolitan areas. The point is:

Although it is easy to visualize cells as a uniform honeycomb, practical systems vary the cell size according to the density of cell phones, and obstructions cause coverage to be irregular, which results in overlaps and gaps.

16.16 Cell Clusters And Frequency Reuse

Cellular communication follows a key principle:

Interference can be minimized if an adjacent pair of cells do not use the same frequency.

To implement the principle, cellular planners employ a *cluster* approach in which a small pattern of cells is replicated. Figure 16.16 illustrates clusters of size 3, 4, 7, and 12 that are commonly used.

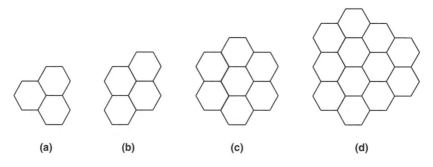

(a)   (b)   (c)   (d)

Figure 16.16 Illustration of typical cell clusters.

In geometric terms, each of the shapes in the figure can be used to tile a plane. That is, by replicating the same shape, it is possible to cover an entire area without leaving any gaps. Furthermore, if each cell in a given shape is assigned a unique frequency, the repeated pattern will not assign the same frequency to any pair of adjacent cells. For example, Figure 16.17 illustrates a replication of the 7-cell cluster with a letter in each cell to denote the frequency assigned to the cell.

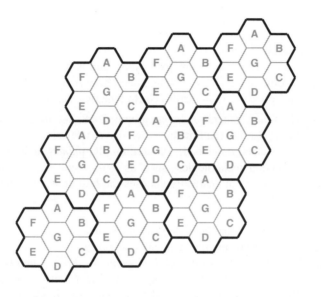

Figure 16.17 Illustration of frequency assignment when a 7-cell cluster is replicated.

In the figure, each letter corresponds to a particular frequency, and each cell within a cluster is assigned a frequency. As the figure shows, when the cluster pattern is replicated, no adjacent cells share a common frequency.

16.17 Generations Of Cellular Technologies

The telecommunications industry divides cellular technologies into four generations that are labeled *1G*, *2G*, *3G*, and *4G*, with intermediate versions labeled *2.5G* and *3.5G*. The generations can be characterized as follows:

- *1G.* The first generation began in the latter 1970s, and extended through the 1980s. The systems, which were originally called *cellular mobile radio telephones,* used analog signals to carry voice.

- *2G* and *2.5G.* The second generation began in the early 1990s and continues to be used. The main distinction between 1G and 2G arises because 2G uses digital signals to carry voice. The label *2.5G* is used for systems that extend a 2G system to include some 3G features.

- *3G* and *3.5G.* The third generation began in the 2000s, and focuses on the addition of higher-speed data services. A 3G system offers download rates of 400 Kbps to 2 Mbps, and is intended to support applications such as web browsing and photo sharing. 3G allows a single telephone to roam across North America, Japan, and Europe.

- *4G.* The fourth generation began around 2008, and focuses on support for real-time multimedia, such as a television program or high-speed video download. In addition, 4G phones include multiple connection technologies, such as Wi-Fi and satellite; at any time, the phone automatically chooses the best connection technology available.

A wide variety of cellular technologies and standards have evolved. When 2G emerged, many groups each attempted to choose an approach and create a standard. The *European Conference Of Postal and Telecommunications Administrators* chose a TDMA technology known as *Global System for Mobile Communications* (*GSM*), and created a system that was intended as a worldwide standard. In the United States, each carrier created a network with its own technology. Motorola invented a TDMA system known as *iDEN.* Most US and Asian carriers adopted a CDMA approach that was standardized as *IS-95A.* Japan created a TDMA technology known as *PDC.* Figure 16.18 summarizes major 2G standards and some of the 2.5G standards that evolved; various other technologies, not listed in the figure, played a minor role.

The standards listed in the figure each provide a basic communication mechanism over which many services can operate. For example, the *General Packet Radio Service* (*GPRS*) is available to subscribers who have GSM or IS-136 access. Once he or she subscribes to GPRS, a user can choose to invoke services that run on GPRS. The *Short Message Service* (SMS) is used for texting, the *Wireless Application Service* (WAP) is used to access the Internet, and the *Multimedia Messaging service* (*MMS*) is used for web access. Typically, service providers charge extra for GPRS service, with the rate usually billed per unit of data transferred (e.g., per megabyte).

After GPRS, digital technologies have been developed that use more sophisticated modulation and multiplexing techniques to increase data rates. *Enhanced Data rate for GSM Evolution* (*EDGE*), which is also known as *Enchanced GPRS* (*EGPRS*), offers a transfer rate of up to 473.6 Kbps. A successor known as *EDGE Evolution* provides a peak data rate of 1 Mbps.

Approach	Standard	Generation
GSM	GSM	2G
	GPRS	2.5G
	EDGE (EGPRS)	2.5G
	EDGE Evolution	2.5G
	HSCSD	2.5G
CDMA	IS-95A	2G
	IS-95B	2.5G
TDMA	iDEN	2G
	IS-136	2G
	PDC	2G

Figure 16.18 Major second-generation cellular technologies.

By the time providers began to think about third generation technologies, it was apparent that customers wanted cell phone service that worked globally. As a result, providers pushed to make technologies interoperable, and the industry consolidated many of the approaches from 2G into a few key standards. IS-136, PDC, IS-95A, and EDGE all influenced the design of *UMTS*, a technology that uses *Wideband CDMA* (*WCDMA*). Meanwhile, IS-95B was extended to produce *CDMA 2000*, as Figure 16.19 indicates.

Approach	Standard	Successor To
WCDMA	UMTS	IS-136, IS-95A, EDGE, PDC
	HSDPA	UMTS
CDMA 2000	1xRTT	IS-95B
	EVDO	1xRTT
	EVDV	1xRTT

Figure 16.19 Third-generation cellular technologies.

Several competing standards evolved for third-generation data services. *EVDO* and *EVDV* emerged at approximately the same time. Each of the two combines CDMA and frequency division multiplexing techniques to increase the overall performance. EVDO, which is either expanded to *Evolution Data Optimized* or *Evolution Data Only*, is the most widely deployed. EVDO comes in two versions that differ in the rate at which data is delivered: 2.4 Mbps or 3.1 Mbps. An alternative named *High-Speed Downlink Packet Access* (*HSDPA*) offers download speeds of 14 Mbps†. Of course, carriers charge more for services that offer a higher data rate.

16.18 VSAT Satellite Technology

Chapter 7 describes the three types of communication satellites (i.e., LEO, MEO, and GEO), and Chapter 14 discusses channel access mechanisms, including reservation mechanisms that are used to provide TDMA across a satellite. This section concludes the discussion by describing specific satellite technologies.

The key to satellite communication is a parabolic antenna design that is known informally as a *dish*. The parabolic shape means that electromagnetic energy arriving from a distant satellite is reflected to a single focus point. By aiming the dish at a satellite and placing a detector at the focus point, a designer can guarantee that a strong signal is received. Figure 16.20 illustrates the design, and shows how incoming energy is reflected from the surface of the dish toward the receiver.

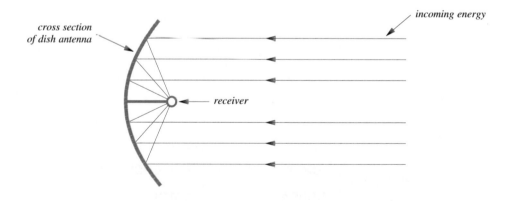

Figure 16.20 Illustration of reflection by a parabolic dish antenna.

To maximize the signal received, early satellite communication used ground stations with large dish antennas more than three meters in diameter. Although they are appropriate for situations such as a transatlantic link used by a telephone company, consumers and small businesses cannot place such ground stations on their property. Thus, a major change occurred with the emergence of a technology known as a *Very Small*

---

†A corresponding *High-Speed Uplink Packet Access* (*HSUPA*) protocol has also been defined, but has received less interest than HSDPA.

Aperture Terminal (*VSAT*) that uses dishes less than three meters in diameter. A typical VSAT antenna is less than one meter in diameter.

Many businesses use VSAT technology to link all their stores. For example, pharmacies such as Walgreens and CVS employ VSAT communication, as do fast-food chains such as Pizza Hut and Taco Bell, and retailers such as Wal Mart. In addition, VSAT services are available to consumers for both entertainment and Internet access.

VSAT satellites use three frequency ranges that differ in the strength of the signal delivered, the sensitivity to rain and other atmospheric conditions, and the area of the earth's surface covered (known as a satellite's *footprint*). Figure 16.21 describes the characteristics of each frequency band.

Band	Frequency	Footprint	Signal Strength	Effect Of Rain
C Band	3 - 7 GHz	Large	Low	Medium
Ku	10 - 18 GHz	Medium	Medium	Moderate
Ka	18 - 31 GHz	Small	High	Severe

Figure 16.21 Frequency bands used by VSAT technology and the characteristics of each.

16.19 GPS Satellites

Satellites in the *Global Positioning System* (*GPS*) provide accurate time and location information. Although it is not part of computer communication, location information is increasingly used in mobile networking. The key features are:

- Accuracy between 20 and 2 meters (military versions have higher accuracy)
- 24 total satellites orbit the earth
- Satellites arranged in six orbital planes
- Provides time synchronization that is used in some communication networks

In one sense, the technique used to obtain position information is straightforward: because all GPS satellites orbit in well-known positions, a receiver can determine a unique location on the earth's surface by finding the distance to three satellites. To see why, consider the set of points distance D_1 from satellite 1. The set defines a sphere. Similarly, the set of points distance D_2 from satellite 2 defines another sphere. A GPS system that is simultaneously D_1 from satellite 1 and D_2 from satellite 2 lies on the circle that is formed by the intersection of the two spheres. If the GPS system is also distance D_3 from satellite 3, the GPS system will be in the intersection of a third sphere with the circle, which results in two possible points. The satellites are arranged so that only one of the two points lies on the Earth's surface and the other is in space, making it easy to choose the correct point.

To compute distance, a GPS system applies the formula from Newtonian physics that specifies distance equals rate times time. The rate is constant (the speed of light, 3×10^9 meters per second). The time is computed by arranging for each GPS system to compute the local time, and for each satellite to have an accurate clock that is used to include a *timestamp* in the information being sent. A receiver can then subtract the timestamp from the local time to determine the time the information has been in transit.

16.20 Software Radio And The Future Of Wireless

The wide variety of wireless technologies described in the chapter each use special-purpose radio hardware. The antenna, transmitter, and receiver in a given device are designed to operate on predetermined frequencies using specific forms of modulation and multiplexing. A cell phone that can use GSM, Wi-Fi, and CDMA networks must have three completely separate radio systems, and must choose among them.

Traditional radios are being replaced by radios that follow a *programmable* paradigm in which features are controlled by software running on a processor. Figure 16.22 lists major radio features that can be controlled in a *software programmable radio*.

Feature	Description
Frequency	The exact set of frequencies used at a given time
Power	The amount of power the transmitter emits
Modulation	The signal and channel coding and modulation
Multiplexing	Any combination of CDMA, TDMA, FDMA and others
Signal Direction	Antennas can be tuned for a specific direction
MAC Protocol	All aspects of framing and MAC addressing

Figure 16.22 Features under control of software in a programmable radio.

The key technologies that enable software radios are: tunable analog filters and multiple antenna management. Analog chips are currently available that provide tunable analog filters. Thus, it is possible to select frequencies and control power. *Digital Signal Processors* (*DSPs*) are available to handle signal coding and modulation. The more interesting aspect of software radios concerns the use of multiple antennas. Instead of merely choosing an antenna to use at a given time, a software radio can use multiple antennas simultaneously to provide *spatial multiplexing*, a technique that allows a signal to be transmitted or received from a given direction. We use the term *Multiple-Input Multiple-Output* (*MIMO*) to denote a system that employs multiple antennas for both transmission and reception (i.e., can aim transmission or reception).

Software programmable radios have emerged from the research lab, and are already being deployed by the U.S. military. In addition, the *Universal Software Radio Peripheral* (*USRP*) and *GNU Radio* are currently available for experimentation. A few details need to be worked out before programmable radios will appear in commercial products. First, the cost is currently too high (approximately $1000 US). Second, policies need to be established for spectrum use. In particular, devices that transmit electromagnetic energy are certified to insure that they do not interfere with other communication (e.g., a cell phone does not interfere with police or emergency communications). If a software radio can be reprogrammed, a consumer might inadvertently download a virus that could cause the radio to jam emergency channels. Thus, techniques are being investigated that will control the amount of power a software radio can generate on certain frequencies.

16.21 Summary

Many wireless communication technologies exist and are used to create wireless LANs, PANs, MANs, and WANs. IEEE has standardized several LAN and MAN technologies. Wi-Fi uses the IEEE 802.11 standards, with variants each assigned a suffix, such as 802.11b or 802.11g. Wireless LANs can be ad hoc or can use an infrastructure architecture with access points; the frame format includes a MAC address for an access point as well as a MAC address for a router beyond the access point.

In addition to LANs, wireless technologies are used for MANs and PANs. The main MAN technology is known as WiMAX, which can be used for backhaul or access. A variety of PAN technologies exist, including Bluetooth, Ultra Wideband, Zigbee, and IrDA. RFID tags provide another form of wireless communication used primarily for inventory and shipping.

Wireless WANs use cellular and satellite technologies. Cellular technologies are classified as 1G (analog), 2G (digital voice), 3G (digital voice plus data), and 4G (high-speed digital voice and data); many technologies exist. VSAT satellite technologies make it possible for businesses and consumers to have dish antennas on their property.

Emerging wireless systems use software programmable radios that allow software to control all aspects of radio transmission. Programmable radios are expensive, and are currently available for military and special uses.

EXERCISES

16.1 What is the Wi-Fi Alliance?

16.2 What features are controllable in a software radio?

16.3 Name three wireless PAN technologies, and give a short description of each.

16.4 What are the three blocks of frequencies used by wireless LANs and PANs?

16.5 Give the numeric prefix IEEE standards use for Wi-Fi networks.

16.6 To what does a cell tower connect?

16.7 What is RFID, and where is it used?

16.8 List three spread spectrum techniques, and give a general description of each.

16.9 Name the four generations of cellular technology, and describe each.

16.10 What is a VSAT satellite?

16.11 Name the three chief frequency bands used by communication satellites, and give the effect of weather on each.

16.12 Why is a satellite dish shaped in the form of a parabola?

16.13 List the IEEE standards that have been proposed or created for wireless LANs.

16.14 What are SIFS and DIFS, and why are they needed?

16.15 Why do most wireless LANs use an infrastructure approach rather than an ad hoc approach?

16.16 How many satellites are used in GPS, and how accurate is a GPS system?

16.17 Why must a wireless computer associate with a specific base station?

16.18 What is Zigbee, and where is it used?

16.19 An 802.11 header contains two destination addresses. Explain the purpose of each.

16.20 Name the two types of WiMAX technologies, and describe the purpose of each.

16.21 Give the characteristics of UWB technology.

16.22 What is a cell cluster, and how does a designer use clusters?

16.23 In addition to position, what does GPS provide?

16.24 What is GSM, and what standards does it comprise?

16.25 Look up OFDM on the Web, and give a one-paragraph description in your own words.

16.26 Does it make sense to use IrDA for applications such as file transfer? Why or why not?

16.27 What are the third-generation cellular technologies that use code-division multiplexing?

Chapter Contents

17

LAN Extensions: Fiber Modems, Repeaters, Bridges, and Switches

17.1 Introduction

Previous chapters describe LAN topologies and wiring schemes. A typical LAN is designed to span a few hundred meters, which means LAN technology works well within a single building or a small campus.

This chapter discusses two important concepts: mechanisms that can extend a LAN across a longer distance and LAN switching. The chapter introduces repeaters, bridges, and the spanning tree algorithm used to prevent forwarding loops.

17.2 Distance Limitation And LAN Design

Distance limitation is a fundamental part of LAN designs. When designing a network technology, engineers choose a combination of capacity, maximum delay, and distance that can be achieved at a given cost. One limitation on distance arises because hardware is engineered to emit a fixed amount of energy — if wiring is extended beyond the design limits, stations will not receive a sufficiently strong signal, and errors will occur. The point is:

> *A maximum length specification is a fundamental part of LAN technology; LAN hardware will not work correctly over wires that exceed the bound.*

17.3 Fiber Modem Extensions

Engineers have developed a variety of ways to extend LAN connectivity. As a general rule, extension mechanisms do not increase the strength of signals, nor do they merely extend cables. Instead, most extension mechanisms use standard interface hardware, and insert additional hardware components that can relay signals across longer distances.

The simplest LAN extension mechanism consists of an optical fiber and a pair of *fiber modems*, used to connect a computer to a remote Ethernet. Figure 17.1 illustrates the interconnection.

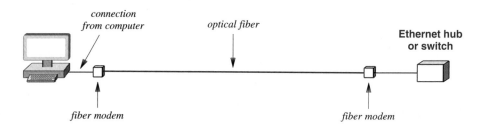

Figure 17.1 Illustration of fiber modems used to provide a connection between a computer and a remote Ethernet.

Each of the fiber modems contains hardware to perform two chores: accept packets over the Ethernet interface and send them over the optical fiber, and accept packets that arrive over the optical fiber and send them over the Ethernet interface†. If the modems offer a LAN interface on each end, standard interfaces can be used on the computer and the LAN device.

To summarize:

> *A pair of fiber modems and optical fibers can be used to provide a connection between a computer and a remote LAN such as an Ethernet.*

---

†In practice, implementations use a pair of fibers to allow simultaneous transmission in both directions.

17.4 Repeaters

A *repeater* is an analog device used to propagate LAN signals over long distances. A repeater does not understand packets or signal coding. Instead, it merely amplifies the signal received, and transmits the amplified version as output.

Repeaters were used extensively with the original Ethernet, and have been used with other LAN technologies. Recently, repeaters have been introduced with infrared receivers to permit a receiver to be located at a longer distance from a computer. For example, consider a situation in which the infrared receiver for a cable television controller must be in a different room than the controller. A repeater can extend the connection, as Figure 17.2 illustrates.

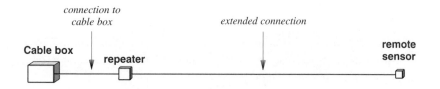

Figure 17.2 Illustration of an infrared sensor extended with a repeater.

To summarize:

> A *repeater* is an analog hardware device used to extend a LAN. The repeater amplifies and sends all incoming signals to the other side.

17.5 Bridges And Bridging

A *bridge* is a mechanism that connects two LAN segments (e.g., two hubs) and transfers packets between them. The bridge listens in *promiscuous mode* on each segment (i.e., receives all packets sent on the segment). When it receives an intact frame from one segment, the bridge forwards a copy of the frame to the other segment. Thus, two LAN segments connected by a bridge appear to behave like a single LAN — a computer connected to either segment can send a frame to any computer on the two segments. Furthermore, a broadcast frame is delivered to all computers on the two segments. Thus, computers do not know whether they are connected to a single LAN segment or a bridged LAN.

Originally, bridges were sold as independent hardware devices that each had two network connections. Currently, bridge technology is incorporated into other devices, such as a cable modem. Figure 17.3 illustrates the conceptual architecture.

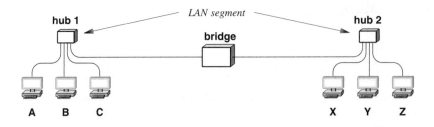

Figure 17.3 Illustration of six computers connected to a pair of bridged LAN segments.

To summarize:

> *A bridge is a mechanism used to connect two LAN segments and forward frames from one segment to another; computers cannot tell whether they are on a single segment or a bridged LAN.*

17.6 Learning Bridges And Frame Filtering

Bridges do not blindly forward a copy of each frame from one LAN to another. Instead, a bridge uses MAC addresses to perform *filtering*. That is, a bridge examines the destination address in a frame, and does not forward the frame onto the other LAN segment unless necessary. Of course, if the LAN supports broadcast or multicast, the bridge must forward a copy of each broadcast or multicast frame to make the bridged LAN operate like a single LAN.

How can a bridge know which computers are attached to which segments? Most bridges are called *adaptive* or *learning* bridges because they learn the locations of computers automatically. To do so, a bridge uses source addresses. When a frame arrives from a given segment, the bridge extracts the source address from the header, and adds the address to a list of computers attached to the segment. Of course, the bridge must then extract the MAC destination address from the frame, and use the address to determine whether to forward the frame. Thus, a bridge learns that a computer is present on a segment as soon as the computer transmits a frame.

To see how a bridge learns the locations of computers as frames are sent, consider the bridge in Figure 17.3. Figure 17.4 lists a sequence of packet transmissions, the location information that the bridge has accumulated at each step, and the disposition of the packet (i.e., the segments over which the packet is sent).

Event	Segment 1	Segment 2	Frame Sent
Bridge boots	–	–	–
A sends to B	A	–	Both Segments
B sends to A	A, B	–	Segment 1 only
X broadcasts	A, B	X	Both Segments
Y sends to A	A, B	X, Y	Both Segments
Y sends to X	A, B	X, Y	Segment 2 only
X sends to Z	A, B	X, Y	Both Segments
Z sends to X	A, B, C	X, Y, Z	Segment 2 only

Figure 17.4 Example of a learning bridge with computers A, B, and C on one
segment and computers X, Y, and Z on another.

We can summarize:

> *An adaptive bridge uses the source MAC address in a packet to
> record the location of the sender, and uses the destination MAC ad-
> dress to determine whether to forward the frame.*

17.7 Why Bridging Works Well

It is important to know that once a bridge learns the locations of all computers, a
bridged network can exhibit higher overall performance than a single LAN. To understand why, it is important to know that a bridge permits simultaneous transmission on
each segment. In Figure 17.3, for example, computer A can send a packet to computer
B at the same time computer X sends a packet to computer Y. Although it receives a
copy of each packet, the bridge will not forward either of them because each packet has
been sent to a destination on the same segment as the source. Thus, the bridge merely
discards the two frames without forwarding them. We can summarize:

> *Because a bridge permits simultaneous activity on attached segments,
> a pair of computers on one segment can communicate at the same
> time as a pair computers on another segment.*

The ability to localize communication makes it possible to bridge between buildings on a campus. Most communication is local (e.g., a computer communicates with a
printer in the same building more often than it communicates with a printer in another

building). Thus, a bridge can provide communication between buildings when needed, but does not send packets needlessly. DSL and cable modems also use the concept of bridging — the modem operates as a bridge between a local network on a subscriber's premise and a network at an ISP.

17.8 Distributed Spanning Tree

Consider Figure 17.5 that shows four LAN segments currently connected by three bridges and a fourth bridge about to be inserted. We assume that computers (not shown in the diagram) are also plugged into each of the hubs.

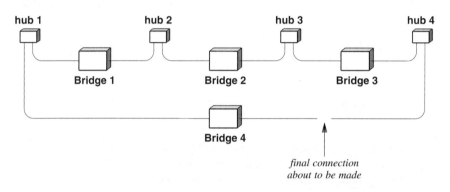

Figure 17.5 Illustration of a bridged network with a fourth bridge about to be inserted.

Before the fourth bridge is inserted, the network operates as expected — any computer can send a unicast frame to another computer, or send a broadcast or multicast frame to all computers. Broadcast and multicast work because a bridge always forwards a copy of a frame sent to a broadcast or multicast address. If a fourth bridge is inserted, a problem arises because a loop will exist. Unless at least one bridge is prevented from forwarding broadcasts, copies of a broadcast frame will continue to flow around the cycle forever, with computers attached to hubs receiving an endless number of copies.

To prevent a cycle from causing an endless loop, bridges implement an algorithm that computes a *Distributed Spanning Tree* (*DST*). That is, the algorithm views bridges as nodes in a graph, and imposes a tree on the graph (a tree is a graph that does not contain cycles). The original approach, developed at Digital Equipment Corporation in 1985, was designed for Ethernet networks, and is known as the *Spanning Tree Protocol* (*STP*). STP consists of three steps:

- Root election

- Shortest path computation

- Forwarding

To use STP, Ethernet bridges communicate among themselves using a multicast address that is reserved for spanning tree†:

01:80:C2:00:00:00

The first step consists of electing a root. The election is straightforward: bridges multicast a packet that contains their *bridge ID*, and the bridge with the smallest ID is chosen. To permit a manager to control the election, a bridge ID consists of two parts: a 16-bit configurable *priority number* and a 48-bit MAC address. When comparing IDs, a bridge compares the priority portion first, and uses the MAC address portion to break a tie. Thus, a manager can insure a bridge becomes the root by assigning a priority that is lower than any other bridge priority.

The second step is a shortest path computation. Each bridge computes a shortest path to the root bridge. The result is that links included in the shortest paths of all bridges form the spanning tree.

Once a spanning tree has been computed, bridges begin forwarding packets. An interface that connects to the shortest path is enabled for forwarding packets; an interface that does not lie on the shortest path is blocked, which means that no user packets can be sent over the interface.

Many variations of spanning tree have been designed and standardized. In 1990, IEEE created a standard named 802.1d; the standard was updated in 1998. IEEE standard 802.1q provides a way to run spanning tree on a set of logically independent networks that share a physical medium without any confusion or interference among the logical networks. Cisco created a proprietary version of spanning tree, *Per-VLAN Spanning Tree* (*PVST*) for use on a VLAN switch‡, and later updated the protocol to *PVST+*, making it compatible with 802.1q. In 1998, IEEE standard 802.1w introduced the *Rapid Spanning Tree Protocol* to reduce the time required for convergence after a topology change. Rapid Spanning Tree has been incorporated in 801.1d-2004, and now replaces STP. Versions known as the *Multiple Instance Spanning Tree Protocol* (*MISTP*) and *Multiple Spanning Tree Protocol* (*MSTP*) were defined to handle more complex VLAN switches; MSTP was incorporated into IEEE standard 802.1q-2003.

17.9 Switching And Layer 2 Switches

The concept of bridging helps explain a mechanism that forms the basis of modern Ethernets: *switching*. An *Ethernet switch*, sometimes called a *Layer 2 switch* is an electronic device that resembles a hub. Like a hub, a switch provides multiple *ports* that each attach to a single computer, and a switch allows computers to send frames to one

---

†By convention, Ethernet addresses are written in hexadecimal with colons separating each pair of hex digits.

‡The next sections describe switching and VLAN switches.

another. The difference between a hub and a switch arises from the way the devices operate: a hub operates as an analog device that forwards signals among computers, while a switch is a digital device that forwards packets. We can think of a hub as simulating a shared transmission medium, and think of a switch as simulating a bridged network that has one computer per LAN segment. Figure 17.6 illustrates the conceptual use of bridges in a switch.

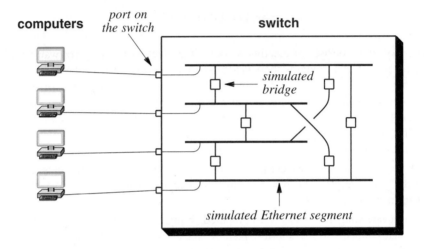

Figure 17.6 Conceptual organization of a switched LAN.

Although the figure provides a conceptual view, a switch does not contain separate bridges. Instead, a switch consists of an *intelligent interface* attached to each port and a central *fabric* that provides simultaneous transfer between pairs of interfaces. An interface contains a processor, memory, and other hardware needed to accept an incoming packet, consult a forwarding table, and send the packet across the fabric to the correct output port. The interface also accepts packets from the fabric, and transmits them out the port. Most important, because it contains memory, an interface can buffer arriving packets when an output port is busy. Thus, if computer 1 and computer 2 send packets to computer 3 simultaneously, either interface 1 or interface 2 will hold a packet while the other interface transmits. Figure 17.7 illustrates the architecture.

Physically, switches are available in many sizes. The smallest consist of an inexpensive, stand-alone device that provides four connections, which are sufficient to interconnect a computer, printer, and two other devices such as a scanner. Businesses use the largest switches to connect tens of thousands of computers and other devices throughout the company.

The chief advantage of using a switched LAN instead of a hub is parallelism. Although a hub can only support one transmission at a time, a switch permits multiple transfers to occur at the same time, provided the transfers are independent (i.e., only one packet is being transferred to a given port at a given time). Thus, if a switch has N ports connected to N computers, $N/2$ transfers can occur at the same time. The point is:

> *Because it handles packets instead of signals and uses a fabric to provide parallel internal paths, a switch with N ports can transfer up to N/2 packets simultaneously.*

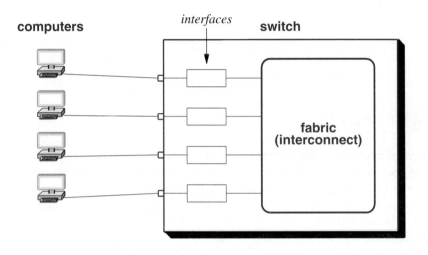

Figure 17.7 Illustration of the architecture of a switch.

17.10 VLAN Switches

Switches have been extended by adding virtualization, and the result is known as a *Virtual Local Area Network switch* (*VLAN switch*). The concept is straightforward: allow a manager to configure a single switch to emulate multiple, independent switches. That is, a manager specifies a set of ports on the switch and designates them to be on virtual LAN 1, designates another set of ports to be on virtual LAN 2, and so on. When a computer on virtual LAN 2 broadcasts a packet, only those computers on the same virtual LAN receive a copy (i.e., once configured, a VLAN switch makes it appear that there are multiple switches).

Dividing computers into separate *broadcast domains* does not appear important until one considers a large company or a service provider. In each case, it may be important to guarantee that a set of computers can communicate without others receiving the packets and without receiving packets from outsiders. For example, a company may choose to provide a firewall between computers in the CEO's office and other computers in the company†. Configuring a separate VLAN for the CEO's computers allows a firewall to be installed.

---

†Chapter 30 describes firewalls.

17.11 Bridging Used With Other Devices

Although our description characterizes a bridge as a stand-alone device, bridging is a fundamental concept that has been incorporated into many devices. For example, a DSL or cable modem provides a form of bridging: the modem provides an Ethernet connection at a subscriber's residence, and transfers Ethernet packets between the subscriber's location and the provider's network. Some wireless technologies also use a form of bridging to transfer frames from a mobile device to a provider's network. Thus,

> *Although vendors no longer sell stand-alone bridge devices, the concept of bridging has been incorporated in network devices, such as modems used in access technologies.*

17.12 Summary

Several mechanisms have been created to extend LANs across a longer geographic distance. A pair of fiber modems can be used to extend the connection between a computer and a LAN. A repeater is an analog device that amplifies electrical signals from one LAN segment and transmits a copy on the other, and vice versa. A bridge is a digital device that connects two LAN segments and transfers packets between them.

To optimize forwarding, a bridge examines MAC addresses in the header of each frame, and learns which computers are attached to each segment. Once a bridge learns the location of a computer, the bridge does not forward frames that are sent to the computer from other computers on the same segment.

An Ethernet switch connects multiple computers, and forwards frames among them. Conceptually, a switch functions like a set of LAN segments interconnected by bridges. In practice, a switch contains a set of intelligent interfaces that use a high-speed hardware interconnection mechanism called a fabric. The chief advantage of a switch over a hub is that a switch can transfer multiple packets simultaneously, provided that only one packet is destined for a given output port. A VLAN switch allows a manager to configure a switch to act like a set of independent switches.

EXERCISES

17.1 Can a bridge connect a Wi-Fi network to an Ethernet? Can a switch? Why or why not?

17.2 Give a precise statement of conditions under which an adaptive bridge will forward a packet.

17.3   Consult the Web to find a description of the spanning tree algorithm, and write a computer program that simulates bridges forming a spanning tree.

17.4   Do computers on a bridged Ethernet receive spanning tree packets? Explain.

17.5   When bridging is used with a satellite link, two bridges are typically used, one on each side. Explain why.

17.6   When an optical fiber is used to extend a connection to a LAN, what additional devices are needed?

17.7   If a television set provides a wired extension for a remote infrared sensor, what technology is likely used?

17.8   Consider a packet sent on a bridged LAN to a nonexistent address. Across how many segments will bridges forward the packet?

17.9   Suppose a network contains three Ethernet segments operating at 100 Mbps connected by two bridges and that each segment contains one computer. If two computers send to a third, what is the maximum data rate a given sender can achieve? The minimum?

17.10   Write a computer program that simulates a bridge function. Let two files of data simulate frames transmitted on two segments to which the bridge attaches. Assume that each simulated frame contains a source and destination address. To perform the simulation, read a frame from the first file, then a frame from the second file, and so on. For each frame, display whether the bridge will forward a copy of the frame to the other LAN segment.

17.11   Extend the program in the previous exercise to simulate a VLAN switch. Have the program begin by reading configuration information that specifies a set of hosts and a set of virtual LANs to which they should be attached. Create a file of frames that each specify the computer sending the frame (i.e., the port on the switch over which the frame arrives) and a destination address. Show how each frame is forwarded.

17.12   According to Figure 17.6, can two computers attached to a switched LAN transmit packets simultaneously? Explain.

17.13   Extend Figure 17.6 to have five ports.

17.14   In the previous exercise, write an equation that gives the number of simulated bridges needed as a function of the number of ports.

17.15   If two computers are connected on a bridged network, are changes required in addressing or in applications? Explain.

17.16   Use a network analyzer to observe traffic on a bridged Ethernet. What do you observe after a bridge reboots?

Chapter Contents

18

WAN Technologies And Dynamic Routing

18.1 Introduction

Chapters in this part of the text describe a variety of wired and wireless packet switching technologies. The previous chapter considered LAN extensions. This chapter considers the structure of a network that spans an arbitrarily large area. The chapter describes the basic components used to build a packet switching system, and explains the fundamental concept of routing. The chapter presents the two basic routing algorithms, and explains the advantages of each. A later chapter extends the discussion of routing to the Internet, and presents routing protocols that use the algorithms described here.

18.2 Large Spans And Wide Area Networks

We said that networking technologies can be classified according to the distance spanned:

- PAN — spans a region near an individual
- LAN — spans a building or campus
- MAN — spans a large metropolitan area
- WAN — spans multiple cities or countries

Consider a company that uses a satellite bridge to connect LANs at two sites. Should the network be classified as a WAN or as an extended LAN? Does the answer change if the company only has a PC and a printer at each site? Yes, it does. The key issue that separates WAN technologies from LAN technologies is *scalability* — a WAN must be able to grow as needed to connect many sites spread across large geographic distances, with many computers at each site. For example, a WAN should be able to connect all the computers in a large corporation that has offices or factories at dozens of locations spread across thousands of square miles. Furthermore, a technology is not classified as a WAN unless it can deliver reasonable performance for a large scale network. That is, a WAN does not merely connect to many computers at many sites — it must provide sufficient capacity to permit all computers to communicate. Thus, a satellite bridge that connects a pair of PCs and printers is merely an extended LAN.

18.3 Traditional WAN Architecture

Traditional WAN technologies were developed before Local Area Networks emerged, before personal computers were available, and before the Internet had been created†. Thus, traditional WAN architectures were designed to connect a set of sites, where each site had a few, large computers.

Without LAN technologies available, WAN designers chose to create a special-purpose hardware device that could be placed at each site. Known as a *packet switch*, the device provides local connections for computers at the site as well as connections for data circuits that lead to other sites.

Conceptually, a packet switch consists of a small computer system with a processor, memory, and I/O devices used to send and receive packets. Early packet switches were constructed from conventional computers; the packet switches used in the highest-speed WANs require special-purpose hardware. Figure 18.1 illustrates the internal architecture.

---

†Early WANs were called *long-haul networks*.

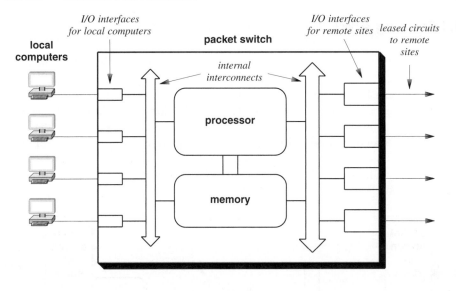

Figure 18.1 Illustration of traditional packet switch architecture.

As the figure shows, a packet switch contains two types of I/O devices. The first, which operates at high-speed, is used to connect the switch to a digital circuit that leads to another packet switch. The second type of I/O device, which operates at a lower speed, is used to connect the switch to an individual computer.

Since the advent of LAN technology, most WANs separate a packet switch into two parts: a Layer 2 switch that connects local computers and a router that connects to other sites. Part 4 of the text discusses Internet routers in detail, and explains how the concepts covered here apply to the Internet; for now, it is sufficient to understand that communication with local computers can be separated from transmission across a WAN. Figure 18.2 illustrates the separation.

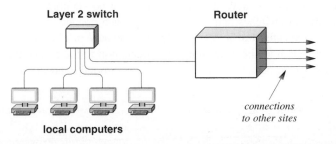

Figure 18.2 Illustration of a modern WAN site with local communication handled by a separate LAN.

18.4 Forming A WAN

Conceptually, a WAN can be formed by interconnecting a set of sites. The exact details of the interconnections depend on the data rate needed, the distance spanned, and the delay that can be tolerated. Many WANs use leased data circuits as described in Chapter 12 (e.g., a T3 circuit or an OC-12 circuit). However, other forms are also available, such as microwave and satellite channels. In addition to choosing the technology for a connection, a designer must choose a topology. For a given set of sites, many topologies are possible. For example, Figure 18.3 illustrates a possible way to interconnect four traditional packet switches and eight computers.

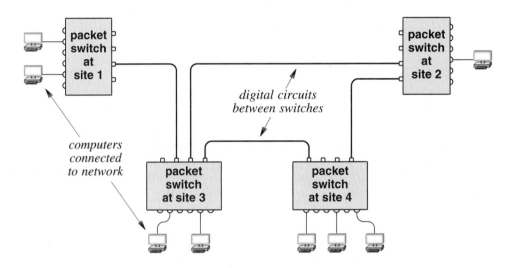

Figure 18.3 An example WAN formed by interconnecting packet switches.

As the figure shows, a WAN does not need to be symmetric — the interconnections among packet switches and the capacity of each connection can be chosen to accommodate the expected traffic and provide redundancy in case of failure. In the figure, the packet switch at site *1* has only one connection to the rest of the network, while the packet switches at other sites have at least two external connections. The point is:

> *A traditional WAN is formed by interconnecting packet switches; a packet switch at each site connects to computers. The topology and capacity of connections are chosen to accommodate expected traffic and need for redundancy.*

18.5 Store And Forward Paradigm

The goal of a WAN is to allow as many computers as possible to send packets simultaneously. The fundamental paradigm used to achieve simultaneous transmission is known as *store and forward*. To perform store and forward processing, a packet switch *buffers* packets in memory. The *store* operation occurs when a packet arrives: I/O hardware inside the packet switch places a copy of the packet in memory. The *forward* operation occurs once a packet has arrived and is waiting in memory. The processor examines the packet, determines its destination, and sends the packet over the I/O interface that leads to the destination.

A system that uses the store and forward paradigm can keep each data link busy, and thus, increase overall performance. More important, if multiple packets are sent to the same output device, the packet switch can accept and hold packets in memory until the device is ready. For example, consider packet transmission on the network in Figure 18.3. Suppose the two computers at site *1* each generate a packet destined for a computer at site *3* at approximately the same time. The two computers can send their packet to the packet switch simultaneously. As each packet arrives, I/O hardware on the packet switch places the packet in memory and informs the packet switch processor. The processor examines each packet's destination, and determines that the packets should be sent to site *3*. If the output interface that leads to site *3* is idle when a packet arrives, transmission starts immediately. If the output device is busy, the processor places the outgoing packet in a queue associated with the device. As soon as it finishes sending a packet, the device extracts and sends the next packet in the queue.

The concept can be summarized:

> *Wide area packet switching systems use the store-and-forward technique in which packets arriving at a packet switch are placed in a queue until the packet switch can forward them on toward their destination. The technique allows a packet switch to buffer a short burst of packets that arrive simultaneously.*

18.6 Addressing In A WAN

From the view of an attached computer, a traditional WAN network operates similar to a LAN. Each WAN technology defines the exact frame format a computer uses when sending and receiving data. Furthermore, each computer connected to a WAN is assigned an address. When sending a frame to another computer, the sender must supply the destination address.

Although details vary, WANs addresses follow a key concept that is used in the Internet: *hierarchical addressing*. Conceptually, hierarchical addressing divides each address into two parts:

$$(\text{site, computer at the site})$$

In practice, instead of a identifying a site, each packet switch is assigned a unique number, which means that the first part of an address identifies a packet switch and the second part identifies a specific computer. For example, Figure 18.4 shows two-part hierarchical addresses assigned to computers connected to a pair of packet switches.

Figure 18.4 Example of an address hierarchy where each address identifies a packet switch and a computer attached to the switch.

The figure shows each address as a pair of decimal integers. For example, a computer connected to port *6* on packet switch *2* is assigned address *[2,6]*. In practice, an address is represented as a single binary value, with some bits of the binary value used to represent a packet switch and others used to identify a computer. In Part 4 of the text, we will see that the Internet uses the same scheme: each Internet address consists of a binary number where a prefix of the bits identify a specific network in the Internet and the remainder of the bits identify a computer attached to the network.

18.7 Next-Hop Forwarding

The importance of hierarchical addressing becomes clear when one considers packet processing. When a packet arrives, a packet switch must choose an outgoing path over which to forward the packet. If a packet is destined for a local computer, the switch sends the packet directly to the computer. Otherwise, the packet must be forwarded over one of the connections that leads to another switch. To make the choice, a packet switch examines the destination address in the packet, and extracts the packet switch number. If the number in the destination address is identical to the packet switch's own ID, the packet is intended for a computer on the local packet switch. Otherwise, the packet is intended for a computer on another packet switch. Algorithm 18.1 explains the computation.

The important idea is that a packet switch does not need to keep complete information about how to reach all possible computers, nor does a switch need to compute the entire route a packet will follow through the network. Instead, a switch bases forwarding on packet switch IDs, which means that a switch only needs to know which outgoing link to use to reach a given switch.

Algorithm 18.1

Given:

    A packet that has arrived at packet switch Q

Perform:

    The next-hop forwarding step

Method:

    Extract the destination address from the packet;

    Divide the address into a packet switch number, P, and a

        computer identification, C;

    if (P == Q) {   /* the destination is local */

        Forward the packet to local computer C;

    } else {

        Select a link that leads to another packet switch, and forward

            the packet over the link;

    }

Algorithm 18.1 The two steps a packet switch uses to forward a packet when using next-hop forwarding.

We say that a switch only needs to compute the *next hop* for a packet. The process is called *next-hop forwarding*, and is analogous to the way airlines list flights. Suppose an airline passenger traveling from San Francisco to Miami finds that the only available itinerary involves three flights: the first from San Francisco to Dallas, the second from Dallas to Atlanta, and the third from Atlanta to Miami. Although the ultimate destination (Miami) remains the same throughout the trip, the next hop changes at each airport. When the passenger leaves San Francisco, the next hop is Dallas. When the passenger is in Dallas, the next hop is Atlanta, and when the passenger is in Atlanta, the next hop is Miami.

To make the computation efficient, packet switches use table lookup. That is, each packet switch contains a *forwarding table*† that lists all possible packet switches and gives a next hop for each. Figure 18.5 illustrates next-hop forwarding with a trivial example.

---

†Although purists insist on the name *forwarding table*, such tables were originally called *routing tables*, and the terminology is still widely used in the networking industry.

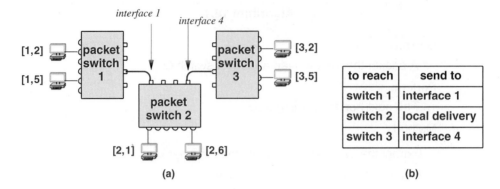

Figure 18.5 (a) A network of three packet switches, and (b) the next-hop forwarding table for switch 2.

To use a forwarding table, a switch extracts a packet's destination address, and
uses the packet switch portion of the address as an index in the forwarding table. For
example, consider the table in Figure 18.5b. If a packet is destined for *[3,5]*, the switch
extracts *3*, consults the table, and forwards the packet to interface *4*, which leads to
switch *3*.

Using only one part of a two-part hierarchical address to forward a packet has two
practical consequences. First, the computation time required to forward a packet is reduced because the forwarding table can be organized as an array that uses indexing instead of searching. Second, the forwarding table contains one entry per packet switch
instead of one entry per destination computer. The reduction in table size can be substantial, especially for a large WAN that has many computers attached to each packet
switch.

In essence, a two-part hierarchical addressing scheme allows packet switches to use
only the first part of the destination address until the packet reaches the final switch
(i.e., the switch to which the destination computer is attached). Once the packet reaches
the final switch, the switch uses the second part of the address to choose a specific computer, as Algorithm 18.1 describes.

To summarize:

> *Only the first part of a destination address is used when forwarding a*
> *packet across a WAN. Once the packet reaches the switch to which*
> *the destination computer attaches, the second part of the address is*
> *used to forward the packet to the correct local computer.*

18.8 Source Independence

Note that next-hop forwarding does not depend on the packet's original source or on the path the packet has taken before it arrives at a particular packet switch. Instead, the next hop to which a packet is sent depends only on the packet's destination. The concept, which is known as *source independence*, is a fundamental idea in networking, and will be implicit in our discussions throughout the chapter and in later chapters that describe Internet forwarding.

Source independence allows the forwarding mechanism in a computer network to be compact and efficient. Because all packets follow the same path, only one table is required. Because forwarding does not use source information, only the destination address needs to be extracted from a packet. Furthermore, a single mechanism handles forwarding uniformly — packets that originate on directly connected computers and packets that arrive from other packet switches use the same mechanism.

18.9 Dynamic Routing Updates In A WAN

For a WAN to operate correctly, each switch must have a forwarding table, and must forward packets. Furthermore, values in the forwarding table must guarantee the following:

- Universal communication. The forwarding table in each switch must contain a valid next-hop route for each possible destination address.

- Optimal routes. In a switch, the next-hop value in the forwarding table for a given destination must point to the shortest path to the destination.

Network failures further complicate forwarding. For example, if two paths exist to a given destination and one of the paths becomes unavailable because hardware fails (e.g., a circuit is disconnected), forwarding should be changed to avoid the unavailable path. Thus, a manager cannot merely configure a forwarding table to contain static values that do not change. Instead, software running on the packet switches continually tests for failures, and reconfigures the forwarding tables automatically. We use the term *routing software* to describe software that automatically reconfigures forwarding tables.

The easiest way to think about route computation in a WAN is to think of a graph that models the network, and imagine software using the graph to compute the shortest path to all possible destinations. Each *node* in the graph corresponds to a packet switch in the network (individual computers are not part of the graph). If the network contains a direct connection between a pair of packet switches, the graph contains an *edge* or *link* between the corresponding nodes†. For example, Figure 18.6 shows an example WAN and the corresponding graph.

---

†Because the relationship between graph theory and computer networking is strong, one often hears a packet switch called a *network node* and a data circuit between two sites called a *link*.

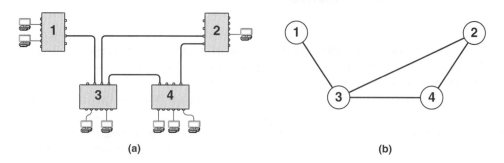

(a)   (b)

Figure 18.6 Illustration of a WAN and the corresponding graph.

As the figure shows, nodes in the graph are given a label that is the same as the number assigned to the corresponding packet switch. A graph representation is especially useful in computing next-hop forwarding because graph theory has been studied and efficient algorithms have been developed. Furthermore, a graph abstracts away details, allowing routing software to deal with the essence of the problem.

When it computes next-hop forwarding for a graph, a routing algorithm must identify a link. Our examples will used the notation (k, j) to denote a link from node k to node j. Thus, when a routing algorithm runs on the graph in Figure 18.6b, the algorithm produces output as shown in Figure 18.7.

to reach	next hop		to reach	next hop		to reach	next hop		to reach	next hop
1	–		1	(2,3)		1	(3,1)		1	(4,3)
2	(1,3)		2	–		2	(3,2)		2	(4,2)
3	(1,3)		3	(2,3)		3	–		3	(4,3)
4	(1,3)		4	(2,4)		4	(3,4)		4	–

node 1   *node 2*   *node 3*   *node 4*

Figure 18.7 A forwarding table for each node in the graph of Figure 18.6b.

18.10 Default Routes

The forwarding table for node *1* in Figure 18.7 raises an important point: a forwarding table may contain many entries that point to the same next hop. An examination of the WAN in Figure 18.6a reveals why all remote entries contain the same next hop: the packet switch has only one connection to the network. Therefore, all outgoing traffic must be sent across the same connection. Consequently, except for the entry that corresponds to the node itself, all entries in node *1*'s forwarding table have a next hop that points to the link from node *1* to node *3*.

In our trivial example, the list of duplicate entries in the forwarding table is short. However a large WAN may contains hundreds of duplicate entries. Most WAN systems include a mechanism that can be used to eliminate the common case of duplicate entries. Called a *default route*, the mechanism allows a single entry in a forwarding table to replace a long list of entries that have the same next-hop value. Only one default entry is allowed in a forwarding table, and the entry has lower priority than other entries. If the forwarding mechanism does not find an explicit entry for a given destination, it uses the default. Figure 18.8 shows the forwarding tables from Figure 18.7 revised to use a default route.

to reach	next hop
1	–
*	(1,3)

to reach	next hop
2	–
4	(2,4)
*	(2,3)

to reach	next hop
1	(3,1)
2	(3,2)
3	–
4	(3,4)

to reach	next hop
2	(4,2)
4	–
*	(4,3)

node 1   *node 2*   *node 3*   *node 4*

Figure 18.8 The forwarding tables from Figure 18.7 with default routes denoted by an asterisk.

Default routing is optional — a default entry is present only if more than one destination has the same next-hop value. For example, the forwarding table for node *3* does not contain a default route because each entry has a unique next hop. However, the forwarding table for node *1* benefits from a default route because all remote destinations have the same next hop.

18.11 Forwarding Table Computation

How is a forwarding table constructed? There are two basic approaches.

- *Static routing.* A program computes and installs routes when a packet switch boots; the routes do not change.
- *Dynamic routing.* A program builds an initial forwarding table when a packet switch boots; the program then alters the table as conditions in the network change.

Each approach has advantages and disadvantages. The chief advantages of static routing are simplicity and low overhead. The chief disadvantage is inflexibility — static routes cannot be changed when communication is disrupted. Because large networks are designed with redundant connections to handle occasional hardware failures, most WANs use a form of dynamic routing.

18.12 Distributed Route Computation

Algorithm 18.2 shows how a forwarding table can be computed after information about a network is encoded in a graph. In practice, WANs need to perform *distributed route computation*. That is, instead of a centralized program computing all shortest paths, each packet switch must compute its own forwarding table locally.

All packet switches must participate in distributed route computation. There are two general forms:

- Link-State Routing (LSR), which uses Dijkstra's algorithm
- Distance-Vector Routing (DVR), which uses another approach

The next sections describe each of the two approaches. Chapter 27 explains how each approach is used to control routes in the Internet.

18.12.1 Link-State Routing (LSR)

Known formally as *link-state routing* or *link-status routing*, the approach has become known as *Shortest Path First* or *SPF* routing. The terminology arises because Dijkstra used it to characterize the way the algorithm works. However, it is somewhat misleading because all routing algorithms find shortest paths.

To use LSR routing, packet switches periodically send messages across the network that carry the status of a link between two packet switches. For example, packet switches *5* and *9* measure the link between them and send a status message, such as "the link between *5* and *9* is up". Each status message is broadcast to all switches. Every switch runs software that collects incoming status messages and uses them to build a graph of the network. Each switch then uses Algorithm 18.2 to produce a forwarding table by choosing itself as the source.

An LSR algorithm can adapt to hardware failures. If a link between packet switches fails, the attached packet switches will detect the failure and broadcast a status message that specifies the link is down. All packet switches receive the broadcast, change their copy of the graph to reflect the change in the link's status, and recompute shortest paths. Similarly, when a link becomes available again, the packet switches connected to the link detect that it is working and start sending status messages that report its availability.

Algorithm 18.2

Given:

    A graph with a nonnegative weight assigned to each edge
    and a designated source node

Compute:

    The shortest distance from the source node to each other
    node and a next-hop routing table

Method:

    Initialize set S to contain all nodes except the source node;
    Initialize array D so that D[v] is the weight of the edge from the
        source to v if such an edge exists, and *infinity* otherwise;
    Initialize entries of R so that R[v] is assigned *v* if an
        edge exists from the source to v, and zero otherwise;

    while (set S is not empty) {
        choose a node u from S such that D[u] is minimum;
        if (D[u] is *infinity*) {
            error: no path exists to nodes in S; quit;
        }
        delete u from set S;
        for each node v such that (u,v) is an edge {
            if (v is still in S) {
                c = D[u] + weight(u,v);
                if (c < D[v]) {
                    R[v] = R[u];
                    D[v] = c;
                }
            }
        }
    }

Algorithm 18.2 A version of Dijkstra's algorithm that computes *R*, a next-hop forwarding table, and *D*, the distance to each node from the specified source node.

18.12.2 Distance Vector Routing (DVR)

The chief alternative to LSR is known as the *Distance-Vector Routing* (*DVR*) approach. As with LSR, each link in the network is assigned a weight, and the *distance* to a destination between two packet switches is defined to be the sum of weights along the path between the two. Like LSR, distance-vector routing arranges for packet switches to exchange messages periodically. Unlike LSR, however, a distance-vector scheme arranges for a packet switch to send a complete list of destinations and the current cost of reaching each. In essence, when it sends a DVR message, a packet switch is sending a series of individual statements, of the form:

"I can reach destination X, and its current distance from me is Y."

DVR messages are not broadcast. Instead, each packet switch periodically sends a DVR message to its neighbors. Each message contains pairs of (*destination, distance*). Thus, each packet switch must keep a list of possible destinations along with the current distance to the destination and the next hop to use. The list of destinations and the next hop for each can be found in the forwarding table. We can think of DVR software as maintaining an extension to the forwarding table that stores a *distance* for each destination.

When a message arrives at a packet switch from neighbor *N*, the packet switch examines each item in the message, and changes its forwarding table if the neighbor has a shorter path to some destination than the path currently being used. For example, if neighbor *N* advertises a path to destination *D* as having cost five and the current path through neighbor *K* has cost one hundred, the current next hop for *D* will be replaced by *N* and the cost to reach *D* will be five plus the cost to reach *N*. Algorithm 18.3 specifies how routes are updated when using the distance-vector approach.

Algorithm 18.3

Given:

   A local forwarding table with a distance for each entry, a
   distance to reach each neighbor, and an incoming DV
   message from a neighbor

Compute:

   An updated forwarding table

Method:

   Maintain a *distance* field in each forwarding table entry;
   Initialize forwarding table with a single entry that has the
      destination equal to the local packet switch, the
      next-hop unused, and the *distance* set to zero;

   Repeat forever {
      Wait for a routing message to arrive over the network
         from a neighbor; let the sender be switch *N*;
      for each entry in the message {
         Let *V* be the destination in the entry and let *D*
            be the distance;
         Compute *C* as *D* plus the weight assigned to the
            link over which the message arrived;
         Examine and update the local routing table:
         if (no route exists to *V*) {
            add an entry to the local routing table for destination
            V with next-hop *N* and distance *C*;
         } else if (a route exists that has next-hop *N*) {
            replace the distance in existing route with *C*;
         } else if (a route exists with distance greater than *C*) {
            change the next-hop to *N* and distance to *C*;
         }
      }
   }

Algorithm 18.3 Distance-vector algorithm for route computation.

18.13 Shortest Path Computation In A Graph

Once a graph has been created that corresponds to a network, software uses a method known as *Dijkstra's Algorithm*† to find the shortest path from a source node to each of the other nodes in the graph; a next-hop forwarding table is constructed during the computation of shortest paths. The algorithm must be run once for each node in the graph. That is, to compute the forwarding table for packet switch *P*, the node that corresponds to *P* is designated as the source node, and the algorithm is run.

Dijkstra's algorithm is popular because it can be used with various definitions of *shortest path*. In particular, the algorithm does not require edges in the graph to represent geographic distance. Instead, the algorithm allows each edge to be assigned a nonnegative value called a *weight*, and defines the distance between two nodes to be the sum of the weights along a path between the nodes. The important point is:

> *Because it uses weights on links when computing shortest paths, Dijkstra's algorithm can be used with measures other than geographic distance.*

Figure 18.9 illustrates the concept of weights by showing an example graph with an integer weight assigned to each edge and a least-weight path between two nodes in the graph.

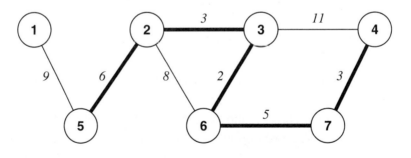

Figure 18.9 An example graph with a weight assigned to each edge and a shortest path between nodes *4* and *5* shown darkened.

Dijkstra's algorithm maintains a set of nodes, *S*, for which the minimum distance and next hop have not been computed. The set is initialized to all nodes except the source. The algorithm then iterates until set *S* is empty. On each iteration, the algorithm removes a node from *S* that has the least distance from the source. As it deletes node *u*, the algorithm examines the current distance from the source to each of the neighbors of *u* that remains in the set. If a path from the source through *u* to the neigh-

---

†The algorithm is named for its inventor, E. Dijkstra.

bor has less weight than the current path, the algorithm updates the distance to the neighbor. After all nodes have been removed from S, the algorithm will have computed the minimum distance to each node and a correct next-hop forwarding table for all possible paths.

Implementation of Dijkstra's algorithm is straightforward. In addition to the data structure used to store information about the graph, Dijkstra's algorithm needs three data structures to store: the current distance to each node, the next hop for the shortest path, and information about the remaining set of nodes. Nodes can be numbered from 1 to n as Figure 18.9 demonstrates, which makes the implementation efficient because a node number can be used as an index into a data structure. In particular, the algorithm can use two arrays, D and R, that are each indexed by the node number. The ith entry in array D stores a current value of the minimum distance from the source to node i. The ith entry in array R stores the next hop used to reach node i along the path being computed. The set S can be maintained as a doubly linked list of node numbers, which facilitates searching the entire set or deleting an entry.

Algorithm 18.2 specifies how to compute shortest paths in a graph. The algorithm uses *weight(i,j)* as a function that returns the weight of the edge from node i to node j. Function *weight* is assumed to return a reserved value *infinity* if no edge exists from node i to node j. In practice, any value can be used to represent infinity provided the value is larger than the sum of weights along any path in the graph. One way to generate a value *infinity* consists of adding one to the sum of all weights on all edges.

Allowing arbitrary weights to be assigned to edges of a graph means one algorithm can be used with different measures of distance. For example, some WAN technologies measure distance by counting the number of packet switches along a path. To use the algorithm for such technologies, each edge in the graph is assigned a weight of 1. In other WAN technologies, weights are assigned to reflect the capacity of the underlying connections. As an alternative, a manager can assign weights to links to control routing. For example, consider a case where two separate paths exist between a pair of packet switches, with one path designated to be the *primary* path, and the other designated to be a *backup path*. To enforce such a policy, a manager can assign the primary link a low weight and the other link a high weight. Routing software will configure forwarding tables to use the path with low weight unless the path is not available, in which case routing software will select the alternative path.

18.14 Routing Problems

In theory, either LSR or DVR routing will compute shortest paths. Furthermore, each approach will eventually *converge*, meaning that the forwarding tables in all packet switches agree. However, problems do occur. For example, if LSR messages are lost, two packet switches can disagree about the shortest path. DVR problems can be more severe because a link failure can cause two or more packet switches to create a *routing loop* in which each packet switch thinks the next packet switch in the set is the shortest path to a particular destination. As a result, a packet can circulate among the packet switches indefinitely.

One of the primary reasons DVR protocols exhibit problems comes from *backwash* (i.e., a packet switch receives information that it sent). For example, suppose a switch tells its neighbors, "I can reach destination D_1 at cost 3". If the connection leading to destination D_1 fails, the switch will remove the entry for D_1 from its forwarding table (or mark the entry invalid). But the switch has told neighbors that a route exists. Imagine that just after the link fails, one of the neighbors sends a DVR message that specifies "I can reach destination D_1 at cost 4". Unfortunately, the message will be believed, and a routing loop will be created.

Most practical routing mechanisms contain constraints and hueristics to prevent problems like routing loops. For example, DVR schemes employ *split horizon*, which specifies that a switch does not send information back to its origin. Furthermore, most practical routing systems introduce hysteresis that prevents the software from making many changes in a short time. However, in a large network where many links fail and recover frequently, routing problems can occur.

18.15 Summary

A Wide Area Network (WAN) technology can be used to form networks that span an arbitrarily long distance and connect arbitrarily many computers. A traditional WAN consists of electronic devices called packet switches interconnected by communication lines. A packet switch contains a processor, memory, and I/O interfaces. An interface either connects to a local computer or another packet switch.

Packet switching networks use a store-and-forward approach in which an arriving packet is placed in the memory of a packet switch until the processor can forward the packet to its destination. Forwarding relies on a data structure known as a forwarding table. The table contains an entry for each destination, and the entry specifies the next hop used to reach that destination. A forwarding table lists packet switches as destinations instead of individual computers.

A WAN can be represented as a graph in which each node corresponds to a packet switch and each edge corresponds to a communication line. The graph representation is useful because it eliminates details and can be used to compute forwarding tables. The two basic approaches used in routing software are Link State Routing (LSR) and Distance-Vector Routing (DVR). LSR arranges for each packet switch to broadcast the status of each directly connected link, and uses Dijkstra's shortest path algorithm to compute shortest paths. DVR arranges for a packet switch to send its neighbors a list of destinations and the cost to reach each. A neighbor examines the list in an incoming DVR message, and replaces items in its forwarding table if a lower-cost route is available.

EXERCISES

18.1   What are the two conceptual parts of a WAN address?

18.2   What are the conceptual parts of a traditional packet switch, and to what does it connect?

18.3   What benefit does dynamic routing offer?

18.4   What is a routing loop?

18.5   When computer programs running on two packet switches exchange distance-vector information, the programs must agree on a message format. Create a specification for an unambiguous message format. Hint: consider differences in the way computers represent information.

18.6   Write a computer program that implements Dijkstra's algorithm for finding shortest paths in a graph.

18.7   Into what two conceptual pieces is a modern packet switch divided?

18.8   Explain the store and forward paradigm.

18.9   Figure 18.4 shows how addresses can be assigned to computers that connect to a packet switch. Suppose the hardware for one of the interfaces on a switch fails and a network administrator moves a computer's connection to an unused interface. Will the new configuration work correctly? Why or why not?

18.10   Write a computer program that takes as input a forwarding table and a series of packets, and generates as output a statement of how each packet should be forwarded. Remember to handle packets that have an incorrect address.

18.11   Consider a WAN with two packet switches. Assume each switch has a forwarding table entry for each local address (i.e., the address of each computer that attaches to the switch) plus a default entry that points to the other switch. Under what circumstances will the scheme work? Under what circumstances will the scheme fail?

18.12   What are the two basic approaches used to perform a distributed route computation, and how does each work?

18.13   When a packet switch receives a distance-vector message from a neighbor, will the switch's forwarding table always change? Explain.

18.14   Can a computer use an Ethernet interface to communicate with a WAN? Explain.

18.15   Extend the previous exercise by implementing a computer program that uses the specified message format. Have another student implement a program from the same specification, and see if they interoperate correctly.

18.16   If a WAN connects N sites, what is the minimum number of digital circuits needed? What is the maximum number that can be present?

Chapter Contents

19

Networking Technologies Past And Present

19.1 Introduction

Previous chapters examine data communications and data networking by considering basic taxonomies. Early chapters consider the division between technologies used for Internet access and those used in the core of the Internet. Chapters in this part of the text use the classic taxonomy of LANs, MANs, and WANs to describe wired and wireless networks.

Over the years, many networking technologies have been defined for each basic type. Some that were once of major importance have faded into obscurity, and others continue to fill a niche. This brief chapter highlights some of the major technologies, and describes the significant features and characteristics of each. The examples illustrate the variety of technologies that have been created, and show how quickly technologies change.

19.2 Connection And Access Technologies

Early chapters describe the most significant access and connection technologies (DSL and cable modems). A variety of additional technologies have been defined, including a technology that delivers data over power lines and wireless access mechanisms. The set of technologies can be summarized as follows:

19.2.1 Synchronous Optical Network or Digital Hierarchy (SONET/SDH)

SONET and the associated TDM hierarchy was originally designed as a system to carry digital voice telephone calls. The technology has become the standard for the digital circuits used throughout the Internet. SONET permits a physical ring to be constructed with the purpose of providing redundancy. The hardware can automatically detect and correct problems — even if one part of the ring is damaged, data can still get through. A device known as an *Add-Drop Multiplexor* is used to connect a site to a SONET ring. The term arises because the Add-Drop Multiplexor either inserts or terminates a set of data circuits that each connect to another Add-Drop Multiplexor on the ring. SONET uses time-division multiplexing to multiplex the circuits onto the underlying fiber. SDH provides the well-known standards for circuits such as a T3 circuit that can be configured across a SONET ring.

19.2.2 Optical Carrier (OC)

The OC standards specify the signaling used on an optical fiber SONET ring. OC standards are associated with higher data rates than the T-series standards provided by SDH. A private company might choose to lease an OC circuit to connect two of the company sites. Tier 1 ISPs use circuits of OC-192 (10 Mbps) and OC-768 (40 Mbps) in the backbone of the Internet.

19.2.3 Digital Subscriber Line (DSL) And Cable Modems

These two technologies have emerged as the principal means of providing broadband Internet access to private residences and small businesses. DSL makes use of existing telephone land lines, and cable modem technology makes use of existing cable television infrastructure. DSL offers data rates of 1 to 6 Mbps, depending on the distance between a central office and a subscriber; cable modems offer up to 52 Mbps, but the bandwidth is shared among a set of users. Both technologies are viewed as transitory until optical fiber is available to the curb or to the home.

19.2.4 WiMAX And Wi-Fi

Wi-Fi comprises a set of wireless technologies that have become widely used to provide Internet access in homes, cafes, airports, hotels, and other locations. Successive generations of Wi-Fi technologies have increased overall data rates.

WiMAX is an emerging wireless technology that can be used to form a MAN. WiMAX provides either access or backhaul† capabilities, and two versions are defined to support fixed and mobile endpoints.

---

†A connection from a remote location or access point back to a provider's central facility.

19.2.5 Very Small Aperture Satellite (VSAT)

VSAT technologies, which have a dish size of less then 3 meters, have made it possible to use satellite to provide Internet access to individuals or small businesses. Although it provides high data rates, VSAT incurs long delays.

19.2.6 Power Line Communication (PLC)

PLC uses high frequencies to send data along power lines. The idea is to use existing infrastructure to deliver Internet access. Although much research has been done, the technology has not enjoyed widespread deployment.

19.3 LAN Technologies

After LANs were invented, many groups proposed designs or built experimental prototypes. The development of new LANs continued for twenty years, and several LAN technologies enjoyed popularity and commercial success. Interestingly, LAN technologies have begun to converge; new LANs are unexpected.

19.3.1 IBM Token Ring

Some of the early work on LANs explored token passing as an access control mechanism. IBM chose to create a token passing LAN technology that was known as *IBM Token Ring*. The original version of IBM's Token Ring operated at 4 Mbps, compared to the competitor, Ethernet, that operated at 10 Mbps. Later, IBM introduced a 16 Mbps version of Token Ring. Despite a lower data rate and high cost, IBM's Token Ring was widely accepted by corporate information technology departments, and was a major LAN technology for many years.

19.3.2 Fiber And Copper Distributed Data Interconnect (FDDI And CDDI)

By the late 1980s, it became apparent that the two chief LAN technologies, Ethernet at 10 Mbps and IBM's Token Ring at 16 Mbps, had insufficient data rates to meet growing demand. The FDDI standard was created to increase LAN data rates to 100 Mbps. At the time, designers argued that higher data rates required the use of optical fiber instead of copper wiring, and suggested rewiring offices to deliver fiber to the desktop. In addition, FDDI used a pair of *counter-rotating rings* to provide redundancy — if an FDDI ring was cut, hardware automatically looped the data path to route traffic around the failure and keep the ring active. Finally, FDDI introduced one of the earliest LAN switches in which each computer connected directly to a central FDDI mechanism. Thus, it was possible to have a physical star topology and a logical ring topology.

Because it offered the highest available data rate and the opportunity for redundancy, FDDI became popular as a high-speed interconnect among computers in a data center. However, the high cost and special expertise needed to install fiber discouraged most organizations from replacing copper wiring. As work on Fast Ethernet progressed, FDDI proponents created a version of FDDI called CDDI that ran over copper wiring. Ultimately, Ethernet proved to have lower cost, and FDDI technologies vanished.

19.3.3 Ethernet

In one sense, Ethernet has won the race and completely dominates the LAN market. Indeed, there are more Ethernets deployed than any other type of LAN. In another sense, Ethernet has disappeared completely, and has been replaced by new technology that is still called Ethernet. One can observe, for example, that there is almost no similarity between the heavy coaxial cable and RF signaling used in early Ethernet and the wiring and signaling used with gigabit Ethernet. In addition to changes in data rate, the physical and logical topologies have changed: hubs replaced cables, Ethernet switches replaced hubs, and VLAN switches replaced switches.

19.4 WAN Technologies

Many technologies have been created for experimental and production use in Wide Area Networks. This section presents a few examples that illustrate some of the diversity.

19.4.1 ARPANET

Packet switched WANs are less than fifty years old. In the late 1960s, the *Advanced Research Projects Agency* (*ARPA*) funded research on networking for the U.S. Department of Defense. A major ARPA research project developed a Wide Area Network to determine whether packet switching technology would be valuable for the military. Known as the *ARPANET*, the network was one of the first packet switched WANs. The ARPANET connected researchers from academia and industry. Although by current standards the ARPANET was slow (leased serial data lines connecting packet switches operated at only 56 Kbps), the project left a legacy of concepts, algorithms, and terminology that are still in use.

When the Internet project began, the ARPANET was used as the backbone over which researchers communicated and experimented. In January of 1983, ARPA ordered everyone connected to the ARPANET to stop using the original protocols and begin using the Internet protocols. Thus, the ARPANET became the first Internet backbone.

19.4.2 X.25

The organization that sets international telephone standards, the *International Telecommunications Union* (*ITU*), developed an early standard for WAN technology that became popular among public carriers. At the time, the ITU was known as the *Consultative Committee for International Telephone and Telegraph* (*CCITT*), and the standard is still known as the *CCITT X.25* standard. X.25 networks enjoyed more popularity in Europe than in the United States.

X.25 used a traditional WAN design — an X.25 network consisted of two or more X.25 packet switches interconnected by leased lines. Computers connected directly to packet switches. X.25 used a connection-oriented paradigm analogous to a telephone call — a computer was required to open a connection before transferring data.

Because X.25 was invented before personal computers became popular, many early X.25 networks were engineered to connect ASCII terminals to remote timesharing computers. As a user entered data on a keyboard, an X.25 network interface captured keystrokes, placed each in an X.25 packet, and transmitted the packets across the network. Similarly, when a program running on a remote computer displayed output, the computer passed the output to the X.25 network interface, which placed the information in X.25 packets for transmission back to the user's screen. Although telephone companies pushed X.25 services, the technology was expensive for the performance it delivered, and has been replaced by other WAN technologies.

19.4.3 Frame Relay

Long-distance carriers have created a series of wide area network technologies that transport data. One such service, *Frame Relay*, was designed to accept and deliver blocks of data, where each block can contain up to 8K octets of data. Part of the motivation for the large data size (and for the name) arises because the inventors envisioned using Frame Relay service to bridge LAN segments. An organization with offices in two cities could obtain a Frame Relay service for each office, and then use the Frame Relay to forward packets from a LAN segment at one site to a LAN segment at the other. The designers chose a connection-oriented paradigm that was acceptable to corporations with multiple offices. Thus, Frame Relay was popular until lower-cost alternatives became available.

Because it was designed to handle data from a LAN segment, the designers envisioned Frame Relay running at speeds between *4* and *100* Mbps (the speed of LANs when Frame Relay was created). In practice, however, the high cost of Frame Relay service led many customers to choose slower connections running at *1.5* Mbps or 56 Kbps.

19.4.4 Switched Multi-megabit Data Service (SMDS)

Like Frame Relay, SMDS is a high-speed wide area data service offered by long-distance carriers. It was based on IEEE standard 802.6DQDB, and is considered a precursor to ATM. Instead of voice traffic, SMDS is designed to carry data. More important, SMDS is optimized to operate at the highest speeds. For example, header information in packets can require a significant amount of the available bandwidth. To minimize header overhead, SMDS uses a small header and constrains each packet to contain no more than 9188 octet of data. SMDS also defined a special hardware interface used to connect computers to the network. The special interface makes it possible to deliver data as fast as a computer can move the data into memory.

As the name implies, SMDS networks often operate at speeds faster than 1 Mbps (i.e., faster than a typical Frame Relay connection). The two services differed in the way they could be used. SMDS was connectionless, which gave it flexibility. However, most telephone companies were more comfortable with connection-oriented technologies, which meant that SMDS was not popular and has been replaced.

19.4.5 Asynchronous Transfer Mode (ATM)

The telecommunications industry designed ATM as an alternative to the Internet, and announced the effort with great fanfare. When the technology emerged in the 1990s, ATM had ambitious goals — designers claimed that it would replace all WAN and LAN technologies and lead to a completely uniform communication system worldwide. In addition to data, ATM was designed to handle video transmission as well as conventional voice telephone traffic. Furthermore, the designers announced, ATM would scale to much higher data rates than other packet switching technologies.

The key new idea introduced in ATM is known as *Label Switching*. ATM is a connection-oriented technology, but packets do not have addresses as usual. Instead, a packet carries a small ID known as a *label*. Furthermore, a label can be changed each time the packet passes through a switch. When a connection is set up, a unique label is chosen for each link in the path, and the labels are placed in tables in the switches. When a packet arrives, the switch looks up the current label, and substitutes a replacement label. In theory, label switching can be performed in hardware at higher speed than conventional forwarding.

To accommodate all possible uses, designers added many features to ATM, including mechanisms to provide end-to-end guarantees on service (e.g., guaranteed bandwidth and bounds on delay). When they began to implement ATM, engineers discovered that the plethora of features meant that the hardware was complex and expensive. Furthermore, the mechanism created to establish label switched paths was so cumbersome that it was not used. Thus, ATM was not accepted, and virtually disappeared.

19.4.6 Multi-Protocol Label Switching (MPLS)

Although not a network system, MPLS is a notable result of the ATM effort — engineers adapted label switching for use in Internet routers†. Instead of completely replacing the underlying hardware as ATM attempted to do, MPLS can be implemented in software as an extra feature. An MPLS router accepts Internet packets, places each packet in a special wrapper, uses label switching to transport the packet across an MPLS path, unwraps the packet, and continues normal forwarding. MPLS is used extensively at the center of the Internet; tier 1 ISPs use MPLS to allow some packets to follow a specific path (e.g., a large customer that pays more can have packets follow a shorter path that is not available to lower-paying customers).

19.4.7 Integrated Services Digital Network (ISDN)

Chapter 12 covers ISDN in detail; this chapter only contains a short summary. Telephone companies created ISDN to provide network service at a higher data rate than could be achieved with a dial-up modem. When it was first proposed, 128 Kbps seemed fast. By the time it was available, the technology seemed slow for the price. In most parts of the world, ISDN has been replaced by DSL, cable modems, or 3G cellular systems, all of which offer much higher data rates.

19.5 Summary

Many networking technologies have been created. Some were too complex, some were too expensive, and others lacked essential features. Even after achieving some commercial success, many were replaced. Ironically, even though Ethernet technology has survived for over thirty years, only the name and frame format have been preserved — the underlying technology has completely changed.

EXERCISES

19.1   What technology has replaced Ethernet hubs?

19.2   What is SONET?

19.3   Which would you expect to have smaller delay, VSAT technology or WiMAX technology? Why?

19.4   What technology overshadowed and eventually edged out FDDI?

19.5   By why name does a consumer know DOCSIS technology?

19.6   Name a WAN technology that adopted Internet protocols in 1983.

---

†Chapter 20 describes Internet architecture and routing.

19.7   Why did ISDN fail to gain a large market?

19.8   Which company was well-known for a token ring technology?

19.9   Name a current technology that arose from ATM.

19.10   What WAN technology was used by banks in the 1980s?

19.11   What does ATM stand for in the networking world?

PART IV

Internetworking Using TCP/IP

Internet architecture, addressing, binding, encapsulation, and protocols in the TCP/IP suite

Chapters

Chapter Contents

20

Internetworking: Concepts, Architecture, and Protocols

20.1 Introduction

Previous chapters describe basic networking, including the hardware components used in LAN and WAN networks as well as general concepts such as addressing and routing. This chapter begins an examination of another fundamental idea in computer communication — an internetworking technology that can be used to connect multiple physical networks into a large, uniform communication system. The chapter discusses the motivation for internetworking, introduces the hardware components used, describes the architecture in which the components are connected, and discusses the significance of the concept. The remaining chapters in this section expand the internetworking concept, and provide additional details about the technology. They examine individual protocols, and explain how each uses techniques from earlier chapters to achieve reliable, error-free communication.

20.2 The Motivation For Internetworking

Each network technology is designed to fit a specific set of constraints. For example, LAN technologies are designed to provide high-speed communication across short distances, while WAN technologies are designed to provide communication across large areas. Consequently,

No single networking technology is best for all needs.

A large organization with diverse networking requirements needs multiple physical networks. More important, if the organization chooses the type of network that is best for each task, the organization will have several types of networks. For example, a LAN technology like Ethernet might be the best solution for connecting computers at a given site, but a leased data circuit might be used to interconnect a site in one city with a site in another.

20.3 The Concept Of Universal Service

The chief problem with multiple networks should be obvious: a computer attached to a given network can only communicate with other computers attached to the same network. The problem became evident in the 1970s as large organizations began to acquire multiple networks. Each network in the organization formed an island. In many early installations, each computer attached to a single network, and employees had to choose a computer appropriate for each task. That is, an employee was given access to multiple screens and keyboards, and the employee was forced to move from one computer to another to send a message across the appropriate network.

Users are neither satisfied nor productive when they must use a separate computer for each network. Consequently, most modern computer communication systems allow communication between any two computers analogous to the way a telephone system provides communication between any two telephones. Known as *universal service*, the concept is a fundamental part of networking. With universal service, a user on any computer in any organization can send messages or data to any other user. Furthermore, a user does not need to change computer systems when changing tasks — all information is available to all computers. As a result, users are more productive. To summarize:

> *A communication system that supplies universal service allows arbitrary pairs of computers to communicate.*

20.4 Universal Service In A Heterogeneous World

Does universal service mean that everyone needs to adopt a single network technology, or is it possible to have universal service across multiple networks that use multiple technologies? Incompatibilities make it impossible to form a large network merely by interconnecting the wires among networks. Furthermore, extension techniques such as bridging cannot be used with heterogeneous network technologies because each technology uses its own packet format and addressing scheme. Thus, a frame created for one network technology cannot be transmitted on a network that uses a different technology. The point can be summarized:

Although universal service is highly desirable, incompatibilities among network hardware, frames, and addresses prevent a bridged network from including arbitrary technologies.

20.5 Internetworking

Despite the incompatibilities among network technologies, researchers have devised a scheme that provides universal service among heterogeneous networks. Called *internetworking*, the scheme uses both hardware and software. Additional hardware systems are used to interconnect a set of physical networks. Software on the attached computers then provides universal service. The resulting system of connected physical networks is known as an *internetwork* or *internet*.

Internetworking is quite general. In particular, an internet is not restricted in size — internets exist that contain a few networks and the global Internet contains tens of thousands of networks. Similarly, the number of computers attached to each network in an internet can vary — some networks have no computers attached, while others have hundreds.

20.6 Physical Network Connection With Routers

The basic hardware component used to connect heterogeneous networks is a *router*. Physically, a router is an independent hardware system dedicated to the task of interconnecting networks. Like a bridge, a router contains a processor and memory as well as a separate I/O interface for each network to which it connects. The network treats a connection to a router the same as a connection to any other computer. Figure 20.1 illustrates that the physical connection of networks with a router is straightforward.

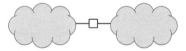

Figure 20.1 Two physical networks connected by a router, which has a separate interface for each network connection. Computers can attach to each network.

The figure uses a cloud to depict each network because router connections are not restricted to a particular network technology. A router can connect two LANs, a LAN and a WAN, or two WANs. Furthermore, when a router connects two networks in the same general category, the networks do not need to use the same technology. For example, a router can connect an Ethernet to a Wi-Fi network. Thus, each cloud represents an arbitrary network technology.

To summarize:

> *An Internet router is a special-purpose hardware system dedicated to the task of interconnecting networks. A router can interconnect networks that use different technologies, including different media, physical addressing schemes, or frame formats.*

20.7 Internet Architecture

Routers make it possible for organizations to choose network technologies appropriate for each need and to use routers to connect all networks into an internet. For example, Figure 20.2 illustrates how three routers can be used to connect four arbitrary physical networks into an internet.

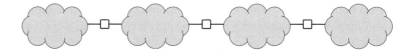

Figure 20.2 An internet formed by using three routers to interconnect four physical networks.

Although the figure shows each router with exactly two connections, commercial routers can connect more than two networks. Thus, a single router could connect all four networks in the example. Despite the feasibility, an organization seldom uses a single router to connect all of its networks. There are two reasons:

- Because the router must forward each packet, the processor in a given router is insufficient to handle the traffic passing among an arbitrary number of networks.

- Redundancy improves internet reliability. To avoid a single point of failure, protocol software continuously monitors internet connections and instructs routers to send traffic along alternative paths when a network or router fails.

Thus, when planning an internet, an organization must choose a design that meets the organization's need for reliability, capacity, and cost. In particular, the exact details of internet topology often depend on the bandwidth of the physical networks, the expected traffic, the organization's reliability requirements, and the cost and performance of available router hardware. To summarize:

*An internet consists of a set of networks interconnected by routers.
The internet scheme allows each organization to choose the number
and type of networks, the number of routers to use to interconnect
them, and the exact interconnection topology.*

20.8 Achieving Universal Service

The goal of internetworking is universal service across heterogeneous networks. To provide universal service among all computers on an internet, routers must agree to forward information from a source on one network to a specified destination on another. The task is complex because frame formats and addressing schemes used by the underlying networks can differ. As a result, protocol software is needed on computers and routers to make universal service possible.

Later chapters describe Internet† protocol software in detail. They show how Internet protocols overcome differences in frame formats and physical addresses to make communication possible among networks that use different technologies. Before considering how Internet protocols work, it is important to understand the effect that an internet system presents to attached computers.

20.9 A Virtual Network

In general, Internet software provides the appearance of a single, seamless communication system to which many computers attach. The system offers universal service: each computer is assigned an address, and any computer can send a packet to any other computer. Furthermore, Internet protocol software hides the details of physical network connections, physical addresses, and routing information — neither users nor application programs are aware of the underlying physical networks or the routers that connect them.

We say that an internet is a *virtual network* system because the communication system is an abstraction. That is, although a combination of hardware and software provides the illusion of a uniform network system, no such network exists. Figure 20.3 illustrates the virtual network concept as well as a corresponding physical structure.

---

†Recall that when written with an uppercase *I*, the term *Internet* refers to the global Internet and the associated protocols.

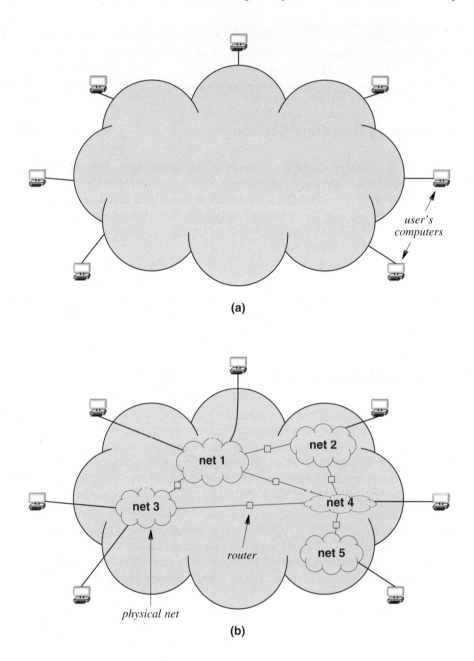

Figure 20.3 The Internet concept. (a) The illusion of a single network provided to users and applications, and (b) the underlying physical structure with routers interconnecting networks.

20.10 Protocols For Internetworking

Although several protocols have been proposed for use with internets, one suite stands out as the most widely used. The suite is formally known as the *TCP/IP Internet Protocols*; most networking professionals simply refer to the suite as *TCP/IP*†.

TCP/IP was developed at the same time as the global Internet. In fact, the same researchers who proposed TCP/IP also proposed the Internet architecture described above. Work on TCP/IP began in the 1970s, approximately the same time that Local Area Networks were being developed, and continued until the early 1990s when the Internet became commercial.

20.11 Review Of TCP/IP Layering

Recall from Chapter 1 that the Internet protocols use a five-layer reference model as Figure 20.4 illustrates.

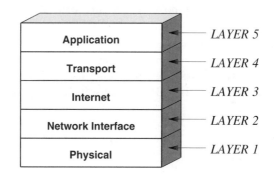

Figure 20.4 The five layers of the TCP/IP reference model.

We have already explored three of the layers. Chapters in part 1 of the text consider applications; chapters in parts 2 and 3 of the text discuss layer 1 and layer 2 protocols. Chapters in this part of the text consider the two remaining layers in detail:

Layer 3: Internet

Layer *3* (IP) specifies the format of packets sent across the Internet as well as the mechanisms used to forward packets from a computer through one or more routers to a final destination.

Layer 4: Transport

Layer *4* (TCP) specifies the messages and procedures that are used to insure reliable transfer.

To summarize:

> *Internet protocols are organized into five conceptual layers, with IP at layer 3 and TCP at layer 4.*

20.12 Host Computers, Routers, And Protocol Layers

We use the term *host computer* to refer to a computer that connects to the Internet and runs applications. A host can be as small as a cell phone or as large as a mainframe. Furthermore, a host's CPU can be slow or fast, the memory can be large or small, and the network to which a host connects can operate at high or low speed. TCP/IP protocols make it possible for any pair of hosts to communicate, despite hardware differences.

Both hosts and routers need TCP/IP protocol software. However, routers do not use protocols from all layers. In particular, a router does not need layer *5* protocols for applications like file transfer because routers do not run conventional applications†. The next chapters discuss TCP/IP protocol software in more detail, and show how Internet layering works.

20.13 Summary

Logically, the Internet appears to be a single, seamless communication system. An arbitrary pair of computers connected to the Internet can communicate as if they were attached to a single network. That is, a computer can send a packet to any other computer that is attached to the Internet. Physically, the Internet is a collection of networks interconnected by devices called *routers*. Each router is a special-purpose device that connects to two or more networks and is dedicated to transferring Internet packets among the networks.

Computers that attach to the Internet are called *hosts*. A host may be a large computer (e.g., a supercomputer) or a small computer (e.g., a cell phone). Each host attaches to one of the physical networks in the Internet.

The illusion of a single communication system is provided by Internet protocol software. Each host or router in the Internet must run the software, which hides the details of the underlying physical connections and takes care of sending each packet to its destination.

---

†Some routers do run special applications that permit a manager to control the router remotely.

The most important protocols developed for internetworking are known as the *TCP/IP Internet Protocols*, usually abbreviated as *TCP/IP*. In addition to being used on private internets, TCP/IP has been used on the global Internet for many years.

EXERCISES

20.1   In the 5-layer reference model used with the TCP/IP Internet protocols, what is the purpose of each of the five layers?

20.2   Will the Internet be replaced by a single networking technology? Why or why not?

20.3   Users view the Internet as a single network. What is the reality, and to what does a user's computer attach?

20.4   What is the chief difficulty in providing universal service?

20.5   What are the two reasons an organization does not use a single router to connect all its networks?

20.6   If a given router can connect to at most K networks, how many routers, R, are required to connect N networks? Write an equation that gives R in terms of N and K.

Chapter Contents

21

IP: Internet Addressing

21.1 Introduction

The previous chapter explains the physical architecture of the Internet in which routers interconnect physical networks. This chapter begins a description of protocol software that makes the Internet appear to be a single, seamless communication system. The chapter introduces the addressing scheme used by the *Internet Protocol (IPv4)*, and discusses the use of address masks for classless and subnet addressing†.

The next chapters expand the description of IP. They each consider one aspect of the protocol in detail. Taken as a group, the chapters define the IP protocol and explain how IP software allows computers to exchange packets across the Internet.

21.2 Addresses For The Virtual Internet

Recall from Chapter 20 that the goal of internetworking is to provide a seamless communication system. To achieve the goal, protocol software must hide the details of physical networks and offer the illusion of a single, large network. From the point of view of an application, the virtual Internet operates like any network, allowing computers to send and receive packets. The chief difference between the Internet and a physical network is that the Internet is an abstraction imagined by its designers and created entirely by protocol software. Thus, the designers chose addresses, packet formats, and delivery techniques independent of the details of the underlying hardware.

Addressing is a critical component of the Internet abstraction. To give the appearance of a single network, all host computers must use a uniform addressing scheme, and each address must be unique. Although each computer has a MAC address, such ad-

---

†Unless otherwise noted, *Internet Protocol* and *IP* refer to version 4 of IP throughout the text.

dresses do not suffice because the Internet can include multiple network technologies and each technology defines its own MAC addresses.

To guarantee uniform addressing, IP defines an addressing scheme that is independent of the underlying MAC addresses. IP addresses are used as destinations in the Internet analogous to the way MAC addresses are used as destinations on a LAN. To send a packet across the Internet, the sender places the destination's IP address in the packet, and passes the packet to IP protocol software for forwarding. IP protocol software uses the destination IP address when it forwards the packet across the Internet to the destination computer.

The advantage of IP addressing lies in uniformity: an arbitrary pair of application programs can communicate without knowing the type of network hardware or MAC addresses being used. The illusion is so complete that some users are surprised to learn that IP addresses are supplied by protocol software and are not part of the underlying network. Interestingly, we will learn that many layers of protocol software use IP addresses. To summarize:

> *To provide uniform addressing in the Internet, IP defines an abstract addressing scheme that assigns each host a unique protocol address; applications use IP addresses to communicate.*

21.3 The IP Addressing Scheme

The IP standard specifies that each host is assigned a unique 32-bit number known as the host's *Internet Protocol address*, *IP address*, or *Internet address*†. When sending a packet across the Internet, the sender must specify its own 32-bit IP address (the source address) as well as the address of the intended recipient (the destination address).

To summarize:

> *An Internet address (IP address) is a unique 32-bit binary number assigned to a host and used for all communication with the host.*

21.4 The IP Address Hierarchy

Analogous to the hierarchical addressing using with WANs, each 32-bit IP address is divided into two parts: a prefix and a suffix. Instead of identifying a packet switch, an IP prefix identifies the physical network to which the host is attached. An IP suffix identifies a specific computer on the network. That is, each physical network in the Internet is assigned a unique *network number*. The network number appears as a prefix in the IP address of each computer attached to the network, and each computer on a given physical network is assigned a unique suffix.

---

†The three terms are used as interchangeable synonyms.

To guarantee uniqueness, no two networks in the Internet can be assigned the same network number and no two computers on a given network can be assigned the same suffix. For example, if an internet contains three networks, they might be assigned network numbers *1*, *2*, and *3*. Three computers attached to network *1* can be assigned suffixes *1*, *3*, and *5*, while three computers attached to network *2* can be assigned suffixes *1*, *2*, and *3*. The assigned values do not need to be contiguous.

The important point is that the IP address scheme guarantees two properties:

- Each computer is assigned a unique address (i.e., a single address is never assigned to more than one computer).

- Although network number assignments must be coordinated globally, suffixes can be assigned locally without global coordination.

The first property is guaranteed because an IP address contains both a prefix and a suffix. If two computers are attached to different physical networks, the prefixes assigned to their addresses will differ. If two computers are attached to the same physical network, their addresses have different suffixes. Thus, the address assigned to a computer is unique.

21.5 Original Classes Of IP Addresses

Once they chose a size for IP addresses and decided to divide each address into two parts, the designers of IP had to determine how many bits to place in each part. The prefix needs sufficient bits to allow a unique network number to be assigned to each physical network in the Internet. The suffix needs sufficient bits to permit each computer attached to a network to be assigned a unique suffix. No simple choice was possible because adding bits to one part means subtracting bits from the other. Choosing a large prefix accommodates many networks, but limits the size of each network; choosing a large suffix means each physical network can contain many computers, but limits the total number of networks.

Because the Internet includes arbitrary network technologies, it contains a few large physical networks and many small networks. Consequently, the designers chose an addressing scheme to accommodate a combination of large and small networks. The original scheme, which is known as *classful IP addressing*, divided the IP address space into three primary *classes*, where each class has a different size prefix and suffix.

The first four bits of an address determined the class to which the address belonged, and specified how the remainder of the address was divided into prefix and suffix. Figure 21.1 illustrates the five address classes, the leading bits used to identify each class, and the division into prefix and suffix. The figure follows the convention used in TCP/IP protocols of numbering bits from left to right and using zero for the first bit.

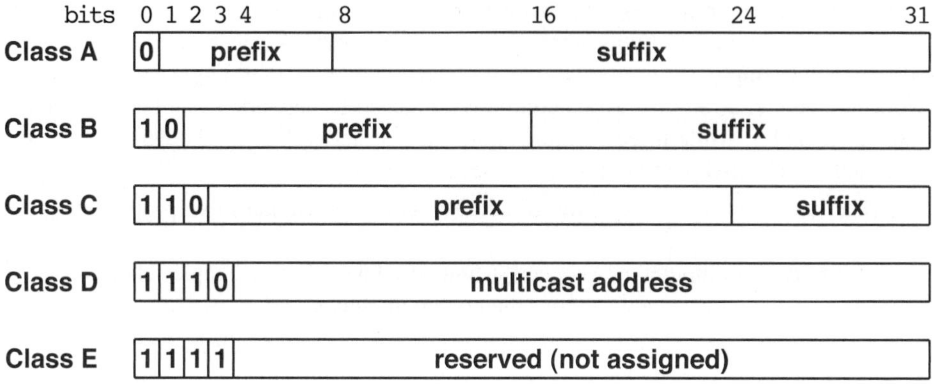

bits   0 1 2 3 4   8   16   24   31

Class A | 0 | prefix | suffix |

Class B | 1 | 0 | prefix | suffix |

Class C | 1 | 1 | 0 | prefix | suffix |

Class D | 1 | 1 | 1 | 0 | multicast address |

Class E | 1 | 1 | 1 | 1 | reserved (not assigned) |

Figure 21.1 The five classes of IP addresses in the original classful scheme.

Although the classful scheme has been superseded, class *D* addresses are still used for multicasting, which allows delivery to a set of computers. Each multicast address corresponds to a group of computers. Once a multicast group has been established, a copy of any packet sent to the multicast address will be delivered to each host in the group. In practice, Internet multicasting has never been available globally, which means that multicasting is restricted to individual sites.

We can summarize:

> *The original IP addressing scheme divided addresses into classes. Class D addresses are still used for multicasting, but multicasting does not work globally.*

21.6 Dotted Decimal Notation

Although IP addresses are 32-bit numbers, users do not enter or read the values in binary. Instead, when interacting with a user, software uses a notation that is more convenient for humans to understand. Called *dotted decimal notation*, the form expresses each 8-bit section of a 32-bit number as a decimal value and uses periods to separate the sections. Figure 21.2 illustrates examples of binary numbers and the equivalent dotted decimal notation.

32-bit Binary Number	Equivalent Dotted Decimal
10000001 00110100 00000110 00000000	129.52.6.0
11000000 00000101 00110000 00000011	192.5.48.3
00001010 00000010 00000000 00100101	10.2.0.37
10000000 00001010 00000010 00000011	128.10.2.3
10000000 10000000 11111111 00000000	128.128.255.0

Figure 21.2 Examples of 32-bit binary numbers and their equivalent in dotted
decimal notation.

Dotted decimal treats each *octet* (each 8-bit value) as an unsigned binary integer†.
As the final example in the figure shows, the smallest possible value, *0*, occurs when all
bits of an octet are zero, and the largest possible value, *255*, occurs when all bits of an
octet are one. Thus, dotted decimal addresses range from *0.0.0.0* through
255.255.255.255. Multicast addresses, class D, occupy the range from 224.0.0.0
through 239.255.255.255.

To summarize:

> *Dotted decimal notation is a syntactic form that IP software uses to
> express 32-bit binary values when interacting with humans. Dotted
> decimal represents each octet in decimal and uses a dot to separate
> octets.*

21.7 Division Of The Address Space

The original classful scheme, which was devised before the PC was invented, before LANs were widely available, and before most companies had a computer network,
divided the address space into unequal sizes. The designers chose an unequal division
to accommodate a variety of scenarios. For example, although it is limited to 128 networks, class *A* contains half of all addresses. The motivation was to allow major ISPs
to each deploy a large network that connected millions of computers. Similarly, the
motivation for class C was to allow an organization to have a few computers connected
on a LAN. Figure 21.3 summarizes the maximum number of networks available in
each class and the maximum number of hosts per network.

---

†IP uses the term *octet* rather than *byte* because the size of a byte depends on the computer. Thus,
although 8-bit bytes have become a de facto standard, octet is unambiguous.

Address Class	Bits In Prefix	Maximum Number of Networks	Bits In Suffix	Maximum Number Of Hosts Per Network
A	7	128	24	16777216
B	14	16384	16	65536
C	21	2097152	8	256

Figure 21.3 The number of networks and hosts per network in each of the original three primary IP address classes.

21.8 Authority For Addresses

Each prefix assigned to an individual network in the Internet must be unique. Therefore a central organization, the *Internet Corporation for Assigned Names and Numbers* (*ICANN*), has been established to handle address assignment and adjudicate disputes. ICANN does not assign individual prefixes. Instead, ICANN authorizes a set of *registrars* to do so. Registrars make blocks of addresses available to ISPs, which provide addresses to subscribers. Thus, to obtain a prefix, a corporation usually contacts an ISP†.

21.9 Subnet And Classless Addressing

As the Internet grew, the original classful addressing scheme became a limitation. Everyone demanded a class A or B address so they would have enough addresses for future growth; many addresses were unused. Although many class C addresses remained, few groups wanted them.

Two new mechanisms were invented to overcome the limitation:

- Subnet addressing
- Classless addressing

The two mechanisms are so closely related that they can be considered to be part of a single abstraction: instead of having three distinct address classes, allow the division between prefix and suffix to occur on an arbitrary bit boundary. Subnet addressing was initially used within large organizations that attached to the global Internet, and classless addressing extended the approach to the entire Internet.

To understand the motivation for using an arbitrary boundary, consider an ISP that hands out prefixes. Suppose a customer of the ISP requests a prefix for a network that contains thirty-five hosts. When classful addressing was used, the ISP would assign a

†Chapter 23 explains how a computer obtains a unique suffix.

class C prefix. In fact, only four bits of host suffix are needed to represent all possible host values, which meant that 219 of the 254 possible suffixes would never be assigned to hosts†. In other words, most of the class C address space is wasted. Classless addressing provides a better solution by allowing the ISP to assign a prefix that is twenty-six bits long. Thus, the suffix is six bits long, meaning that only twenty-seven addresses will be unused.

Another way to look at the situation is to assume the ISP owns a class C prefix. Classful addressing assigns the entire prefix to one organization. With classless addressing, however, the ISP can divide the prefix into several longer prefixes, and assign each to a subscriber. Figure 21.4 illustrates how classless addressing allows an ISP to divide a class C prefix into four longer prefixes that each accommodate a network of up to sixty-two hosts.

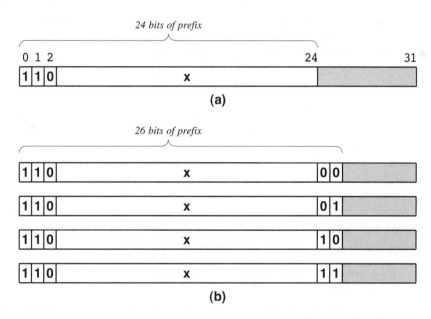

Figure 21.4 (a) A class C prefix, and (b) the same prefix divided into four classless prefixes.

In the figure, the host portion of each prefix is shown in gray. The original class C address has eight bits of suffix, and each of the classless addresses has six bits of suffix. Assuming that the original class C prefix was unique, each of the classless prefixes will also be unique. Thus, instead of wasting addresses, the ISP can assign each of the four classless prefixes to a subscriber.

---

†The number 254 arises because a class C address has 256 possible suffixes and the all 0s and all 1s suffixes are reserved for subnet broadcast as described later in the chapter.

21.10 Address Masks

How can an IP address be divided at an arbitrary boundary? The classless and subnet addressing schemes require hosts and routers that process addresses to store an additional piece of information: a value that specifies the exact boundary between the network prefix and the host suffix. To mark the boundary, IP uses a 32-bit value known as an *address mask*, which was originally called a *subnet mask*. An address mask has one bits to mark the network prefix and zero bits to mark the host portion.

Why store the boundary size as a bit mask? A mask makes processing efficient. In particular, we will see that when they handle an IP packet, hosts and routers need to compare the network prefix portion of the address to a value in their forwarding tables. The bit-mask representation makes the comparison efficient. To see how, suppose a router is given a destination address, D, a network prefix represented as a 32-bit value, N, and a 32-bit address mask, M. That is, assume the top bits of N contain a network prefix, and the remaining bits have been set to zero. To test whether the destination lies on the specified network, the router tests the condition:

$$N == (D\ \&\ M)$$

That is, the router uses the mask with a "logical and" operation to set the host bits of address D to zero, and then compares the result with the network prefix N.

As an example, consider the following 32-bit network prefix:

> 10000000   00001010   00000000   00000000

which has the dotted decimal value *128.10.0.0*. Also consider a 32-bit mask that has sixteen one bits followed by 16 zero bits, which can be denoted in dotted decimal as *255.255.0.0*:

> 11111111   11111111   00000000   00000000

Now consider a 32-bit destination address *128.10.2.3*, which has a binary equivalent of:

> 10000000   00001010   00000010   00000011

A logical *and* between the destination address and the address mask extracts the high-order sixteen bits, which produces the binary result:

> 10000000   00001010   00000000   00000000

which is equal to the network prefix *128.10.0.0*.

21.11 CIDR Notation

The classless addressing scheme is formally known as *Classless Inter-Domain Routing (CIDR)*. The name is unfortunate because CIDR only specifies addressing and forwarding. When the CIDR addressing scheme was created, the designers wanted to make it easy for a human to specify a mask. To understand the difficulty, consider the mask needed for the example in Figure 21.4b, which has twenty-six 1 bits followed by six 0 bits. In dotted decimal, the mask is:

$$255.255.255.192$$

To make it easier for humans to specify and interpret mask values, dotted decimal notation was extended. In the extended version, which is known as *CIDR notation*, an address and a mask can be specified by giving a dotted decimal address followed by a slash and a decimal number that specifies the number of contiguous, left-justified one bits in the mask. That is, the general form is:

$$ddd.ddd.ddd.ddd\,/\,m$$

where *ddd* is the decimal value for an octet of the address, and *m* is the number of one bits in the mask. Thus, one might write the following:

$$192.5.48.69\,/\,26$$

which specifies a mask of 26 bits. Figure 21.5 lists address masks in CIDR notation along with the dotted decimal equivalent of each. Note that some of the CIDR address masks correspond to the original classful assignments.

21.12 A CIDR Example

As an example of CIDR, assume an ISP has the following address block available to assign:

$$128.211.0.0\,/\,16$$

Further suppose the ISP has two customers, one customer needs twelve IP addresses and the other customer needs nine. The ISP can assign one customer CIDR prefix:

$$128.211.0.16\,/\,28$$

and can assign the other customer:

$$128.211.0.32\,/\,28$$

Length (CIDR)	Address Mask				Notes
/0	0 .	0 .	0 .	0	All 0s (equivalent to no mask)
/1	128 .	0 .	0 .	0	
/2	192 .	0 .	0 .	0	
/3	224 .	0 .	0 .	0	
/4	240 .	0 .	0 .	0	
/5	248 .	0 .	0 .	0	
/6	252 .	0 .	0 .	0	
/7	254 .	0 .	0 .	0	
/8	255 .	0 .	0 .	0	Original Class A mask
/9	255 .	128 .	0 .	0	
/10	255 .	192 .	0 .	0	
/11	255 .	224 .	0 .	0	
/12	255 .	240 .	0 .	0	
/13	255 .	248 .	0 .	0	
/14	255 .	252 .	0 .	0	
/15	255 .	254 .	0 .	0	
/16	255 .	255 .	0 .	0	Original Class B mask
/17	255 .	255 .	128 .	0	
/18	255 .	255 .	192 .	0	
/19	255 .	255 .	224 .	0	
/20	255 .	255 .	240 .	0	
/21	255 .	255 .	248 .	0	
/22	255 .	255 .	252 .	0	
/23	255 .	255 .	254 .	0	
/24	255 .	255 .	255 .	0	Original Class C mask
/25	255 .	255 .	255 .	128	
/26	255 .	255 .	255 .	192	
/27	255 .	255 .	255 .	224	
/28	255 .	255 .	255 .	240	
/29	255 .	255 .	255 .	248	
/30	255 .	255 .	255 .	252	
/31	255 .	255 .	255 .	254	
/32	255 .	255 .	255 .	255	All 1s (host specific mask)

Figure 21.5 A list of address masks in CIDR notation and in dotted decimal.

Although both customers have the same mask size (28 bits), the prefixes differ. The binary value assigned to one customer is:

$$10000000 \quad 11010011 \quad 00000000 \quad 0001 \quad 0000$$

and the binary value assigned to the other customer is:

$$10000000 \quad 11010011 \quad 00000000 \quad 0010 \quad 0000$$

Thus, there is no ambiguity — each customer has a unique prefix. More important, the ISP retains most of the original address block, which it can allocate to other customers.

21.13 CIDR Host Addresses

Consider computing the range of addresses in a CIDR block. Once an ISP assigns a customer a CIDR prefix, the customer can assign host addresses. For example, suppose an organization is assigned *128.211.0.16/28* as described above. Figure 21.6 illustrates that the organization will have four bits to use as a host address field, and shows the highest and lowest addresses in both binary and dotted decimal. The example avoids assigning the all 1s and all 0s host addresses.

Network Prefix 128.211.0.16 / 28

0																											28			31
1	0	0	0	0	0	0	0	1	1	0	1	0	0	1	1	0	0	0	0	0	0	0	0	0	0	1	0	0	0	0

Address Mask 255.255.255.240

0																											28			31
1	1	1	1	1	1	1	1	1	1	1	1	1	1	1	1	1	1	1	1	1	1	1	1	1	1	1	0	0	0	0

Lowest Host Address 128.211.0.17

0																											28			31
1	0	0	0	0	0	0	0	1	1	0	1	0	0	1	1	0	0	0	0	0	0	0	0	0	0	1	0	0	0	1

Highest Host Address 128.211.0.30

0																											28			31
1	0	0	0	0	0	0	0	1	1	0	1	0	0	1	1	0	0	0	0	0	0	0	0	0	0	1	1	1	1	0

Figure 21.6 Illustration of CIDR addressing for an example / 28 prefix.

Figure 21.6 illustrates a disadvantage of classless addressing — because the host suffix can start on an arbitrary boundary, values are not easy to read in dotted decimal. For example, when combined with the network prefix, the fourteen possible host suffixes result in dotted decimal values from *128.211.0.17* through *128.211.0.30*.

21.14 Special IP Addresses

In addition to assigning an address to each computer, it is convenient to have addresses that can be used to denote networks or sets of computers. IP defines a set of special address forms that are *reserved*. That is, special addresses are never assigned to hosts. This section describes both the syntax and semantics of each special address form.

21.14.1 Network Address

One of the motivations for defining special address forms can be seen in Figure 21.6 — it is convenient to have an address that can be used to denote the prefix assigned to a given network. IP reserves host address zero, and uses it to denote a *network*. Thus, the address *128.211.0.16/28* denotes a network because the bits beyond the 28th are zero. A network address should never appear as the destination address in a packet†.

21.14.2 Directed Broadcast Address

Sometimes, it is convenient to send a copy of a packet to all hosts on a physical network. To simplify broadcasting, IP defines a *directed broadcast address* for each physical network. When a packet is sent to a network's directed broadcast address, a single copy of the packet travels across the Internet until it reaches the specified network. The packet is then delivered to all hosts on the network.

The directed broadcast address for a network is formed by adding a suffix that consists of all *1* bits to the network prefix. Thus, the host suffix that consists of all *1* bits is reserved — if an administrator inadvertently assigns the all-ones suffix to a specific computer, software may malfunction.

How does broadcast work? If network hardware supports broadcast, a directed broadcast will be delivered using the hardware broadcast capability. If a particular network does not have hardware support for broadcast, software must send a separate copy of the packet to each host on the network.

---

†Section 21.16 discusses the Berkeley broadcast address form, which is a nonstandard exception.

21.14.3 Limited Broadcast Address

The term *limited broadcast* refers to a broadcast on a directly-connected network; informally, we say that the broadcast is limited to a "single wire". Limited broadcast is used during system startup by a computer that does not yet know the network number.

IP reserves the address consisting of thirty-two *1* bits to refer to limited broadcast. Thus, IP will broadcast any packet sent to the all-ones address across the local network.

21.14.4 This Computer Address

Because each Internet packet contains the address of the source as well as the destination, a computer needs to know its IP address before it can send or receive Internet packets. In Chapter 23, we will learn that TCP/IP contains protocols a computer can use to obtain its IP address automatically when the computer boots. Interestingly, the startup protocols use IP to communicate. When using such startup protocols, a computer cannot supply a correct IP source address. To handle such cases, IP reserves the address that consists of all zeroes to mean *this computer*†.

21.14.5 Loopback Address

IP defines a *loopback address* used to test network applications. Programmers often use loopback for preliminary debugging after a network application has been created. To perform a loopback test, a programmer must have two application programs that are intended to communicate across a network. Each application includes the code needed to interact with TCP/IP protocol software. Instead of executing each program on a separate computer, the programmer runs both programs on a single computer and instructs them to use a loopback address when communicating. When one application sends data to another, data travels down the protocol stack to the IP software, which forwards it back up through the protocol stack to the second program. Thus, the programmer can test the program logic quickly without needing two computers and without sending packets across a network.

IP reserves the network prefix *127/8* for use with loopback. The host address used with *127* is irrelevant — all host addresses are treated the same. By convention, programmers often use host number *1*, making *127.0.0.1* the most popular loopback address.

During loopback testing no packets ever leave a computer — the IP software forwards packets from one application program to another. Consequently, the loopback address never appears in a packet traveling across a network.

---

†The meaning of *this computer* only applies when the address appears in a datagram. An all-zeroes entry may appear as the default route in a forwarding table along with an all-zeroes address mask. However, the use in a forwarding table is unrelated to the use in a datagram.

21.15 Summary Of Special IP Addresses

The table in Figure 21.7 summarizes the special IP address forms.

Prefix	Suffix	Type Of Address	Purpose
all-0s	all-0s	this computer	used during bootstrap
network	all-0s	network	identifies a network
network	all-1s	directed broadcast	broadcast on specified net
all-1s	all-1s	limited broadcast	broadcast on local net
127/8	any	loopback	testing

Figure 21.7 Summary of the special IP address forms.

We said that special addresses are reserved and should never be assigned to host computers. Furthermore, each special address is restricted to certain uses. For example, a broadcast address must never appear as a source address, and the all-*0*s address must not be used after a host completes the startup procedure and has obtained an IP address.

21.16 The Berkeley Broadcast Address Form

The University of California at Berkeley developed and distributed an early implementation of TCP/IP protocols as part of BSD UNIX†. The BSD implementation contained a nonstandard feature that has affected many subsequent implementations. Instead of using a host suffix of all ones to represent a directed broadcast address, the Berkeley implementation uses a host suffix that contains all zeroes (i.e., identical to the network address). The address form is known informally as *Berkeley broadcast*.

Unfortunately, many computer manufacturers derived their early TCP/IP software from the Berkeley implementation, and a few sites still use Berkeley broadcast. TCP/IP implementations often include a configuration parameter that can select between the TCP/IP standard and the Berkeley form; many implementations are built to accept both standard and Berkeley broadcast address forms. Thus, a network manager must choose the form to be used on each network (if directed broadcast is allowed).

---

†BSD stands for the *Berkeley Software Distribution*.

21.17 Routers And The IP Addressing Principle

In addition to assigning an Internet address to each host, the Internet Protocol specifies that routers should be assigned IP addresses as well. In fact, each router is assigned two or more IP addresses, one for each network to which the router attaches. To understand why, recall two facts:

- A router has connections to multiple physical networks.
- Each IP address contains a prefix that specifies a physical network.

Thus, a single IP address does not suffice for a router because each router connects to multiple networks and each network has a unique prefix. The IP scheme can be explained by a fundamental principle:

> *An IP address does not identify a specific computer. Instead, each IP address identifies a connection between a computer and a network. A computer with multiple network connections (e.g., a router) must be assigned one IP address for each connection.*

Figure 21.8 illustrates the idea with an example that shows IP addresses assigned to two routers that connect three networks.

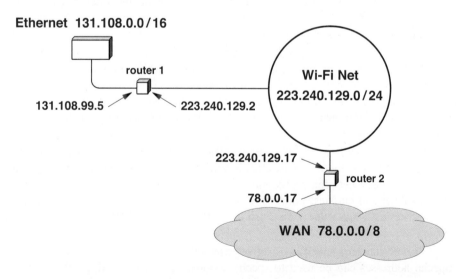

Figure 21.8 An example of IP addresses assigned to two routers.

IP does not require that the same suffix be assigned to all the interfaces of a router. In the figure, for example, the router connecting the Ethernet and Wi-Fi network has suffixes *99.5* (connection to the Ethernet) and *2* (connection to the Wi-Fi network). However, IP does not prevent using the same suffix for all connections. Thus, the example shows that the administrator has chosen to use the same suffix, *17*, for both interfaces of the router that connects the Wi-Fi network to the WAN. As a practical matter, using the same suffix can help humans who manage the networks because a single number is easier to remember.

21.18 Multi-Homed Hosts

Can a host connect to multiple networks? Yes. A host computer with multiple network connections is said to be *multi-homed*. Multi-homing is sometimes used to increase reliability — if one network fails, the host can still reach the Internet through the second connection. Alternatively, multi-homing is used to increase performance — connections to multiple networks can make it possible to send traffic directly and avoid routers, which are sometimes congested. Like a router, a multi-homed host has multiple protocol addresses, one for each network connection.

21.19 Summary

To give the appearance of a large, seamless network, the Internet uses a uniform addressing scheme. Each computer is assigned a unique IP address; all Internet applications use the address when communicating with the computer.

The Internet Protocol specifies addressing. IP divides each Internet address into a two-level hierarchy: a prefix identifies the network to which a computer attaches, and a suffix identifies a specific computer on the network. To ensure that addresses remain unique throughout a given internet, a central authority assigns network prefixes. Once a prefix has been assigned, a local network administrator assigns each host on the network a unique suffix.

An IP address is a 32 bit number. The original addressing scheme divided addresses into classes; the multicast class is still used. Classless and subnet addressing allow the boundary between prefix and suffix to occur on an arbitrary bit boundary. To do so, subnet and classless addressing (CIDR) store a 32-bit mask along with each address. The mask has value *1* for each bit in the prefix, and value *0* for each bit in the suffix.

The IP standard specifies a set of reserved addresses that have special meaning. Special addresses can be used to specify loopback (used for testing), the address of a network, broadcast on the local physical network, and broadcast on a remote network.

Although it is convenient to think of an IP address as specifying a computer, each IP address identifies a connection between a computer and a network. Routers and multi-homed hosts, which have connections to multiple physical networks, each have multiple IP addresses.

EXERCISES

21.1   What does the Internet address hierarchy allow a local manager to do?

21.2   Suppose you are an ISP that owns a / 22 address block. Can you accommodate requests from six customers who need addresses for 9, 15, 20, 41, 128, and 260 computers, respectively? If so, how? If not, explain why.

21.3   Write a computer program that reads as input a network prefix in CIDR notation and a request for a number of hosts. Assume the request has been given to the ISP that owns the prefix, and assign a CIDR prefix that accommodates the request without wasting addresses.

21.4   Can a host have more than one IP address? Explain.

21.5   Could IP be redesigned to use hardware addresses instead of the 32-bit addresses it currently uses? Why or why not?

21.6   In the original classful address scheme, was it possible to determine the class of an address from the address itself? Explain.

21.7   If an ISP assigned you a / 28 address block, how many computers could you assign an address?

21.8   Suppose you are an ISP with a / 24 address block. Explain whether you accommodate a request from a customer who needs addresses for 255 computers. (Hint: consider the special addresses.)

21.9   Write a computer program that reads an address in CIDR notation and prints the resulting address and mask in binary.

21.10   What is a Berkeley broadcast address?

21.11   Write a computer program that accepts a dotted decimal address as input and displays a string of 32 bits.

21.12   How many IP addresses are assigned to a router? Explain.

21.13   Write a computer program that reads an IP address in dotted decimal form and determines whether the address is a multicast address.

21.14   Write a computer program that translates between CIDR slash notation and an equivalent dotted decimal value.

21.15   Suppose you are an ISP that owns a / 22 address block. Show the CIDR allocation you would use to allocate address blocks to four customers who need addresses for 60 computers each.

21.16   Is the CIDR prefix 1.2.3.4 / 29 valid? Why or why not?

21.17   If an ISP offers a / 17 address block for N dollars per month and a / 16 address block for 1.5 N dollars per month, which has the cheapest cost per computer?

21.18   Write a computer program that reads a 32-bit host address and a 32-bit mask in CIDR notation and tells whether the address is one of the special addresses.

Chapter Contents

22

Datagram Forwarding

22.1 Introduction

Previous chapters describe the architecture of the Internet and Internet addressing. This chapter discusses the fundamental communication service in the Internet. It describes the format of packets that are sent across the Internet, and discusses the key concepts of datagram encapsulation, forwarding, and fragmentation and reassembly. Later chapters extend the discussion by considering additional protocols that form a complete service.

22.2 Connectionless Service

The goal of internetworking is to provide a packet communication system that allows a program running on one computer to send data to a program running on another computer. In a well-designed internet, application programs remain unaware of the underlying physical networks — they can send and receive data without knowing the details of the local network to which a computer connects, the remote network to which the destination connects, or the interconnection between the two.

One of the fundamental questions that must be considered when designing an internet concerns the services that will be offered. In particular, designers must decide whether to offer a *connection-oriented* service, a *connectionless* service, or both.

TCP/IP designers chose to include protocols for both connectionless and connection-oriented service. They chose to make the fundamental delivery service connectionless, and to add a reliable connection-oriented service that uses the underlying connectionless service. The design was successful, and forms the basis for all Internet communication.

22.3 Virtual Packets

Connectionless service is a straightforward extension of packet switching — the service allows a sender to transmit individual packets of data across the Internet. Each packet travels independently, and contains information that identifies the intended recipient.

How does a packet pass across the Internet? In general, the answer is that routers handle most of the forwarding. A host creates a packet, places the destination address in the packet header, and then sends the packet to a nearby router. When a router receives a packet, the router uses the destination address to select the next router on the path to the destination, and then forwards the packet. Eventually, the packet reaches a router that can deliver the packet to its final destination.

What format is used for an Internet packet? Because the Internet consists of heterogeneous networks that use incompatible frame formats, the Internet cannot adopt any of the hardware frame formats. More important, a router cannot simply reformat the frame header because the two networks may use incompatible addressing (e.g., the addresses in an incoming frame may make no sense on another network).

To overcome heterogeneity, the Internet Protocol defines a packet format that is independent of the underlying hardware. The result is a *universal, virtual* packet that can be transferred across the underlying hardware intact. As the term *virtual* implies, the Internet packet format is not tied directly to any hardware. In fact, the underlying hardware does not understand or recognize an Internet packet. As the term *universal* implies, each host or router in the Internet contains protocol software that recognizes Internet packets. We can summarize:

> *Because it includes incompatible networks, the Internet cannot adopt a particular hardware packet format. To accommodate heterogeneity, the Internet Protocol defines a hardware-independent packet format.*

22.4 The IP Datagram

TCP/IP protocols use the name *IP datagram* to refer to an Internet packet. Surprisingly, an IP datagram has the same general format as a hardware frame: the datagram begins with a header followed by a data (or *payload*) area. Figure 22.1 illustrates the datagram format.

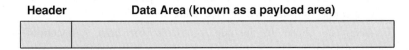

Figure 22.1 The general form of an IP datagram with a header followed by a payload.

To summarize:

> *A packet sent across a TCP/IP internet is called an IP datagram.*
> *Each datagram consists of a header followed by data area, which is*
> *known as the payload.*

The amount of data carried in a datagram is not fixed. A sender chooses an amount of data that is appropriate to a particular purpose. For example, an application that transmits keystrokes across a network can place each keystroke in a separate datagram, while an application that transfers large files can send large datagrams. The point is:

> *The size of a datagram is determined by the application that sends*
> *data. Allowing the size of datagrams to vary makes IP adaptable to a*
> *variety of applications.*

In the current version of the Internet Protocol (IP version 4), a datagram can contain as little as a single octet of data or at most 64K octets, including the header. In most datagrams, the header is much smaller than the payload. A header represents overhead — because the size of the datagram header is fixed, sending large datagrams results in more data octets transmitted per unit of time (i.e., higher throughput).

22.5 The IP Datagram Header Format

What does a datagram header contain? Similar to a frame header, a datagram header contains information used to forward the datagram. In particular, the header contains the address of the source (the original sender), the address of the destination (the ultimate recipient), and a field that specifies the type of data being carried in the payload area. Each address in the header is an IP address; MAC addresses for the sender and recipient do not appear in the datagram.

Each field in an IP datagram header has a fixed size, which makes header processing efficient. Figure 22.2 shows the fields of an IP datagram header, and the subsequent text describes each field.

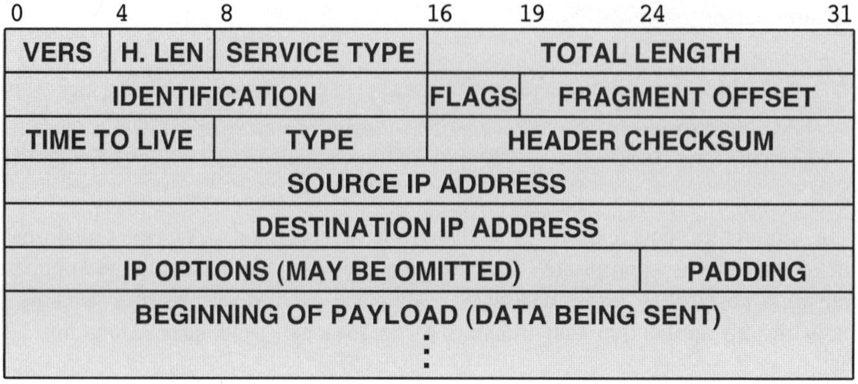

```
0        4        8               16      19      24              31
┌────────┬────────┬───────────────┬───────┬───────────────────────┐
│ VERS   │ H. LEN │ SERVICE TYPE  │        TOTAL LENGTH            │
├────────┴────────┴───────────────┼───────┬───────────────────────┤
│       IDENTIFICATION             │ FLAGS │   FRAGMENT OFFSET      │
├─────────────────┬───────────────┼───────┴───────────────────────┤
│  TIME TO LIVE   │     TYPE      │       HEADER CHECKSUM          │
├─────────────────┴───────────────┴───────────────────────────────┤
│                   SOURCE IP ADDRESS                              │
├─────────────────────────────────────────────────────────────────┤
│                 DESTINATION IP ADDRESS                           │
├─────────────────────────────────────────────┬───────────────────┤
│        IP OPTIONS (MAY BE OMITTED)           │      PADDING       │
├─────────────────────────────────────────────┴───────────────────┤
│        BEGINNING OF PAYLOAD (DATA BEING SENT)                    │
│                              ⋮                                   │
└─────────────────────────────────────────────────────────────────┘
```

Figure 22.2 Fields in the IP version 4 datagram header.

VERS. Each datagram begins with a 4-bit protocol version number (the figure shows a version *4* header).

H.LEN. The 4-bit header length field specifies the number of 32-bit quantities in the header. If no options are present, the value is 5.

SERVICE TYPE. An 8-bit field that carries a class of service for the datagram (seldom used in practice). Chapter 28 explains the DiffServ interpretation of the service type field.

TOTAL LENGTH. A 16-bit integer that specifies the total number of bytes in the datagram, including both the header and the data.

IDENTIFICATION. A unique 16-bit number (usually sequential) assigned to the datagram that is used to gather all fragments for reassembly.

FLAGS. A 3-bit field with individual bits specifying whether the datagram is a fragment and if so, whether the fragment corresponds to the rightmost piece of the original datagram.

FRAGMENT OFFSET. A 13-bit field that specifies where in the original datagram the data in this fragment belongs. The value of the field is multiplied by eight to obtain an offset.

TIME TO LIVE. An 8-bit integer initialized by the original sender and decremented by each router that processes the datagram. If the value reaches zero, the datagram is discarded and an error message is sent back to the source.

TYPE. An 8-bit field that specifies the type of the payload.

HEADER CHECKSUM. a 16-bit ones-complement checksum of header fields computed according to Algorithm 8.1†.

SOURCE IP ADDRESS. The 32-bit Internet address of the original sender (the addresses of intermediate routers do not appear in the header).

---

†Algorithm 8.1 can be found on page 144.

DESTINATION IP ADDRESS. The 32-bit Internet address of the ultimate destination. The addresses of intermediate routers do not appear in the header.

IP OPTIONS. Optional header fields used to control routing and datagram processing. Most datagrams do not contain any options, which means the IP OPTIONS field is omitted from the header.

PADDING. If options do not end on a 32-bit boundary, zero bits of padding are added to make the header a multiple of 32 bits.

22.6 Forwarding An IP Datagram

We said that a datagram traverses the Internet by following a path from its initial source through routers to the final destination. The Internet uses next-hop forwarding. Each router along the path receives the datagram, extracts the destination address from the header, and uses the destination address to determine a next hop to which the datagram should be sent. The router then forwards the datagram to the next hop, either the final destination or another router.

To make the selection of a next hop efficient, an IP router uses a *forwarding table*. A forwarding table is initialized when the router boots, and must be updated if the topology changes or hardware fails.

Conceptually, the forwarding table contains a set of entries that each specify a destination and the next hop used to reach that destination. Figure 22.3 shows an example internet and the contents of a forwarding table in one of the three routers that are used to interconnect the networks.

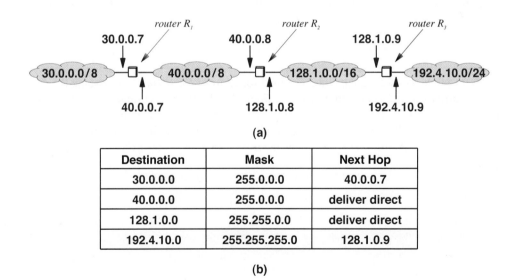

Destination	Mask	Next Hop
30.0.0.0	255.0.0.0	40.0.0.7
40.0.0.0	255.0.0.0	deliver direct
128.1.0.0	255.255.0.0	deliver direct
192.4.10.0	255.255.255.0	128.1.0.9

(b)

Figure 22.3 (a) An example internet with four networks, and (b) the forwarding table found in router R_2.

In the figure, each router has been assigned two IP addresses, one for each interface. Router R_2, which connects directly to networks *40.0.0.0/8* and *128.1.0.0/16*, has been assigned addresses *40.0.0.8* and *128.1.0.8*. Recall that IP does not require the suffix to be the same on all interfaces — a network administrator has chosen the same suffix for each interface to make it easier for humans who manage the network.

The important point to note is the forwarding table size, which is crucial in the global Internet:

> *Because each destination in a forwarding table corresponds to a network, the number of entries in a forwarding table is proportional to the number of networks in the Internet, not the number of hosts.*

22.7 Network Prefix Extraction And Datagram Forwarding

The process of using a forwarding table to select a next hop for a given datagram is called *forwarding*. Recall from Chapter 21 that the *mask* field in a forwarding table entry is used to extract the network portion of an address during lookup. When a router encounters a datagram with destination IP address D, the forwarding function must find an entry in the forwarding table that specifies a next hop for D. To do so, the software examines each entry in the table by using the mask in the entry to extract a prefix of address D and comparing the resulting prefix to the *Destination* field of the entry. If the two are equal, the datagram will be forwarded to the *Next Hop* in the entry.

The bit mask representation makes extraction efficient — the computation consists of a Boolean *and* between the mask and destination address, D. Thus, the computation to examine the ith entry in the table can be expressed as:

if ((Mask[i] & D) == Destination[i]) forward to NextHop[i];

As an example, consider a datagram destined for address *192.4.10.3*, and assume the datagram arrives at the center router, R_2, in Figure 22.3. Further assume the forwarding procedure searches entries of the table in order. The first entry fails because *255.0.0.0 & 192.4.10.3* is not equal to *30.0.0.0*. After rejecting the second and third entries in the table, the routing software eventually chooses next hop *128.1.0.9* because

255.255.255.0 & 192.4.10.3 == 192.4.10.0

22.8 Longest Prefix Match

Figure 22.3 contains a trivial example. In practice, Internet forwarding tables can be extremely large, and the forwarding algorithm is complex. For example, analogous to WAN forwarding described in Chapter 18, Internet forwarding tables can contain a *default* entry that provides a path for all destinations that are not explicitly listed. In addition, Internet forwarding allows a manager to specify a *host-specific route* that directs traffic destined to a specific host along a different path than traffic for other hosts on the same network (i.e., to specify a forwarding table entry with a 32-bit mask, which requires the entire host address to match).

An important feature of Internet forwarding arises because address masks can overlap. For example, suppose a router's forwarding table contains entries for the following two network prefixes:

$$128.10.0.0/16$$

$$128.10.2.0/24$$

Consider what happens if a datagram arrives destined to 128.10.2.3. Surprisingly, the matching procedure described above succeeds for both of the entries. That is, a Boolean *and* of a 16-bit mask will produce 128.10.0.0, and a Boolean *and* with a 24-bit mask will produce 128.10.2.0. Which entry should be used?

To handle ambiguity that arises from overlapping address masks, Internet forwarding uses a *longest prefix match*. That is, instead of examining the entries in arbitrary order, forwarding software arranges to examine entries with the longest prefix first. In the example above, Internet forwarding will choose the entry that corresponds to 128.10.2.0/24. The point is:

> *To resolve ambiguity that can arise when more than one entry matches a destination, Internet forwarding examines entries with the longest prefix first.*

22.9 Destination Address And Next-Hop Address

What is the relationship between the destination address in a datagram header and the address of the next hop to which the datagram is forwarded? The *DESTINATION IP ADDRESS* field in a datagram contains the address of the ultimate destination; it does not change as the datagram passes through the Internet. When a router receives a datagram, the router uses the ultimate destination, D, to compute the address of the next router to which the datagram should be sent, N. Although the router forwards a datagram to the next hop, N, the header in the datagram retains destination address D. In other words:

The destination address in a datagram header always refers to the ultimate destination; at each point, a next hop is computed, but the next hop address does not appear in the datagram header.

22.10 Best-Effort Delivery

In addition to defining the format of Internet datagrams, the Internet Protocol defines the semantics of communication, and uses the term *best-effort* to describe the service it offers. In essence, the standard specifies that although IP makes a best-effort to deliver each datagram, IP does not guarantee that it will handle all problems. Specifically, the IP standard acknowledges that the following problems can occur:

- Datagram duplication
- Delayed or out-of-order delivery
- Corruption of data
- Datagram loss

It may seem strange for IP to specify that errors can occur. However, there is an important reason: IP is designed to run over any type of network. We know from earlier chapters that network equipment can experience interference from noise, which can result in corruption or loss. In a system where routes can change, packets following one path may take longer than those following another path, which can result in out-of-order delivery. The point is

Because IP is designed to operate over all types of network hardware, including hardware that experiences problems, IP datagrams may be lost, duplicated, delayed, delivered out of order, or delivered with corrupted data.

Fortunately, we will see that the TCP/IP protocol suite includes additional protocols that handle many of the problems. We will also learn that some applications prefer to use a best-effort service rather than a service that detects and corrects problems.

22.11 IP Encapsulation

How can a datagram be transmitted across a physical network that does not understand the datagram format? The answer lies in a technique known as *encapsulation*. When an IP datagram is encapsulated in a frame, the entire datagram is placed in the payload area of a frame. The network hardware treats a frame that contains a datagram exactly like any other frame. In fact, the hardware does not examine or change the contents of the payload. Figure 22.4 illustrates the concept.

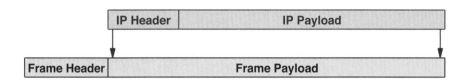

Figure 22.4 Illustration of an IP datagram encapsulated in a frame.

How does a receiver know whether the payload of an incoming frame contains an IP datagram or other data? The sender and receiver must agree on the value used in the frame type field. When it places a datagram in a frame, software on the sending computer assigns the frame type field the special value that is reserved for *IP*. When a frame arrives with the IP value in its type field, the receiver knows that the payload area contains an IP datagram. For example, the Ethernet standard specifies that the type field of an Ethernet frame carrying an IP datagram is assigned *0x0800*.

A frame that carries an IP datagram must have a destination address. Therefore, in addition to placing a datagram in the payload area of a frame, encapsulation requires the sender to supply the MAC address of the next computer to which the datagram should be sent. To compute the appropriate address, IP on the sending computer must bind the next-hop IP address to an equivalent MAC address, which is the destination in the frame header. The next chapter describes the ARP protocol used to perform the binding.

To summarize:

> *A datagram is encapsulated in a frame for transmission across a physical network. The destination address in the frame is the MAC address of the next hop to which the datagram is being sent; the address is obtained by translating the IP address of the next hop to an equivalent MAC address.*

22.12 Transmission Across An Internet

Encapsulation applies to one transmission at a time. After the sender selects a next hop, the sender encapsulates the datagram in a frame and transmits the result across the physical network. When the frame reaches the next hop, the receiving software removes the IP datagram and discards the frame. If the datagram must be forwarded across another network, a new frame is created. Figure 22.5 illustrates how a datagram is encapsulated and unencapsulated as it travels from a source host to a destination host through three networks and two routers. Each network can use a different hardware technology than the others, meaning that the frame formats and frame header sizes can differ.

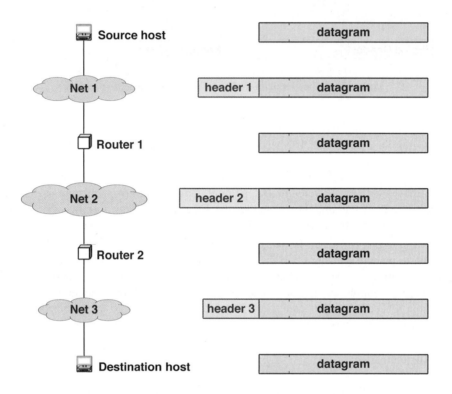

Figure 22.5 An IP datagram as it travels across the Internet.

As the figure shows, hosts and routers store a datagram in memory with no additional header. When the datagram passes across a physical network, the datagram is encapsulated in a frame suitable for the network. The size of the frame header that appears before the datagram depends on the network technology. For example, if *Net 1* represents an Ethernet, the header in frame *1* is an Ethernet header. Similarly, if *Net 2* represents a Wi-Fi network, the header in frame *2* corresponds to a Wi-Fi header.

It is important to observe that frame headers do not accumulate during a trip through the Internet. When a datagram arrives, the datagram is removed from the incoming frame before being encapsulated in an outgoing frame. Thus, when the datagram reaches its final destination, the only frame header on the datagram is the header of the last network over which the datagram arrived. Once the header is removed, the result is the original datagram. The point is:

> *When a datagram arrives in a network frame, the receiver extracts the datagram from the frame payload area and discards the frame header.*

22.13 MTU And Datagram Fragmentation

Each hardware technology specifies the maximum amount of data that a frame can carry. The limit is known as a *Maximum Transmission Unit (MTU)*. There is no exception to the MTU limit — network hardware is not designed to accept or transfer frames that carry more data than the MTU allows. Thus, a datagram must be smaller or equal to the network MTU, or it cannot be encapsulated for transmission.

In an internet that contains heterogeneous networks, MTU restrictions create a problem. In particular, because a router can connect networks with different MTU values, a datagram that a router receives over one network can be too large to send over another network. For example, Figure 22.6 illustrates a router that interconnects two networks with MTU values of *1500* and *1000*.

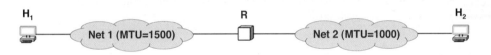

Figure 22.6 Illustration of a router that connects two networks with different MTUs.

In the figure, host H_1 attaches to a network with an MTU of *1500*, and can send a datagram that is up to *1500* octets. Host H_2 attaches to a network that has an MTU of *1000*, which means that it cannot send or receive a datagram larger than *1000* octets. If host H_1 sends a *1500*-octet datagram to host H_2, router R will not be able to encapsulate the datagram for transmission across network 2.

To solve the problem of heterogeneous MTUs, a router uses a technique known as *fragmentation*. When a datagram is larger than the MTU of the network over which it must be sent, the router divides the datagram into smaller pieces called *fragments*, and sends each fragment independently.

Surprisingly, a fragment has the same format as other datagrams — a bit in the *FLAGS* field of the header indicates whether a datagram is a fragment or a complete datagram†. Other fields in the header are assigned information that the ultimate destination uses to *reassemble* fragments to reproduce the original datagram. In particular, the *FRAGMENT OFFSET* field in the header of a fragment specifies where in the original datagram the fragment belongs.

---

†The datagram header format can be found in Figure 22.2 on page 366.

To fragment a datagram for transmission across a network, a router uses the network MTU and the header size to calculate the maximum amount of data that can be sent in each fragment and the number of fragments that will be needed. The router then creates the fragments. It uses fields from the original header to create a fragment header. For example, the router copies the *IP SOURCE* and *IP DESTINATION* fields from the datagram into the fragment header. Finally, the router copies the appropriate data from the original datagram into the fragment, and transmits the result. Figure 22.7 illustrates the division.

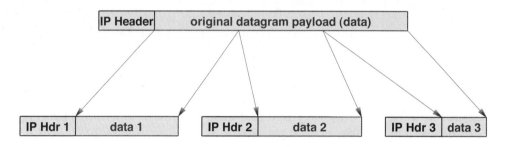

Figure 22.7 An IP datagram divided into three fragments, with the final fragment smaller than the others.

To summarize:

> *Each network has an MTU that specifies the maximum amount of data a frame can carry. When a router receives a datagram that is larger than the MTU of the network over which it is to be sent, the router divides the datagram into smaller pieces called* fragments. *Each fragment uses the IP datagram format, but carries only part of the original payload.*

22.14 Reassembly Of A Datagram From Fragments

The process of recreating a copy of the original datagram from fragments is called *reassembly*. Because each fragment begins with a copy of the original datagram header†, all fragments have the same destination address as the original datagram from which they were derived. The fragment that carries the final piece of data has an additional bit set in the header. Thus, a host performing reassembly can tell whether all fragments have arrived successfully.

Interestingly, IP specifies that the ultimate destination should reassemble fragments. For example, consider the configuration in Figure 22.8.

---

†The only header fields that differ between the original datagram and a fragment are fields that specify fragmentation.

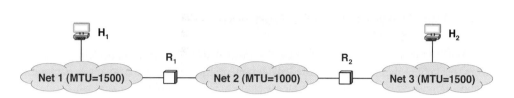

Figure 22.8 Illustration of three networks connected by two routers.

In the figure, if host H_1 sends a *1500*-octet datagram to host H_2, router R_1 will divide the datagram into two fragments, which it will forward to R_2. Router R_2 does not reassemble the fragments. Instead R_2 uses the destination address in a fragment to forward the fragment as usual. The ultimate destination host, H_2, collects the fragments, and reassembles them to produce the original datagram.

Requiring the ultimate destination to reassemble fragments has two advantages.

- First, it reduces the amount of state information in routers. When forwarding a datagram, a router does not need to know whether the datagram is a fragment.

- Second, it allows routes to change dynamically. If an intermediate router were to reassemble fragments, all fragments would need to reach the router.

By postponing reassembly until the ultimate destination, IP is free to pass some fragments from a datagram along differents routes than other fragments. That is, the Internet can change routes at any time (e.g., to route around a hardware failure).

22.15 Collecting The Fragments Of A Datagram

Recall that IP does not guarantee delivery. Thus, individual fragments, which are forwarded exactly like other datagrams, can be lost or arrive out of order. More important, if a given source sends multiple datagrams to the same destination, fragments from multiple datagrams can arrive in arbitrary order.

How does IP software reassemble fragments that arrive out of order? A sender places a unique identification number in the *IDENTIFICATION* field of each outgoing datagram. When a router fragments a datagram, the router copies the identification number into each fragment. A receiver uses the identification number and IP source address in an incoming fragment to determine the datagram to which the fragment belongs. In addition, the *FRAGMENT OFFSET* field tells a receiver where data in the fragment belongs in the original datagram.

22.16 The Consequence Of Fragment Loss

We said that IP does not guarantee fragment delivery — if an underlying network drops packets, either an encapsulated datagram or fragment can be lost. A datagram cannot be reassembled until all fragments arrive. Thus, a problem arises when one or more fragments from a datagram arrive, and other fragments are delayed or lost. Although the datagram cannot be reassembled, the receiver must save the fragments that have arrived in case missing fragments are only delayed.

A receiver cannot hold fragments an arbitrarily long time because fragments occupy space in memory. To avoid exhausting memory, IP specifies a maximum time to hold fragments. When the first fragment arrives from a given datagram, the receiver starts a *reassembly timer*. If all fragments of a datagram arrive before the timer expires, the receiver cancels the timer and reassembles the datagram. However, if the timer expires before all fragments arrive, the receiver discards the fragments that have arrived.

The result of IP's reassembly timer is all-or-nothing: either all fragments arrive and IP reassembles the datagram, or IP discards the incomplete datagram. In particular, there is no mechanism for a receiver to tell the sender which fragments have arrived. The design makes sense because the sender does not know about fragmentation. Furthermore, if the sender did retransmit the datagram, routes may be different, which means a retransmission would not necessarily traverse the same routers. Hence, there is no guarantee that a retransmitted datagram would be fragmented in the same way as the original.

22.17 Fragmenting A Fragment

After performing fragmentation, a router forwards each fragment on to its destination. What happens if a fragment eventually reaches a network that has a smaller MTU? The fragmentation scheme has been planned carefully to make it possible to fragment a fragment. A router along the path divides the fragment into smaller fragments. If networks are arranged in a sequence of decreasing MTUs, each router along the path must further fragment each fragment. Of course, designers work carefully to insure that such situations do not occur in the Internet.

In any case, IP does not distinguish between original fragments and subfragments. In particular, a receiver cannot know whether an incoming fragment is the result of one router fragmenting a datagram or multiple routers fragmenting fragments. The advantage of making all fragments the same is that a receiver can perform reassembly of the original datagram without first reassembling subfragments. Doing so saves CPU time, and reduces the amount of information needed in the header of each fragment.

22.18 Summary

The Internet protocol defines an IP datagram to be the basic unit of transfer across a TCP/IP internet. Each datagram resembles a hardware frame because the datagram contains a header followed by a payload area. Like a hardware frame, a datagram header contains information used to transfer the datagram to a specific destination. Unlike a hardware frame, a datagram header contains IP addresses rather than MAC addresses.

IP software in routers uses a table of routes to determine the next hop to which a datagram should be sent. Each entry in a forwarding table corresponds to one destination network, making the size of the forwarding table proportional to the number of networks in the Internet. When selecting a route, IP compares the network prefix of a destination address to each entry in the table. To avoid ambiguity, IP specifies that if a forwarding table contains two entries that match a given destination, forwarding should match the longest prefix.

Although IP selects a next hop to which a datagram must be sent, the address of the next hop does not appear in the datagram header. Instead, the header always specifies the address of the ultimate destination.

An IP datagram is encapsulated in a frame for transmission. Each network technology specifies an MTU (Maximum Transmission Unit), the maximum payload size; when a datagram exceeds the network MTU, IP fragments the datagram. A fragment may be further fragmented, if necessary. The ultimate destination reassembles fragments, using a timer to discard a datagram if one or more fragments are lost.

EXERCISES

22.1   Read RFCs 1149 and 1217. Are they serious network standards? (Hint: consider the dates.)

22.2   If two prefixes in a forwarding table both match a given destination address, which will the forwarding algorithm use?

22.3   What are the two basic communication paradigms that designers consider when designing an internet?

22.4   If a datagram contains one 8-bit data value and no header options, what values will be found in header fields *H. LEN* and *TOTAL LENGTH*?

22.5   Write a program to extract all fields from an IP datagram header. Print the values in hexadecimal or dotted decimal as appropriate.

22.6   What is the MTU of a network?

22.7   Does a destination address in an IP datagram ever refer to an intermediate router? Explain.

22.8   Build an Internet emulation gateway that randomly drops, duplicates, and delays packets.

22.9   In the Internet, where are fragments reassembled?

22.10   If a datagram has a payload of 1480 bytes and must be sent over a network with an MTU of 500 bytes, how many fragments will be sent? Explain.

22.11   Write a computer program to extract the source and destination addresses from an IP datagram, and print them in dotted decimal notation.

22.12   Write a computer program that takes as input an IP forwarding table as in Figure 22.3b and a sequence of destination addresses. For each destination address, search the table sequentially to find the correct next hop, and output the results.

22.13   How does the Internet design accommodate heterogeneous networks that each have their own packet format?

22.14   What problems can occur as an IP datagram passes through the Internet?

22.15   If one captures an IP datagram passing across a network in the middle of the Internet, how many frame headers will appear before the datagram?

22.16   Where in a frame does an IP datagram travel?

22.17   What is the maximum length of an IP datagram?

22.18   Assume two routers are misconfigured to form a routing loop for some destination, D. Explain why a datagram destined for D will not go around the loop forever.

22.19   If a fragment is lost, does a receiver request a new copy? Explain.

22.20   When reassembling fragments, how does a host know whether incoming fragments belong to the same datagram?

Chapter Contents

23

Support Protocols And Technologies

23.1 Introduction

Chapters in this part of the text discuss the Internet and associated technologies. After a description of the internetworking concept and Internet architecture, chapters describe the IP addressing scheme and classless addressing, the IP datagram format, and IP forwarding. The previous chapter introduces encapsulation, fragmentation, and reassembly.

This chapter continues the discussion of internetworking by introducing four key support technologies: address binding, error reporting, bootstrapping, and address translation. Each technology handles one small problem. When combined with other protocols, each makes a significant contribution to the overall functionality of the Internet. Future chapters extend the discussion of internetworking by focusing on transport layer protocols and Internet routing protocols.

23.2 Address Resolution

Recall from Chapter 22 that as a datagram travels across the Internet, the initial sender and each router along the path uses the destination IP address in the datagram to select a next-hop address, encapsulates the datagram in a hardware frame, and transmits the frame across one network. A crucial step of the forwarding process requires a translation: forwarding uses IP addresses, and a frame transmitted across a physical network must contain the MAC address of the next hop. Thus, IP software must translate the next-hop IP address to an equivalent MAC address. The principle is:

> *IP addresses are abstractions provided by protocol software. Because physical network hardware does not know how to locate a computer from its IP address, the next-hop address must be translated to an equivalent MAC address before a frame can be sent.*

Translation from a computer's IP address to an equivalent hardware address is known as *address resolution*, and an IP address is said to be *resolved* to the correct MAC address. Address resolution is local to a network. One computer can resolve the address of another computer only if both computers attach to the same physical network — a computer never resolves the address of a computer on a remote network. Address resolution is always restricted to a single network. For example, consider the simple internet in Figure 23.1.

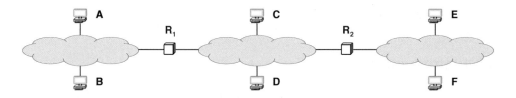

Figure 23.1 An example internet of three networks and computers connected to each.

In the figure, if router R_1 forwards a datagram to router R_2, router R_1 will resolve R_2's IP address to a MAC address. Similarly, hosts A and B attach to the same physical network. If an application on host A sends data to an application on host B, protocol software on A must resolve B's IP address to B's MAC address, and use the MAC address to send the frame directly.

However, if an application on host A sends a message to an application on host F, which attaches to a remote network, protocol software on A will not attempt to resolve F's address. Instead, IP software on A determines that the packet must travel through router R_1, and then resolves the address of R_1. Once it has computed R_2 as the next hop, IP software on R_1 resolves the address of R_2. Similarly, R_2 resolves the address of F.

To summarize:

Mapping between a protocol address and a hardware address is called address resolution. *A host or router uses address resolution when it needs to send a packet to another computer on the same physical network. A computer never attempts to resolve the address of a computer that attaches to a remote network.*

23.3 The Address Resolution Protocol (ARP)

What algorithm does software use to translate a high-level protocol address into an address that the hardware understands? The answer depends on the protocol and hardware addressing schemes. In the Internet, we are only concerned with the resolution of IP addresses. Furthermore, because most hardware has adopted the 48-bit Ethernet addressing scheme, one approach for address resolution dominates. It is the technique that was originally designed for use with Ethernet: the *Address Resolution Protocol (ARP)*.

The idea of ARP is straightforward. Suppose computer *B* needs to resolve the IP address of computer *C*. Computer *B* broadcasts a request that says "I'm looking for the MAC address of a computer that has IP address *C*". The broadcast only travels across one network. When it receives a copy of the request, computer *C* sends a directed reply back to *B* that says, "I'm the computer with IP address *C*, and my MAC address is *M*". Figure 23.2 illustrates the message exchange.

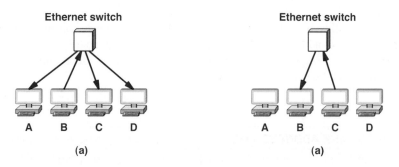

Figure 23.2 Illustration of the ARP message exchange when computer *B* resolves the address of computer *C*.

The figure shows that although an ARP request message reaches all computers on a network, a reply does not. We will see that the sender supplies information in the broadcast request that all computers receive when they process the request.

23.4 ARP Message Format

Rather than restricting ARP to IP and Ethernet, the designers created ARP to be general. Thus, instead of specifying a fixed message format, the standard describes a general form for ARP messages, and specifies how the format is adapted for each type of protocol address and each type of network hardware. The motivation for adapting ARP messages to the hardware arises because the designers realized that they could not choose a fixed size for a hardware address because new network technologies might be invented that have addresses larger than the size chosen. Consequently, the designers included a fixed-size field at the beginning of an ARP message to specify the size of the hardware addresses being used. For example, when ARP is used with an Ethernet, the hardware address length is set to 6 octets because an Ethernet address is 48 bits long. To increase the generality of ARP, the designers also included an address length field for protocol addresses as well as for hardware addresses.

The point is that ARP is not restricted to IP addresses or specific hardware addresses — in theory, the protocol can be used to bind an arbitrary high-level address to an arbitrary hardware address. In practice, the generality of ARP is seldom used: most implementations of ARP are used to bind IP addresses to Ethernet addresses. We can summarize:

> *Although the ARP message format is sufficiently general to allow arbitrary protocol and hardware addresses, ARP is almost always used to bind an IP address to a 48-bit Ethernet address.*

Figure 23.3 illustrates the format of an ARP message when the protocol is used with an IP version 4 address (4 octets) and Ethernet hardware address (6 octets). Each line of the figure corresponds to 32 bits of an ARP message. Subsequent paragraphs describe each of the fields.

0	8	16	24	31
HARDWARE ADDRESS TYPE		PROTOCOL ADDRESS TYPE		
HADDR LEN	PADDR LEN	OPERATION		
SENDER HADDR (first 4 octets)				
SENDER HADDR (last 2 octets)		SENDER PADDR (first 2 octets)		
SENDER PADDR (last 2 octets)		TARGET HADDR (first 2 octets)		
TARGET HADDR (last 4 octets)				
TARGET PADDR (all 4 octets)				

Figure 23.3 The format for an ARP message when binding an IPv4 address to an Ethernet address.

HARDWARE ADDRESS TYPE. A 16-bit field that specifies the type of hardware address being used; the value is *1* for Ethernet.

PROTOCOL ADDRESS TYPE. A 16-bit field that specifies the type of protocol address being used; the value is *0x0800* for IPv4.

HADDR LEN. An 8-bit integer that specifies the size of a hardware address in bytes.

PADDR LEN. An 8-bit integer that specifies the size of a protocol address in bytes.

OPERATION. A 16-bit field that specifies whether the message is a request (the field contains *1*) or a response (the field the contains 2).

SENDER HADDR. A field that extends for *HADDR LEN* bytes and contains the sender's hardware address.

SENDER PADDR. A field that extends for *PADDR LEN* bytes and contains the sender's protocol address.

TARGET HADDR. A field that extends for *HADDR LEN* bytes and contains the target's hardware address.

TARGET PADDR. A field that extends for *PADDR LEN* bytes and contains the target's protocol address.

As the figure shows, an ARP message contains fields for two address bindings. One binding corresponds to the sender, and the other corresponds to the intended recipient, which ARP calls the *target*. When a request is sent, the sender does not know the target's hardware address (that is the information being requested). Therefore, field *TARGET HADDR* in an ARP request can be filled with zeroes because the contents are not used. In a response, the target binding refers to the initial computer that sent the request. Thus, the target address pair in a response serves no purpose; the inclusion of the target fields has survived from an early version of the protocol.

23.5 ARP Encapsulation

When it travels across a physical network, an ARP message is encapsulated in a hardware frame. As with IP, an ARP message is treated as data being transported — the underlying network does not parse the ARP message or interpret fields. Figure 23.4 illustrates ARP encapsulation in an Ethernet frame.

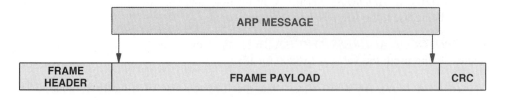

Figure 23.4 Illustration of ARP encapsulation in an Ethernet frame.

The *type field* in the frame header specifies that the frame contains an ARP message. A sender must assign the appropriate value to the type field before transmitting the frame, and a receiver must examine the type field in each incoming frame. Ethernet uses type field *0x806* to denote an ARP message. The same type value is used for both ARP requests and responses. Thus, the frame type does not distinguish between types of ARP messages — a receiver must examine the *OPERATION* field in the message to determine whether an incoming message is a request or a response.

23.6 ARP Caching And Message Processing

Although ARP is used to bind addresses, sending an ARP request for each datagram is inefficient — three frames traverse the network for each datagram (an ARP request, ARP response, and the datagram). More important, because most computer communication involves a sequence of packets, a sender is likely to repeat the exchange many times.

To reduce network traffic, ARP software extracts and saves the information from a response so it can be used for subsequent packets. The software does not keep the information indefinitely. Instead, ARP maintains a small table of bindings in memory. ARP manages the table as a *cache* — an entry is replaced when a response arrives, and the oldest entry is removed whenever the table runs out of space or after an entry has not been updated for a long period of time (e.g., 20 minutes). When it needs to bind an address, ARP starts by searching the cache. If the binding is present in the cache, ARP uses the binding without transmitting a request. If the binding is not present in the cache, ARP broadcasts a request, waits for a response, updates the cache, and then proceeds to use the binding.

Note that unlike most caching schemes, an ARP cache is not updated when a lookup occurs (i.e., when an entry is referenced). Instead, the cache is only updated when an ARP message arrives over the network (either a request or a response). Algorithm 23.1 outlines the procedure for handling an incoming ARP message.

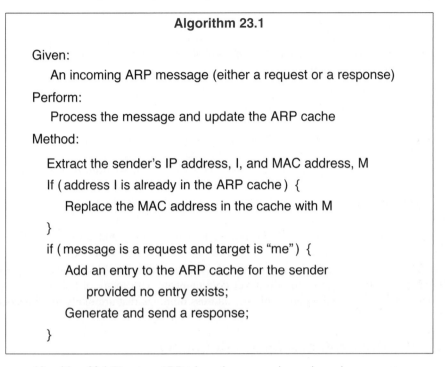

Algorithm 23.1

Given:

An incoming ARP message (either a request or a response)

Perform:

Process the message and update the ARP cache

Method:

Extract the sender's IP address, I, and MAC address, M

If (address I is already in the ARP cache) {

Replace the MAC address in the cache with M

}

if (message is a request and target is "me") {

Add an entry to the ARP cache for the sender

provided no entry exists;

Generate and send a response;

}

Algorithm 23.1 The steps ARP takes when processing an incoming message.

As the algorithm specifies, ARP performs two basic steps to process a message. First, the receiver extracts the sender's address binding and updates the cache if the cache already contains an entry for the sender. Updating the cache handles the case where the sender's hardware address has changed. In the second step, the receiver examines the *OPERATION* field of the message to determine whether the message is a request or a response. If the message is a response, the receiver must have previously issued a request, and is waiting for the binding (i.e., the cache contains an entry for the sender, which was filled in during the first step). If the message is a request, the receiver compares field *TARGET PADDR* with the local protocol address. If the two are identical, the computer is the target of the request, and must send an ARP response. To form the response, ARP begins with the incoming message, reverses the sender's and target's bindings, inserts its hardware address in field *SENDER HADDR*, and changes the *OPERATION* field to 2, indicating a response.

ARP contains a further optimization: when it encounters a request to which it must reply, a computer extracts the sender's address binding from the request and adds the binding to its cache for later use. To understand the optimization, it is necessary to know two facts:

- Most computer communication involves two-way traffic — if a message travels from *A* to *B*, probability is high that a reply will travel from *B* back to *A*.

- Because each address binding requires memory, a computer cannot store an arbitrary number of address bindings.

The first fact explains why extracting the sender's address binding optimizes ARP performance. Computer *A* only sends an ARP request for target *B* when *A* has a packet to deliver to *B*. Thus, when *B* finds itself a target of a request from *A*, it is likely that after the packet arrives, a packet will be sent from *B* to *A*. Arranging for *B* to extract *A*'s binding from the incoming ARP request eliminates the need for a later ARP request from *B* to *A*.

The second fact explains why a new cache entry is only added to the ARP cache by a computer that is the target of an ARP request and not by other computers that receive a request: if all computers inserted the information, their caches would quickly fill, even though most of them will never communicate with many of the computers on the network. Thus, ARP records only the address bindings that are likely to be needed.

23.7 The Conceptual Address Boundary

Recall from Chapter 1 that TCP/IP uses a five-layer reference model. Address resolution is an example of a function associated with the network interface layer, (i.e., layer 2). ARP provides an important conceptual boundary between MAC addresses and IP addresses: ARP hides the details of hardware addressing, and allows higher layers of software to use IP addresses. Thus, there is an important conceptual boundary imposed between the network interface layer and all higher layers: applications as well as higher-layers of protocol software are built to use protocol addresses. Figure 23.5 illustrates the addressing boundary.

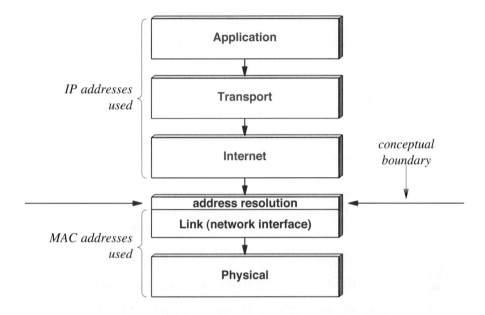

Figure 23.5 Illustration of the boundary between the use of IP addresses and MAC addresses.

The important idea is:

> *ARP forms a conceptual boundary in the protocol stack — layers above ARP use IP addresses, and layers below ARP use MAC addresses.*

23.8 Internet Control Message Protocol (ICMP)

We said that IP defines a best-effort communication service in which datagrams can be lost, duplicated, delayed, or delivered out of order. It may seem that a best-effort service does not need error detection. It is important to realize, however, that a best-effort service is not careless — IP attempts to avoid errors and to report problems when they occur. In fact, we have already seen one example of error detection in IP: a header checksum that is used to detect transmission errors. When a host creates an IP datagram, the host includes a checksum that covers the entire header. Whenever a datagram is received, the checksum is verified to ensure that the header arrived intact. Similarly, the IP header contains a *TIME TO LIVE* field used to prevent a datagram from circulating forever if the forwarding tables in routers incorrectly introduce a circular path.

The action taken in response to a checksum error is straightforward: the datagram must be discarded immediately without further processing. The receiver cannot trust any fields in the datagram header because the receiver cannot know which bits were altered. In particular, the receiver cannot send an error message back to the computer that sent the datagram because the receiver cannot trust the source address in the header. Thus, the receiver has no option but to discard the damaged datagram.

For problems that are less severe than checksum errors, IP includes a companion protocol, the *Internet Control Message Protocol* (*ICMP*), that is used to report errors back to the original source (i.e., the computer that sent the datagram). Interestingly, IP and ICMP are co-dependent — IP depends on ICMP to report errors, and ICMP uses IP to carry error messages.

Although over twenty ICMP messages have been defined, only a few are used. Figure 23.6 lists key ICMP messages and the purpose of each.

Number	Type	Purpose
0	Echo Reply	Used by the ping program
3	Dest. Unreachable	Datagram could not be delivered
5	Redirect	Host must change a route
8	Echo	Used by the ping program
11	Time Exceeded	TTL expired or fragments timed out
12	Parameter Problem	IP header is incorrect
30	Traceroute	Used by the traceroute program

Figure 23.6 Examples of ICMP messages with the message number and purpose.

As the figure illustrates, ICMP contains two message types: messages used to report errors and messages used to obtain information. For example, the *Time Exceeded* and *Destination Unreachable* messages each report an error when a datagram cannot be delivered successfully. A destination address is unreachable if no route exists to the address; a datagram times out if either the TTL count in the header expires or fragments of the datagram do not arrive before the reassembly timer expires. In contrast, the *Echo Request* and *Echo Reply* messages do not correspond to an error. Instead, they are used by the *ping* application to test connectivity — when it receives an *echo request* message, ICMP software on a host or router sends an *echo reply* that carries the same data as the request. Thus, a ping application sends a request to a remote host, waits for a reply, and either declares that the host is reachable, or after a suitable timeout, declares that the host is unreachable.

23.9 ICMP Message Format And Encapsulation

ICMP uses IP to transport each error message: when a router has an ICMP message to send, it creates an IP datagram and encapsulates the ICMP message in the datagram. That is, the ICMP message is placed in the payload area of the IP datagram. The datagram is then forwarded as usual, with the complete datagram being encapsulated in a frame for transmission. Figure 23.7 illustrates the two levels of encapsulation.

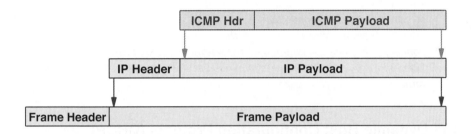

Figure 23.7 Two levels of encapsulation used with an ICMP message.

Datagrams carrying ICMP messages do not have special priority — they are forwarded like any other datagram, with one minor exception. If a datagram carrying an ICMP error message causes an error, no error message is sent. The reason should be clear: the designers wanted to avoid the Internet becoming congested carrying error messages about error messages. We can summarize:

> *The Internet Control Message Protocol includes both messages about errors and informational messages. ICMP encapsulates messages in IP for transmission, and IP uses ICMP to report problems.*

23.10 Protocol Software, Parameters, And Configuration

Our discussion of Internet protocols has described their operation once a host or router has been powered on, the operating system has started, and the protocol software has been initialized. The question arises: how does the protocol software in a host or router begin operation? For a router, the answer is mundane: a manager must specify initial values for items such as the IP address for each network connection, the protocol software to run, and initial values for a forwarding table. The configuration is saved on disk, and a router loads the values during startup.

Host configuration is more complex, and usually uses a two-step process known as *bootstrapping*†. The first step occurs when a computer boots. The operating system fills in a basic set of configuration parameters that allow the protocol software to com-

---

†The term is derived from the phrase "pulling oneself up by one's bootstraps."

municate over a local network. In the second step, the protocol software fills in additional information such as the computer's IP address, the address mask, and the address of a local DNS server. In essence, protocol software consists of a binary image that is *parameterized*, and initialization fills in a set of parameters. Thus, the same binary image can be used on many computers, and an image does not need to change if a computer's network connection changes. We say that protocol software can be *configured* for a particular situation. To summarize:

> *Protocol software is parameterized to allow a compiled binary image to run on multiple computers in a variety of network environments without change. When a copy of the software is started on a given computer, it must be configured by setting a set of parameters that supply information about the computer and the network(s) to which it attaches.*

23.11 Dynamic Host Configuration Protocol (DHCP)

Various mechanisms have been created to allow a host computer to obtain parameters. An early mechanism known as the *Reverse Address Resolution Protocol* (*RARP*) allowed a computer to obtain an IP address from a server. ICMP, described above, includes *Address Mask Request* and *Router Discovery* messages that can obtain the address mask used on a given network and the address of a router. Each of the early mechanisms was used independently, requests were broadcast and a host typically configured layers from lowest to highest.

In the evolution of the Internet protocols, a single protocol was invented to allow a host to obtain multiple parameters with a single request. Known as the *Bootstrap Protocol* (*BOOTP*), the mechanism provided the computer's IP address, the address mask to use, and the address of a default router. Thus, in a single step, a host could obtain most of the information needed to configure a working IP stack.

Like other configuration protocols, BOOTP arranged for a host to broadcast a request. Unlike other configuration protocols, however, BOOTP used IP to communicate with a server — a request was sent to the all-1's *Destination Address*, and used the all-0's address as a *Source Address*. A BOOTP server used the MAC address on an incoming frame to send a response via unicast. Thus, a host that did not know its IP address could communicate with a BOOTP server.

The initial version of BOOTP used a fixed address assignment in which a server had a database of the IP address assigned to each host. A request from the host included a unique ID (usually the host's MAC address), and the server used the ID to find the IP address of the host. The point is that BOOTP required manual administration — before a computer could use BOOTP to obtain an address, a network administrator had to configure a BOOTP server to know the computer's IP address.

Although it works when a set of computers remains fixed, manual specification does not suffice if a set of computers changes rapidly. For example, consider a Wi-FI access point in a coffee shop that provides access to arbitrary customers. To handle such cases, the IETF extended BOOTP and changed the name to the *Dynamic Host Configuration Protocol (DHCP)*.

DHCP provides a mechanism that allows an arbitrary computer to join a new network and obtain an IP address automatically. The concept has been termed *plug-and-play networking*. The point can be summarized:

> *DHCP allows a computer to move to a new network and obtain configuration information without requiring an administrator to make manual changes to a database.*

In fact, DHCP closely follows the same approach as BOOTP. When a computer boots, the computer broadcasts a *DHCP Request* to which a server sends a *DHCP Reply*†. An administrator can configure a DHCP server to supply two types of addresses: permanently assigned addresses as provided by BOOTP or a pool of dynamic addresses to be allocated on demand. Typically, a permanent address is assigned to a server, and a dynamic address is assigned to an arbitrary host. In fact, addresses assigned on demand are not given out for an arbitrary length of time. Instead, DHCP issues a *lease* on the address for a finite period‡. The use of leases allows a DHCP server to reclaim addresses, if necessary. When the lease expires, the server returns the address to the pool of available addresses, which allows the address to be assigned to another computer. Leasing is essential for continuous operation of a server because it allows a server to control resources and reclaim addresses even if a host that is holding an address crashes.

When a lease expires, a host can choose to relinquish the address or renegotiate with DHCP to extend the lease. Negotiation occurs concurrent with other activity. Normally, DHCP approves each lease extension, and the computer continues to operate without any interruption to running application programs or ongoing network communication. However, a server may be configured to deny lease extension for administrative or technical reasons. For example, consider a network in a university classroom. In such cases, a server can be configured so that all leases expire at the end of the class period (to permit the set of addresses to be reassigned to the next class). DHCP grants absolute control of leasing to a server — if a server denies an extension request, the host must stop using the address.

---

†DHCP uses the term *offer* to denote the message a server sends, and we say that the server is *offering* an address to the client.

‡An administrator specifies the lease time for each address when establishing a pool of addresses.

23.12 DHCP Protocol Operation And Optimizations

Although the protocol is straightforward, DHCP includes several important details that optimize performance. The three most significant are:

- Recovery from loss or duplication
- Caching of a server address
- Avoidance of synchronized flooding

The first item means DHCP is designed to insure that missing or duplicate packets do not result in misconfiguration — if no response is received, a host retransmits its request, and if a duplicate response arrives, a host ignores the extra copy. The second item means that once a host uses a *DHCP Discover* message to find a DHCP server, the host caches the server's address. Thus, lease renewal is efficient.

The third item means that DCHP takes steps to prevent synchronized requests. For example, synchronized requests might occur if all computers on a network reboot simultaneously after a power failure. To avoid having all hosts on a network flood the DHCP server with simultaneous requests, DHCP requires each host to delay a random time before transmitting (or retransmitting) a request.

23.13 DHCP Message Format

Because it was designed as an extension of BOOTP, DHCP adopted a slightly modified version of the BOOTP message format. Figure 23.8 illustrates the DHCP message format.

Except for *OPTIONS*, each field in a DHCP message has a fixed size. The first seven fields contain information used to process the message. The *OP* field specifies whether the message is a *Request* or a *Response*. To distinguish among various messages that a client uses to discover servers or request an address or that a server uses to acknowledge or deny a request, DHCP includes an *OPTION* for a specific *message type*. That is, the *OP* field tells whether the message is traveling from the client to the server or the server to the client, and one of the *OPTIONS* gives the exact type of the message.

The *HTYPE* and *HLEN* fields specify the network hardware type and the length of a hardware address. A client uses the *FLAGS* field to specify whether it can receive broadcast or directed replies. The *HOPS* field specifies how many servers forwarded the request, and the *TRANSACTION IDENTIFIER* field provides a value that a client can use to determine if an incoming response matches its request. The *SECONDS ELAPSED* field specifies how many seconds have elapsed since the host began to boot. Finally, if it knows its IP address (e.g., the address was obtained through another mechanism rather than through DHCP), a host fills in the *CLIENT IP ADDRESS* field in a request.

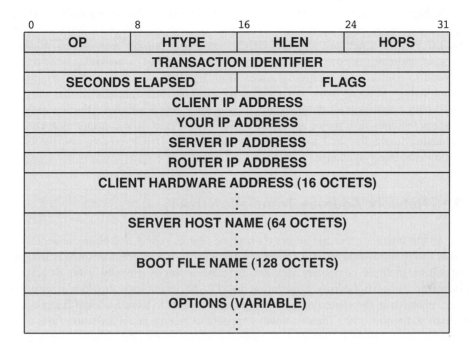

Figure 23.8 The DHCP message format.

Later fields in the message are used in a response to carry information back to the host that sent a request. If a host does not know its IP address, the server uses field *YOUR IP ADDRESS* to supply the value. In addition, the server uses fields *SERVER IP ADDRESS* and *SERVER HOST NAME* to give the host information about the location of a server. Field *ROUTER IP ADDRESS* contains the IP address of a default router.

In addition to protocol configuration, DHCP allows a computer to negotiate to find a boot image. To do so, the host fills in field *BOOT FILE NAME* with a request (e.g., the host can request the LINUX operating system). The DHCP server does not send an image. Instead, the server determines which file contains the requested image, and uses field *BOOT FILE NAME* to return the name of the file. Once a DHCP response arrives, a host must use a separate protocol (e.g., *TFTP*) to download the image.

23.14 Indirect DHCP Server Access Through A Relay

Although it broadcasts on the local network to find a server, DHCP does not require each individual network to have a server. Instead, a *DHCP relay agent* forwards requests and responses between a client and the server. At least one relay agent must be present on each network, and the relay agent must be configured with the address of the appropriate DHCP server. When the server responds, the relay agent forwards the response to the client.

It may seem that using multiple relay agents is no better than using multiple DHCP servers. However, network managers prefer to manage multiple relay agents for two reasons. First, in a network with one DHCP server and multiple relay agents, administration of addresses is centralized into a single device. Thus, a network manager does not need to interact with multiple devices to change the lease policy or determine the current status. Second, many commercial routers contain a mechanism that provides DHCP relay service on all the networks to which the router attaches. Furthermore, relay agent facilities in a router are usually easy to configure (the configuration consists of enabling forwarding and specifying the address of a DHCP server), and the configuration is unlikely to change.

23.15 Network Address Translation (NAT)

As the Internet grew and addresses became scarce, subnet and classless addressing (CIDR) were introduced to help conserve addresses†. A third mechanism was invented that allows multiple computers at a site to share a single, globally valid IP address. Known as *Network Address Translation (NAT)*, the technology provides *transparent* communication in the sense that a host at the site appears to have a normal Internet connection, and a host in the Internet always appears to receive communication from a single computer rather than from one of many computers at the site. That is, hosts at the site run conventional TCP/IP software and applications, and communicate across the Internet as usual.

NAT runs as an in-line service, which means that NAT must be placed on the connection between the Internet and a site. Although NAT is conceptually separate from other facilities and services, most implementations embed NAT in another device such as a Wi-Fi wireless access point or an Internet router. Figure 23.9 illustrates a typical arrangement of a site that uses NAT.

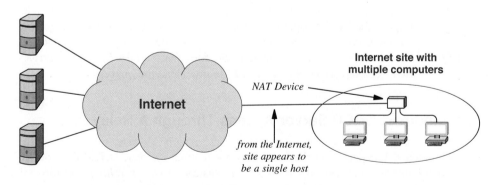

Figure 23.9 The conceptual architecture used with NAT.

---

†A description of subnet and classless addressing can be found in Chapter 21.

23.16 NAT Operation And Private Addresses

The goal of NAT is to provide an illusion. When viewed from the Internet, the site appears to consist of a single host computer that has been assigned a valid IP address — all datagrams sent from the site appear to originate from one host, and all datagrams sent to the site appear to be sent to one host. When viewed from a host in the site, the Internet appears to accept and route private addresses.

Of course, a single IP address cannot be assigned to multiple computers — if two or more computers use the same address, conflicts arise because multiple computers will respond to an ARP request. Thus, to ensure correctness, each computer on a given network must be assigned a unique IP address. NAT solves the problem by using two types of addresses. The NAT device itself is assigned a single globally-valid IP address as if the NAT device were a host on the Internet. Each computer at the site is assigned a unique *private address*, also known as a *nonroutable address*. Figure 23.10 lists address blocks that the IETF has designated as private.

Block	Description
10.0.0.0/8	Class A private address block
169.254.0.0/16	Class B private address block
172.16.0.0/12	16 contiguous Class B blocks
192.168.0.0/16	256 contiguous Class C blocks

Figure 23.10 Blocks of private (nonroutable) addresses used by NAT.

As an example, assume a particular NAT device is using the 192.168.0.0 address block to assign private addresses to hosts within the site. To insure that each address within the site is unique (i.e., to prevent conflicts), hosts might be assigned addresses 192.168.0.1, 192.168.0.2, and so on.

Unfortunately, private addresses are not valid on the global Internet, and routers in the Internet are configured to reject datagrams that specify nonroutable addresses. Thus, private addressing is only used inside a site — before a datagram from the site can be allowed onto the Internet, NAT must translate the private IP address into a globally valid IP address. Similarly, NAT must translate the globally valid IP address in an incoming packet to a private address before transferring a datagram to a host at the site.

The most basic form of NAT translates the source address as a datagram passes from the site to the Internet and the destination address as a datagram passes from the Internet to the site. For example, assume that a NAT device has been assigned a globally valid IP address of 128.210.24.6, and consider the translations that occur if a host with private address 192.168.0.1 sends a datagram to a host on the Internet with address 198.133.219.25 and receives a reply. Figure 23.11 illustrates the translations that occur in each direction.

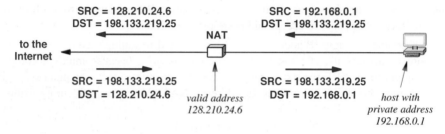

Figure 23.11 Illustration of basic NAT translation that changes the source address of an outgoing datagram and the destination address of an incoming datagram.

To summarize:

> *The most basic form of NAT replaces the IP source address in datagrams passing from the site to the Internet, and replaces the IP destination address in datagrams passing from the Internet to the site.*

Most implementations of NAT use a *translation table* to store the information needed to rewrite addresses. For example, Figure 23.12 shows a translation table that corresponds to the address mapping in Figure 23.11.

Direction	Field	Old Value	New Value
out	IP Source	192.168.0.1	128.210.24.6
	IP Destination	198.133.219.25	-- no change --
in	IP Source	198.133.219.25	-- no change --
	IP Destination	128.210.24.6	192.168.0.1

Figure 23.12 Example NAT translation table for the mapping in Figure 23.11.

How are values placed in a translation table? Although values can be configured manually by a system administrator, most NAT systems operate automatically. That is, NAT places an entry in the translation table whenever a host at the site sends a packet to the Internet. For example, when computer 192.168.0.1 first sends a datagram to destination 198.133.219.25, NAT adds an entry to its table. Later, when it receives a reply from 198.133.219.25, NAT finds the entry in the table, and translates the destination address to 192.168.0.1.

23.17 Transport-Layer NAT (NAPT)

The basic version of NAT described above only handles situations in which each host at a site communicates with a unique server in the Internet. If two hosts at the site attempt to communicate with remote server, X, the translation table will contain multiple entries for X, and NAT will not be able to route incoming datagrams. Basic NAT also fails in situations when two or more applications running on a given host at a site attempt simultaneous communication with different destinations on the Internet.

The most widely used variation of NAT handles both problems: it allows a site to have arbitrary numbers of applications running on arbitrary hosts, all communicating simultaneously with arbitrary destinations throughout the Internet. Although it is technically known as *Network Address and Port Translation (NAPT)*, the mechanism is so popular that most networking professionals assume the term *NAT* means *NAPT*.

The key to understanding NAPT is to recall that applications use *protocol port numbers* to distinguish among services. In particular, Chapters 25 and 26 describe the UDP and TCP transport protocols that each use port numbers. In addition to keeping a table of source and destination addresses, NAPT uses port numbers to associate each datagram with a TCP or UDP flow. That is, instead of stopping at the IP-layer, NAPT operates on transport-layer headers. As a consequence, entries in the translation table used by NAPT contain a 4-tuple of source and destination IP addresses and protocol port numbers.

For example, consider the translation table that might result if a browser on computer 192.168.0.1 and a browser on computer 192.168.0.2 each use local port 30000, and each forms a TCP connection to a web server at port 80 through a NAPT device that uses address 128.10.24.6. To avoid a conflict, NAPT must choose an alternative TCP source port for the connections. Figure 23.13 shows one possibility.

Dir.	Fields	Old Value	New Value
out	IP SRC:TCP SRC	192.168.0.1:30000	128.10.24.6:40001
out	IP SRC:TCP SRC	192.168.0.2:30000	128.10.24.6:40002
in	IP DEST:TCP DEST	128.10.19.20:40001	192.168.0.1:30000
in	IP DEST:TCP DEST	128.10.19.20:40002	192.168.0.2:30000

Figure 23.13 An example NAPT translation table for two TCP connections to
the same web server.

In the figure, the applications on both local computers are using local port 3000. Because an operating system cycles through port numbers, having two identical port numbers is unlikely. However, NAPT handles such extreme cases without confusion. In the example, NAPT chooses port 40001 for one connection and 40002 for the other.

23.18 NAT And Servers

We said that a NAT system builds a translation table automatically by watching outgoing traffic and establishing a new mapping whenever an application at the site initiates communication. Unfortunately, automatic table construction does not work well for communication initiated from the Internet to the site. For example, if multiple computers at a site each run a web server, the NAT device cannot know which computer should receive an incoming web connection. A variant of NAT called *Twice NAT* has been created to allow a site to run multiple servers. Twice NAT arranges for the NAT system to interact with the site's Domain Name System server. When an application on the Internet looks up the domain name of a computer at the site, the DNS server at the site returns the valid IP address that has been assigned to the NAT device, and also creates a new entry in the NAT translation table. Thus, the translation table is initialized before the first packet arrives. Although it is not elegant, Twice NAT works for most cases. Twice NAT fails, however, if a client application uses the IP address directly without performing a domain name lookup or if the client uses a DNS proxy to resolve domain names.

23.19 NAT Software And Systems For Use At Home

NAT is especially useful at a residence or small business that has a broadband connection because it allows a set of computers to share the connection without requiring the customer to purchase additional IP addresses from the ISP. In addition to software that allows a PC to act as a NAT device for additional PCs, dedicated NAT hardware systems are available at low cost. Such systems are usually called *wireless routers†*. For example, Linksys sells a dedicated system that provides NAT among four wired Ethernet and Wi-Fi wireless connections. Figure 23.14 illustrates how such a router is connected.

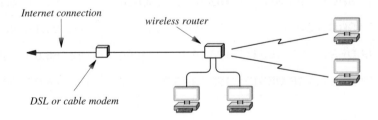

Figure 23.14 Illustration of the connections for a wireless router.

---

†The terminology is slightly misleading because such routers also provide wired connections for host computers.

23.20 Summary

IP uses the Address Resolution Protocol, ARP, to bind a next-hop IP address to an equivalent MAC address. ARP defines the format of messages that computers exchange to resolve an address, the encapsulation, and the rules for handling ARP messages. Because hardware addressing differs among networks, ARP only specifies a general pattern for message format and allows the details to be determined by the MAC addressing scheme. ARP specifies that a computer should broadcast a request message, but that a response should be directed. Furthermore, ARP uses caching to avoid sending a request for each packet.

The Internet Protocol includes a companion error reporting mechanism known as the Internet Control Message Protocol (ICMP). Routers use ICMP when a datagram arrives with incorrect values in header fields or when a datagram cannot be delivered. ICMP messages are always sent back to the original source of a datagram, never to intermediate routers. In addition to messages that report errors, ICMP includes informational messages such as the Echo Request and Echo Reply messages used by the ping application. Each type of ICMP message has a unique format; a type field in the header allows a receiver to divide a given message into appropriate fields. An ICMP message is encapsulated in an IP datagram for transmission.

Originally, separate protocols were used to obtain each of the configuration parameters needed at startup. The Dynamic Host Configuration Protocol (DHCP), which extends the Bootstrapping Protocol (BOOTP), allows a host to obtain all necessary information with a single request. A DHCP response can provide an IP address, the address of a default router, and the address of a name server. When it allocates an IP address automatically, DCHP offers the host a lease during which the address can be used. Once a lease expires, the host must extend the lease, or stop using the address.

The NAT mechanism allows a site to have multiple computers using the Internet through a single IP address. NAT rewrites header fields in each datagram that passes out to the Internet or into the site. For client applications, NAT translations can be established automatically when the NAT device finds the first outgoing packet of the communication. Several variations of NAT exist. The most popular form, NAPT, operates on transport-layer headers, and translates protocol port numbers as well as IP addresses. NAPT allows an arbitrary number of applications running on arbitrary computers within a site to communicate with arbitrary destinations on the Internet simultaneously.

FOR FURTHER STUDY

For details on NAPT refer to RFC 2663 and RFC 2766.

EXERCISES

23.1 Suppose a user specified a directed broadcast address as a destination for ping. What results are possible? Explain.

23.2 Expand Figure 23.13 to show the mappings that will be used if a third application also attempts to reach the same web server.

23.3 When a router uses a forwarding table to look up a next-hop address, the result is an IP address. What must happen before the datagram can be sent?

23.4 What is the chief purpose of NAT?

23.5 When using a wireless router, what are the possible IP addresses that can be assigned to hosts?

23.6 How many responses does a computer expect to receive when it broadcasts an ARP request? Explain.

23.7 Given an Ethernet frame, what fields does a host need to examine to determine whether the frame contains an ICMP message?

23.8 As an alternative to DHCP, devise a distributed algorithm that implements a bidding scheme. Assume that one copy of the algorithm will run on each computer, and have the algorithm assign each computer a unique host address.

23.9 To optimize reassembly, some versions of the Linux operating system send the last fragment of an IP datagram first, and then send the remaining fragments in order. Explain why sending the last fragment first does not work well with NAPT.

23.10 Suppose a computer receives two ARP replies for a single request. The first reply claims that the MAC address is M_1, and the second reply claims that the MAC address is M_2. How does ARP handle the replies?

23.11 What is the chief difference between BOOTP and DHCP?

23.12 What term is used to describe the mapping between a protocol address and a hardware address?

23.13 Make a list of the key network information that can be configured when a computer boots.

23.14 Some network applications defer configuration until a service is needed. For example, a computer can wait until a user attempts to print a document before the software searches for available printers. What is the chief advantage of deferred configuration? The chief disadvantage?

23.15 How many octets does an ARP message occupy when used with IP and Ethernet addresses?

23.16 Many NAT devices choose the 10.0.0.0 /8 address block from Figure 23.10 because it provides the most generality. Explain why.

23.17 What crucial information used by NAPT is not available in most IP fragments?

23.18 How does a computer know whether an arriving frame contains an IP datagram or an ARP message?

23.19 What types of addresses are used in layers below ARP?

23.20 If a datagram has an incorrect value in one of the header fields, which ICMP error message will be received?

23.21 DHCP permits a server to be located on a remote network. How can the computer send DHCP messages to a server on another network?

23.22 In Figure 23.11, the ISP has assigned one IP address to the site. Which is the assigned address?

23.23 Create a NAPT translation table for a case where three computers at a site have TCP connections to three separate web servers in the Internet.

23.24 When does Algorithm 23.1 create a new entry in an ARP cache?

23.25 ARP only permits address resolution to occur on a single network. Does it make sense to send an ARP request to a remote server in an IP datagram? Why or why not?

23.26 Some versions of the *traceroute* program send ICMP messages and others send UDP messages. Experiment with the version on your computer to determine which it sends.

23.27 If a routing loop exists, which ICMP error message will be sent? Explain the process.

23.28 Can ARP be used on a network that does not provide broadcast? Why or why not?

Chapter Contents

24

The Future IP (IPv6)

24.1 Introduction

Previous chapters discuss the current version of the Internet Protocol, IPv4. The chapters describe an IP datagram as a header followed by data. The header contains information such as a destination address that IP software uses to deliver the datagram; each header field has a fixed size to make processing efficient. Chapter 22 describes how an IP datagram is encapsulated in a network frame as it travels across a physical network.

This chapter concentrates on the future of the Internet Protocol. It begins by assessing the strengths and limitations of the current version of IP, and then considers a new version of IP that the IETF has developed. The chapter explains features of the new version, and shows how they overcome some of the limitations of the current version.

24.2 The Success Of IP

The current version of IP has been extremely successful. IP has made it possible for the Internet to handle heterogeneous networks, dramatic changes in hardware technology, and extreme increases in scale. Internet protocols provide a set of abstractions that allow applications to communicate without knowledge of the Internet architecture or underlying hardware. To accommodate heterogeneous hardware, IP defines a network-independent addressing scheme, datagram format, encapsulations, and a fragmentation strategy.

The versatility and scalability of IP are evident from the applications that use IP and from the size of the global Internet. More important, IP has accommodated dramatic changes in hardware. Although it was defined before local area network technologies became popular, the original protocol design has continued to work well through several generations of technologies. In addition to higher data rates, IP has accommodated increases in the size of frames.

To summarize:

> *The success of the current version of IP is incredible — the protocol has accommodated changes in hardware technologies, heterogeneous networks, and extremely large scale.*

24.3 The Motivation For Change

If IP works so well, why change? When IP was defined, only a few computer networks existed. The designers decided to use 32 bits for an IP address because doing so allowed the Internet to include over a million networks. However, the global Internet is growing exponentially, with the size doubling in less than a year. At the current growth rate, each of the possible network prefixes will eventually be assigned, and no further growth will be possible. Thus, the primary motivation for defining a new version of IP arose from the address space limitation — larger addresses are necessary to accommodate continued growth of the Internet.

Secondary motivations for changes in IP have arisen from the perception that special facilities are needed for some applications. Consequently, various groups argue that when IP is replaced, the new version should have more features. For example, consider applications that send real-time audio and video. Such applications deliver data at regular intervals, and need a guarantee of low jitter. Unfortunately, a change in routes usually changes end-to-end latency, which means an increase in jitter. Although the current IP datagram header includes a field that can be used to request a type of service, the protocol does not define a real-time service. Thus, is has been argued that a new version of IP should provide a mechanism that allows datagrams carrying real-time traffic to avoid route changes.

Another group argues that a new version of IP should accommodate more complex addressing and routing capabilities. In particular, it should be possible to configure IP addressing and routing to handle replicated services. For example, Google maintains many data centers around the world. When a user enter *google.com* into a browser, the groups argue, it would be beneficial if IP passed datagrams to the nearest Google data center. In addition, many current applications allow a set of users to *collaborate*. To make collaboration efficient, the Internet needs a mechanism that allows groups to be created or changed and a way to send a copy of a packet to each participant in a given group.

24.4 The Hourglass Model And Difficulty Of Change

Although the apparent scarcity of remaining addresses was considered crucial when work began on a new version of IP in 1993, no emergency occurred, and IP has not been changed. To understand why, think of the importance of IP and the cost to change. In terms of importance, IP lies at the center of Internet communication — all applications use IP, and IP runs over all underlying network technologies. Networking professionals say that Internet communication follows an *hourglass model*, and that IP lies at the position where the hourglass is thin. Figure 24.1 illustrates the concept.

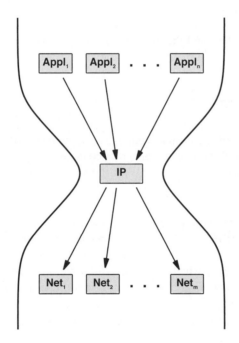

Figure 24.1 The hourglass model of Internet communication with IP at the center.

An important point arises from dependency on IP and the consequent inertia IP introduces:

> *Because IP is central to all Internet communication, changing IP requires a change to the entire Internet.*

24.5 A Name And A Version Number

When researchers began working on a new version of IP, they needed a name for the project. Borrowing from a popular television show, they selected *IP — The Next Generation*, and early reports referred to the new protocol as *IPng*. Unfortunately, many competing proposals were made for IPng, and the name became ambiguous.

When a specific protocol was defined, the designers needed to distinguish the protocol from all other proposals. They decided to use an official version number in the header of the final standardized protocol. The version number that was selected was a surprise. Because the current IP version number is *4*, the networking community expected the next official version to be *5*. However, version *5* had been assigned to an experimental protocol known as *ST*. Consequently, the new version of IP received *6* as its official version number, and the protocol became known as *IPv6*. To distinguish it from IPv6, the current version of IP became known as *IPv4*.

24.6 IPv6 Features

IPv6 retains many of the design features that have made IPv4 so successful. Like IPv4, IPv6 is connectionless — each datagram contains a destination address, and each datagram is routed independently. Like IPv4, the header in a datagram contains a maximum number of hops the datagram can take before being discarded. More important, IPv6 retains most of the general facilities provided by the IPv4 options.

Despite retaining the basic concepts from the current version, IPv6 changes all the details. For example, IPv6 uses larger addresses and an entirely new datagram header format. Furthermore, IPv6 divides header information into a series of fixed-length headers. Thus, unlike IPv4, which places key information in fixed fields of the header and only appends variable-length options for less important information, the IPv6 header is always a variable size.

The new features in IPv6 can be grouped into five broad categories:

- *Address Size*. Instead of 32 bits, each IPv6 address contains 128 bits. The resulting address space is large enough to accommodate continued growth of the world-wide Internet for many decades.

- *Header Format*. The IPv6 datagram header is completely different than the IPv4 header. Almost every field in the header has been changed; some have been replaced.

- *Extension Headers*. Unlike IPv4, which uses a single header format for all datagrams, IPv6 encodes information into separate headers. A datagram consists of the base IPv6 header followed by zero or more extension headers, followed by data.

- *Support For Real-Time Traffic.* IPv6 includes a mechanism that allows a sender and receiver to establish a high-quality path through the underlying network and to associate datagrams with that path. Although the mechanism is intended for use with audio and video applications that require high performance guarantees, the mechanism can also be used to associate datagrams with low-cost paths.

- *Extensible Protocol.* Unlike IPv4, IPv6 does not specify all possible protocol features. Instead, the designers have provided a scheme that allows a sender to add additional information to a datagram. The extension scheme makes IPv6 more flexible than IPv4, and means that new features can be added to the design as needed.

The next sections explain how the new features are implemented by showing the organization of an IPv6 datagram and the addressing structure.

24.7 IPv6 Datagram Format

An IPv6 datagram contains a series of headers. As Figure 24.2 illustrates, each datagram begins with a *base header*, which is followed by zero or more *extension headers* followed by the payload.

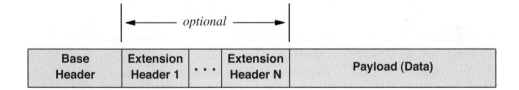

Figure 24.2 The general form of an IPv6 datagram.

Although the figure illustrates the general structure, fields are not drawn to scale. In particular, some extension headers are larger than the base header, and others are smaller. In many datagrams, the size of the payload is much larger than the size of the headers.

24.8 IPv6 Base Header Format

Although it is twice as large as an IPv4 header, the IPv6 base header contains less information. Figure 24.3 illustrates the format.

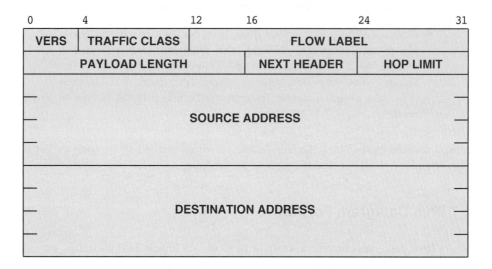

Figure 24.3 The format of the base header in an IPv6 datagram.

As the figure shows, most of the space in the header is devoted to the *SOURCE ADDRESS* and *DESTINATION ADDRESS* fields, each of which occupies sixteen octets, four times more than an IPv4 address. As in IPv4, a source address identifies the original source, and the destination address identifies the ultimate recipient.

In addition to the source and destination addresses, the base header contains six fields. The *VERS* field identifies the protocol as version 6. The *TRAFFIC CLASS* field specifies the *traffic class* using a definition of traffic types known as *differentiated services* to specify general characteristics that the datagram needs. For example, to send interactive traffic (e.g., keystrokes and mouse movements), one might specify a class that has low latency. To send real-time audio across the Internet, however, a sender might request a path with low jitter. The *PAYLOAD LENGTH* field corresponds to IPv4's datagram length field. Unlike IPv4, the *PAYLOAD LENGTH* specifies only the size of the data being carried (i.e., the payload); the size of the header is excluded. The *HOP LIMIT* corresponds to the IPv4 *TIME-TO-LIVE* field. IPv6 interprets the *HOP LIMIT* strictly — the datagram will be discarded if the *HOP LIMIT* counts down to zero before the datagram arrives at its destination. Field *FLOW LABEL* was originally intended to associate a datagram with a particular underlying network path. Since IPv6 was defined, the use of end-to-end flow labels has fallen out of favor, and the *FLOW LABEL* has become less important.

The *NEXT HEADER* field is used to specify the type of information that follows the current header. For example, if the datagram includes an extension header, the *NEXT HEADER* field specifies the type of the extension header. If no extension header exists, the *NEXT HEADER* field specifies the type of data being carried in the payload. Figure 24.4 illustrates the *NEXT HEADER* field.

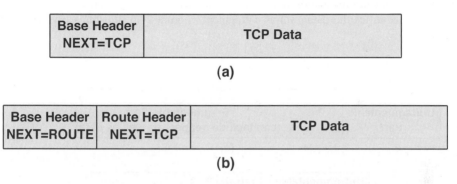

Figure 24.4 The NEXT HEADER field in (a) an IPv6 datagram that has a base header and TCP payload, and (b) a datagram with a base header, route header, and TCP payload.

24.9 Implicit And Explicit Header Size

Because the standard specifies a unique value for each possible header type, there is never ambiguity about the interpretation of the *NEXT HEADER* field. A receiver processes headers sequentially, using the *NEXT HEADER* field in each header to determine what follows.

Some header types have a fixed size. For example, a base header has a fixed size of exactly forty octets. To move to the item following a base header, IPv6 software simply adds *40* to the address of the base header. Some extension headers do not have a fixed size. In such cases, the header must contain sufficient information to allow IPv6 to determine where the header ends. For example, Figure 24.5 illustrates the general form of an IPv6 *options header* that carries information similar to the options in an IPv4 datagram.

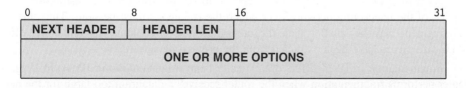

Figure 24.5 Illustration of the IPv6 options extension header with an explicit length.

24.10 Fragmentation, Reassembly, And Path MTU

Although IPv6 fragmentation resembles IPv4 fragmentation, the details differ. Like IPv4, a prefix of the original datagram is copied into each fragment, and the payload length is modified to be the length of the fragment. Unlike IPv4, however, IPv6 does not include fields for fragmentation information in the base header. Instead, IPv6 places the fragment information in a separate fragment extension header; the presence of the header identifies the datagram as a fragment. Figure 24.6 illustrates IPv6 fragmentation.

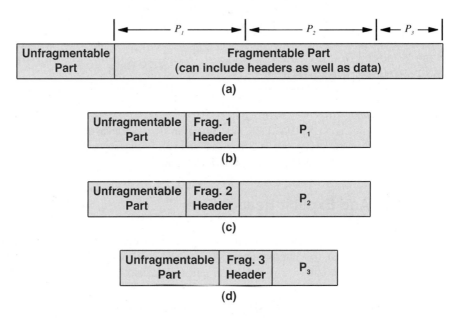

Figure 24.6 Illustration of IPv6 fragmentation with a datagram (a) divided into fragments (b) through (d).

In the figure, the *Unfragmentable Part* denotes the base header plus headers that control routing. To insure that all fragments are routed identically, the unfragmentable part is replicated in every fragment.

As with IPv4, the fragment size is chosen to be the Maximum Transmission Unit (MTU) of the underlying network over which the fragments must be sent. Thus, the final fragment may be smaller than the others because it contains the remainder after MTU-size pieces have been extracted from the original datagram.

Fragmentation in IPv6 differs dramatically from fragmentation in IPv4. In IPv4, a router performs fragmentation when the router receives a datagram too large for the network over which the datagram must be sent. In IPv6, a sending host is responsible for fragmentation. That is, hosts are expected to choose a datagram size that will not require fragmentation; a router along the path that receives a datagram that is larger than the network MTU will send an error message and discard the datagram.

How can a host choose a datagram size that will not result in fragmentation? The host must learn the MTU of each network along the path to the destination, and must choose a datagram size to fit the smallest. The minimum MTU along a path from a source to a destination is known as the *path MTU*, and the process of learning the path MTU is known as *path MTU discovery*. In general, path MTU discovery is an iterative procedure. A host sends a sequence of various-size datagrams to the destination to see if they arrive without error. If fragmentation is required, the sending host will receive an ICMP error message†. Once a datagram is small enough to pass through without fragmentation, the host chooses a datagram size equal to the path MTU.

To summarize:

> In IPv6, fragmentation is performed by the sending host, and not by routers. If fragmentation is required, the sending host receives an ICMP error message, and reduces the fragment size until fragments can be sent to the destination.

24.11 The Purpose Of Multiple Headers

Why does IPv6 use separate extension headers? There are two reasons:

- Economy
- Extensibility

Economy is easiest to understand: partitioning the datagram functionality into separate headers is economical because it saves space. Although IPv6 includes many features, designers expect a given datagram to use only a small subset. Having separate headers makes it possible to define a large set of features without requiring each datagram header to have at least one field for each feature. For example, although many IPv4 datagrams are not fragmented, the IPv4 header has fields used to hold fragmentation information. In contrast, IPv6 does not waste space on fields for fragmentation unless the datagram is fragmented. Because most datagrams only need a few headers, avoiding unnecessary header fields can save considerable space. Smaller datagrams also take less time to transmit. Thus, reducing datagram size also reduces the bandwidth consumed.

To understand extensibility, consider adding a new feature to a protocol. A protocol like IPv4 that uses a fixed header format requires a complete change — the header must be redesigned to accommodate fields needed to support the new feature. In IPv6, however, existing protocol headers can remain unchanged. A new *NEXT HEADER* type is defined as well as a new header format.

---

†IPv6 includes a new version of ICMP.

Another advantage of placing new functionality in a new header lies in the ability to experiment with a new feature before changing all computers in the Internet. For example, suppose the owners of two computers wish to test a new datagram encryption technique. The two must agree on the details of an experimental encryption header. The sender adds the new header to a datagram, and the receiver interprets the header in incoming datagrams. As long as the new header appears after the headers used for routing, routers in the Internet between the sender and receiver can pass the datagram without understanding the experimental header†. Once an experimental feature proves useful, it can be incorporated in the standard.

24.12 IPv6 Addressing

Like IPv4, IPv6 assigns a unique address for each connection between a computer and a physical network. Thus, if a computer (e.g., a router) connects to three physical networks, the computer is assigned three IPv6 addresses. Also like IPv4, IPv6 separates each such address into a prefix that identifies the network and a suffix that identifies a particular computer on the network.

Despite adopting the same approach for assigning computer addresses, IPv6 addressing differs from IPv4 addressing in significant ways. First, address details are completely different. Like CIDR addresses, the division between prefix and suffix can occur on an arbitrary boundary. Unlike IPv4, IPv6 includes addresses with a multi-level hierarchy. Although the address assignments are not fixed, one can assume that the highest level corresponds to an ISP, the next level corresponds to an organization (e.g., a company), the next to a site, and so on. Second, IPv6 defines a set of special addresses that differ from IPv4 special addresses. In particular, IPv6 does not include a special address for broadcasting on a given remote network. Instead, each IPv6 address is one of the three basic types listed in Figure 24.7.

As the figure shows, IPv6 retains unicast and multicast addressing. Directed broadcast was eliminated because it poses a security problem. To handle limited broadcast (broadcast on the local network), IPv6 defines a special multicast group that corresponds to all hosts and routers on the local network.

Anycast addressing was originally known as *cluster* addressing. The motivation for such addressing arises from a desire to allow replication of services. For example, a corporation that offers a service over the network assigns an anycast address to several computers that provide the service. When a user sends a datagram to the anycast address, IPv6 routes the datagram to one of the computers in the set (i.e., in the cluster). If a user from another location sends a datagram to the anycast address, IPv6 can choose to route the datagram to a different member of the set, allowing both computers to process requests at the same time.

---

†If an experimental header is incorrectly placed before routing headers, a router will discard the datagram.

Type	Purpose
unicast	The address corresponds to a single computer. A datagram sent to the address is routed along a shortest path to the computer.
multicast	The address corresponds to a set of computers, and membership in the set can change at any time. IPv6 delivers one copy of the datagram to each member of the set.
anycast	The address corresponds to a set of computers that share a common prefix. A datagram sent to the address is delivered to exactly one of the computers (e.g., the computer closest to the sender).

Figure 24.7 The three types of IPv6 addresses.

24.13 IPv6 Colon Hexadecimal Notation

Because an IPv6 address occupies 128 bits, writing such numbers can be unwieldy. For example, consider a 128-bit number written in the dotted decimal notation that IPv4 uses:

105.220.136.100.255.255.255.255.0.0.18.128.140.10.255.255

To help reduce the number of characters used to write an address, the designers of IPv6 chose a more compact syntactic form known as *colon hexadecimal notation*, usually abbreviated *colon hex*, in which each group of 16 bits is written in hexadecimal with a colon separating groups. For example, when the above number is written in colon hex, it becomes:

69DC:8864:FFFF:FFFF:0:1280:8C0A:FFFF

As the example illustrates, colon hex notation requires fewer characters to express an address. An additional optimization known as *zero compression* further reduces the size. Zero compression replaces sequences of zeroes with two colons. For example, the address:

FF0C:0:0:0:0:0:0:B1

can be written:

FF0C::B1

The large IPv6 address space and the proposed address allocation scheme make zero compression especially important because the designers expect many IPv6 addresses to contain strings of zeroes. In particular, to help ease the transition to the new protocol, the designers mapped existing IPv4 addresses into the IPv6 address space. Any IPv6 address that begins with *96* zero bits contains an IPv4 address in the low-order *32* bits.

24.14 Summary

Although the current version of IP has worked well for many years, exponential growth of the Internet means that the 32-bit address space will eventually be exhausted. The IETF has designed a new version of IP that uses 128 bits to represent each address. To distinguish the new version of IP from the current version, the two protocols are named using their version number. The current version of IP is IPv4, and the new version is IPv6.

IPv6 retains many of the concepts from IPv4, but changes all the details. For example, like IPv4, IPv6 provides a connectionless service in which two computers exchange short messages called datagrams. However, unlike an IPv4 datagram in which the header contains fields for each function, IPv6 defines separate headers for each function. Each IPv6 datagram consists of a base header followed by zero or more extension headers, followed by data.

Like IPv4, IPv6 defines an address for each network connection. Thus, as in IPv4, a computer that connects to multiple physical networks (e.g., a router) has multiple addresses. However, special addresses are redefined in IPv6. Instead of IPv4's notion of network broadcast, IPv6 defines multicast and anycast (cluster) addresses, both of which correspond to a set of computers. A multicast address corresponds to a set of computers at multiple sites that are treated as a single entity — each computer in the set will receive a copy of any datagram sent to the set. An anycast address permits replication of services — a datagram sent to an anycast address will be delivered to exactly one member of the group (e.g., the member that is closest to the sender).

To make IPv6 addresses easier for people to use, the designers created colon hexadecimal notation. Colon hex notation expresses groups of *16* bits in hexadecimal, with a colon separating groups. Zero compression eliminates long runs of zeroes. The resulting notation is more compact than the dotted decimal form used in IPv4.

EXERCISES

24.1   What is the fragmentable part of an IPv6 datagram?

24.2   What is the primary motivation for a change from IPv4 to IPv6?

24.3   Extend the program in the previous exercise to implement zero compression.

24.4   How large is the smallest IPv6 datagram header?

24.5   What is the hourglass model of Internet communication?

24.6   Write a computer program that reads a 128-bit binary number and prints the number in colon hex notation.

24.7   List the major features of IPv6, and give a short description of each.

24.8   What does the *NEXT HEADER* field specify in an IPv6 datagram header?

24.9   List the three IPv6 address types, and give a brief explanation of each.

24.10 Why does IPv6 use separate extension headers instead of fields in a single, fixed header?

Chapter Contents

25

UDP: Datagram Transport Service

25.1 Introduction

Previous chapters describe the connectionless packet delivery service provided by IP and the companion protocol used to report errors. This chapter considers UDP, one of the two major transport-layer protocols used in the Internet and the only connectionless transport service. The chapter discusses the UDP packet format and the ways UDP can be used. We will see that although UDP is efficient and flexible, it has the surprising property of using best-effort delivery semantics. In addition to discussing UDP, the chapter covers the important concept of protocol port numbers.

The next chapter continues the discussion by focusing on the other major transport-layer protocol, TCP. Later chapters discuss Internet routing and network management, which each use transport protocols.

25.2 Transport Protocols And End-To-End Communication

As previous chapters show, the Internet Protocol provides a packet delivery service that spans the Internet (i.e., a datagram can pass from the sending host, across one or more physical networks, to the receiving host). Despite its ability to pass traffic across the Internet, IP lacks an essential feature: IP cannot distinguish among multiple application programs running on a given host. If a user runs an email application and a web browser at the same time or runs multiple copies of a given application, they must be able to communicate independently.

IP is incapable of supporting multiple applications because fields in the datagram header only identify computers. That is, from IP's point of view, the source and destination fields in a datagram identify a host computer; an IP address does not contain additional bits to identify an application program on the host. We say that IP treats a computer as an *endpoint* of communication. In contrast, transport-layer protocols are known as *end-to-end protocols* because a transport protocol allows an individual application program to be an endpoint of communication. Instead of adding additional features to IP to identify applications, the designers of the TCP/IP protocols placed end-to-end protocols in a separate layer, Layer 4.

25.3 The User Datagram Protocol

As we will see, the TCP/IP suite contains two transport protocols, the *User Datagram Protocol* (*UDP*) and the *Transmission Control Protocol* (*TCP*), that differ dramatically in the service they offer to applications. UDP is less complex and easiest to understand. The simplicity and ease of understanding come with a cost — UDP does not provide the type of service a typical application expects.

UDP can be characterized as:

- *End-to-end.* UDP is a transport protocol that can distinguish among multiple application programs running on a given computer.

- *Connectionless.* The interface that UDP supplies to applications follows a connectionless paradigm.

- *Message-oriented.* An application that uses UDP sends and receives individual messages.

- *Best-effort.* UDP offers applications the same best-effort delivery semantics as IP.

- *Arbitrary Interaction.* UDP allows an application to send to many other applications, receive from many other applications, or communicate with exactly one other application.

- *Operating System Independent.* UDP provides a means of identifying application programs that does not depend on identifiers used by the local operating system.

The most important characteristic of UDP, its best-effort semantics, arises because UDP uses IP for transmission. In fact, UDP is sometimes characterized as a *thin* protocol layer that provides applications with the ability to send and receive IP datagrams. We can summarize:

> *UDP provides an end-to-end service that allows an application pro-*
> *gram to send and receive individual messages, each of which travels*
> *in a separate datagram. An application can choose to restrict com-*
> *munication to one other application program or communicate with*
> *multiple applications.*

25.4 The Connectionless Paradigm

UDP uses a *connectionless* communication paradigm, which means that an application using UDP does not need to preestablish communication before sending data, nor does the application need to inform the network when finished. Instead, an application can generate and send data at any time. Moreover, UDP allows an application to delay an arbitrarily long time between the transmission of two messages. UDP does not maintain state, and does not use control messages; communication consists only of the data messages themselves. In particular, if a pair of applications stop sending data, no other packets are exchanged. As a result, UDP has extremely low overhead. To summarize:

> *UDP is connectionless, which means that an application can send*
> *data at any time and UDP does not transmit any packets other than*
> *the packets that carry user data.*

25.5 Message-Oriented Interface

UDP offers application programs a *message-oriented* interface. Each time an application requests that UDP send a block of data, UDP places the data in a single message for transmission. UDP does not divide a message into multiple packets, and does not combine messages for delivery — each message that an application sends is transported across the Internet and delivered to the receiver.

The message-oriented interface has several important consequences for programmers. On the positive side, applications that use UDP can depend on the protocol to preserve data boundaries — each message UDP delivers to a receiving application will be exactly the same as was transmitted by the sender. On the negative side, each UDP message must fit into a single IP datagram. Thus, the IP datagram size forms an absolute limit on the size of a UDP message. More important, UDP message size can lead to inefficient use of the underlying network. If an application sends extremely small messages, the resulting datagrams will have a large ratio of header octets to data octets. If an application sends extremely large messages, the resulting datagrams may be larger than the network MTU, and will be fragmented by IP.

Allowing UDP messages to be large produces an interesting anomaly. Normally, an application programmer can achieve higher efficiency by using large transfers. For example, programmers are encouraged to declare large I/O buffers, and to specify transfers that match the buffer size. With UDP, however, sending large messages leads to less efficiency because large messages cause fragmentation. Even more surprising, the fragmentation can occur on the sending computer — an application sends a large message, UDP places the entire message in a user datagram and encapsulates the user datagram in an Internet datagram, and IP must perform fragmentation before the datagram can be sent. The point is:

> *Although a programmer's intuition suggests that using larger messages will increase efficiency, if a UDP message is larger than the network MTU, IP will fragment the resulting datagram, which reduces efficiency.*

As a consequence, many programmers who use UDP choose a message size that produces datagrams that fit in a standard MTU. In particular, because most parts of the Internet now support an MTU of 1500 octets, programmers often choose a message size of 1400 or 1450 to leave plenty of space for IP and UDP headers.

25.6 UDP Communication Semantics

UDP uses IP for all delivery. Furthermore, UDP provides applications with exactly the same best-effort delivery semantics as IP, which means messages can be:

- Lost
- Duplicated
- Delayed
- Delivered out-of-order
- Corrupted

Of course, UDP does not purposefully introduce delivery problems. Instead, UDP merely uses IP to send messages, and does not detect or correct delivery problems. UDP's best-effort delivery semantics have important consequences for applications. An application must either be immune to the problems or the programmer must take additional steps to detect and correct problems. As an example of an application that can tolerate packet errors, consider an audio transmission. If the sender places a small amount of audio in each message, the loss of a single packet produces a small gap in the playback, which will be heard as a pop or click. Although it is not desirable, the noise is merely annoying. At the opposite extreme, consider an on-line shopping application. Such applications are not written to use UDP because packet errors can have serious consequences (e.g., duplication of a message that carries a catalog order can result in two orders, with double charges being made to the buyer's credit card).

We can summarize:

> *Because UDP offers the same best-effort delivery semantics as IP, a UDP message can be lost, duplicated, delayed, delivered out-of-order or bits can be corrupted in transit. UDP only suffices for applications such as voice or video that can tolerate delivery errors.*

25.7 Modes Of Interaction And Broadcast Delivery

UDP allows four styles of interaction:

- 1-to-1
- 1-to-many
- Many-to-1
- Many-to-many

That is, an application using UDP has a choice. An application can choose a 1-to-1 interaction in which the application exchanges messages with exactly one other application, a 1-to-many interaction in which the application sends a message to multiple recipients, or a many-to-1 interaction in which the application receives messages from multiple senders. Finally, a set of applications can establish a many-to-many interaction in which they exchange messages with one another.

Although a 1-to-many interaction can be achieved by arranging to send an individual copy of a message to each intended recipient, UDP allows the exchange to be efficient. Instead of requiring an application to repeatedly send a message to multiple recipients, UDP allows an application to transmit the message via IP multicast or broadcast. To do so, the sender uses an IP broadcast address as the destination IP address. For example, local broadcast can be specified by using IP's limited broadcast address, 255.255.255.255. Similarly, UDP allows an application to multicast messages. Delivery via broadcast or multicast is especially useful for Ethernet networks because the underlying hardware supports both types efficiently.

25.8 Endpoint Identification With Protocol Port Numbers

Exactly how should UDP identify an application program as an endpoint? It might seem that UDP could use the same mechanism that the operating system uses. Unfortunately, because UDP must span heterogeneous computers, no common mechanism exists. For example, some operating systems use process identifiers, others use job names, and others use task identifiers. Thus, an identifier that is meaningful on one system may not be meaningful on another.

To avoid ambiguity, UDP defines an abstract set of identifiers called *protocol port numbers* that are independent of the underlying operating system. Each computer that implements UDP must provide a mapping between protocol port numbers and the program identifiers that the operating system uses. For example, the UDP standard defines protocol port number seven as the port for an *echo* service and port number thirty-seven as the port for a *timeserver* service. All computers running UDP recognize the standard protocol port numbers, independent of the underlying operating system. Thus, when a UDP message arrives for port seven, UDP protocol software must know which program on the local computer implements the echo service and must pass the incoming message to the program.

The communication mode is determined by the way an application fills in addresses and protocol port numbers for a socket. To engage in 1-to-1 communication, for example, an application specifies the local port number, remote IP address, and remote protocol port number; UDP only passes the application messages that arrive from the specified sender. To engage in many-to-1 communication, the application specifies the local port number, but informs UDP that the remote endpoint can be any system. UDP then passes the application all messages that arrive for the specified port†.

25.9 UDP Datagram Format

Each UDP message is called a *user datagram* and consists of two parts: a short header that specifies the sending and receiving application programs and a payload that carries the data being sent. Figure 25.1 illustrates the user datagram format.

0	16	31
UDP SOURCE PORT	UDP DESTINATION PORT	
UDP MESSAGE LENGTH	UDP CHECKSUM	
PAYLOAD (MESSAGE DATA)		
...		

Figure 25.1 The format of a UDP user datagram with an 8-octet header.

†Only one application can request all messages for a given port.

The first two fields of the UDP header contain 16-bit protocol port numbers. Field *UDP SOURCE PORT* contains the port number of the sending application, and field *UDP DESTINATION PORT* contains the port number of the application to which the message is being sent. Field *UDP MESSAGE LENGTH* specifies the total size of the UDP message, measured in 8-bit bytes.

25.10 The UDP Checksum And The Pseudo Header

Although the UDP header contains a sixteen-bit field named *UDP checksum* the checksum is optional. A sender can either choose to compute a checksum or set all bits of the checksum field to zero. When a message arrives at the destination, UDP software examines the checksum field, and only verifies the checksum if the value is nonzero†.

Note that the UDP header does not contain any identification of the sender or receiver other than the protocol port numbers. In particular, UDP assumes that the IP source and destination addresses are contained in the IP datagram that carries UDP. Thus, IP addresses are not carried in the UDP header.

Omitting the source and destination IP addresses makes UDP smaller and more efficient, but introduces the possibility of error. In particular, if IP malfunctions and delivers a UDP message to an incorrect destination, UDP cannot use header fields to determine that an error occurred.

To allow UDP to verify that messages reach the correct destination without incurring the overhead of additional header fields, UDP extends the checksum. When computing the checksum, UDP software includes a *pseudo header* that contains the source, destination, and type (i.e. PROTO) fields from the IP datagram and a UDP datagram length. That is, the sender computes a checksum as if the UDP header contained extra fields. Similarly, to verify a checksum, a receiver must obtain the UDP length, and the source, destination, and type fields from the IP datagram; the receiver appends them to the UDP message before verifying the checksum. Figure 25.2 illustrates fields in the pseudo header.

0	16	31
IP SOURCE ADDRESS		
IP DESTINATION ADDRESS		
ZERO	PROTO	UDP LENGTH

Figure 25.2 Illustration of the pseudo header used to calculate the UDP checksum.

---

†Like IP, UDP uses a ones-complement checksum; if the computed checksum has a value of zero, a sender uses the all-ones form of zero.

25.11 UDP Encapsulation

Like ICMP, each UDP datagram is encapsulated in an IP datagram for transmission across the Internet. Figure 25.3 illustrates the encapsulation.

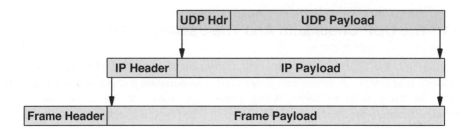

Figure 25.3 The encapsulation of a UDP message in an IP datagram.

25.12 Summary

The User Datagram Protocol provides end-to-end message transport from an application running on one computer to an application running on another computer. UDP offers the same best-effort delivery semantics as IP, which means that messages can be lost, duplicated, or delivered out-of-order. One advantage of a connectionless approach arises from the ability to have 1-to-1, 1-to-many, and many-to-1 interactions among applications.

To remain independent of the underlying operating systems, UDP uses small integer protocol port numbers to distinguish among application programs. Protocol software on a given computer must map each protocol port number to the appropriate mechanism (e.g., process ID) used on the computer.

The UDP checksum is optional — if a sender fills the checksum field with zero, the receiver does not verify the checksum. To verify that the UDP datagram arrived at the correct location, a UDP checksum is computed over the datagram plus a pseudo header

UDP requires two levels of encapsulation. Each UDP message is encapsulated in an IP datagram for transmission across the Internet. The datagram is encapsulated in a frame for transmission across an individual network.

EXERCISES

25.1   Given an Ethernet frame, what fields must be examined to determine whether the frame carries a UDP message?

25.2   Do applications need to exchange UDP control messages before exchanging data? Explain.

25.3   If an application uses UDP to send an 8K byte message across an Ethernet, how many frames will traverse the network?

25.4   What endpoint values must be specified by an application that engages in 1-to-1 communication? In 1-to-many? In many-to-1?

25.5   What is the conceptual difference between IP and end-to-end protocols?

25.6   What happens if a UDP message containing a payload of 1500 data bytes is sent across an Ethernet?

25.7   List the features of UDP.

25.8   Calculate the size of the largest possible UDP message. (Hint: the entire UDP message must fit in an IP datagram.)

25.9   What is a pseudo header, and when is one used?

25.10   What are the semantics of UDP?

Chapter Contents

26

TCP: Reliable Transport Service

26.1 Introduction

Previous chapters describe the connectionless packet delivery service provided by IP and the User Datagram Protocol that runs over IP. This chapter considers transport protocols in general, and examines TCP, the major transport protocol used in the Internet. The chapter explains how the TCP protocol provides reliable delivery.

TCP achieves a seemingly impossible task: it uses the unreliable datagram service offered by IP when sending across the Internet, but provides a reliable data delivery service to application programs. TCP must compensate for loss, delay, duplication, and out-of-order delivery, and it must do so without overloading the underlying networks and routers. After reviewing the service that TCP provides to applications, the chapter examines the techniques TCP uses to achieve reliability.

26.2 The Transmission Control Protocol

Programmers are trained to think that reliability is fundamental in a computer system. For example, when writing an application that sends data to an I/O device such as a printer, a programmer assumes the data will arrive correctly or the operating system will inform the application that an error has occurred. That is, a programmer assumes the underlying system guarantees that data will be delivered reliably.

To allow programmers to follow conventional techniques when creating applications that communicate across the Internet, protocol software must provide the same semantics as a conventional computer system: the software must guarantee prompt, reliable communication. Data must be delivered in exactly the same order that it was sent, and there must be no loss or duplication.

In the TCP/IP suite, the *Transmission Control Protocol* (*TCP*) provides reliable transport service. TCP is remarkable because it solves a difficult problem well — although other protocols have been created, no general-purpose transport protocol has proved to work better. Consequently, most Internet applications are built to use TCP.

To summarize:

> *In the Internet, the Transmission Control Protocol (TCP) is a transport-layer protocol that provides reliability.*

26.3 The Service TCP Provides To Applications

The service offered by TCP has seven major features:

- *Connection Orientation.* TCP provides connection-oriented service in which an application must first request a connection to a destination, and then use the connection to transfer data.

- *Point-To-Point Communication.* Each TCP connection has exactly two endpoints.

- *Complete Reliability.* TCP guarantees that the data sent across a connection will be delivered exactly as sent, complete and in order.

- *Full Duplex Communication.* A TCP connection allows data to flow in either direction, and allows either application program to send data at any time.

- *Stream Interface.* TCP provides a stream interface in which an application sends a continuous sequence of octets across a connection. TCP does not group data into records or messages, and does not guarantee to deliver data in the same size pieces that were transferred by the sending application.

- *Reliable Connection Startup.* TCP allows two applications to reliably start communication.

- *Graceful Connection Shutdown.* Before closing a connection, TCP insures that all data has been delivered and that both sides have agreed to shut down the connection.

To summarize:

> *TCP provides a reliable, connection-oriented, full-duplex stream transport service that allows two application programs to form a connection, send data in either direction, and then terminate the connection. Each TCP connection is started reliably and terminated gracefully.*

26.4 End-To-End Service And Virtual Connections

Like UDP, TCP is classified as an *end-to-end* protocol because it provides communication between an application on one computer to an application on another computer. It is *connection oriented* because applications must request that TCP form a connection before they can transfer data, and must close the connection when transfer is complete.

The connections provided by TCP are called *virtual connections* because they are achieved in software. Indeed, the underlying Internet does not provide hardware or software support for connections. Instead, the TCP software modules on two machines exchange messages to achieve the illusion of a connection.

Each TCP message is encapsulated in an IP datagram and sent across the Internet. When the datagram arrives on the destination host, IP passes the contents to TCP. Note that although TCP uses IP to carry messages, IP does not read or interpret the messages. In fact, IP treats each TCP message as data to be transferred. Conversely, TCP treats IP as a packet communication system that provides communication between the TCP modules at each end of a connection. Figure 26.1 illustrates how TCP views the underlying Internet.

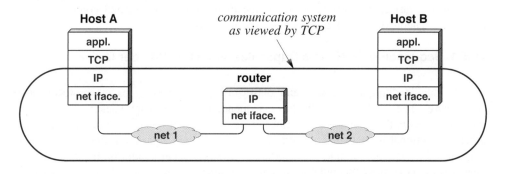

Figure 26.1 Illustration of how TCP views the underlying Internet.

As the figure shows, TCP software is needed at each end of a virtual connection, but not on intermediate routers. From TCP's point of view, the entire Internet is a communication system that can accept and deliver messages without changing or interpreting their contents.

26.5 Techniques That Transport Protocols Use

An end-to-end transport protocol must be carefully designed to achieve efficient, reliable transfer. The major problems are:

- *Unreliable Communication.* Messages sent across the Internet can be lost, duplicated, corrupted, delayed, or delivered out of order.

- *End System Reboot.* At any time during communication, either of the two end systems might crash and reboot. There must be no confusion between sessions; some embedded systems can reboot in less time than it takes a packet to cross the Internet.

- *Heterogeneous End Systems.* A powerful sender can generate data so fast that it overruns a slow receiver.

- *Congestion In The Internet.* If senders aggressively transmit data, intermediate switches and routers can become overrun with packets, analogous to a congested highway.

We have already seen examples of basic techniques data communications systems use to overcome some of the problems. For example, to compensate for bits that are changed during transmission, a protocol might include *parity bits*, a *checksum*, or a *cyclic redundancy check* (*CRC*). Transport protocols do more than detect errors — they employ techniques that can repair or circumvent problems. In particular, transport protocols use a variety of tools to handle some of the most complicated communication problems. The next sections discuss basic mechanisms.

26.5.1 Sequencing To Handle Duplicates And Out-Of-Order Delivery

To handle duplicate packets and out-of-order deliveries, transport protocols use *sequencing*. The sending side attaches a sequence number to each packet. The receiving side stores both the sequence number of the last packet received in order as well as a list of additional packets that arrived out of order. When a packet arrives, the receiver examines the sequence number to determine how the packet should be handled. If the packet is the next one expected (i.e., has arrived in order), the protocol software delivers the packet to the next highest layer, and checks its list to see whether additional packets can also be delivered. If the packet has arrived out of order, the protocol software adds the packet to the list. Sequencing also solves the problem of duplication — a receiver checks for duplicates when it examines the sequence number of an arriving packet. If the packet has already been delivered or the sequence number matches one of the packets waiting on the list, the software discards the new copy.

26.5.2 Retransmission To Handle Lost Packets

To handle packet loss, transport protocols use *positive acknowledgement with retransmission*. Whenever a frame arrives intact, the receiving protocol software sends a small *acknowledgement (ACK)* message that reports successful reception. The sender takes responsibility for ensuring that each packet is transferred successfully. Whenever it sends a packet, the sending-side protocol software starts a timer. If an acknowledgement arrives before the timer expires, the software cancels the timer; if the timer expires before an acknowledgement arrives, the software sends another copy of the packet and starts the timer again. The action of sending a second copy is known as *retransmitting*, and the copy is commonly called a *retransmission*.

Of course, retransmission cannot succeed if a hardware failure has permanently disconnected the network or if the receiving computer has crashed. Therefore, protocols that retransmit messages usually bound the maximum number of retransmissions. When the bound has been reached, the protocol stops retransmitting and declares that communication is impossible.

Note that if packets are delayed, retransmission can introduce duplicate packets. Thus, transport protocols that incorporate retransmission are usually designed to handle the problem of duplicate packets.

26.5.3 Techniques To Avoid Replay

Extraordinarily long delays can lead to *replay errors* in which a delayed packet affects later communication. For example, consider the following sequence of events.

- Two computers agree to communicate at *1* PM.
- One computer sends a sequence of ten packets to the other.
- A hardware problem causes packet *3* to be delayed.
- Routes change to avoid the hardware problem.
- Protocol software on the sending computer retransmits packet *3*, and sends the remaining packets without error.
- At 1:05 PM the two computers agree to communicate again.
- After the second packet arrives, the delayed copy of packet *3* arrives from the earlier conversation.
- Packet *3* arrives from the second conversation.

Unless a transport protocol is designed carefully to avoid such problems, a packet from an earlier conversation might be accepted in a later conversation and the correct packet discarded as a duplicate.

Replay can also occur with control packets (i.e., packets that establish or terminate communication). To understand the scope of the problem, consider a situation in which two application programs form a TCP connection, communicate, close the connection, and then form a new connection. The message that specifies closing the connection might be duplicated and one copy might be delayed long enough for the second connection to be established. A protocol should be designed so the duplicate message will not cause the second connection to be closed.

To prevent replay, protocols mark each session with a unique ID (e.g., the time the session was established), and require the unique ID to be present in each packet. The protocol software discards any arriving packet that contains an incorrect ID. To avoid replay, an ID must not be reused until a reasonable time has passed (e.g., hours).

26.5.4 Flow Control To Prevent Data Overrun

Several techniques are available to prevent a fast computer from sending so much data that it overruns a slow receiver. We use the term *flow control* to refer to techniques that handle the problem. The simplest form of flow control is a *stop-and-go* system in which a sender waits after transmitting each packet. When the receiver is ready for another packet, the receiver sends a control message, usually a form of acknowledgement.

Although stop-and-go protocols prevent overrun, they result in extremely low throughput. To understand why, consider what happens on a network that has a packet size of 1000 octets, a throughput capacity of 2 Mbps, and a delay of 50 milliseconds. The network hardware can transport 2 Mbps from one computer to another. However, after transmitting a packet, the sender must wait 100 msec before sending another packet (i.e., 50 msec for the packet to reach the receiver and 50 msec for an acknowledgement to travel back). Thus, the maximum rate at which data can be sent using stop-and-go is one packet every 100 milliseconds. When expressed as a bit rate, the maximum rate that stop-and-go can achieve is 80,000 bps, which is only 4% of the hardware capacity.

To obtain high throughput rates, transport protocols use a flow control technique known as *sliding window*. The sender and receiver are programmed to use a fixed *window size*, which is the maximum amount of data that can be sent before an acknowledgement arrives. For example, the sender and receiver might agree on a window size of four packets. The sender begins with the data to be sent, extracts data to fill four packets (i.e., the first window), and transmits a copy of each packet. In most transport protocols, the sender retains a copy in case retransmission is needed. The receiver must have preallocated buffer space for the entire window. If a packet arrives in sequence, the receiver passes the packet to the receiving application and transmits an acknowledgement to the sender. When an acknowledgement arrives, the sender discards its copy of the acknowledged packet and transmits the next packet. Figure 26.2 illustrates why the mechanism is known as a *sliding window*.

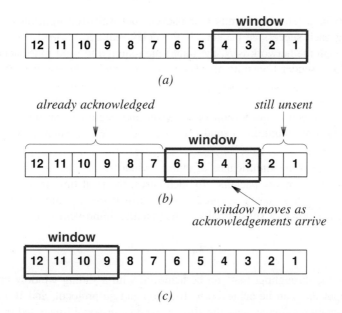

(a)

(b)

(c)

Figure 26.2 An illustration of a sliding window in (a) initial, (b) intermediate, and (c) final positions.

Sliding window can increase throughput dramatically. To understand why, compare the sequence of transmissions with a stop-and-go scheme and a sliding window scheme. Figure 26.3 contains a comparison for a 4-packet transmission.

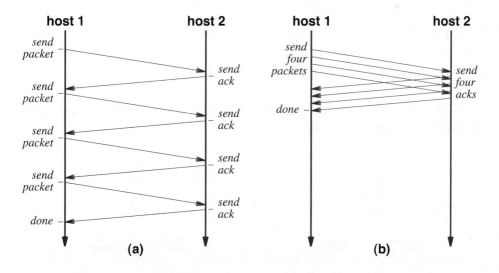

Figure 26.3 Comparison of transmission using (a) stop-and-go, and (b) sliding window.

In Figure 26.3a, a sender transmits four packets, but waits for an acknowledgement before sending each successive packet. If the delay required to send a single packet on one trip through the network is *N*, the total time required to send four packets is *8N*. In Figure 26.3b, a sender transmits all packets in the window before it waits. The figure shows a small delay between successive packet transmissions because transmission is never instantaneous — a short time (usually a few microseconds) is required for the hardware to complete transmission of a packet and begin to transmit the next packet. Thus, the total time required to send four packets is $2N + \varepsilon$, where ε denotes the small delay.

To understand the significance of sliding window, imagine an extended communication that involves many packets. In such cases, the total time required for transmission is so large that ε can be ignored. For such networks, a sliding window protocol can increase performance substantially. The potential improvement is:

$$T_W = T_g \times W \qquad\qquad (26.1)$$

where T_W is the throughput that can be achieved with a sliding window protocol, T_g is the throughput that can be achieved with a stop-and-go protocol, and W is the window size. The equation explains why the sliding window protocol illustrated in Figure 26.3b has approximately four times the throughput of the stop-and-go protocol in Figure 26.3a. Of course, throughput cannot be increased arbitrarily merely by increasing the window size. The bandwidth of the underlying network imposes an upper bound — bits cannot be sent faster than the hardware can carry them. Thus, the equation can be rewritten:

$$T_W = min(B, T_g \times W) \qquad\qquad (26.2)$$

where *B* is the underlying hardware bandwidth.

26.6 Techniques To Avoid Congestion

To understand how easily congestion can occur, consider four hosts connected by two switches as Figure 26.4 illustrates.

Figure 26.4 Four hosts connected by two switches.

Assume each connection in the figure operates at 1 Gbps, and consider what happens if both computers attached to switch 1 attempt to send data to a computer attached to switch 2. Switch 1 receives data at an aggregate rate of 2 Gbps, but can only forward 1 Gbps to switch 2. The situation is known as *congestion*. Even if a switch temporarily stores packets in memory, congestion results in increased delay. If congestion persists, the switch will run out of memory and begin discarding packets. Although retransmission can be used to recover lost packets, retransmission sends more packets into the network. Thus, if the situation persists, an entire network can become unusable; the condition is known as *congestion collapse*. In the Internet, congestion usually occurs in routers. Transport protocols attempt to avoid congestion collapse by monitoring the network and reacting quickly once congestion starts. There are two basic approaches:

- Arrange for intermediate systems (i.e., routers) to inform a sender when congestion occurs
- Use increased delay or packet loss as an estimate of congestion

The former scheme is implemented either by having routers send a special message to the source of packets when congestion occurs or by having routers set a bit in the header of each packet that experiences delay caused by congestion. When the second approach is used, the computer that receives the packet includes information in the acknowledgement to inform the original sender†.

Using delay and loss to estimate congestion is reasonable in the Internet because:

> *Modern network hardware works well; most delay and loss results from congestion, not hardware failure.*

The appropriate response to congestion consists of reducing the rate at which packets are being transmitted. Sliding window protocols can achieve the effect of reducing the rate by temporarily reducing the window size.

26.7 The Art Of Protocol Design

Although the techniques needed to solve specific problems are well-known, protocol design is nontrivial for two reasons. First, to make communication efficient, details must be chosen carefully — small design errors can result in incorrect operation, unnecessary packets, or delays. For example, if sequence numbers are used, each packet must contain a sequence number in the packet header. The field must be large enough so sequence numbers are not reused frequently, but small enough to avoid wasting unnecessary bandwidth. Second, protocol mechanisms can interact in unexpected ways. For example, consider the interaction between flow control and congestion control mechanisms. A sliding window scheme aggressively uses more of the underlying network bandwidth to improve throughput. A congestion control mechanism does the op-

---

†A long delay can occur between the time congestion occurs and the original sender is informed.

posite by reducing the number of packets being inserted to prevent the network from collapsing; the balance between sliding window and congestion control can be tricky, and a design that does both well is difficult. That is, aggressive flow control can cause congestion and conservative congestion control can lower the throughput more than necessary. Designs that attempt to switch from aggressive to conservative behavior when congestion occurs tend to oscillate — they slowly increase their use of bandwidth until the network begins to experience congestion, decrease use until the network becomes stable, and then begin to increase again.

Computer system reboot poses another serious challenge to transport protocol design. Imagine a situation where two application programs establish a connection, begin sending data, and then the computer receiving data reboots. Although protocol software on the rebooted computer has no knowledge of a connection, protocol software on the sending computer considers the connection valid. If a protocol is not designed carefully, a duplicate packet can cause a computer to incorrectly create a connection and begin receiving data in midstream.

26.8 Techniques Used In TCP To Handle Packet Loss

Which of the aforementioned techniques does TCP use to achieve reliable transfer? The answer is complex because TCP uses a variety of schemes that are combined in novel ways. As expected TCP uses *retransmission* to compensate for packet loss. Because TCP provides data flow in both directions, both sides of a communication participate in retransmission. When TCP receives data, it sends an *acknowledgement* back to the sender. Whenever it sends data, TCP starts a timer, and retransmits the data if the timer expires. Thus, basic TCP retransmission operates as Figure 26.5 illustrates.

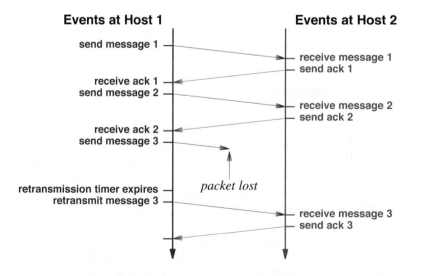

Figure 26.5 Illustration of TCP retransmission after a packet loss.

TCP's retransmission scheme is the key to its success because it handles communication across an arbitrary path through the Internet. For example, one application might send data across a satellite channel to a computer in another country, while another application sends data across a local area network to a computer in the next room. TCP must be ready to retransmit any message that is lost on either connection. The question is: how long should TCP wait before retransmitting? Acknowledgements from a computer on a local area network are expected to arrive within a few milliseconds, but a satellite connection requires hundreds of milliseconds. On one hand, waiting too long for such an acknowledgement leaves the network idle and does not maximize throughput. Thus, on a local area network, TCP should not delay a long time before retransmitting. On the other hand, retransmitting quickly does not work well on a satellite connection because the unnecessary traffic consumes network bandwidth and lowers throughput.

TCP faces a more difficult challenge than distinguishing between local and remote destinations: bursts of datagrams can cause congestion, which causes transmission delays along a given path to change rapidly. In fact, the total time required to send a message and receive an acknowledgement can increase or decrease by an order of magnitude in a few milliseconds. To summarize:

> *The delay required for data to reach a destination and an acknowledgement to return depends on traffic in the Internet as well as the distance to the destination. Because TCP allows multiple application programs to communicate with multiple destinations concurrently and traffic conditions affect delay, TCP must handle a variety of delays that can change rapidly.*

26.9 Adaptive Retransmission

Before TCP was invented, transport protocols used a fixed value for retransmission delay — the protocol designer or network manager chose a value that was large enough for the expected delay. Designers working on TCP realized that a fixed timeout would not operate well for the Internet. Thus, they chose to make TCP's retransmission *adaptive*. That is, TCP monitors current delay on each connection, and adapts (i.e., changes) the retransmission timer to accommodate changing conditions.

How can TCP monitor Internet delays? In fact, TCP cannot know the exact delays for all parts of the Internet at all times. Instead, TCP estimates *round-trip delay* for each active connection by measuring the time needed to receive a response. Whenever it sends a message to which it expects a response, TCP records the time at which the message was sent. When a response arrives, TCP subtracts the time the message was sent from the current time to produce a new estimate of the round-trip delay for that connection. As it sends data packets and receives acknowledgements, TCP generates a sequence of round-trip estimates and uses a statistical function to produce a weighted average. In addition to a weighted average, TCP keeps an estimate of the variance, and uses a linear combination of the estimated mean and variance when computing the time at which retransmission is needed.

Experience has shown that TCP adaptive retransmission works well. Using the variance helps TCP react quickly when delay increases following a burst of packets. Using a weighted average helps TCP reset the retransmission timer if the delay returns to a lower value after a temporary burst. When the delay remains constant, TCP adjusts the retransmission timeout to a value that is slightly longer than the mean round-trip delay. When delays start to vary, TCP adjusts the retransmission timeout to a value greater than the mean to accommodate peaks.

26.10 Comparison Of Retransmission Times

To understand how adaptive retransmission helps TCP maximize throughput on each connection, consider a case of packet loss on two connections that have different round-trip delays. For example, Figure 26.6 illustrates traffic on two such connections.

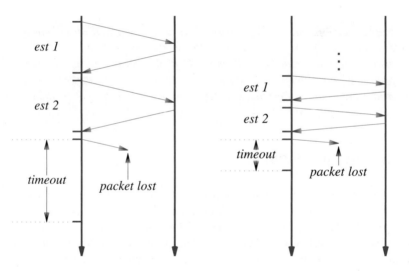

Figure 26.6 Timeout and retransmission on two TCP connections that have different round-trip delays.

As the figure shows, TCP sets the retransmission timeout to be slightly longer than the mean round-trip delay. If the delay is large, TCP uses a large retransmission timeout; if the delay is small, TCP uses a small timeout. The goal is to wait long enough to determine that a packet was lost, without waiting longer than necessary.

26.11 Buffers, Flow Control, And Windows

TCP uses a *window* mechanism to control the flow of data. Unlike the simplistic packet-based window scheme described above, a TCP window is measured in bytes. When a connection is established, each end of the connection allocates a buffer to hold incoming data and sends the size of the buffer to the other end. As data arrives, the receiving TCP sends acknowledgements, which specify the remaining buffer size. TCP uses the term *window* to refer to the amount of buffer space available at any time; a notification that specifies the size of the window is known as a *window advertisement*. A receiver sends a window advertisement with each acknowledgement.

If the receiving application can read data as quickly as it arrives, a receiver will send a positive window advertisement along with each acknowledgement. However, if the sending side operates faster than the receiving side (e.g., because the CPU is faster), incoming data will eventually fill the receiver's buffer, causing the receiver to advertise a *zero window*. A sender that receives a zero window advertisement must stop sending until the receiver again advertises a positive window. Figure 26.7 illustrates window advertisements.

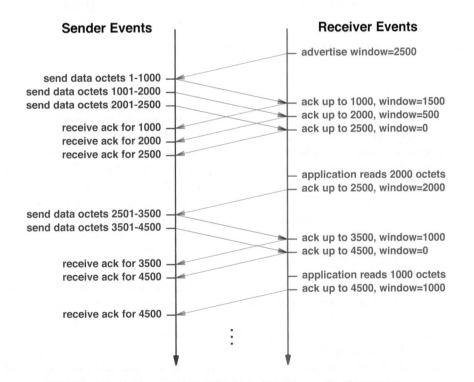

Figure 26.7 A sequence of messages that illustrates TCP flow for a maximum segment size of *1000* bytes.

In the figure, the sender uses a maximum segment size of *1000* bytes. Transfer begins when the receiver advertises an initial window size of *2500* bytes. The sender immediately transmits three segments, two that contain *1000* bytes of data and one that contains *500* bytes. As the segments arrive, the receiver generates an acknowledgement with the window size reduced by the amount of data that has arrived.

In the example, the first three segments fill the receiver's buffer faster than the receiving application can consume data. Thus, the advertised window size reaches zero, and the sender cannot transmit additional data. After the receiving application consumes *2000* bytes of data, the receiving TCP sends an additional acknowledgement that advertises a window size of *2000* bytes. The window size is always measured beyond the data being acknowledged, so the receiver is advertising that it can accept *2000* bytes beyond the *2500* it has already received. The sender responds by transmitting two additional segments. As each segment arrives, the receiver sends an acknowledgement with the window size reduced by *1000* bytes (i.e., the amount of data that has arrived).

Once again, the window size reaches zero, causing the sender to stop transmission. Eventually, the receiving application consumes some of the data, and the receiving TCP transmits an acknowledgement with a positive window size. If the sender had more data waiting to be sent, the sender could proceed to transmit another segment.

26.12 TCP's Three-Way Handshake

To guarantee that connections are established or terminated reliably, TCP uses a *3-way handshake* in which three messages are exchanged. During the 3-way handshake to start a connection, each side sends a control message that specifies an initial buffer size (for flow control) and a sequence number. Scientists have proved that TCP's 3-way exchange is necessary and sufficient to ensure unambiguous agreement despite packet loss, duplication, delay, and replay events†. Furthermore, the handshake insures that TCP will not open or close a connection until both ends have agreed.

TCP uses the term *synchronization segment* (*SYN segment*) to describe the control messages used in a 3-way handshake to create a connection, and the term *FIN segment* (short for *finish segment*) to describe control messages used in a 3-way handshake to close a connection. Figure 26.8 illustrates the 3-way handshake used to create a connection.

A key aspect of the 3-way handshake used to create a connection involves the selection of sequence numbers. TCP requires each end to generate a random 32-bit sequence number that becomes the initial sequence for data sent. If an application attempts to establish a new TCP connection after a computer reboots, TCP chooses a new random number. Because the probability of selecting a random value that matches the sequence used on a previous connection is low, TCP avoids replay problems. That is, if a pair of application programs uses TCP to communicate, closes the connection, and then establishes a new connection, the sequence numbers on the new connection will differ from the sequence numbers used on the old connection, allowing TCP to reject any delayed packets that arrive.

†Like other TCP packets, messages used for a 3-way handshake can be retransmitted.

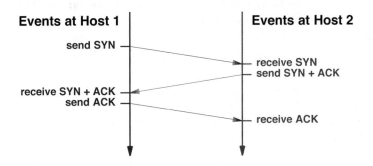

Figure 26.8 The 3-way handshake used to create a TCP connection.

The 3-way handshake used to close a connection uses *FIN* segments. An acknowledgement is sent in each direction along with a FIN to guarantee that all data has arrived before the connection is terminated. Figure 26.9 illustrates the exchange.

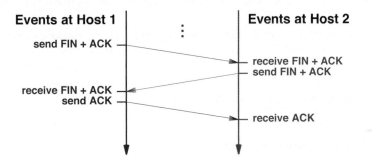

Figure 26.9 The 3-way handshake used to close a connection.

26.13 TCP Congestion Control

One of the most interesting aspects of TCP is a mechanism for *congestion control*. Recall that in the Internet, delay or packet loss is more likely to be caused by congestion than a hardware failure, and that retransmission can exacerbate the problem of congestion by injecting additional copies of a packet. To avoid congestion collapse, TCP uses changes in delay as a measure of congestion, and responds to congestion by reducing the rate at which it retransmits data.

Although we think of reducing the rate of transmission, TCP does not compute a data rate. Instead, TCP bases transmission on buffer size. That is, the receiver advertises a window size, and the sender can transmit data to fill the receiver's window before an ACK is received. To control the data rate, TCP imposes a restriction on the window size — by temporarily reducing the window size, the sending TCP effectively reduces the data rate. The important concept is:

> *Conceptually, a transport protocol should reduce the rate of transmission when congestion occurs. Because it uses a variable-size window, TCP can achieve a reduction in data rate by temporarily reducing the window size. In the extreme case where loss occurs, TCP temporarily reduces the window to one-half of its current value.*

TCP uses a special congestion control mechanism when starting a new connection or when a message is lost. Instead of transmitting enough data to fill the receiver's buffer (i.e., the receiver's window size), TCP begins by sending a single message containing data. If an acknowledgement arrives without additional loss, TCP doubles the amount of data being sent and sends two additional messages. If both acknowledgements arrive, TCP sends four messages, and so on. The exponential increase continues until TCP is sending half of the receiver's advertised window. When one-half of the original window size is reached, TCP slows the rate of increase, and increases the window size linearly as long as congestion does not occur. The approach is known as *slow start*.

TCP's congestion control mechanisms respond well to increases in traffic. By backing off quickly, TCP is able to alleviate congestion. In essence, TCP avoids adding retransmissions when the Internet becomes congested. More important, if all TCPs follow the standard, the congestion control scheme means that all senders back off when congestion occurs and congestion collapse is avoided.

26.14 TCP Segment Format

TCP uses a single format for all messages, including messages that carry data, those that carry acknowledgements, and messages that are part of the 3-way handshake used to create or terminate a connection (SYN and FIN). TCP uses the term *segment* to refer to a message. Figure 26.10 illustrates the TCP segment format.

To understand the segment format, it is necessary to remember that a TCP connection contains two streams of data, one flowing in each direction. If the applications at each end are sending data simultaneously, TCP can send a single segment that carries outgoing data, the acknowledgement for incoming data, and a window advertisement that specifies the amount of additional buffer space available for incoming data. Thus, some of the fields in the segment refer to the data stream traveling in the forward direction, while other fields refer to the data stream traveling in the reverse direction.

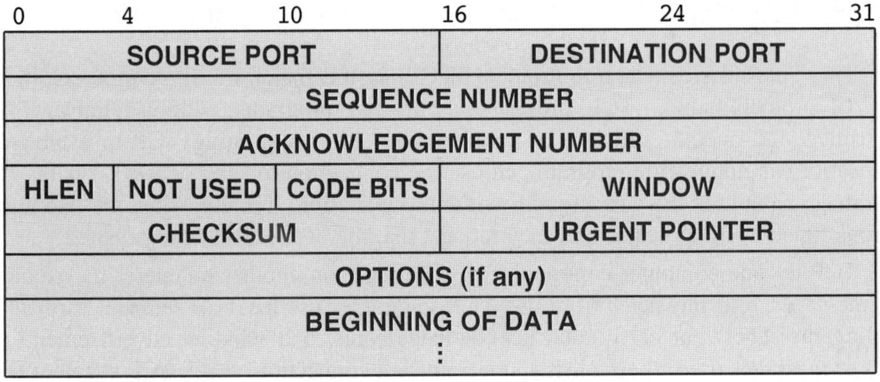

0	4	10	16	24	31

SOURCE PORT			DESTINATION PORT		
SEQUENCE NUMBER					
ACKNOWLEDGEMENT NUMBER					
HLEN	NOT USED	CODE BITS	WINDOW		
CHECKSUM			URGENT POINTER		
OPTIONS (if any)					
BEGINNING OF DATA					

Figure 26.10 The TCP segment format used for both data and control messages.

When a computer sends a segment, the *ACKNOWLEDGEMENT NUMBER* and *WINDOW* fields refer to incoming data: the *ACKNOWLEDGEMENT NUMBER* specifies the sequence number of the data that is expected next, and the *WINDOW* specifies how much additional buffer space is available beyond the acknowledged data. The acknowledgement always refers to the first position for which data is missing; if segments arrive out of order, a receiving TCP generates the same acknowledgement multiple times until the missing data arrives. The *SEQUENCE NUMBER* field refers to outgoing data. It gives the sequence number of the first byte of data being carried in the segment. A receiver uses the sequence number to reorder segments that arrive out of order and to compute an acknowledgement number. Field *DESTINATION PORT* identifies which application program on the receiving computer should receive the data, while field *SOURCE PORT* identifies the application program that sent the data. Finally, the *CHECKSUM* field contains a checksum that covers the TCP segment header and the data.

The key ideas regarding sequence and acknowledgement numbering are:

The SEQUENCE NUMBER field in a TCP segment gives the sequence number for the first byte of data carried in the segment in the forward direction; an ACKNOWLEDGEMENT NUMBER gives the first sequence number for which data is missing in the reverse direction.

26.15 Summary

The Transmission Control Protocol (TCP) is the major transport protocol in the TCP/IP protocol suite. TCP provides application programs with a reliable, flow-controlled, full-duplex, stream transport service. After requesting TCP to establish a connection, an application program can use the connection to send or receive data; TCP guarantees to deliver the data in order without duplication. Finally, when the two applications finish using a connection, they request that the connection be terminated.

TCP on one computer communicates with TCP on another computer by exchanging messages. All messages from one TCP to another use the TCP segment format, including messages that carry data, acknowledgements, and window advertisements, as well as messages used to establish and terminate a connection. Each TCP segment travels in an IP datagram.

In general, transport protocols use a variety of mechanisms to insure reliable service. TCP has a particularly complex combination of techniques that have proven to be extremely successful. In addition to a checksum in each segment, TCP retransmits any message that is lost. To be useful in the Internet where delays vary over time, TCP's retransmission timeout is adaptive — TCP measures the current round-trip delay separately for each connection, and uses a weighted average of the round-trip time to choose a timeout for retransmission.

EXERCISES

26.1 Is the TCP checksum necessary, or can TCP depend on the IP checksum to insure integrity? Explain.

26.2 Assume that messages sent between two programs can be lost, duplicated, delayed, or delivered out of order. Design a protocol that reliably allows the two programs to agree to communicate. Give your design to someone, and see if they can find a sequence of loss, duplication, and delay that makes the protocol fail.

26.3 What happens to throughput if a protocol waits too long to retransmit? If a protocol does not wait long enough to retransmit?

26.4 When using a sliding window of size N, how many packets can be sent without requiring a single ACK to be received?

26.5 How does TCP handle packet loss?

26.6 Write a computer program to extract and print fields in a TCP segment header.

26.7 What layers of a protocol stack are used on a router? A host?

26.8 What is a *SYN*? A *FIN*?

26.9 What are the techniques a transport protocol uses?

26.10 How does TCP compute a timeout for retransmission?

26.11 List the features of TCP.

26.12 What are the main problems a transport protocol must solve to achieve reliable transfer?

26.13 What does the TCP window size control?

26.14 Suppose two programs use TCP to establish a connection, communicate, terminate the connection, and then open a new connection. Further suppose a *FIN* message sent to shut down the first connection is duplicated and delayed until the second connection has been established. If a copy of the old *FIN* is delivered, will TCP terminate the new connection? Why or why not?

26.15 What problem in a network causes TCP to reduce its window size temporarily?

26.16 Why does a stop-and-go protocol have especially low throughput over a GEO satellite channel that operates at two megabits per second?

26.17 Extend the diagrams in Figure 26.3 to show the transmission of sixteen successive packets.

26.18 What is the chief cause of packet delay and loss in the Internet?

Chapter Contents

27

Internet Routing And Routing Protocols

27.1 Introduction

Previous chapters describe the fundamental concept of datagram forwarding, and explain how IP uses a forwarding table to select a next-hop for each datagram. This chapter explores an important aspect of internetworking technology: the propagation of routing information that is used to create and update forwarding tables. The chapter discusses how forwarding tables are built, and explains how routing software updates the tables, as needed.

The chapter focuses on the propagation of routing information in the Internet. It describes several routing update protocols that are used, and explains the distinction between interior and exterior routing protocols.

27.2 Static Vs. Dynamic Routing

IP routing can be partitioned into two broad categories:

- Static routing
- Dynamic routing

The term *static routing* characterizes an approach that creates a forwarding table when the system starts and does not change entries unless an administrator manually alters them. In contrast, the term *dynamic routing* characterizes an approach in which *route propagation software* runs on the system and continuously updates the forwarding table to insure that each datagram follows an optimum route. That is, the software communicates with other systems to learn optimum routes to each destination, and continually checks for network failures that cause routes to change. Ironically, dynamic routing begins exactly like static routing by loading an initial set of routes into a forwarding table when the system boots.

27.3 Static Routing In Hosts And A Default Route

Static routing is straightforward, easy to specify, and does not require extra routing software. It does not consume bandwidth, and no CPU cycles are required to propagate routing information. However, static routing is relatively inflexible; it cannot accommodate network failures or changes in topology.

Where is static routing used? Most hosts use static routing, especially in cases where the host has one network connection and a single router connects the network to the rest of the Internet. For example, consider the architecture that Figure 27.1 illustrates. Four hosts are attached to an Ethernet, which connects to the rest of the Internet through router R_1.

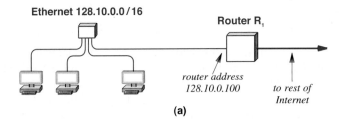

(a)

Net	Mask	Next hop
128.10.0.0	255.255.0.0	direct
default	0.0.0.0	128.10.0.100

(b)

Figure 27.1 (a) A typical connection to the Internet, and (b) the static forwarding table used in each host.

As the figure shows, a static forwarding table with two entries suffices for a typical host. One entry specifies the address of the directly connected network, and the other entry specifies that router R_1 provides a *default route* for all other destinations. When an application generates a datagram for a computer on the local net (e.g., a local printer), the first entry in the forwarding table directs IP to deliver the datagram directly to its destination. When a datagram is destined for any other destination in the Internet, the second entry in the table directs IP to send the datagram to the router, R_1.

The point is:

> *Most Internet hosts use static routing. The host's forwarding table contains two entries: one for the network to which the host attaches and a* default *entry that directs all other traffic to a specific router.*

27.4 Dynamic Routing And Routers

Can a router in the Internet use static routing the same way a host does? Although cases exist where a router uses static routing, most routers use dynamic routing. To understand an exceptional case where static routing does suffice for a router, look at Figure 27.1 again. We can imagine that the figure corresponds to a small organization that is a customer of an ISP. All traffic leaving the customer's site through router R_1 must travel to the ISP (e.g., across a DSL connection). Because routes never change, the forwarding table in router R_1 can be static. Furthermore, the forwarding table in R_1 can use a default route just as the forwarding table in a host does.

Despite a few exceptions, static routing and default routes do not suffice for most routers; the use is limited to special configurations such as the one above. When two ISPs interconnect, both need to exchange routing information dynamically. To see why, consider three networks interconnected by two routers as Figure 27.2 illustrates.

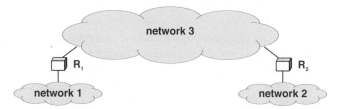

Figure 27.2 Illustration of an architecture that requires dynamic routing.

Each router knows about directly connected networks. Thus, router R_1 knows about networks 1 and 3, and R_2 knows about networks 2 and 3. However, router R_1 does not know about network 2, and R_2 does not know about network 1 because there is no direct connection. For the trivial example, it may seem that static routing will suffice. However, the static approach does not scale to handle thousands of networks. In particular, each time an ISP adds a new customer's network, the information must be passed throughout the Internet. More important, a manual process is far too slow to accommodate network failures and congestion in the Internet. Consequently, to ensure that all routers obtain information about how to reach each possible destination, each router runs software that uses a route propagation protocol to exchange information with other routers. When it learns about changes in routes, the routing software updates the local forwarding table. Furthermore, because routers exchange information periodically, the local forwarding table is updated continuously.

In Figure 27.2, for example, routers R_1 and R_2 will exchange routing information across network 3. As a result, routing software in R_2 will install a route to network 1 and software running in R_1 will install a route to network 2. If router R_2 crashes, the route propagation software in R_1 will detect that network 2 is no longer reachable, and will remove the route from its forwarding table. Later, when R_2 comes back on line, the routing software in R_1 will determine that network 2 is reachable again, and will reinstall the route.

To summarize:

> *Each router runs routing software that learns about destinations other routers can reach, and informs other routers about destinations that it can reach. The routing software uses incoming information to update the local forwarding table continuously.*

27.5 Routing In The Global Internet

So far, we have described routing for the most trivial connectivity (i.e., situations that involve only a few routers). This section looks at a broader issue: routing in the global Internet. The section considers general principles; later sections explain specific route propagation protocols.

We said that a route propagation protocol allows one router to exchange routing information with another. However, such a scheme cannot scale to the entire Internet — if a router in the Internet attempted to exchange routing information with all other routers, the resulting traffic would overwhelm the core of the Internet. To limit routing traffic, the Internet uses a routing hierarchy. Routers and networks in the Internet are divided into groups. All routers within a group exchange routing information. Then, at least one router (possibly more) in each group summarizes the information before passing it to other groups.

How large is a group? What protocol do routers use within a group? How is routing information represented? What protocol do routers use between groups? The designers of the Internet routing system did not dictate an exact size nor did they specify an exact data representation or protocol. Instead, the designers purposefully kept the architecture flexible enough to handle a wide variety of organizations. For example, to accommodate organizations of various size, the designers avoided specifying a minimum or maximum size for a group. To accommodate arbitrary routing protocols, the designers decided to permit each organization to choose a routing protocol independently.

27.6 Autonomous System Concept

To capture the concept of groups of routers, we use the term *Autonomous System* (*AS*). Intuitively, one can think of an autonomous system as a contiguous set of networks and routers all under control of one administrative authority. There is no exact meaning for *administrative authority* — the term is sufficiently flexible to accommodate many possibilities. For example, an autonomous system can correspond to an ISP, an entire corporation, or a university. Alternatively, a large organization with multiple sites may choose to define one autonomous system for each site. In particular, each ISP is usually a single autonomous system, but it is possible for a large ISP to divide itself into multiple autonomous systems.

The choice of autonomous system size can be made for economic, technical, or administrative reasons. For example, consider a multi-national corporation. It may be less expensive for the corporation to divide into multiple autonomous systems, each of which has a connection to an ISP in a given country than to act as a single autonomous system with one connection to the rest of the Internet. Another reason for a specific size arises from the routing protocol to be used — a protocol may generate excessive routing traffic when used on many routers (i.e., the routing traffic may grow as the square of the number of routers).

To summarize:

> *The Internet is divided into a set of* autonomous systems; *routers within an autonomous system exchange routing information, which is then summarized before being passed to another group.*

27.7 The Two Types Of Internet Routing Protocols

Now that we understand the autonomous system concept, Internet routing can be defined more precisely. All Internet routing protocols fall into one of two categories:

- Interior Gateway Protocols (IGPs)
- Exterior Gateway Protocols (EGPs)

After defining the two categories, we will examine a set of example routing protocols that illustrate each category.

27.7.1 Interior Gateway Protocols (IGPs)

The routers within an autonomous system use an *Interior Gateway Protocol* (*IGP*) to exchange routing information. Several IGPs are available; each autonomous system is free to choose its own IGP. Usually, an IGP is easy to install and operate, but an IGP may limit the size or routing complexity of an autonomous system.

27.7.2 Exterior Gateway Protocols (EGPs)

A router in one autonomous system uses an *Exterior Gateway Protocol* (*EGP*) to exchange routing information with a router in another autonomous system. EGPs are usually more complex to install and operate than IGPs, but EGPs offer more flexibility and lower overhead (i.e., less traffic). To save traffic, an EGP summarizes routing information from an autonomous system before passing it to another autonomous system. More important, an EGP implements *policy constraints* that allow a system manager to determine exactly what information is released outside the organization.

27.7.3 Illustration Of How IGPs And EGPs Are Used

Figure 27.3 illustrates the two-level routing hierarchy used in the Internet by showing two routers in two autonomous systems.

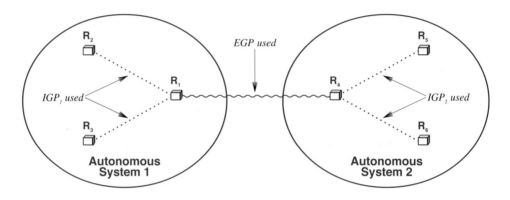

Figure 27.3 Illustration of Internet routing with an IGP used in each autonomous system and an EGP used between autonomous systems.

In the figure, Autonomous System 1 (AS_1) has chosen IGP_1 to use internally, and Autonomous System 2 (AS_2) has chosen IGP_2. All routers in AS_1 communicate using IGP_1, and all routers in AS_2 communicate using IGP_2. Routers R_1 and R_4 use an EGP to communicate between the two autonomous systems. That is, R_1 must summarize information from its autonomous system and send the summary to R_4. In addition, R_1 accepts a summary from R_4, and uses IGP_1 to propagate the information to routers in AS_1. R_4 performs the same service for AS_2.

27.7.4 Optimal Routes, Routing Metrics, and IGPs

It may seem that instead of merely discovering one path to each destination, routing software should find all possible paths and then choose one that is optimal. Although the Internet usually has multiple paths between any source and destination, there is no universal agreement about which path is optimal. To understand why, consider the requirements of various applications. For a remote desktop application, a path with least delay is optimal. For a browser downloading a large graphics file, a path with maximum throughput is optimal. For an audio webcast application that receives real-time audio, a path with least jitter is optimal.

We use the term *routing metric* to refer to a measure of the path that routing software uses when choosing a route. Although it is possible to use throughput, delay, or jitter as a routing metric, most Internet routing software does not. Instead, typical Internet routing uses a combination of two metrics: *administrative cost* and *hop count*. In Internet routing, a hop corresponds to an intermediate network (or router). Thus, the hop count for a destination gives the number of intermediate networks on the path to the destination. Administrative costs are assigned manually, often to control which paths traffic can use. For example, suppose in a corporation two paths connect the accounting department to the payroll department: a 2-hop path that includes a network designated to be used for customer traffic and a 3-hop path that includes networks for internal corporate traffic. That is, the shortest path violates the corporate policy by traversing a network designated to serve customers. In such cases, a network administrator can override the actual cost of the 2-hop path by assigning the path an administrative cost of four hops (i.e., the manager replaces the actual cost with an administrative value to achieve the desired effect). Routing software will choose the path with the lower cost (i.e., the path with a metric of three hops). Thus, traffic will follow the corporate policy. The point is:

> *Although most Internet routing protocols are designed to use a hop-count metric, it is possible for a network administrator to override the metric to enforce a policy.*

IGPs and EGPs differ in an important way with respect to routing metrics: IGPs use routing metrics, but EGPs do not. That is, each autonomous system chooses a routing metric and arranges internal routing software to send the metric with each route so receiving software can use the metric to choose optimal paths. Outside an autonomous system, however, an EGP does not attempt to choose an optimal path. Instead, the EGP merely finds a path. The reason is simple: because each autonomous system is free to choose a routing metric, an EGP cannot make meaningful comparisons. For example, suppose one autonomous system reports the number of hops along a path to destination D and another autonomous system reports the throughput along a different path to D. An EGP that receives the two reports cannot choose which of the two paths has least cost because there is no way to convert from hops to throughput. Thus, an EGP can only report the existence of a path and not its cost. We can summarize:

> *Within an autonomous system, IGP software uses a routing metric to choose an optimal path to each destination. EGP software finds a path to each destination, but cannot find an optimal path because it cannot compare routing metrics from multiple autonomous systems.*

27.8 Routes And Data Traffic

An aphorism in networking suggests that the response to a routing advertisement is data. The concept is straightforward: data traffic for a given destination flows in exactly the opposite direction of routing traffic. For example, suppose an autonomous system owned by ISP_1 contains network N. Before traffic can arrive destined for N, ISP_1 must advertise a route to N. That is, when the routing advertisement flows out, data will begin to flow in. Figure 27.4 illustrates the flow of data in response to routing advertisements.

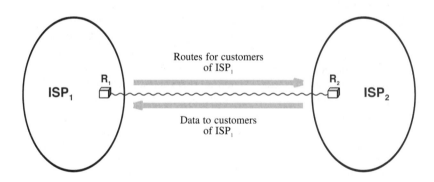

Figure 27.4 The flow of data after a router in an ISP advertises routes.

27.9 The Border Gateway Protocol (BGP)

One particular protocol has emerged as the most widely used Exterior Gateway Protocol in the Internet. Known as the *Border Gateway Protocol* (*BGP*), the protocol has survived three major revisions. Version 4 is the current standard, and is officially abbreviated *BGP-4*. In practice, the version number has remained unchanged for so long that networking professionals use the term *BGP* to refer to version 4.

BGP has the following characteristics:

- *Routing Among Autonomous Systems.* Because it is intended for use as an Exterior Gateway Protocol, BGP provides routing information at the autonomous system level. That is, all routes are given as a path of autonomous systems. For example, the path to a given destination may consist of autonomous systems *17*, *2*, *56*, and *12*. There is no use of routing metrics, and no way for BGP to provide details about the routers within each autonomous system on the path.

- *Provision For Policies.* BGP allows the sender and receiver to enforce policies. In particular, a manager can configure BGP to restrict which routes BGP advertises to outsiders.

- *Facilities For Transit Routing.* BGP classifies each autonomous system as a *transit* system if it agrees to pass traffic through to another autonomous system, or as a *stub* system if it does not. Similarly, traffic passing through on its way to another AS is classified as transit traffic. The classification allows BGP to distinguish between ISPs and other autonomous systems. More important, BGP allows a corporation to classify itself as a stub even if it is *multi-homed* (i.e., a corporation with multiple external connections can refuse to accept transit traffic).

- *Reliable Transport.* BGP uses TCP for all communication. That is, a BGP program on a router in one autonomous system forms a TCP connection to a BGP program on a router in another autonomous system, and then sends data across the connection. TCP ensures that the data arrives in the correct order and that no data is missing.

BGP provides the glue that holds Internet routing together — at the center of the Internet, Tier-1 ISPs use BGP to exchange routing information and learn about each other's customers. To summarize:

> *The Border Gateway Protocol (BGP) is the Exterior Gateway Protocol that Tier-1 ISPs use to exchange routing information among autonomous systems at the center of the Internet; the current version is BGP-4.*

27.10 The Routing Information Protocol (RIP)

The *Routing Information Protocol* (*RIP*) was among the first Interior Gateway Protocols used in the Internet. RIP has the following characteristics:

- *Routing Within An Autonomous System.* RIP is designed as an Interior Gateway Protocol used to pass information among routers within an autonomous system.

- *Hop Count Metric.* RIP measures distance in network *hops*, where each network between the source and destination counts as a single hop; RIP counts a directly connected network as one hop away.

- *Unreliable Transport.* RIP uses UDP to transfer messages among routers.

- *Broadcast Or Multicast Delivery.* RIP is intended for use over Local Area Network technologies that support broadcast or multicast (e.g., Ethernet). Version 1 of RIP broadcasts messages; version 2 allows delivery via multicast.

- *Support For CIDR And Subnetting.* RIP version 2 includes an address mask with each destination address.

- *Support For Default Route Propagation.* In addition to specifying explicit destinations, RIP allows a router to advertise a *default route*.

- *Distance Vector Algorithm.* RIP uses the *distance-vector* approach to routing defined in Algorithm 18.3†.

- *Passive Version For Hosts.* Although only a router can propagate routing information, RIP allows a host to listen passively and update its forwarding table. Passive RIP is useful on networks where a host selects among multiple routers.

To understand how RIP propagates routes, recall how distance vector routing works. Each outgoing message contains an advertisement that lists the networks the sender can reach along with a distance to each. When it receives an advertisement, RIP software uses the list of destinations to update the local forwarding table. Each entry in a RIP advertisement consists of a pair:

(destination network, distance)

where *distance* is the number of *hops* to the destination. When a message arrives, if the receiver does not have a route to an advertised destination or if an advertised distance is shorter than the distance of the current route, the receiver replaces its route with a route to the sender.

---

†Algorithm 18.3 can be found on page 319.

The chief advantage of RIP is simplicity. RIP requires little configuration — a manager merely starts RIP running on each router in the organization and allows the routers to broadcast messages to one another. After a short time, all routers in the organization will have routes to all destinations.

RIP also handles the propagation of a default route. The organization merely needs to configure one of its routers to have a default (typically, an organization chooses a router that connects to an ISP). RIP propagates the default route to all other routers in the organization, which means that any datagram sent to a destination outside the organization will be forwarded to the ISP.

27.11 RIP Packet Format

The RIP message format helps explain how a distance vector routing protocol operates. Figure 27.5 illustrates a RIP update message.

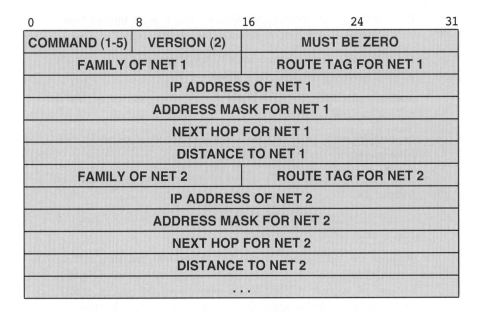

Figure 27.5 The format of a RIP version 2 update message.

As the figure shows, each entry contains the IP address of a destination and a distance to that destination. In addition, to permit RIP to be used with CIDR or subnet addressing, an entry contains a 32-bit address mask. Each entry also has a next hop address, and two 16-bit fields that identify the entry as an IP address and provide a tag used to group entries together. In all, each entry contains twenty octets. We can summarize:

> *RIP is an Interior Gateway Protocol that uses a distance vector algorithm to propagate routing information.*

27.12 The Open Shortest Path First Protocol (OSPF)

The RIP message format illustrates a disadvantage of distance-vector protocols: the size of a message is proportional to the number of networks that can be reached. Sending RIP messages introduces delay, and processing RIP messages consumes many CPU cycles. The delay means that route changes propagate slowly, one router at a time. Thus, although RIP works well among a few routers, it does not scale well.

To satisfy demand for a routing protocol that can scale to large organizations, the IETF devised an IGP known as the *Open Shortest Path First Protocol* (*OSPF*). The name is derived from the use of Dijkstra's SPF algorithm which computes shortest paths. OSPF has the following characteristics:

- *Routing Within An Autonomous System.* OSPF is an Interior Gateway Protocol used within an autonomous system.

- *CIDR Support.* To accommodate CIDR addressing, OSPF includes a 32-bit address mask with each address.

- *Authenticated Message Exchange.* A pair of routers using OSPF can authenticate each message.

- *Imported Routes.* OSPF allows a router to introduce routes learned from another means (e.g., from BGP).

- *Link-State Algorithm.* OSPF uses *link-state routing* as described in Chapter 18.

- *Support For Metrics.* OSPF allows an administrator to assign a cost to each route.

- *Support For Multi-access Networks.* Traditional link state routing is inefficient across a multi-access network, such as an Ethernet, because all routers attached to the network broadcast link status. OSPF optimizes by designating a single router to broadcast on the network.

To summarize:

> *OSPF is an Interior Gateway Protocol that uses a link-state algorithm to propagate routing information. Routers use Dijkstra's SPF algorithm to compute shortest paths.*

27.13 An Example OSPF Graph

Recall from Chapter 18 that link-state routing uses a graph-theoretic abstraction. Although OSPF allows a complex relationship between networks and a graph, a simple example will help explain the basic concept†. Consider the network and associated graph illustrated in Figure 27.6.

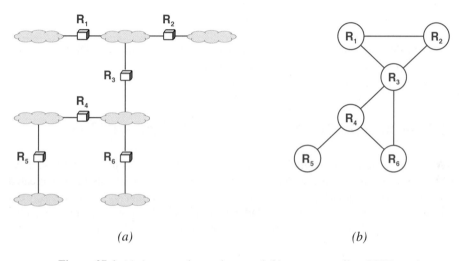

(a)   *(b)*

Figure 27.6 (a) An example topology, and (b) a corresponding OSPF graph.

The figure shows a typical OSPF graph in which each node corresponds to a router. An edge in the graph corresponds to a connection between a pair of routers (i.e., a network). To follow a link-state algorithm, each pair of routers connected by a network periodically probe one another and then broadcast a link-state message to other routers. All routers receive the broadcast message; each uses the message to update its local copy of the graph, and recomputes shortest paths when the status changes.

27.14 OSPF Areas

One particular feature that makes OSPF more complex than other routing protocols also makes it more powerful: hierarchical routing. To achieve a hierarchy, OSPF allows an autonomous system to be partitioned for routing purposes. That is, a manager can divide routers and networks in an autonomous system into subsets that OSPF calls *areas*. Each router is configured to know the area boundary (i.e., exactly which other routers are in its area). When OSPF runs, routers within a given area exchange link-state messages periodically.

---

†In practice, OSPF graphs are more complex than shown.

In addition to exchanging information within an area, OSPF allows communication between areas. One router in each area is configured to communicate with a router in one or more other area(s). The two routers summarize routing information they have learned from other routers within their respective area, and then exchange the summary. Thus, instead of broadcasting to all routers in the autonomous system, OSPF limits link-state broadcasts to routers within an area. As a result of the hierarchy, OSPF can scale to handle much larger autonomous systems than other routing protocols.

The point is:

> *Because it allows a manager to partition the routers and networks in an autonomous system into multiple areas, OSPF can scale to handle a larger number of routers than other IGPs.*

27.15 Intermediate System - Intermediate System (IS-IS)

Originally designed by Digital Equipment Corporation to be part of DECNET V, the *IS-IS* (*Intermediate System to Intermediate System*†) is an IGP. IS-IS was created around the same time as OSPF, and the two protocols are similar in many ways. Both use the link-state approach and employ Dijkstra's algorithm to compute shortest paths. In addition, both protocols require two adjacent routers to periodically test the link between them and broadcast a status message.

The chief differences between OSPF and the original IS-IS can be summarized as:

- IS-IS was proprietary (owned by Digital) and OSPF was created as an *open* standard, available to all vendors.

- OSPF was designed to run over IP; IS-IS was designed to run over CLNS (part of the ill-fated OSI protocol stack).

- OSPF was designed to propagate IPv4 routes (IPv4 addresses and address masks); IS-IS was designed to propagate routes for OSI protocols.

- Over time, OSPF gained many features. As a result, IS-IS now has less overhead.

When the protocols were initially invented, OSPF's openness and dedication to IP made it much more popular than IS-IS. In fact, IS-IS was almost completely forgotten. As the years progressed, OSPF's popularity encouraged the IETF to add additional features. Ironically, in the early 2000's, ten years after the protocols were designed, several things changed to give IS-IS a second chance. Digital Equipment Corporation had dissolved, and IS-IS was no longer considered valuable proprietary property. A

---

†The naming follows Digital's terminology in which a router was called an *Intermediate System* and a host was called an *End System*.

newer version of IS-IS was defined to integrate it with IP and the Internet. Because OSPF was built for IPv4, a completely new version had to be developed to handle larger IPv6 addresses. The largest ISPs have grown to a size where the extra overhead in OSPF makes IS-IS more attractive. As a result, IS-IS has started to make a comeback.

27.16 Multicast Routing

27.16.1 IP Multicast Semantics

So far, we have discussed unicast routing. That is, we have considered routing protocols that propagate information about destinations that each have a static address and a location that does not change. One of the design goals for unicast route propagation is *stability* — continual changes in routes are undesirable because they lead to higher jitter and datagrams arriving out of order. Thus, once a unicast routing protocol finds a shortest path, it usually retains the route until a failure makes the path unusable.

Propagating *multicast routing* information differs dramatically from unicast route propagation. The difference arises because Internet multicast allows dynamic group membership and anonymous senders. Dynamic group membership means that an application can choose to participate in a group at any time and remain a participant for an arbitrary duration. That is, the IP multicast abstraction allows an application running on an arbitrary computer to:

- Join a multicast group at any time and begin receiving a copy of all packets sent to the group. To join a group, a host informs a nearby router. If multiple applications on the same host decide to join a group, the host receives one copy of each datagram sent to the group and makes a local copy for each application.

- Leave a multicast group at any time. A host periodically sends group membership messages to the local router. Once the last application on the host leaves the group, the host informs the local router that it is no longer participating in the group.

An IP multicast group is anonymous in two ways. First, neither a sender nor a receiver knows (nor can they find out) the identity or the number of group members. Second, routers and hosts do not know which applications will send a datagram to a group because an arbitrary application can send a datagram to any multicast group at any time. That is, membership in a multicast group only defines a set of receivers — a sender does not need to join a multicast group before sending a message to the group.

To summarize:

> *Membership in an IP multicast group is dynamic: a computer can join or leave a group at any time. Group membership defines a set of receivers; an arbitrary application can send a datagram to the group, even if the application is not a group member.*

27.16.2 IGMP

How does a host join or leave a multicast group? A standard protocol exists that allows a host to inform a nearby router whenever the host needs to join or leave a particular multicast group. Known as the *Internet Group Multicast Protocol (IGMP)*, the protocol is used only on the network between a host and a router. Furthermore, the protocol defines the host, not the application, to be a group member, and specifies nothing about applications. If multiple applications on a given host join a multicast group, the host must make copies of each datagram it receives for local applications. When the last application on a host leaves a group, the host uses IGMP to inform the local router that it is no longer a member of the group.

27.16.3 Forwarding And Discovery Techniques

When a router learns that a host on one of its networks has joined a multicast group, the router must establish a path to the group and propagate datagrams it receives for the group to the host. Thus, routers, not hosts, have responsibility for the propagation of multicast routing information.

Dynamic group membership and support for anonymous senders makes general-purpose multicast routing extremely difficult. Moreover, the size and topology of groups vary considerably among applications. For example, teleconferencing often creates small groups (e.g., between two and five members) who may be geographically dispersed or in the same organization. A webcast application can potentially create a group with millions of members that span the globe.

To accommodate dynamic membership, multicast routing protocols must be able to change routes quickly and continually. For example, if a user in France joins a multicast group that has members in the U.S. and Japan, multicast routing software must first find other members of the group, and then create an optimal forwarding structure. More important, because an arbitrary user can send a datagram to the group, information about routes must extend beyond group members. In practice, multicast protocols have followed three different approaches for datagram forwarding:

- Flood-And-Prune
- Configuration-And-Tunneling
- Core-Based Discovery

Flood-And-Prune. Flood-and-prune is ideal in a situation where the group is small and all members are attached to contiguous Local Area Networks (e.g., a group within a corporation). Initially, routers forward each datagram to all networks. That is, when a multicast datagram arrives, a router transmits the datagram on all directly attached LANs via hardware multicast. To avoid routing loops, flood-and-prune protocols use a technique known as *Reverse Path Broadcasting* (*RPB*) that breaks cycles. While the flooding stage proceeds, routers exchange information about group membership. If a router learns that no hosts on a given network are members of the group, the router stops forwarding multicast to the network (i.e., "prunes" the network from the set).

Configuration-And-Tunneling. Configuration-and-tunneling is ideal in a situation where the group is geographically dispersed (i.e., has a few members at each site, with sites separated by long distances). A router at each site is configured to know about other sites. When a multicast datagram arrives, the router at a site transmits the datagram on all directly attached LANs via hardware multicast. The router then consults its configuration table to determine which remote sites should receive a copy, and uses IP-in-IP tunneling to transfer a copy of the multicast datagram to each of the remote sites.

Core-Based Discovery. Although flood-and-prune and configuration-and-tunneling each handle extreme cases well, a technique is needed that allows multicast to scale gracefully from a small group in one area to a large group with members at arbitrary locations. To provide smooth growth, some multicast routing protocols designate a *core* unicast address for each multicast group. Whenever a router R_1 receives a multicast datagram that must be transmitted to a group, R_1 encapsulates the multicast datagram in a unicast datagram and forwards the unicast datagram to the group's core unicast address. As the unicast datagram travels through the Internet, each router examines the contents. When the datagram reaches a router R_2 that participates in the group, R_2 removes and processes the multicast message. R_2 uses multicast routing to forward the datagram to members of the group. Requests to join the group follow the same pattern — if it receives a request to join a group, R_2 adds a new route to its multicast forwarding table and begins to forward a copy of each multicast datagram to R_1. Thus, the set of routers receiving a particular multicast group grows from the core outward. In graph theoretic terms, the routers form a *tree*.

27.16.4 Multicast Protocols

Although many multicast routing protocols have been proposed; no Internet-wide multicast routing currently exists. A few of the proposed protocols are:

Distance Vector Multicast Routing Protocol (*DVMRP*). A protocol used by the UNIX program *mrouted* and the Internet *Multicast backBONE* (*MBONE*), DVMRP performs local multicast, and uses IP-in-IP encapsulation to send multicast datagrams from one site on the Internet to another. More information about the MBONE can be found at:

http://www.lbl.gov/web/Computers-and-Networks.html#MBONE

Core Based Trees (CBT). A particular protocol in which routers build a delivery tree from a central point for each group. CBT relies on unicast routing to reach a central point.

Protocol Independent Multicast – Sparse Mode (PIM-SM). A protocol that uses the same approach as CBT to form a multicast routing tree. The designers chose the term *protocol independent* to emphasize that although unicast datagrams are used to contact remote destinations when establishing multicast forwarding, PIM-SM does not depend on any particular unicast routing protocol.

Protocol Independent Multicast – Dense Mode (PIM-DM). A protocol designed for use within an organization. Routers that use PIM-DM broadcast (i.e. flood) multicast packets to all locations within the organization. Each router that has no member of a particular group sends back a message to *prune* the multicast routing tree (i.e., a request to stop the flow of packets). The scheme works well for short-lived multicast sessions (e.g., a few minutes) because it does not require setup before transmission begins.

Multicast Extensions To The Open Shortest Path First Protocol (MOSPF). Rather than a general-purpose multicast routing protocol, MOSPF is designed to pass multicast routes among routers within an organization. Thus, instead of a general-purpose multicast approach, MOSPF builds on OSPF and uses the LSR facilities.

Figure 27.7 summarizes the multicast routing protocols described above.

Protocol	Type
DVMRP	Configuration-and-Tunneling
CBT	Core-Based-Discovery
PIM-SM	Core-Based-Discovery
PIM-DM	Flood-And-Prune
MOSPF	Link-State (within an organization)

Figure 27.7 Multicast routing protocols and the approach each uses.

Despite twenty years of research and many experiments, general-purpose Internet multicast has not been successful. Even collaborative applications have not provided sufficient incentive. We can summarize the results as follows:

> *The dynamic characteristics of Internet multicast make the problem of multicast route propagation difficult. Although many protocols have been proposed, the Internet does not currently have an Internet-wide multicast routing facility.*

27.17 Summary

Most hosts use static routing in which the forwarding table is initialized at system startup; routers use dynamic routing in which route propagation software updates the forwarding table continuously. In terms of routing, the Internet is divided into a set of autonomous systems. Protocols used to pass routes between autonomous systems are known as Exterior Gateway Protocols (EGPs); protocols used to pass routing information inside an autonomous system are known as Interior Gateway Protocols (IGPs).

The Border Gateway Protocol (BGP) is the primary EGP in the Internet; Tier-1 ISPs use BGP to inform each other about their customers. IGPs include RIP, OSPF, and IS-IS.

Because Internet multicast allows dynamic group membership and an arbitrary source can send to a multicast group without being a member, the problem of multicast route propagation is difficult. Although several multicast routing protocols have been proposed, no Internet-wide multicast technology exists.

EXERCISES

27.1   Suppose you and two friends at distant colleges want to participate in a 3-way teleconference using IP multicast. Which multicast routing protocols would work best? Why?

27.2   Write a computer program that reads a RIP update message and prints the contents of each field.

27.3   Which multicast protocols allow a multicast message to be sent before the protocol has established routes?

27.4   List the characteristics of RIP.

27.5   List the two broad categories of Internet routing, and explain each.

27.6   List and explain the characteristics of BGP.

27.7   Suppose that all routers in the Internet contain a default route; show that a routing loop must exist.

27.8   Although each IP multicast group needs a unique IP multicast address, using a central server to allocate unique addresses creates a central bottleneck. Devise a scheme that allows a set of computers to choose a multicast address at random and resolve a conflict, if one should arise.

27.9   What is the meaning of "Open" in OSPF?

27.10   List the characteristics of OSPF.

27.11   Is multicast widely deployed in the Internet? Explain.

27.12   What two entries are needed in the forwarding table of a typical host?

27.13   Suppose a router in an organization uses a routing protocol to declare that a given destination is ten hops away when the destination is only three hops away. Is the declaration necessarily an error? Explain.

27.14   List and explain the two types of Internet routing protocols.

27.15   When a router receives a RIP message, how does the router divide each IP address into a prefix and suffix?

27.16   What is the main purpose of IGMP, and where is it used?

27.17   Why does OSPF have multiple areas?

27.18   What are the three main approaches used to forward multicast datagrams?

27.19   The traffic generated by flood-and-prune limits the size of the network region over which it can be used. Estimate the total traffic on one network if G multicast groups each generate traffic at a rate of P packets per second, each packet contains B bits, N networks constitute the intranet, and each network contains at least one listener for each group.

27.20   Where is BGP used?

27.21   What type of routing algorithm does RIP employ, and where is RIP used?

27.22   Which protocol has lower overhead, OSPF or IS-IS? Which has more features?

27.23   What is the expected consequence when a router advertises routes to a given destination?

27.24   What is an autonomous system?

27.25   RIP limits distance values to a maximum of 16 hops. Devise an example corporate intranet that has more than 16 routers and more than 16 networks but can still use RIP.

PART V

Other Aspects
Of Computer Networking

Network Performance, QoS, Security, Management, And Emerging Technologies

Chapters

Chapter Contents

28

Network Performance (QoS and DiffServ)

28.1 Introduction

Early chapters consider the fundamental properties of data communications systems, and discuss the relationships among signals, frequencies, bandwidth, channel coding, and data transmission. The chapters explain measures of underlying data transmission systems, discuss data network size, and explain that each networking technology is classified as a PAN, LAN, MAN, or WAN.

This chapter continues the discussion by considering the topic of network performance. The chapter discusses quantitative measures of networks, and explains how protocols and packet forwarding technologies can implement mechanisms that provide priority for some traffic.

28.2 Measures Of Performance

Informally, we use the term *speed* to describe network performance, and refer to *low-speed* or *high-speed* networks. However, such definitions are inadequate because network technologies change so rapidly that a network classified as "high speed" can become medium or low speed in as little as three or four years. Thus, in place of qualitative descriptions, scientists and engineers use formal, quantitative measures to specify network performance precisely. After reviewing basic measures, we will explain how they are used to implement tiered services. Although beginners often prefer informal descriptions, quantitative measures are important because they make it possible to compare the exact features of two networks and to build mechanisms that provide higher

471

priority for some traffic. Figure 28.1 lists the major measures of network performance, and successive sections explain each.

Measure	Description
Latency (delay)	The time required to transfer data across a network
Throughput (capacity)	The amount of data that can be transferred per unit time
Jitter (variability)	The changes in delay that occur and the duration of the changes

Figure 28.1 Key measures of data network performance.

28.3 Latency Or Delay

The first property of networks that can be measured quantitatively is *latency* or *delay*. Latency specifies how long it takes for data to travel across a network from one computer to another; it is measured in fractions of seconds. Delays across the Internet depend on the underlying infrastructure as well as the location of the specific pair of computers that communicate. Although users care about the total delay of a network, engineers need more precise measurements. Thus, engineers usually report both the maximum and average delays, and divide a delay into several constituent parts. Figure 28.2 lists the various types of delay.

Type	Explanation
Propagation Delay	The time required for a signal to travel across a transmission medium
Access Delay	The time needed to obtain access to a transmission medium (e.g., a cable)
Switching Delay	The time required to forward a packet
Queuing Delay	The time a packet spends in the memory of a switch or router waiting to be selected for transmission
Server Delay	The time required for a server to respond to a request and send a response

Figure 28.2 Various types of delay and an explanation of each.

Propagation Delay. Some delay in a network arises because a signal requires a small amount of time to travel across a transmission medium. In general, propagation delays are proportional to the distance spanned. Even with long cable runs, a typical LAN used within a single building has a propagation delay under a millisecond. Although such delays seem irrelevant to a human, a modern computer can execute over one hundred thousand instructions in a millisecond. Thus, a millisecond delay is significant when a set of computers need to coordinate (e.g., in the financial industry, where the exact time a stock order arrives determines whether an order is accepted). A network that uses a GEO satellite has much higher delay — even at the speed of light, it takes hundreds of milliseconds for a bit to travel to the satellite and back to earth.

Access Delay. Many networks use shared media. The set of computers that share a medium must contend for access. For example, a Wi-Fi wireless network uses a CSMA/CA approach to medium access. Such delays are known as *access delays*. Access delays depend on the number of stations that contend for access and the amount of traffic each station sends. Access delays remain small and fixed unless the medium is overloaded.

Switching Delay. An electronic device in a network (e.g., a Layer 2 switch or router) must compute a next-hop for each packet before transmitting the packet over an output interface. The computation often involves table lookup, which means memory access. In some devices, additional time is needed to send the packet over an internal communication mechanism such as a bus or fabric. The time required to compute a next hop and begin transmission is known as a *switching delay*. Fast CPUs and special-purpose hardware have made switching delays among the least significant delays in a computer network.

Queuing Delay. The store-and-forward paradigm used in packet switching means that a device such as a router collects the bits of a packet, places them in memory, chooses a next-hop, and then waits until the packet can be sent before beginning transmission. Such delays are known as *queueing delays*. In the simplest case, a packet is placed in a FIFO output queue, and the packet only needs to wait until packets that arrived earlier are sent; more complex systems implement a selection algorithm that gives priority to some packets. Queuing delays are variable — the size of a queue depends entirely on the amount of traffic that has arrived recently. Queuing delays account for most delays in the Internet. When queuing delays become large, we say that the network is congested.

Server Delay. Although not part of a network per se, servers are essential to most communication. The time required for a server to examine a request and compute and send a response constitutes a significant part of overall delay. Servers queue incoming requests, which means that server delay is variable and depends on the current load. In many cases, a user's perception of Internet delay arises from server delay rather than network delays.

28.4 Throughput, Capacity, And Goodput

A second fundamental property of networks that can be measured quantitatively is the *capacity* of a network, which is often expressed as the maximum *throughput* that the network can sustain. Throughput is a measure of the rate at which data can be sent through the network, specified in *bits per second* (*bps*). Most data communication networks offer a throughput rate of more than 1 Mbps, and the highest-speed networks operate faster than 1 Gbps. As we have seen, however, special cases arise where a network has throughput less than 1 Kbps.

Because throughput can be measured several ways, one must be careful to specify exactly what has been measured. There are several possibilities:

- Capacity of a single channel
- Aggregate capacity of all channels
- Theoretical capacity of the underlying hardware
- Effective data rate achieved by an application (goodput)

Vendors often advertise the theoretical capacity of their equipment and the throughput achieved under optimal conditions. The hardware capacity is often cited as an approximation of the potential throughput because the capacity gives an upper bound on performance — it is impossible for a user to send data faster than the rate at which the hardware can transfer bits.

Users do not care about the capacity of the underlying hardware — they are only interested in the rate at which data can be transferred. Users typically assess the *effective data rate* that an application achieves by measuring the amount of data transferred per unit time; the term *goodput* is sometimes used to describe the measure. The goodput rate is less than the capacity of the hardware because protocols impose overhead — some network capacity is not available to user data because protocols:

- Send packet headers, trailers, and control information
- Impose a limit on the window size (receive buffer)
- Use protocols to resolve names and addresses
- Use a handshake to initiate and terminate communication
- Reduce the transmission rate when congestion is detected
- Retransmit lost packets

The disadvantage of using goodput as a measure arises because the amount of overhead depends on the protocol stack being used. In addition to Transport, Internet, and Layer 2 protocols, goodput depends on the application protocol. For example, consider using the *File Transfer Protocol* (*FTP*) to measure goodput across an Ethernet. FTP uses TCP, which uses IP. Furthermore, FTP does not compress data before transmission. Instead, FTP places user data in TCP segments, TCP encapsulates each segment in an IP datagram, and IP encapsulates each datagram in an Ethernet frame.

Thus, each frame has an Ethernet header and CRC field, an IP datagram header, and a TCP header. If a user chooses an alternative file transfer application or an alternative protocol stack is used, the goodput may change. The point is:

> *Although it provides a measure of the effective rate at which data can be transferred over a network, the goodput depends on the application.*

28.5 Understanding Throughput And Delay

In practice, the terminology that networking professionals use to describe network throughput or network capacity can be confusing. For example, chapters on data communications define the bandwidth of a channel, and explain the relationship between the hardware bandwidth and the maximum data rate. Unfortunately, networking professionals often use the terms *bandwidth* and *speed* as synonyms for throughput. Thus, one might hear someone say that a particular network has a "speed of 1 Gbps." Alternatively, some advertisements use the phrase "bandwidth of 1 Gbps." In an attempt to distinguish between the two uses of *bandwidth*, engineers reserve *bandwidth* to mean *analog bandwidth*, and use the term *digital bandwidth* as a synonym for *throughput*. Although such statements are common, they can be confusing because throughput, delay, and bandwidth are separate properties.

In fact, throughput is a measure of capacity, not speed. To understand the relationship, imagine a network to be a road between two locations and packets traveling across the network to be cars traveling down the road. The throughput determines how many cars can enter the road each second, and the propagation delay determines how long it takes a single car to travel the road from one town to another. For example, a road that can accept one car every five seconds has a throughput of *0.2* cars per second. If a car requires *30* seconds to traverse the entire road, the road has a propagation delay of *30* seconds. Now consider what happens if a second lane is opened on the road (i.e., the capacity doubles). It will be possible for two cars to enter every five seconds, so the throughput has doubled to *0.4* cars per second. Of course, the *30* second delay will remain unchanged because each car must still traverse the entire distance. Thus, when thinking about measures of networks, remember that:

> *Propagation delay specifies the time a single bit remains in transit in a network. Throughput, which specifies how many bits can enter the network per unit time, measures network capacity.*

Networking professionals have an interesting aphorism:

> *You can always buy more throughput, but you cannot buy lower delay.*

The analogy to a road helps explain the aphorism: adding more lanes to a road will increase the number of cars that can enter the road per unit of time, but will not decrease the total time required to traverse the road. Networks follow the same pattern: adding more parallel transmission paths will increase the throughput of the network, but the propagation delay, which depends on the distance spanned, will not decrease.

28.6 Jitter

A third measure of networks is becoming important as networks are used for the transmission of real-time voice and video. The measure, which is known as a network's *jitter*, assesses the variance in delay. Two networks can have the same average delay, but different values of jitter. In particular, if all packets that traverse a given network have exactly the same delay, D, the network has no jitter. However, if packets alternate between a delay of $D+\varepsilon$ and $D-\varepsilon$, the network has the same average delay, but has a nonzero jitter.

To understand why jitter is important, consider sending voice over a network. On the sending side, the analog signal is sampled and digitized and an eight-bit digital value is emitted every 125 μ seconds. The samples are collected into packets, which are then transferred across the network. At the receiving side, the digital values are extracted and converted back to analog output. If the network has zero jitter (i.e., each packet takes exactly the same time to transit the network), the audio output will exactly match the original input; otherwise, the output will be flawed. There are two general approaches to handling jitter:

- Design an isochronous network with no jitter
- Use a protocol that compensates for jitter

A traditional telephone system uses the first approach: the phone system implements an *isochronous network* which guarantees the delay along all paths is the same. Thus, if digitized data from a phone call is transmitted over two paths, the hardware is configured so that both paths have exactly the same delay.

Transmission of voice or video over the Internet takes the second approach: although the underlying network may have substantial jitter, voice and video applications rely on *real-time protocols* to compensate for jitter†. Because using real-time protocols is much less expensive than building an isochronous network, phone companies are relaxing the strict requirements for isochrony. Of course, a protocol cannot compensate for arbitrary jitter — if the variance in delay becomes excessive, output will be affected. Thus, even when using the second approach, service providers attempt to minimize jitter in their networks.

---

†The next chapter discusses the transmission of real-time data over the Internet.

28.7 The Relationship Between Delay And Throughput

In theory, the delay and throughput of a network are independent. In practice, however, they can be related. To understand why, think of the road analogy discussed above. If cars enter the road at even time intervals, cars traveling along the road at uniform speed are spaced at uniform intervals. If a car slows down for any reason (e.g., at an intersection), others behind it will slow down as well, causing temporary traffic congestion. Cars that enter the road when congestion is occurring will experience longer delays than cars traveling on an uncongested road. A similar situation occurs in networks. If a router has a queue of packets waiting when a new packet arrives, the new packet will be placed on the tail of the queue, and will need to wait while the router forwards the previous packets. If congestion occurs, the packets will experience longer delays than data entering an idle network.

28.7.1 Utilization As An Estimate Of Delay

Computer scientists have studied the relationship between delay and congestion, and have found that in many cases, the expected delay can be estimated from the current percentage of the network capacity being used. If D_0 denotes the delay when a network is idle, and U is a value between *0* and *1* that denotes the current *utilization*, the effective delay, D, is given by a simple formula:

$$D \; = \; \frac{D_0}{(1 - U)} \tag{28.1}$$

When a network is completely idle, U is zero, and the effective delay is D_0. When a network operates at $1/2$ its capacity, the effective delay doubles. As traffic approaches the network capacity (i.e., as U becomes close to *1*), the delay approaches infinity. Although the formula only provides an estimate of effective delay, we can conclude:

> *Throughput and delay are not completely independent. As traffic in a computer network increases, delays increase; a network that operates at close to 100% of its throughput capacity experiences severe delay.*

In practice, network managers understand that extremely high utilization can produce disastrous delay. Thus, most managers work to keep utilization low, and measure the traffic on each network constantly. When the average or peak utilization begins to climb above a preset threshold, the manager increases the capacity of the network. For example, if utilization becomes high on a 100 Mbps Ethernet, the manager might choose to replace it with a Gigabit Ethernet. Alternatively, the manager might choose to divide a network in two, placing half the hosts on one network and half the hosts on the other (such division is extremely easy with a VLAN switch).

How high should the utilization threshold be? There is no simple answer; many managers choose a conservative value. For example, one major ISP that runs a large backbone network keeps utilization on all its digital circuits under 50%. Others set thresholds at 80% to save money. In any case, managers generally agree that a network should not be operated above 90% of capacity.

28.7.2 Delay-Throughput Product

Once a network's delay and throughput are known, it is possible to compute another interesting quantity, the *delay-throughput product†*. To understand the meaning of the delay-throughput product, think of the road analogy: when cars are entering a road at a fixed rate of T cars per second and it takes a car D seconds to traverse the road, then $T \times D$ additional cars will enter the road by the time the first car has made a complete trip. Thus, a total of $T \times D$ cars can be on the road. In terms of networks, the number of bits traveling through a network at any time is given by:

$$Bits\ present\ in\ a\ network\ =\ D \times T \qquad (28.2)$$

where D is the delay measured in seconds, and T is the throughput measured in bits per second. To summarize:

> *The product of delay and throughput measures the volume of data that can be present on the network. A network with throughput* T *and delay* D *can have a total of* T $\times$ D *bits in transit at any time.*

The delay-throughput product is important for any network with especially long delay or large throughput because it affects transmission — a sending application can transmit a large volume of data before the destination receives the first bit.

28.8 Measuring Delay, Throughput, And Jitter

The techniques used to measure throughput and jitter are relatively straightforward. To assess throughput, a sender transfers a large volume of data. A receiver records the time from the start of data arriving until all data has arrived, and calculates the throughput as the amount of data sent per unit of time. The technique for measuring jitter is known as a *packet train*: a sender emits a series of packets with a small, fixed delay between packets. Typically, packets in the train are sent back-to-back. A receiver records the time at which each packet arrives, and uses the sequence of times to compute the differences in delay.

Unlike measurements of throughput or jitter, a precise measurement of the delay on a path from host A to host B requires that the two hosts have synchronized clocks.

---

†When used as a measure of the underlying hardware, the delay-throughput product is often called the *delay-bandwidth product*.

Furthermore, to measure delay over a short distance (e.g., a LAN), the clocks must be extremely accurate. Instead of using synchronized clocks, many network measurement tools choose an easier approach: measure the round-trip time and divide by two. For example, *ping* can be used.

Measuring network performance can be surprisingly difficult for four reasons:

- Routes can be asymmetric
- Conditions change rapidly
- Measurement can affect performance
- Traffic is bursty

The first point explains why it may not be possible to use round-trip times to approximate delay. Asymmetric routing means that the delay along a path from *B* to *A* can differ substantially from the delay along a path from *A* to B. Thus, one-half of the round-trip time may not give an accurate measure.

The second point explains why an accurate measure of network performance can be difficult to obtain: conditions change rapidly. For example, consider a shared network. If only one host is sending data, the host will enjoy low delay, high throughput, and low jitter. As other hosts begin to use the network, utilization increases, which will increase delay and jitter and decrease throughput. Furthermore, because conditions change rapidly, delays can vary widely in as little as a second. Thus, even if measurements are taken every ten seconds, a measurement can miss a major shift in performance.

The third point suggests that sending test traffic to measure a network can affect network performance. On the PlanetLab research testbed, for example, so many researchers used ping to measure performance that ping traffic completely dominated other traffic. The situation became so severe that administrators established a policy to discourage the use of ping.

The fourth point is fundamental: data networks exhibit *bursty* behavior, which means that traffic is uneven. If we consider the traffic sent by a given host computer, the pattern of burstiness is obvious: most hosts remain silent until a user runs an application that communicates over the Internet. When a user enters a URL in a web browser, the browser fetches all parts of the page, and then stops communicating until the user requests another page. Similarly, if a user downloads email, the host computer communicates with an email system, downloads a copy of the user's mailbox, and then waits for the user.

Interestingly, aggregate data traffic is also bursty. One might expect that the burstiness is a local phenomenon and when traffic from millions of Internet users is combined, the result will be a smooth pattern of use. After all, users do not all read email at exactly the same time; so, while one user is downloading, another user might be reading email that was downloaded previously. Indeed, measurements of the voice telephone network show that telephone traffic from millions of users results in a smooth aggregate. When the traffic from a million Internet users is combined, however, the result is not a smooth aggregate. Instead, the aggregate is bursty in the sense that the total traffic has peaks and low points. In fact, statisticians say that data traffic is *self similar*, which means that the traffic is analogous to a *fractal*, where the same statistics profile is evident at any granularity. Thus, if an enterprise examines a LAN, traffic from local hosts will appear bursty. If an intermediate ISP measures traffic from one thousand users or a large ISP measures traffic from ten million users, the traffic will have large absolute quantities, but will exhibit the same overall statistical pattern as the traffic on a LAN.

We can summarize:

> *Unlike voice telephone traffic, data traffic is bursty. Data traffic is said to be self-similar because aggregates of data traffic exhibit the same pattern of burstiness.*

28.9 Passive Measurement, Small Packets, And NetFlow

Network managers who measure networks distinguish between two forms of measurement:

- Active
- Passive

We have discussed the disadvantage of *active* measurement techniques: by injecting traffic into a network, the measurement traffic can change the performance of the network. The alternative is *passive* measurement that monitors a network and counts packets, but does not inject additional traffic. For example, an ISP can count the bytes that are transferred over a link in a given amount of time to produce an estimate of the link utilization. That is, the ISP arranges a passive monitor station that observes a network over an interval of time and accumulates a total of the bytes in all packets.

Interestingly, an ISP may choose to measure the number of packets sent as well as the number of data bytes. To understand why, observe that because link utilization is measured as a percentage of capacity and capacity is measured in bits per second, an ISP needs to measure the total data bits sent per unit time. However, the capacity of switches and routers is measured in packets per second. That is, because a router or switch performs next-hop forwarding once per packet, the computational effort expended is proportional to the number of packets processed rather than the number of bits in a packet. If a stream of data arrives at 1 Gbps, a switch or router performs less work if the stream is divided into a few large packets than it does if the stream is divided into many small packets. Networking equipment vendors understand the concept, and some vendors make performance claims about the data rate rather than the packet rate (i.e., they measure the performance of their products using large packets).

We can summarize:

> *To assess link utilization, an ISP measures the total data transferred over a link per unit time; to assess the impact on a router or switch, an ISP measures the number of packets transferred per unit time.*

One of the most widely used passive measurement techniques was originally created by Cisco and is now an IETF standard: *NetFlow*. A router that implements NetFlow statistically samples packets according to parameters established by the network administrator (e.g., samples one of every one-thousand packets). Information is extracted from the header of each sampled packet, the information is summarized, and the summary is sent to a network management system where it is processed (often, data is saved on disk for later analysis). Typically, NetFlow extracts source and destination IP addresses, the datagram type, and protocol port numbers. To insure that it is passive, a router running NetFlow must send the NetFlow summaries over a special management port rather than route them across one of the networks that handles user data.

28.10 Quality Of Service (QoS)

The counterpart of network measurement is *network provisioning*: designing a network to provide a specific level of service. The remainder of the chapter considers mechanisms that can be used to implement service guarantees. Broadly, the topic is known as *Quality of Service (QoS)*.

To understand QoS, consider the contract between a service provider and a customer. The simplest contracts define a service by specifying the data rate that the provider guarantees. For example, a provider that offers a DSL connection to the Internet might guarantee a data rate of 2.2 Mbps. More complex contracts define *tiered services*, where the level of service received depends on the amount paid. For example, a provider might choose a *priority* approach that guarantees packets from a customer who subscribes to the platinum level of service will have priority over packets from customers who subscribe to a silver level of service.

Large corporate customers often demand more stringent *service guarantees*. The financial industry typically creates service contracts with bounds on the delay between specific locations. For example, a brokerage firm might need a service contract that specifies packets must be transferred from the company's main office to the New York Stock Exchange in less than 10 milliseconds; a company that backs up their entire data center each night might need a service contract that guarantees a throughput of not less than 1 Gbps on the TCP connections used for backup.

28.11 Fine-Grain And Coarse-Grain QoS

How can a provider specify QoS guarantees, and what technologies does a provider use to enforce QoS? Figure 28.3 lists the two general approaches that have been proposed for service specification. As the figure indicates, the approaches differ in their granularity and whether a provider or a customer selects parameters.

Approach	Description
Fine-Grain	A provider allows a customer to state specific QoS requirements for a given instance of communication; a customer makes a request each time a flow is created (e.g., for each TCP connection)
Coarse-Grain	A provider specifies a few broad classes of service that are each suitable for one type of traffic; a customer must fit all traffic into the classes

Figure 28.3 Two approaches that have been proposed for specification of QoS services.

28.11.1 Fine-Grain QoS And Flows

Much of the early work on QoS arose from telephone companies. The designers assumed a connection-oriented data network modeled after the telephone system: when a customer needed to communicate with a remote site (e.g., a web server), the customers would create a connection. Furthermore, the designers assumed a customer would issue QoS requirements for each connection, and a provider would compute a charge according to the distance spanned and QoS used.

The phone companies incorporated many QoS features in the design of *Asynchronous Transmission Mode (ATM)*. Although ATM did not survive and providers do not generally charge for each connection, some of the terminology that ATM created for fine-grain QoS still persists with minor modifications. Instead of specifying the QoS on a connection, we now use the term *flow*. A flow generally refers to transport-layer communication such as a TCP connection, a set of UDP packets traveling between a pair of applications, or a VoIP telephone call. Figure 28.4 lists four main categories of service that were present in ATM, and explains how they relate to flows.

Abbreviation	Expansion	Meaning
CBR	**Constant Bit Rate**	**Data enters the flow at a fixed rate, such as data from a digitized voice call entering at exactly 64 Kbps**
VBR	**Variable Bit Rate**	**Data enters the flow at a variable rate within specified statistical bounds**
ABR	**Available Bit Rate**	**The flow agrees to use whatever data rate is available at a given time**
UBR	**Unspecified Bit Rate**	**No bit rate is specified for the flow; the application is satisfied with best-effort service**

Figure 28.4 Four main categories of QoS service.

As the figure indicates, CBR service is appropriate for a flow that transfers data at a fixed rate, with digitized voice being the canonical example. VBR service is appropriate for a flow that uses a variable-rate encoding. For example, some video codecs send differential encodings, where the amount of data sent for a frame is proportional to the difference between the previous frame and the current frame. In such cases, a customer can specify the average data rate that is expected as well as a maximum data rate and the length of time the maximum rate will occur. VBR asks users to specify:

- Sustained Bit Rate (SBR)
- Peak Bit Rate (PBR)
- Sustained Burst Size (SBS)
- Peak Burst Size (PBS)

ABR service implies sharing: a customer is willing to pay for any amount of service that is available. If other customers send data, the amount available will be lower (and presumably the provider will charge less). Finally, UBR service means the customer does not want to pay higher fees and is satisfied with best-effort service.

When Internet QoS was first considered, telephone companies argued that fine-grain services would be needed before the quality of voice telephone calls over a packet network would be acceptable. Consequently, in addition to the work on ATM, the research community began to explore fine-grain QoS on the Internet. The research was known as *Integrated Services (IntServ)*.

28.11.2 Coarse-Grain QoS And Classes Of Service

The alternative to fine-grain QoS is a coarse-grain approach in which traffic is divided into *classes* and QoS parameters are assigned to the class rather than individual flows. To understand the motivation for the coarse-grain approach, it is necessary to consider an implementation of QoS on a core router. The connections to routers can each operate at 10 Gbps, which means packets arrive at an extremely high rate; special hardware is needed to perform forwarding because conventional processors are too slow. Furthermore, because it carries traffic among major ISPs, a core router can handle millions of simultaneous flows. QoS requires many additional resources. The router must maintain state for millions of flows, and must perform a complex computation for each packet. Memory accesses slow down processing. In addition, a router must allocate resources when a flow begins, and deallocate them when a flow ends.

After many years of research on Integrated Services and the creation of several protocols, the research community and the IETF concluded that a fine-grain approach was generally both impractical and unnecessary. On one hand, an average user will not have sufficient understanding of QoS to choose parameters. After all, what throughput requirements would one specify for a connection to a typical web site? On the other hand, core routers have insufficient processing power to implement per-flow QoS. Thus, most work on QoS concentrates on defining a few broad classes of service rather than trying to provide end-to-end QoS for each individual flow. We can summarize:

> *Despite many years of research and standards work, the fine-grain approach to QoS has been relegated to a few special cases.*

28.12 Implementation Of QoS

Figure 28.5 illustrates the four steps a switch or router uses to implement QoS.

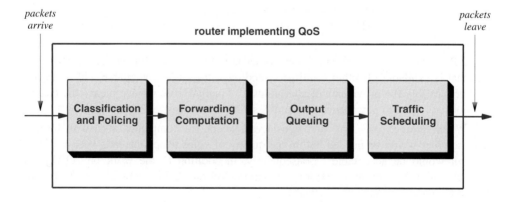

Figure 28.5 The four key steps used to implement QoS.

Classification And Policing. When a packet arrives, a router *classifies* the packet by assigning the packet a flow identifier. For a fine-grain system, the identifier specifies an individual connection; for a coarse-grain system, the identifier specifies a traffic class. Once an identifier has been assigned, the router performs *policing*, which means that the router verifies that the packet does not violate parameters for the flow. In particular, if a customer sends data faster than the maximum rate for which the customer is paying, a policer begins to discard packets. One technique used for policing is *Random Early Discard (RED)* in which packets on a given flow are dropped probabilistically. A queue is established for the flow, and the current size of the queue is used to determine the probability of drop. When the queue is less than half full, the probability is set to zero. When the queue is completely full, the probability is set to one. At queue sizes in between, the probability is linearly proportional to the number of packets in the queue. Using RED helps avoid a cyclic problem caused by *tail drop* in which all incoming packets are discarded once a queue fills, many TCP sessions each back off and begin slow start, traffic increases until the queue fills again, and the cycle repeats.

Forwarding Computation. When computing a next-hop, a router or switch can use the flow identifier. In some cases, the flow identifier determines the path to be followed (e.g., all voice traffic is sent out port 54 to a voice switch). In other cases, the flow identifier is ignored and the destination address in each packet is used to select a next hop. The exact details of forwarding depend on the purpose of a particular switch or router and the manager's QoS policies.

Output Queuing. Most implementations of QoS create a set of queues for each output port. Once the forwarding computation selects an output port for the packet, the output queueing mechanism uses the flow identifier to place the packet in one of the queues associated with the port. A coarse-grain system typically uses one queue per class. Thus, if a manager establishes eight QoS classes, each output port will have eight queues. A fine-grain system often has one queue per connection, with queues arranged in a hierarchy. For example, one network processor chip provides 256,000 queues arranged in a multi-level hierarchy.

Traffic Scheduling. A *traffic scheduler* implements the QoS policies by selecting a packet to send whenever a port is idle. For example, a manager might specify that three customers each receive 25% of the capacity and all other customers share the remaining capacity. To implement such a policy, a traffic scheduler might use four queues and a *round-robin* approach to select packets. Thus, if all customers are sending data, the three designated customers will each receive one quarter of the capacity, as specified.

More sophisticated packet selection algorithms can be used to implement complex proportional sharing. Complexity arises because a traffic scheduler must maintain long-term policies even though packets arrive in bursts. Thus, a traffic scheduler must adapt to situations where a given queue temporarily exceeds its allotted data rate provided the long-term average meets the specified bounds. Similarly, a traffic scheduler must adapt to a situation where one or more queues is temporarily empty by dividing the unused capacity among other queues.

Many traffic scheduling algorithms have been proposed and analyzed. It is not possible to create a practical algorithm that achieves perfection; each is a compromise between fairness and computational overhead. Figure 28.6 lists traffic management algorithms that have been proposed and studied.

Algorithm	Description
Leaky Bucket	Allows a queue to send packets at a fixed rate by incrementing a packet counter periodically and using the counter to control transmission
Token Bucket	Allows a queue to send data at a fixed rate by incrementing a byte counter periodically and using the counter to control transmission
Weighted Round Robin	Selects packets from a set of queues according to a set of weights that divide the capacity into fixed percentages, assuming a uniform packet size
Deficit Round Robin	A variant of the round-robin approach that accounts for bytes sent rather than packets transferred, and allows a temporary deficit caused by a large packet

Figure 28.6 Example traffic scheduling algorithms.

28.13 Internet QoS Technologies

The IETF has designed a series of technologies and protocols related to QoS. Three significant efforts are:

- RSVP and COPS
- DiffServ
- MPLS

RSVP and COPS. As it explored IntServ, the IETF developed two protocols to provide QoS: the *Resource ReSerVation Protocol* (*RSVP*) and the *Common Open Policy Services* (*COPS*) protocol. RSVP is a fine-grained version of QoS. Thus, RSVP is needed for each TCP or UDP session. To use RSVP, an application sends a request that specifies the desired QoS. Each router along the path from the source to the destination reserves the requested resources and passes the request to the next router. Eventually, the destination host must agree to the request. When every hop along the path has agreed to honor the request, a flow identifier is generated and returned. Traffic can then be sent along the reserved path. COPS is a companion protocol for RSVP used to specify and enforce policies. A router that implements policing uses COPS to communicate with a policy server and obtain information about the flow parameters. Because it is designed to provide fine-grain, per-flow QoS, RSVP is seldom used.

DiffServ. Once it abandoned IntServ and fine-grain QoS, the IETF created *Differentiated Services (DiffServ)* to define a coarse-grain QoS mechanism. The DiffServ effort produced a definition of how classes can be specified and how the *TYPE OF SERVICE* field in an IPv4 or IPv6 header can be used to specify the class of a datagram. Although various ISPs have experimented with DiffServ, the technology does not enjoy widespread acceptance.

MPLS. Chapter 19 describes *MultiProtocol Label Switching (MPLS)* as a connection-oriented communication mechanism built on top of IP. To use MPLS, a manager configures forwarding paths through a set of MPLS-capable routers. At one end of a path, each datagram is encapsulated in an MPLS header and injected into the MPLS path; at the other end, each datagram is extracted, the MPLS header is removed, and the datagram is forwarded to its destination. In many cases, a traffic scheduling policy is assigned to an MPLS path, which means that when a datagram is inserted in a particular path, QoS parameters are set for the datagram. Thus, an ISP might set up an MPLS path for voice data that is separate from the MPLS path used for other data.

28.14 Summary

The two primary measures of network performance are delay, the time required to send a bit from one computer to another, and throughput, the number of bits per second that can be transmitted across the network. Although throughput is commonly called speed, throughput is a measure of network capacity. The delay-throughput product measures the amount of data that can be in transit at a given instant. Delay and throughput are not independent — as throughput approaches 100% of capacity, delays increase rapidly.

Jitter, a measure of variance in delay, is becoming important in data networks. Low jitter can be achieved with an isochronous network or with a protocol that handles the transmission of real-time audio and video; the Internet uses the protocol approach.

Measuring network performance can be difficult. Asymmetric routes mean synchronized clocks are needed to measure delay; bursty traffic means performance can change rapidly. Because additional traffic from measurement can alter network conditions, many managers prefer passive measurement technologies, such as NetFlow.

Both fine-grain and coarse-grain QoS have been studied; fine-grain efforts have generally been abandoned. ATM defined categories of service, and the acronyms are still used: Constant, Variable, Available, and Unspecified Bit Rate (CBR, VBR, ABR, and UBR).

To implement QoS, a switch or router classifies and polices incoming data, forwards and places each packet on an output queue, and uses a traffic scheduler to select a packet to send when an output port becomes free. Several traffic scheduling algorithms have been proposed and analyzed; each is a tradeoff between optimal fairness and computational overhead.

The IETF defined RSVP and COPS as part of the IntServ effort; when emphasis shifted away from fine-grain QoS, the IETF defined DiffServ. The IETF also defined MPLS as a traffic engineering technology. QoS parameters can be associated with each MPLS tunnel, meaning that once a datagram has been classified, its MPLS association defines its QoS parameters.

EXERCISES

28.1 Which of delay or throughput provides the most fundamental limit on performance? Why?

28.2 If two users create a chat session over the Internet, what category of QoS will they be using?

28.3 Explain why ISPs count the number of packets received per unit time instead of merely the number of bytes received per unit time.

28.4 List and describe the three primary measures of network performance.

28.5 Estimate the computational power needed to implement fine-grain QoS in the core of the Internet: assume a 10 Gbps link delivering 1000 byte packets and N arithmetic operations per packet, and calculate the number of operations a processor needs to perform per second.

28.6 Provide an explanation of delay and throughput in terms of bits being transmitted.

28.7 Compare the throughput of a 100 Mbps network and a 1 Gbps network.

28.8 Professionals sometimes refer to a "knee" in the delay curve. To understand what they mean, plot the effective delay for values of utilization between 0 and 0.95. Can you find a value of utilization for which the curve appears to increase sharply?

28.9 Give five types of delay along with an explanation of each.

28.10 Give examples of processing that make goodput less than the channel capacity.

28.11 How does MPLS forwarding differ from conventional IP forwarding?

28.12 What are the two types of QoS?

28.13 Consider a web browser. What type of QoS would be appropriate for a typical flow where the browser downloads a web page? Why?

28.14 Explain the four steps used to implement QoS.

28.15 How can throughput be measured?

28.16 Use *ping* to measure network latency to local and distant sites. What is the minimum and maximum Internet delay you can find?

28.17 Would you expect access delays to be longer on a LAN or on a WAN? Queuing delays? Why?

28.18   If your ISP uses leaky bucket to schedule packet transmission, will your throughput be higher with large packets or small packets? Explain.

28.19   What is DiffServ?

28.20   If one pings IP address 127.0.0.1, the latency is extremely low. Explain.

28.21   What is jitter, and what are the two approaches used to overcome jitter?

28.22   Why is measurement of network performance difficult?

28.23   Download a copy of the program *ttcp* and use it to measure throughput on a local Ethernet. What is the goodput? Estimate the link utilization achieved.

28.24   What name is used for the form of throughput that is the most meaningful to a user?

28.25   How much data can be "in flight" between a sending ground station, a satellite, and a receiving station? To find out, compute the delay-throughput product for a GEO satellite network that operates at 3 Mbps. Assume that the satellite orbits at 20,000 miles above the earth, and that radio transmissions propagate at the speed of light.

28.26   How does data traffic differ from voice traffic?

28.27   List the four main categories of QoS that were derived from ATM, and give the meaning of each.

28.28   What four parameters are used to characterize a VBR flow?

Chapter Contents

29

Multimedia And IP Telephony (VoIP)

29.1 Introduction

Chapters in this part of the text consider a variety of networking technologies and uses. The previous chapter discusses network performance and QoS. The chapter points out the two basic ways that networks can be designed to provide service that is used for real-time applications such as voice: an isochronous infrastructure or the use of protocols that compensate for jitter.

This chapter continues the discussion by examining the transfer of multimedia over the Internet. The chapter examines how multimedia can be sent over a best-effort communication mechanism, describes a general-purpose protocol for real-time traffic, and considers the transmission of voice telephone calls in detail.

29.2 Real-Time Data Transmission And Best Effort Delivery

We use the term *multimedia* to refer to data that contains audio or video, and may include text. The phrase *real-time multimedia* refers to multimedia data that must be reproduced at exactly the same rate that it was captured (e.g., a television news program that includes audio and video of an actual event).

A question arises, how can the Internet be used for transmission of real-time multimedia? To understand the difficulty, recall that the Internet offers best-effort delivery service. Thus, packets can be lost, delayed, or delivered out-of-order — if audio or video is digitized, sent across the Internet without special treatment, and then displayed exactly as it arrives, the resulting output will be unacceptable. Early multimedia systems solved the problem by creating communication networks specifically designed to handle audio or video. The analog telephone network uses an isochronous network to provide high-quality reproduction of audio, and analog cable television systems are designed to deliver multiple channels of broadcast video with no interruptions or loss.

Instead of requiring the underlying networks to handle real-time transmission, the Internet uses additional protocol support. Interestingly, the most significant problem to be handled is jitter, not packet loss. To see why, consider a live webcast. If a protocol uses timeout-and-retransmission to resend the packet, the retransmitted packet will arrive too late to be useful — the receiver will have played the video and audio from successive packets, and it makes no sense to insert a snippet of the webcast that was missed earlier.

The important point is:

> *Unlike conventional transport protocols, a protocol that transfers real-time data only handles the problem of jitter, and does not retransmit lost packets.*

29.3 Delayed Playback And Jitter Buffers

To overcome jitter and achieve smooth playback of real-time data, two chief techniques are employed:

- *Timestamps.* A sender provides a timestamp for each piece of data. A receiver uses the timestamps to handle out-of-order packets and to display the data in the correct time sequence.
- *Jitter Buffer.* To accommodate jitter (i.e., small variances in delay), a receiver buffers data and delays playback.

The implementation of a jitter buffer is straightforward. A receiver maintains a list of data items, and uses timestamps to order the list. Before it begins playback, a receiver delays for d time units, which means the data being played is d time units behind the data that is arriving. Thus, if a given packet is delayed less than d, the contents of the packet will be placed in the buffer before it is needed for playback. In other words, items are inserted into a jitter buffer with some variation in rate, but the playback process extracts data from a jitter buffer at a fixed rate. Figure 29.1 illustrates the organization of a real-time playback system.

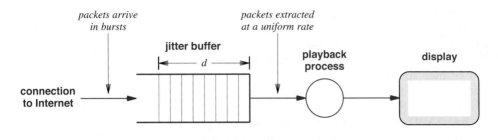

Figure 29.1 Illustration of a jitter buffer with delay *d*.

29.4 Real-time Transport Protocol (RTP)

In the Internet protocol suite, the *Real-time Transport Protocol* (*RTP*) provides the mechanism used to transmit real-time data across the Internet. The term *Transport* is a misnomer because RTP sits above the transport layer. Thus, despite the name, one should think of RTP as a transfer protocol.

RTP does not ensure timely delivery of data, and it does not include a jitter buffer or playback mechanism. Instead, it provides three items in each packet that permit a receiver to implement a jitter buffer:

- A *sequence number* that allows a receiver to place incoming packets in the correct order and to detect missing packets
- A *timestamp* that allows a receiver to play the data in the packet at the correct time in the multimedia stream
- A series of *source identifiers* that allow a receiver to know the source(s) of the data

Figure 29.2 illustrates how the sequence number, timestamp, and source identifier fields appear in an RTP packet header.

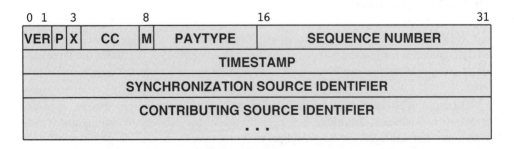

Figure 29.2 The basic header that appears at the start of each RTP packet.

Field *VER* gives the RTP version number, which is currently 2. Field *P* specifies whether the payload is zero-padded (some encodings require a fixed block size). Field *X* specifies whether a header extension is present, and *CC* gives a count of sources that have been combined to produce the stream as described below. *M* is a marker bit that can be used to mark some frames. In particular, some video encodings send a full frame followed by a series of incremental changes; the *M* bit is only set if an RTP packet carries a full frame. The *PAYTYPE* field specifies the payload type; a receiver uses the PAYTYPE value to interpret the remainder of the packet.

Each packet includes a *SEQUENCE NUMBER*; the sequence is incremented by one for each packet. As with TCP, a sender chooses a random starting sequence to help avoid replay problems. A *TIMESTAMP* field that is independent of the sequence provides a receiver with information about playback timing. Keeping the timestamp independent of the sequence is important in cases where time is not linearly related to packet sequence (e.g., a variable-size video encoding that sends fewer packets when the picture does not change rapidly).

An RTP *TIMESTAMP* does not encode a date and time. Instead, RTP chooses a random initial timestamp, and then makes each successive timestamp relative to the initial value. Furthermore, RTP does not specify whether time is measured in seconds, milliseconds, or other units — the payload type determines the granularity of the timestamp. No matter what time granularity is used, a sender must increment the time continuously, even when no packets are being sent (e.g., if a codec suppresses transmission during silent periods of an audio stream).

The two fields *SYNCHRONIZATION SOURCE IDENTIFIER* and *CONTRIBUTING SOURCE IDENTIFIER* identify the sources of the data. The reason a source must be identified arises from the multicast delivery mechanism: a host may receive data from multiple sources and may receive multiple copies of a given packet. The reason multiple sources are identified arises from a technique known as *mixing* in which an intermediate system combines data from multiple real-time streams to produce a new stream. For example, a mixer can combine separate video and audio streams from a movie, and then multicast the combined stream.

29.5 RTP Encapsulation

RTP uses UDP for message transport. Thus, each RTP message is encapsulated in a UDP datagram for transmission over the Internet. Figure 29.3 illustrates the three levels of encapsulation that are used when an RTP message is transferred over a single network.

Because RTP uses UDP encapsulation, the resulting messages can be sent via broadcast or multicast. Multicast is especially useful for delivery of entertainment programming that appeals to a large audience. For example, if a cable provider offers a television program or a sports event, multiple customers can watch simultaneously. In such cases, instead of sending a copy of a message to each subscriber, RTP allows a provider to reach customers by multicasting a copy of an RTP message across each logical subnet. If a given multicast reaches an average of *N* customers, the amount of traffic will be reduced by a factor of *N*.

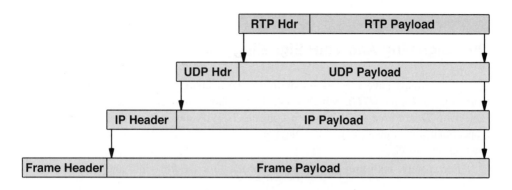

Figure 29.3 The three levels of encapsulation used with RTP.

29.6 IP Telephony

The term *IP telephony*† or *Voice over IP* (*VoIP*) is used to describe one of the most widespread multimedia applications. Telephone companies around the world are replacing traditional telephone switches with IP routers. The motivation is economic: routers cost much less than traditional telephone switches. Enterprises have also begun to use IP telehones for economic reasons: sending both data and voice in IP datagrams lowers cost because the underlying network infrastructure is shared — a single set of equipment, wiring, and network connections suffices for all communication, including telephone calls.

The basic idea behind IP telephony is straightforward: continuously sample audio, convert each sample to digital form, send the resulting digitized stream across an IP network in packets, and convert the stream back to analog for playback. However, many details complicate the task. A sender cannot wait to fill a large packet because doing so delays transmission by several seconds. The system must handle call setup: when a caller dials, the system must translate the phone number to an IP address, and locate the specified party. When a call begins, the called party must accept and answer the call. Similarly, when a call ends, the two parties must agree on how to terminate communication.

The most significant complications arise because IP telephony strives to be backward compatible with the existing *Public Switched Telephone Network* (*PSTN*). That is, instead of restricting calls to IP telephones, mechanisms allow a caller or callee to use a telephone anywhere on the PSTN, including an international location or a cellular connection. Thus, an IP telephone system must be prepared to handle calls that originate

---

†Pronounced *I-P te-lef'-oh-nee.*

on the PSTN and terminate at an IP telephone, or vice versa. Users expect an IP telephone system to provide existing telephone services such as *call forwarding*, *call waiting*, *voicemail*, *conference calls*, and *caller ID*. In addition, businesses that currently operate a *Private Branch Exchange* (*PBX*) may require an IP telephone system to offer services equivalent to a PBX.

29.7 Signaling And VoIP Signaling Standards

Two groups have created standards for IP telephony: the *International Telecommunications Union* (*ITU*), which controls telephone standards, and the *Internet Engineering Task Force* (*IETF*), which controls TCP/IP standards. After considering the conceptual components of an IP telephone system, we will review the protocols that each group has chosen.

Fortunately, both groups agree on the basics for the encoding and transmission of audio:

- Audio is encoded using *Pulse Code Modulation* (*PCM*)

- RTP is used to transfer the digitized audio

The main complexity of IP telephony (and the reason that multiple standards have been proposed) lies in call setup and call management. In telephone terminology, the process of establishing and terminating a call is known as *signaling*, and includes mapping a phone number to a location, finding a route to the called party, and handling other details such as call forwarding. The mechanism used in the traditional telephone system to handle call management is known as *Signaling System 7* (*SS7*).

One of the fundamental questions about IP telephony centers on the approach to be taken for signaling — should the signaling system be centralized like the current phone system, or should it be distributed like the current mapping from domain names to IP addresses? Proponents of a distributed approach argue that it should be possible for two IP telephones, at arbitrary points on the Internet, to find one another and communicate exactly like current Internet applications (i.e., an IP telephone acts as a server to accept incoming calls, and as a client to place outgoing calls). In a distributed approach, no further infrastructure is needed beyond DNS and the IP forwarding services that are currently available for data communications. The distributed approach is especially pertinent for a local IP telephone system (e.g., a system that allows calls between two IP telephones within a single company). Proponents of a centralized approach argue that a conventional telephone model works best because giving telephone companies control of call setup allows them to provide service guarantees.

To be compatible with existing telephones, new protocols must be able to interact with SS7, both to place outgoing calls and to accept incoming calls. As the debate over the basic approach proceeded, four sets of signaling protocols were proposed for use with IP telephony: the IETF proposed the *Session Initiation Protocol* (*SIP*) and the

Media Gateway Control Protocol (MGCP), the ITU proposed a large, comprehensive set of protocols under the general umbrella of *H.323*, and the two groups jointly proposed *Megaco (H.248)*. The point is:

> *The processes of call setup and termination are known as signaling; multiple signaling protocols have been proposed for use with IP telephony.*

29.8 Components Of An IP Telephone System

Figure 29.4 lists the four main components of an IP telephone system, and Figure 29.5 illustrates how they are used to interconnect networks.

Component	Description
IP telephone	Operates like a conventional telephone, but uses IP to send digitized voice
Media Gateway Controller	Provides control and coordination between IP telephones for services such as call setup, call termination, and call forwarding
Media Gateway	Provides a connection between two networks that use different encodings, and translates as a call passes between them
Signaling Gateway	Connects to two networks that use different signaling mechanisms, and translates call management requests and responses

Figure 29.4 The four main building blocks of an IP telephone system.

An *IP telephone* connects to a network, uses IP for all communication, and offers a traditional telephone interface that allows a user to place or receive telephone calls. An IP phone can be a stand-alone hardware unit (i.e., a conventional telephone), or can consist of a computer with a microphone, speaker, and IP telephony software. The connection between an IP telephone and the rest of the world can consist of a wired or wireless network (e.g., Ethernet or 802.11b).

A *Media Gateway Controller*, which is also known as a *Gatekeeper* or *Softswitch*, provides overall control and coordination between a pair of IP telephones, allowing a caller to locate a callee or access services such as call forwarding.

A *Media Gateway* provides translation of audio as a call passes across the boundary between an IP network and the PSTN or the boundary between two IP networks that use different encodings. For example, a media gateway on the boundary between the PSTN and the Internet moves digitized audio between the TDM encoding used on a conventional voice circuit and the packet encoding used on the Internet.

A *Signaling Gateway* also spans the boundary between a pair of disparate networks, and provides translation of signaling operations, allowing either side to initiate a call (e.g., to allow an IP telephone on the Internet to place a call to a phone on the PSTN). A media gateway controller coordinates the operation of the media and signaling gateways. Figure 29.5 illustrates how the components are used to interconnect the Internet and the PSTN.

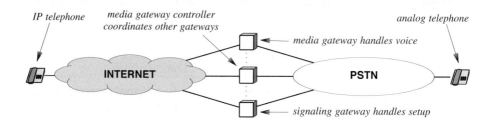

Figure 29.5 Connections among IP telephone components.

The concepts and terminology defined above present a straightforward and somewhat simplified view of IP telephony that derives from work in the IETF and ITU on the *Megaco* and *Media Gateway Control Protocol* (*MGCP*). Practical implementations of IP telephone service are more complex. The next sections give examples.

29.8.1 SIP Terminology And Concepts

The *Session Initiation Protocol* (*SIP*) minimizes the need for additional protocols by using existing protocols whenever possible. For example, SIP uses the Domain Name System to map a telephone number to an IP address. As a result, SIP defines three new elements that constitute a signaling system:

- User Agent
- Location Server
- Support Servers (proxy, redirect, registrar)

User Agent. SIP documents refer to a device that makes or terminates phone calls as a *user agent*. A SIP user agent can be implemented in an IP telephone, a laptop computer, or a PSTN gateway that allows an IP telephone to make calls to the PSTN.

A user agent contains two parts: a *User Agent Client* that places outgoing calls, and a *User Agent Server* that handles incoming calls.

Location Server. A SIP location server manages a database of information about each user such as a set of IP addresses, services to which the user subscribes, and the user's preferences. The location server is contacted during call setup to obtain information about the location or locations that will accept a given call.

Proxy Server. SIP includes the concept of a proxy that can forward requests from user agents to another location. Proxies handle optimal routing, and enforce policies (e.g., ensure that the caller is authorized to make the call).

Redirect Server. SIP uses a redirect server to handle tasks such as call forwarding and 800-number connections. The redirect server receives a request from a user agent, and returns an alternate location for the user agent to contact.

Registrar Server. SIP uses a registrar server to receive registration requests and update the database that location servers consult. A registrar is responsible for authenticating registration requests and ensuring that the underlying database remains consistent.

29.8.2 H.323 Terminology And Concepts

The H.323 standard from the ITU, which defines alternative terminology and additional concepts, focuses on PSTN interaction. Although it is extremely broad and covers many details, H.323 can be summarized as follows:

Terminal. An H.323 terminal provides the IP telephone function, which may also include facilities for video and data transmission.

Gatekeeper. An H.323 gatekeeper provides location and signaling functions, and coordinates the operation of the gateway that provides a connection to the PSTN.

Gateway. H.323 uses a single gateway to interconnect the IP telephone system with the PSTN; the gateway handles both signaling and media translation.

Multipoint Control Unit (MCU). An MCU provides services such as multipoint conferencing.

29.8.3 ISC Terminology And Concepts

Because the ITU and IETF spawned several variations of terminology and concepts, vendors formed the *International Softswitch Consortium* (*ISC*) to create a uniform, comprehensive functional model that incorporates all models of IP telephony into a single framework. To do so, the ISC defined the functionality that may be needed, including signaling between various types of systems, translation of encodings, support for services such as call forwarding, and management functions such as accounting and billing. The ISC then defined a list of functions that suffices for all situations:

Media Gateway Controller Function (MGC-F). The MGC-F maintains state information in endpoints; it provides call logic and call control.

Call Agent Function (CA-F). The CA-F is a subset of the MGC-F that maintains call state. Examples of CA-F are SIP, H.323, and Q.931.

InterWorking Function (IW-F). The IW-F is a subset of the MGC-F that handles signaling between heterogeneous networks such as SS7 and SIP.

Routing Function and *Accounting Function (R-F/A-F).* The R-F handles routing of calls for the MGC-F, and the A-F collects information used for accounting and billing.

Signaling Gateway Function (SG-F). The SG-F handles signaling between an IP network and the PSTN.

Access Gateway Signaling Function (AGS-F). The AGS-F handles signaling between an IP network and a circuit-switched access network such as the PSTN.

Application Server Function (AS-F). The AS-F handles a set of application services such as voicemail.

Service Control Function (SC-F). The SC-F is called when an AS-F must control (i.e., change) the logic of a service (e.g., install a new mapping).

Media Gateway Function (MG-F). The MG-F handles translation of digitized audio between two forms, and may also include detection of events such as whether a phone is off-hook and recognition of *Dual Tone Multi-Frequency (DTMF)* signals, the audio signaling standard that is known as *Touch Tone* encoding.

Media Server Function (MS-F). The MS-F manipulates a media packet stream on behalf of an AS-F application.

29.9 Summary Of Protocols And Layering

Because multiple groups have proposed protocols for IP telephony, competing protocols exist at most layers of the protocol stack. Figure 29.6 lists some of the proposed protocols along with their position in the Internet 5-layer reference model.

Layer	Call Process.	User multimedia	User Data	Support	Routing	Signal Transport
5	H.323 Megaco MGCP SIP	RTP	T.120	RTCP RTSP NTP SDP	ENUM TRIP	SIGTRAN†
4	TCP UDP	UDP	TCP	TCP UDP		SCTP
3	IP, RSVP, and IGMP					

Figure 29.6 A summary of IP telephony protocols.

---

†*SIGTRAN* allows transfer of PSTN signals (e.g., SS7, DTMF) across an IP network; SCTP multiplexes multiple input streams over a single transport-layer flow.

29.10 H.323 Characteristics

Instead of a single protocol, the *H.323* standard, created by the ITU, consists of a set of protocols that work together to handle all aspects of telephone communication. The highlights of H.323 are:

- Handles all aspects of a digital telephone call

- Includes signaling to set up and manage the call

- Allows the transmission of video and data while a call is in progress

- Sends binary messages that are defined by *ASN.1* and encoded using *Basic Encoding Rules* (*BER*)

- Incorporates protocols for security

- Uses a special hardware unit known as a *Multipoint Control Unit* to support conference calls

- Defines servers to handle tasks such as *address resolution* (i.e., mapping the called party's phone number into an IP address), *authentication, authorization* (i.e., determining whether a user is allowed to access a given service), *accounting*, and *features*, such as call forwarding

29.11 H.323 Layering

H.323 protocols use both TCP and UDP for transport — audio can travel over UDP, while a data transfer proceeds over TCP. Figure 29.7 illustrates the basic layering in the H.323 standard.

Layer	Signaling	Registration	Audio	Video	Data	Security
5	H.225.0-Q.931 H.250-Annex G H.245 H.250	H.225.9-RAS	G.711 G.763 G.722 G.723 G.728	H.261 H.323	T.120	H.235
			RTP, RTCP			
4	TCP, UDP	UDP			TCP	TCP, UDP
3	IP, RSVP, and IGMP					

Figure 29.7 The layering of major protocols in the H.323 standard.

29.12 SIP Characteristics And Methods

Highlights of IETF's *Session Initiation Protocol* (*SIP*) are:

- Operates at the application layer
- Encompasses all aspects of signaling, including location of a called party, notification and setup (i.e., ringing a phone), determination of availability (i.e., whether the party accepts the call), and termination
- Provides services such as call forwarding
- Relies on multicast for conference calls
- Allows the two sides to negotiate capabilities and choose the media and parameters to be used†

A SIP URI contains a user's name and a domain name at which the user can be found. For example, a user named *Smith* who works at *Somecompany, Inc.* might be assigned the SIP URI:

$$sip : smith @ somecompany.com$$

SIP defines six basic message types and seven extensions. The basic message types are known as *methods*. Figure 29.8 lists the basic SIP methods.

Method	Purpose
INVITE	Session creation: an endpoint is invited to participate in the session
ACK	Acknowledgment response to INVITE
BYE	Session termination: call is ended
CANCEL	Pending request cancellation (no effect if request has been completed)
REGISTER	Registration of user's location (i.e., a URL at which the user can be reached)
OPTIONS	Query to determine capabilities of called party

Figure 29.8 The six basic methods that SIP uses.

---

†SIP uses the *Session Description Protocol* (*SDP*) to describe capabilities and parameters.

29.13 An Example SIP Session

An example of the messages sent during a SIP session will clarify some of the details and help explain the general idea behind most IP telephony. Figure 29.9 lists a sequence of messages sent when a user agent, *A*, contacts a DNS server, and then communicates with a proxy server, which invokes a location server†. Once the call has been established, the two IP phones communicate directly. Finally, SIP is used to terminate the call.

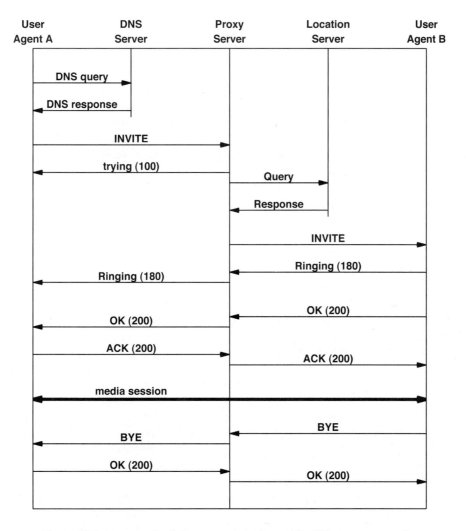

Figure 29.9 An example of the messages exchanged by SIP to manage a telephone call.

---

†In practice, SIP supports *call forking*, which allows a location server to return multiple locations for a user (e.g., home and office), and allows a User Agent to attempt simultaneous contact.

Typically, a user agent is configured with the IP address of one or more DNS servers (used to map the domain name in a SIP URI to an IP address) and one or more proxy servers. Similarly, each proxy server is configured with the address of one or more location servers. Thus, if a given server is unavailable, SIP can find an alternate quickly.

29.14 Telephone Number Mapping And Routing

How should IP telephone users be named and located? The PSTN follows ITU standard E.164 for telephone numbers, and SIP uses IP addresses. The problem of locating users is complicated because multiple types of networks may be involved. For example, consider an integrated network that consists of two PSTN networks interconnected by an IP network. Designers define two subproblems: locate a user in the integrated network, and find an efficient route to the user. The IETF has proposed two protocols that correspond to the mappings needed for the two subproblems:

- ENUM — converts a telephone number to a URI
- TRIP — finds a user in an integrated network

ENUM. The IETF protocol *ENUM* (short for *E.164 NUMbers*) solves the problem of converting an E.164 telephone number into a *Uniform Resource Identifier* (*URI*). In essence, ENUM uses the Domain Name System to store the mapping. A phone number is converted into a special domain name in the domain:

e164.arpa

The conversion consists of treating the phone number as a string, reversing the string, and writing individual digits as segments of a domain name. For example, the telephone number 1-800-555-1234 produces the domain name:

4.3.2.1.5.5.5.0.0.8.1.e164.arpa

An ENUM mapping can be 1-to-1 like a conventional telephone numbering scheme, or can be 1-to-many, which means a user's desk phone and mobile phone can be assigned the same phone number. When a number corresponds to multiple hosts, a DNS server returns a list of the hosts along with the protocol used to reach each; a User Agent proceeds to contact hosts on the list until a host responds.

TRIP. The IETF protocol *Telephone Routing over IP* (*TRIP*) solves the problem of finding a user in an integrated network. A location server or other network element can use TRIP to advertise routes. Thus, two location servers use TRIP to inform each other about external routes that they each know. Because it is independent of the signaling protocol, TRIP can be used with SIP or other signaling mechanisms.

TRIP divides the world into a set of *IP Telephone Administrative Domains* (*ITAD*s). In essence, a TRIP advertisement identifies an egress point — a location server informs another location server about a path to a signaling gateway that interconnects to another ITAD. Because IP telephony is new and routing information may change in the future, TRIP is designed to be extensible.

29.15 Summary

The Real-Time Transport Protocol accommodates the transfer of real-time multimedia over the Internet. An RTP message includes a sequence number and a separate timestamp as well as an identification of the data source(s). A receiver uses the timestamp to place data in a jitter buffer before playback. RTP is encapsulated in UDP for transmission, which permits multicasting and broadcasting. No retransmission is used because packets received beyond the playback window cannot be played.

The terms IP telephony and VoIP refer to digitized voice telephone calls transmitted over the Internet. One of the greatest challenges in building an IP telephone system arises from backward compatibility — gateways must be invented that connect an IP telephone system to the traditional PSTN. Gateways must provide both media translation (i.e., translation among digital voice encodings) and signaling (i.e., translation of call setup).

The ITU and IETF have each created standards for IP telephony. ITU standard H.323 includes many protocols that provide call setup and management, authorization and accounting, and user services such as call forwarding, as well as the transmission of voice, video, and data over a telephone call. IETF standard SIP provides signaling capability that includes location of a user, call setup, and allows each side to specify capabilities. SIP uses a set of servers that handle various aspects of signaling: a Domain Name Server, proxy servers, and location servers. The Internet Softswitch Consortium (ISC) has defined an additional framework that is intended to encompass all IP telephony models.

Two additional IETF protocols provide support functions. ENUM uses the Domain Name System to map an E.164 telephone number into a Uniform Resource Identifier (usually a SIP URI). TRIP provides routing among IP telephone administrative domains; a SIP location server can use TRIP to inform other location servers about gateways that form network egress points.

FOR FURTHER STUDY

RFC 3216 defines SIP; RFC 2916 considers E.164 numbers and DNS; and RFC 3219 defines TRIP. RTP and the related control protocol RTCP are documented in RFC 1889. Related concepts and protocols can also be found in RFCs 2915, 2871, 3015, 3435, and 3475.

EXERCISES

29.1   Because it travels in UDP, an RTP message can be duplicated. Does a receiver need to keep a copy of all previously received messages to determine whether an incoming message is a duplicate? Why or why not?

29.2   If voice is converted to digital form using PCM, how many bits of data will be produced in one-half second?

29.3   When H.323 is used to send data along with audio or video, which transport protocol is used?

29.4   Look up the e164.arpa domain. Which organization is responsible for the domain?

29.5   Explain how a jitter buffer permits the playback of an audio stream even if the Internet introduces jitter.

29.6   Define multimedia data. What are the two techniques used to overcome jitter?

29.7   If an RTP message is intercepted as it travels across the Internet, can the timestamp field be interpreted? If so, how? If not, why not?

29.8   Which aspects of IP telephony does H.323 handle?

29.9   RTP contains a companion protocol known as the *Real-Time Control Protocol* (*RTCP*) that allows a receiver to report the quality of messages received to a sender. How can adaptive video encoding use the status of received messages?

29.10   What are the six basic methods used with SIP?

29.11   Consider the operation of an IP telephone and an analog telephone. Which would be better during time of war? Why?

29.12   Read the RFC about SIP, and modify Figure 29.9 to show the messages exchanged when call forwarding occurs. Hint: look at SIP *redirection* messages.

29.13   What are the purposes of the ENUM and TRIP protocols?

29.14   Extend the previous exercise. Estimate the size (in octets) of an IP datagram that carries one-quarter of a second of audio encoded in PCM, placed in an RTP packet, and encapsulated in UDP. Hint: RFC 1889 defines the size of an RTP header.

Chapter Contents

30

Network Security

30.1 Introduction

Previous chapters describe the hardware and software systems that constitute the Internet and explain how client and server applications use the underlying facilities to communicate. This chapter considers the important aspect of network security. The chapter describes types of crime that have been perpetrated over the Internet, discusses key aspects of security, and explains technologies used to increase network security.

30.2 Criminal Exploits And Attacks

Whenever a new technology appears, criminals ask how they can use the technology to commit crimes. The Internet is no exception — as most users are aware, the Internet has been used for criminal activities as reported in the press. Although Internet crimes, such as scams and identity theft, can affect individuals, the most significant crimes pose a threat to businesses. In addition to outright theft of goods or services, businesses are especially concerned with threats to the long-term viability of the company. Thus, damage to reputation, loss of customer confidence, stolen intellectual property, and prevention of customer access are all important to a business.

Several questions arise regarding security:

- What are the major Internet security problems and threats?
- What technical aspects of protocols do criminals exploit?
- What are the key aspects of security?
- What technologies are available to help increase security?

Figure 30.1 summarizes some of the major security problems that exist on the Internet.

Problem	Description
Phishing	Masquerading as a well-known site such as a bank to obtain a user's personal information, typically an account number and access code
Misrepresentation	Making false or exaggerated claims about goods or services, or delivering fake or inferior products
Scams	Various forms of trickery intended to deceive naive users into investing money or abetting a crime
Denial of Service	Intentionally blocking a particular Internet site to prevent or hinder business activities and commerce
Loss of Control	An intruder gains control of a computer system and uses the system to perpetrate a crime
Loss of Data	Loss of intellectual property or other valuable proprietary business information

Figure 30.1 Major security problems prevalent on the Internet.

When considering security, it is important to distinguish between a conventional crime that is committed using the Internet in an incidental way and a crime that is specific to the Internet. For example, consider a crime in which a criminal uses a VoIP telephone to communicate with a co-conspirator, a scam in which a criminal intentionally deceives and fleeces an unsuspecting victim, or an incident in which a criminal uses the Internet to order tools that are used to commit a crime. Although law enforcement agencies must handle each, such cases have little to do with networking technologies — one could easily find alternative communication mechanisms that can be used in place of the Internet. Two of the most widespread crimes experienced on the Internet are conventional crimes that happen to use the Internet: misrepresentation of goods offered in an auction is a form of false advertising, and failure to deliver goods purchased through an auction is analogous to conventional mail-order fraud.

Our discussion will focus on ways that criminals exploit technology and the technologies that have been created to make crime more difficult or expensive. Figure 30.2 lists specific techniques that attackers use.

Technique	Description
Wiretapping	Making a copy of packets as they traverse a network to obtain information
Replay	Sending packets captured from a previous session (e.g., a password packet from a previous login)
Buffer overflow	Sending more data than a receiver expects in order to store values in variables beyond the buffer
Address Spoofing	Faking the IP source address in a packet to trick a receiver into processing the packet
Name Spoofing	Using a misspelling of a well-known name or poisoning a name server with an incorrect binding
DoS and DDoS	Flooding a site with packets to prevent the site from successfully conducting normal business
SYN flood	Sending a stream of random TCP SYN segments to exhaust a receiver's set of TCP connections
Key Breaking	Automatically guessing a decryption key or a password to gain unauthorized access to data
Port Scanning	Attempting to connect to each possible protocol port on a host to find a vulnerability
Packet interception	Removing a packet from the Internet which allows substitution and man-in-the middle attacks

Figure 30.2 Techniques used in security attacks.

Wiretapping and the related *replay* techniques are obvious. Interestingly, *buffer overflow* is among the most exploited weaknesses of a computer system. It is a symptom of poor engineering: a programmer fails to check the buffer size when performing an input operation. A typical attack either sends a jumbo packet (larger than the standard permits) or sends a sequence of back-to-back packets that overflow the input buffer.

Spoofing attacks are used to impersonate a trusted host. The simplest form of address spoofing uses ARP: an attacker broadcasts an ARP reply that binds an arbitrary IP address, *A*, to the attacker's MAC address. When any host on the network sends a packet to *A*, the packet will be forwarded to the attacker instead. Other forms of spoofing involve using a routing protocol to send incorrect routes, sending a DNS message that stores an incorrect binding in a DNS server, and using a slight misspelling of a well-known domain name to give a user the impression that they have reached a trusted web site.

A *Denial of Service* (*DoS*) attack floods a host (usually a web server) with a stream of packets. Although the server continues to operate, the attack effectively consumes all resources, meaning that other users experience long delays or have their connections rejected. Because a manager can spot and disable a stream of packets from a single source, a *Distributed Denial of Service* (*DDoS*) attack arranges for a large set of hosts throughout the Internet to each send a stream of packets, as Figure 30.3 illustrates. Typically, an attacker first commandeers hosts on the Internet, loads software onto the hosts, and then uses the hosts to attack a server. Thus, none of the packets sent by a DDoS come directly from the attacker's computer.

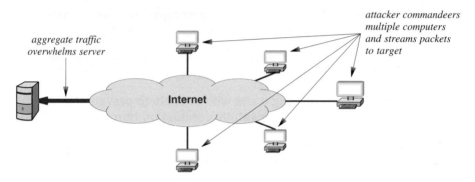

Figure 30.3 Illustration of a Distributed Denial of Service attack.

SYN flooding is a specific technique used to deny service to TCP — each incoming packet contains a TCP *SYN* message that requests a new TCP connection. A receiver allocates a TCP control block for the connection, sends a *SYN + ACK*, and waits for a response. Eventually, all control blocks are allocated, and no further connections can be opened.

Packet Interception makes it possible to launch *man-in-the-middle* attacks in which an intermediary can modify packets as they pass from source to destination. Although it is among the most difficult attacks to engineer, packet interception has the greatest potential for damage, as Figure 30.4 illustrates.

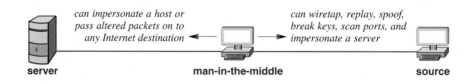

Figure 30.4 A man-in-the middle configuration and the attacks it permits.

30.3 Security Policy

What is a secure network? Although the concept of a secure network is appealing to most users, networks cannot be classified simply as secure or not secure because the term is not absolute — each organization defines the level of access that is permitted or denied. For example, an organization that keeps valuable trade secrets may need to prevent outsiders from accessing the organization's computers. An organization that has a web site which makes information available may define a secure network as one that allows arbitrary access to data, but includes mechanisms that prevent outsiders from changing the data. Other organizations focus on keeping communication confidential: they define a secure network as one in which no one other than the sender or intended recipient can intercept and read a message. Finally, a large organization may need a complex definition of security that allows access to selected data or services and prevents access or modification of sensitive or confidential data and services.

Because no absolute definition of *secure network* exists, the first step an organization must take to achieve a secure system is to define the organization's *security policy*. The policy does not specify how to achieve protection. Instead, it states clearly and unambiguously the items that are to be protected.

Security policies are complex because they involve human behavior as well as computer and network facilities (e.g., a visitor who transports a Flash ROM out of an organization, a wireless network that can be detected outside a building, or employees who work at home). Assessing the costs and benefits of various security policies also adds complexity. In particular, a security policy cannot be defined unless an organization understands the value of its information. In many cases, the value of information is difficult to assess. Consider, for example, a simple payroll database that contains a record for each employee, the hours the employee worked, and the rate of pay. If they were able to access the information, some employees might become upset and either demand higher wages or threaten to leave. If competitors obtained the information, they might use it to lure away employees. More important, a competitor might be able to use the information in unexpected ways (e.g., to assess the effort spent on a particular project).

To summarize:

> *Devising a network security policy can be complex because a rational policy requires an organization to relate network and computer security to human behavior and to assess the value of information.*

Defining a security policy is also complicated because each organization must decide which aspects of protection are most important, and often must compromise between security and ease of use. For example, an organization can consider:

- *Data Integrity.* Integrity refers to protection from change: is the data that arrives at a receiver identical to the data that was sent?

- *Data Availability.* Availability refers to protection against disruption of service: does data remain accessible for legitimate uses?

- *Data Confidentiality.* Confidentiality refers to protection against unauthorized data access (e.g., via snooping or wiretapping): is data protected against unauthorized access?

- *Privacy.* Privacy refers to the ability of a sender to remain anonymous: is the sender's identity revealed?

30.4 Responsibility And Control

In addition to the items above, an organization must specify exactly how responsibility for information is assigned or controlled. The issue of responsibility for information has two aspects:

- *Accountability.* Accountability refers to how an audit trail is kept: which group is responsible for each item of data? How does the group keep records of access and change?

- *Authorization.* Authorization refers to responsibility for each item of information and how such responsibility is delegated to others: who is responsible for where information resides, and how does a responsible person approve access and change?

The critical issue underlying both accountability and authorization is *control* — an organization must control access to information analogous to the way the organization controls access to physical resources such as offices, equipment, and supplies. A key aspect of control concerns *authentication*, which refers to validation of identity. For example, suppose an organization specifies an authorization policy that gives an employee more privilege than a visitor. The authorization policy is meaningless unless the organization has an authentication mechanism that distinguishes between a visitor and an employee. Authentication extends beyond humans to include computers, devices, and application programs. The point is:

Authorization policies are meaningless without an authentication mechanism that can unambiguously verify the identity of a requester.

30.5 Security Technologies

Many security products exist that perform a variety of functions for both individual computers and a set of computers in an organization. Figure 30.5 summarizes the techniques such products use. The next sections explain each of the technologies.

Technique	Purpose
Hashing	Data integrity
Encryption	Privacy
Digital Signatures	Message authentication
Digital Certificates	Sender authentication
Firewalls	Site integrity
Intrusion Detection Systems	Site integrity
Deep Packet Inspection & Content Scanning	Site integrity
Virtual Private Networks (VPNs)	Data privacy

Figure 30.5 Major techniques used to enforce security policies.

30.6 Hashing: An Integrity And Authentication Mechanism

Earlier chapters discuss techniques such as *parity bits*, *checksums*, and *cyclic redundancy checks (CRCs)* used to protect data against accidental damage. Such techniques do not provide data integrity for two reasons. First, a malfunction can change a checksum as well as a data value, which means the altered checksum may be valid for the altered data. Second, if data changes result from a planned attack, the attacker can create a valid checksum for the altered data. Therefore, additional mechanisms have been created to guarantee the integrity of messages against intentional change.

One method supplies a *message authentication code (MAC)* that an attacker cannot break or forge. Typical encoding schemes use *cryptographic hashing* mechanisms. One hashing scheme relies on a *secret key* known only to the sender and receiver. The sender takes a message as input, uses the key to compute a hash, H, and transmits H along with the message. H is a short string of bits, and the length of H is independent of the message size. The receiver uses the key to compute a hash of the message, and compares the hash to H. If the two agree, the message has arrived intact. An attacker, who does not have the secret key, will be unable to modify the message without introducing an error. Thus, H provides message authentication because a receiver knows that a message that arrives with a valid hash is authentic.

30.7 Access Control And Passwords

An *access control* mechanism controls which users or application programs can access data. For example, some operating systems implement an *access control list (ACL)* for each object that specifies who is allowed to access the object. In other systems, each user is assigned a *password* for each protected resource. When a user needs to access a protected resource, the user is asked to enter the password.

When extending access control lists and passwords across a network, steps must be taken to prevent unintentional disclosure. For example, if a user at one location sends an unencrypted password across a network to a computer at another location, anyone who wiretaps the network can obtain a copy of the password. Wiretapping is especially easy when packets travel across a wireless LAN because a physical connection is not required — anyone within range of the transmission can capture a copy of each packet. In addition, steps must be taken to assure that passwords are not easy to guess because a network allows an attacker to automate attempts to break a password. Thus, managers enforce rules for choosing passwords such as a minimum length and a prohibition of using common words (i.e., words found in a dictionary).

30.8 Encryption: A Fundamental Security Technique

Cryptography is a fundamental tool in security because encryption can guarantee data confidentiality (sometimes called *privacy*), message authenticity, data integrity, and can prevent replay attacks. In essence, a sender applies encryption to scramble the bits of the message in such a way that only the intended recipient can unscramble them. Someone who intercepts a copy of an encrypted message will not be able to extract information. Furthermore, an encrypted message can include information such as the message length; an attacker cannot truncate the message without being discovered.

The terminology used with encryption defines four items:

- Plaintext — an original message before it has been encrypted
- Cyphertext — a message after it has been encrypted
- Encryption key — a short bit string used to encrypt a message
- Decryption key — a short bit string used to decrypt a message

As we will see, in some technologies, the encryption key and the decryption key are identical; in others, they differ.

Mathematically, we think of encryption as a function, *encrypt*, that takes two arguments: a key, K_1, and a plaintext message to be encrypted, M. The function produces an encrypted version of the message, cyphertext C:

$$C = encrypt(K_1, M)$$

A *decrypt* function reverses the mapping to produce the original message†:

$$M \;=\; decrypt(K_2, C)$$

Mathematically, *decrypt* is the inverse of *encrypt*:

$$M \;=\; decrypt(K_2, encrypt(K_1, M))$$

30.9 Private Key Encryption

Many encryption technologies exist, and they can be divided into two broad categories that are defined by the way they use keys:

- Private Key
- Public Key

In a *private key* system, each pair of communicating entities share a single key that serves as both an *encryption key* and a *decryption key*. The name arises because the key must be kept secret — if a third party obtains a copy of the key, the third party will be able to decrypt messages passing between the pair. Private key systems are *symmetric* in the sense that each side can send or receive messages. To send a message, the key is used to produce cyphertext, which is then sent across a network. When a message arrives, the receiving side uses the secret key to decode the cyphertext and extract the original (plaintext) message. Thus, in a private key system, a sender and receiver each use the same key, K, which means that:

$$M \;=\; decrypt(K, encrypt(K, M))$$

30.10 Public Key Encryption

The chief alternative to private key encryption is known as *public key encryption*. A public key system assigns each entity a pair of keys. For purposes of discussion, we will assume that each entity is a single user. One of the user's keys, called the *private key*, is kept secret, while the other, called the *public key*, is published along with the name of the user, so everyone knows the value of the key. The encryption function has the mathematical property that a plaintext message encrypted with the public key cannot be decrypted except with the private key, and a plaintext message encrypted with the private key cannot be decrypted except with the public key.

The relationship between encryption and decryption with the two keys can be expressed mathematically. Let M denote a plaintext message, *public_u1* denote user *1*'s

---

†Decryption may or may not use the same key as encryption.

public key, and *private_u1* denote user *1*'s private key. The encryption functions can be expressed as:

$$M = decrypt\ (public\_u1,\ encrypt\ (private\_u1,\ M\ ))$$

and

$$M = decrypt\ (private\_u1,\ encrypt\ (public\_u1,\ M\ ))$$

Figure 30.6 illustrates why a public key system is classified as *asymmetric* by showing the keys used to encrypt messages sent in each direction.

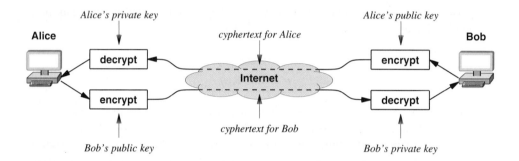

Figure 30.6 Illustration of asymmetry in a public key encryption system.

Revealing a public key is safe because the functions used for encryption and decryption have a *one way property*. That is, telling someone the public key does not allow the person to forge a message that is encrypted with the private key.

Public key encryption can be used to guarantee confidentiality. A sender who wishes communication to remain confidential uses the receiver's public key to encrypt the message. Obtaining a copy of the cyphertext as it passes across the network does not enable someone to read the contents because decryption requires the receiver's private key. Thus, the scheme ensures that data remains confidential because only the receiver can decrypt the message.

30.11 Authentication With Digital Signatures

An encryption mechanism can also be used to authenticate the sender of a message. The technique is known as a *digital signature*. To sign a message, the sender encrypts the message using a key known only to the sender†. The recipient uses the inverse function to decrypt the message. The recipient knows who sent the message because only the sender has the key needed to perform the encryption. To ensure that en-

---

†If confidentiality is not required, the message does not need to be encrypted. Instead, a more efficient form of digital signature can be used in which a hash of the message is encrypted.

crypted messages are not copied and resent later, the original message can contain the time and date that the message was created.

Consider how a public key system can be used to provide a digital signature. To sign a message, a sender encrypts the message using his or her private key. To verify the signature, the recipient looks up the sender's public key and uses it to decrypt the message. Because only the sender knows the private key, only the sender can encrypt a message that can be decoded with the public key.

Interestingly, a message can be encrypted two times to guarantee authentication and confidentiality. First, the message is signed by using the sender's private key to encrypt it. Second, the encrypted message is encrypted again using the recipient's public key. Mathematically, the two encryption steps can be expressed as:

$$X = encrypt(public\_u2, encrypt(private\_u1, M))$$

where M denotes a plaintext message to be sent, X denotes the cyphertext string that results from the double encryption, $private\_u1$ denotes the sender's private key, and $public\_u2$ denotes the recipient's public key.

At the receiving end, the decryption process is the reverse of the encryption process. First, the recipient uses their private key to decrypt the message. The decryption removes one level of encryption, but leaves the message digitally signed. Second, the recipient uses the sender's public key to decrypt the message again. The process can be expressed as:

$$M = decrypt(public\_u1, decrypt(private\_u2, X))$$

where X denotes the cyphertext that was transferred across the network, M denotes the original plaintext message, $private\_u2$ denotes the recipient's private key, and $public\_u1$ denotes the sender's public key.

If a meaningful message results from the two steps, it must be true that the message was confidential and authentic. The message must have reached its intended recipient because only the intended recipient has the correct private key needed to remove the outer encryption. The message must have been authentic because only the sender has the private key needed to encrypt the message so the sender's public key will correctly decrypt it.

30.12 Key Authorities And Digital Certificates

One of the fundamental questions surrounding public key technology arises from the way in which a public key is obtained. Although it is possible to use a conventional publication (analogous to a telephone book), doing so is cumbersome and prone to error because humans would need to enter the keys into their computers manually. The question arises: can an automated system be devised to distribute public keys? Of course, the distribution system must be secure — if the public key given to a user is incorrect, security is broken, and no further encryption can be trusted. The problem is known as the *key distribution problem*, and the formation of a viable key distribution system has been an obstacle to widespread adoption of public key systems.

Several key distribution mechanisms have been proposed, including one that uses the Domain Name System. In each case, a simple principle underlies the scheme: by knowing one key — the public key of a key authority — it is possible to obtain other public keys in a secure manner. Thus, an administrator only needs to configure one public key. Figure 30.7 illustrates the message exchange when a user decides to interact with a new web site, *W*.

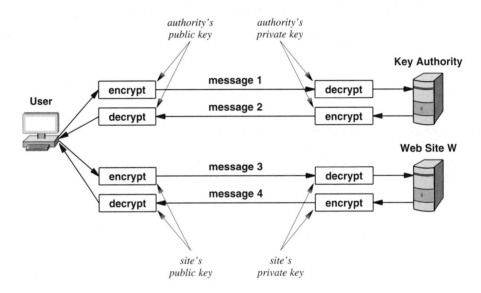

Figure 30.7 Illustration of using a key authority to obtain a public key.

In the figure, a site needs to conduct a secure transaction with a web site, *W*. Each of the four messages is confidential. Message 1 can only be read by the key authority because it has been encrypted using the key authority's well-known public key. Message 2 must have been generated by the key authority because only the key authority has the private key that matches the public key. Once the user has obtained the public key for site W, the user can send a confidential request and know that only the specified web site can generate a response (because only the site has the private key).

Although many variations are possible, the important principle is:

It is possible to create a secure key distribution system that only requires manual configuration of one public key.

30.13 Firewalls

Although encryption technology helps solve many security problems, a second technology is needed. Known as an *Internet firewall†*, the technology helps protect an organization's computers and networks from unwanted Internet traffic. Like a conventional firewall, an Internet firewall is designed to keep problems in the Internet from spreading to an organization's computers.

A firewall is placed between an organization and the rest of the Internet, and all packets entering or leaving the organization pass through the firewall. Figure 30.8 illustrates the architecture.

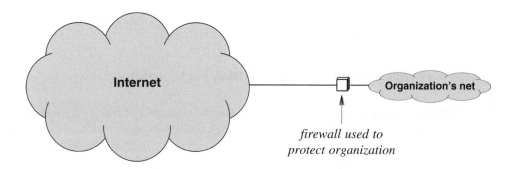

*firewall used to
protect organization*

Figure 30.8 Illustration of a firewall on the path between the Internet and an
organization.

If an organization has multiple Internet connections, a firewall must be placed on each, and all the organization's firewalls must be configured to enforce the organization's security policy. Furthermore, the firewall itself must be secure against tampering. To summarize:

- All traffic entering the organization passes through the firewall
- All traffic leaving the organization passes through the firewall
- The firewall implements the security policy and drops packets that do not adhere to the policy
- The firewall itself is immune to security attacks

Firewalls are the most important security tool used to handle the connection between two organizations that do not trust each other. By placing a firewall on each external network connection, an organization can define a *secure perimeter* that prevents outsiders from interfering with the organization's computers. In particular, a firewall can prevent outsiders from discovering computers in an organization, flooding

---

†The term is derived from the fireproof physical boundary placed between two parts of a structure to prevent fire from moving between them.

the organization's networks with unwanted traffic, or attacking a computer by sending a sequence of IP datagrams that is known to cause the computer to misbehave (e.g., to crash). Furthermore, a firewall can prevent unwanted data export (e.g., a user in the organization inadvertently imports a virus that sends a copy of the user's disk to someone outside the organization).

A firewall has a key advantage over other security schemes: it centralizes control, and thereby improves security dramatically. To provide security without a firewall, an organization must make each of its computers secure. Furthermore, each computer must implement the same policies. The cost of hiring staff to administer many computers is high, and an organization cannot depend on individual users to configure their computers correctly. With a firewall, a manager can restrict all Internet traffic to a small set of computers, and use the staff to configure and monitor the set. In the extreme case, all outside access can be restricted to a single computer. Thus, a firewall allows an organization to save money and achieve better security.

30.14 Firewall Implementation With A Packet Filter

Although a firewall can consist of a stand-alone device, most firewalls are embedded in a switch or router. In either case, the underlying mechanism used to build a firewall is known as a *packet filter*. A filter consists of a configurable mechanism that examines fields in each packet header and decides whether to allow the packet to pass through the router or to discard the packet. A manager configures the packet filter by specifying which packets can pass in each direction. (It is more secure to specify the set of packets that are allowed rather than to specify the set of packets that are denied.)

For TCP/IP, a packet filter specification usually includes a frame type of 0800 (for IP), an IP *source address* or *destination address* (or both), a datagram type, and a protocol port number. For example, to allow outsiders to reach the organization's web server, a packet filter might allow an incoming frame that contains an IP datagram carrying TCP from an arbitrary IP source address and source port to destination port 80 and a destination IP address equal to the web server's IP address.

Because it allows a manager to specify combinations of source and destination addresses and services, the packet filter in a firewall allows a manager to control access to specific services on specific computers. For example, a manager might choose to allow incoming traffic to access a web server on one computer, an email server on another, and a DNS server on a third. Of course, a manager must also install firewall rules that permit reply packets to flow out from the site. Figure 30.9 illustrates a firewall configuration for such a site.

The ability to selectively allow packets for a particular service means that a manager can carefully control the services that are externally visible. Thus, even if a user inadvertently (or intentionally) starts an email server on their computer, outsiders will be unable to contact the server.

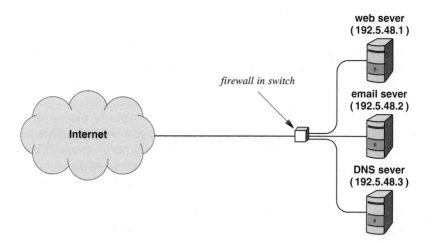

Dir	Frame Type	IP Src	IP Dest	IP Type	Src Port	Dst Port
in	0800	*	192.5.48.1	TCP	*	80
in	0800	*	192.5.48.2	TCP	*	25
in	0800	*	192.5.48.3	TCP	*	53
in	0800	*	192.5.48.3	UDP	*	53
out	0800	192.5.48.1	*	TCP	80	*
out	0800	192.5.48.2	*	TCP	25	*
out	0800	192.5.48.3	*	TCP	53	*
out	0800	192.5.48.3	*	UDP	53	*

Figure 30.9 Example firewall configuration for a site with three servers, with an asterisk used to denote a wildcard entry that matches any value.

We can summarize:

A firewall uses packet filtering to prevent unwanted communication. Each filter specification gives a combination of header fields, including source and destination IP addresses and port numbers as well as the transport protocol type.

30.15 Intrusion Detection Systems

An *Intrusion Detection System* (*IDS*) monitors all packets arriving at a site and no-
tifies the site administrator if a security violation is detected. An IDS provides an extra
layer of security awareness — even if a firewall prevents an attack, an IDS can notify
the site administrator that a problem is occurring.

Most IDSs can be configured to watch for specific types of attacks. For example,
an IDS can be configured to detect a *port scanning* attack where an attacker either sends
UDP datagrams to successive UDP protocol ports or attempts to open a TCP connection
on successive TCP protocol ports. Similarly, an IDS can be configured to detect a potential SYN flooding attack by watching for repeated SYNs from a given source. In
some cases, an IDS and firewall are interconnected to provide automated filtering: instead of merely notifying a site administrator about a problem, the IDS creates a
firewall rule that blocks packets that are causing the problem. For example, if an IDS
detects a SYN flood coming from a given source, the IDS can install a firewall rule that
blocks packets from the source. The reason for using an automated approach is speed
— it takes a human many seconds to respond after being notified of a problem and on a
gigabit network, over 50,000 packets can arrive per second. Thus, a rapid response is
needed to prevent a problem from becoming overwhelming.

The chief difference between an IDS and a firewall arises because an IDS includes
state information. Unlike a firewall that applies rules to a single packet at a time, an
IDS can keep a history of packets. Thus, although a firewall can determine whether to
admit a given SYN packet, an IDS can observe that many SYNs are arriving from a single source. Of course, because it requires more computation and memory access than a
firewall, an IDS cannot handle as many packets per second.

30.16 Content Scanning And Deep Packet Inspection

Although it can handle many security problems, a firewall has a severe limitation:
it only examines fields in a packet header. That is, a firewall cannot test the payload of
a packet. To see why the contents of packets can be important, consider computer
viruses. One of the most common ways a virus is introduced into an organization is
through an email attachment — an attacker sends an email message with a computer
program as an attachment. If an unsuspecting user opens the attachment, the program
can install arbitrary software on the user's computer, including *malware*† such as a
virus.

How can a site prevent problems such as the installation of a virus? The answer
lies in *content analysis*. There are two types of content analysis:

- File scanning
- Deep Packet Inspection (DPI)

---

†Malicious software.

File Scanning. The most straightforward approach to analyze content operates on entire files. File scanning is a well-known technique used by the security software installed on a typical PC. In essence, a file scanner takes a file as input and looks for patterns of bytes that indicate a problem. For example, many virus scanners look for strings of bytes known as a *fingerprint*. That is, a company that sells a virus scanner collects copies of viruses, places each in a file, finds sequences of bytes that are uncommon, and creates a list of all sequences. When a user runs virus scanner software, the software searches files on the user's disk to see if any file contains sequences of bytes that match items on the list. File scanning works well to catch common problems. Of course, file scanning can produce a *false positive* if an ordinary file happens to contain a string on the list, and can produce a *false negative* if a new virus exists that does not contain any of the strings on the list.

Deep Packet Inspection (DPI). The second form of content analysis operates on packets instead of files. That is, instead of merely examining the headers in packets that pass into the site, a DPI mechanism also examines the data in the packet payload. Note that DPI does not exclude header examination — in many cases, the contents of a payload cannot be interpreted without examining fields in the packet header.

As an example of DPI, consider an attack where a slight misspelling of a domain name is used to trick a user into trusting a site. An organization that wants to prevent such attacks can *black-list* a set of URLs that are known to be a security risk. The proxy approach requires every user at the site to configure their browser to use a *web proxy* (i.e., an intermediate web system that checks a URL before fetching the requested page). As an alternative, a Deep Packet Inspection filter can be set up to inspect each outgoing packet and watch for an HTTP request to any of the black-listed sites.

The chief disadvantage of DPI arises from computational overhead. Because a packet payload in an Ethernet frame can be over twenty times larger than a packet header, DPI can require twenty times more processing than header inspection. Furthermore, the payload is not divided into fixed fields, which means that DPI mechanisms must parse contents during an inspection. As a result:

> *Because they examine packet payloads which are much larger than packet headers and not organized into fixed fields, Deep Packet Inspection mechanisms are limited to lower-speed networks.*

30.17 Virtual Private Networks (VPNs)

One of the most important and widely-used security technologies uses encryption to provide secure access to an organization's intranet from remote sites. Known as a *Virtual Private Network (VPN)*, the technology was originally designed to provide a low-cost interconnection among multiple geographic sites of an organization. To undersand the motivation, consider the interconnection alternatives:

- *Private Network Connections.* An organization leases data circuits to connect its sites. Each leased connection extends from a router at one of the organization's sites to a router at another site; data passes directly from a router at one site to a router at another site.

- *Public Internet Connections.* Each site contracts with a local ISP for Internet service. Data sent from one corporate site to another passes across the Internet.

Figure 30.10 illustrates two possibilities for an organization with three sites.

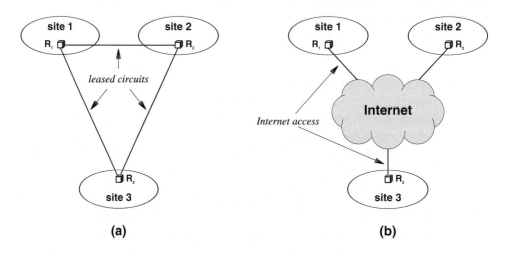

Figure 30.10 Sites connected by (a) leased circuits and (b) the Internet.

The chief advantage of using leased circuits to interconnect sites arises because the resulting network is completely *private* (i.e., confidential). No other organization has access to a leased circuit, so no other organization can read the data that passes from one site to another. The chief advantage of using Internet connections is low cost — instead of paying for lines to connect sites, the organization only needs to pay for Internet service at each site. Unfortunately, the Internet cannot guarantee confidentiality. As it travels from source to destination, a datagram passes across intermediate networks that may be shared. As a consequence, outsiders may be able to obtain copies of the datagram and examine the contents.

A VPN combines the best of both approaches by using the Internet to transfer data among sites and taking additional steps to ensure that the data cannot be accessed by outsiders. That is, in place of an expensive leased connection, a VPN uses encryption — all packets forwarded between an organization's sites are encrypted before being sent.

To make a VPN even more impervious to attacks, an organization can devote dedicated routers to the VPN function and use a firewall to prohibit the VPN routers from accepting any unauthorized packets. For example, assume each of the routers in Figure 30.10b are dedicated to the VPN function (i.e., assume the site has additional routers that handle normal traffic to and from the Internet). A firewall protecting the VPN router at site 1 can restrict all incoming packets to have an IP source address of the VPN router at site 2 or the VPN router at site 3. Similarly, a firewall at each of the other two sites restricts incoming packets at that site. The restrictions help make the resulting system more immune to address spoofing and DoS attacks.

30.18 The Use of VPN Technology For Telecommuting

Although originally designed to interconnect sites, VPN technology has become extremely popular among employees who *telecommute* (i.e., work from a remote location). There are two forms of VPN:

- Stand-alone device
- VPN software

Stand-alone Device. The organization issues an employee a physical device that is sometimes called a *VPN router*. The device connects to the Internet, automatically establishes secure communication to a VPN server at the organization's site, and provides Local Area Network connections to which the user can connect computers and IP telephones. Logically, the VPN device extends the organization's network to the user's site, allowing computers attached to the VPN device to operate as if they were attached to the corporate network. Thus, when the user's computer boots and obtains an IP address, the address will be issued by a DHCP server at the organization. Similarly, the forwarding table in the user's computer is set up as if the computer were located at the organization's site — whenever the computer sends a packet, the VPN encrypts the packet and sends the encrypted version over the Internet to the organization. Whenever a packet arrives from the organization, the VPN device decrypts the packet and transmits the result to the user's computer.

VPN Software. Although a stand-alone device works well for an employee who works at home or in a remote office, such devices are cumbersome for employees who travel. To handle such cases, an organization uses *VPN software* that runs in the user's personal computer. A user connects to the Internet, and then launches the VPN application. When it starts, the VPN application interjects itself in the connection to the Internet. That is, the VPN software arranges to capture all outgoing and incoming packets. It encrypts each outgoing packet and sends the encrypted packet to the corporate VPN server, and decrypts each incoming packet.

30.19 Packet Encryption Vs. Tunneling

The above discussion of VPNs raises an interesting question: how should data be encrypted for transmission across the Internet? There are three main options:

- Payload Encryption
- IP-in-IP Tunneling
- IP-in-TCP Tunneling

Payload Encryption. To keep the contents of a datagram confidential, the *payload encryption* approach encrypts the payload area of a datagram, but leaves the header untouched. Because header fields are not encrypted, outsiders will be able to learn source and destination addresses that are being used as well as protocol port numbers. For example, suppose the chief financial officer (CFO) is at one site and the company president is at another. Further suppose that the CFO sends a short email message to the president whenever the financial news is good, but a long explanation whenever the financial news is not good. An outsider may be able to observe that soon after a short message flows between two specific computers, the stock price increases.

IP-in-IP Tunneling. Some VPNs use an *IP-in-IP tunneling* approach that keeps header information hidden as datagrams pass across the Internet from one site to another. When it encounters an outgoing datagram, the sending VPN software encrypts the entire datagram, including the header, and places the result inside another datagram for transmission. For example, consider the connections in Figure 30.10 shown on page 526. Suppose a computer X at site 1 creates a datagram for a computer Y at site 2. The datagram is forwarded through site 1 to router R_1 (i.e., the router that connects site 1 to the Internet). The VPN facility on R_1 encrypts the original datagram and encapsulates it in a new datagram for transmission to router R_2, the router at site 2. When the encapsulated datagram arrives, VPN software on R_2 decrypts the payload to extract the original datagram, and then forwards it to destination Y. Figure 30.11 illustrates the encapsulation.

In the figure, (a) shows the original datagram, (b) shows the cyphertext that results from encryption, and (c) shows the outer datagram that is sent from R_1 to R_2. Note that internal addresses are hidden because all datagrams traveling across the Internet between sites 1 and 2 list routers R_1 and R_2 as source and destination addresses.

To summarize:

> *When a VPN uses IP-in-IP encapsulation, all fields in the original datagram are encrypted, including the original header.*

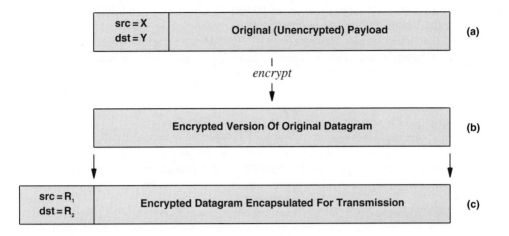

Figure 30.11 Illustration of IP-in-IP encapsulation used with a VPN.

IP-in-TCP Tunneling. The third possible alternative used to keep data confidential involves the use of a TCP tunnel. That is, two parties establish a TCP connection, and then use the connection to send encrypted datagrams. When a datagram must be sent, the entire datagram is encrypted, a small header is added to mark the boundary between datagrams, and the result is send across the TCP connection. Typically, the header consists of a two-byte integer that specifies the length of the datagram. On the other end of the TCP connection, the receiving VPN software reads the header, and then reads the specified number of additional bytes to obtain the datagram. Once the entire cyphertext for a datagram has been received, the receiver decrypts it and processes the original datagram.

The chief advantage of using IP-in-TCP rather than IP-in-IP arises from reliable delivery: TCP insures that all datagrams sent between two sites arrive reliably and in order. The chief disadvantage of using IP-in-TCP is head-of-line blocking: because all datagrams must be delivered in order, if one TCP segment is lost or delayed, TCP cannot deliver data from successive segments, even if they have arrived correctly. If we think of a VPN as transferring a queue of packets, the entire queue remains blocked until the first datagram has been delivered.

A final issue arises regarding VPN tunneling: performance. There are three aspects:

- Latency
- Throughput
- Overhead And Fragmentation

Latency. To understand the issue of latency, consider an organization on the West Coast of the United States, and assume an employee travels to the East Coast, approximately 3,000 miles away. Remember that VPN software merely transfers datagrams back to the home organization — once it reaches the organization, a datagram must be routed to its destination. For example, if the employee browses a web page, each request must travel from the employee's current location to the organization's VPN server, and from there to the web server. The reply must travel back to the organization's VPN server, and finally to the employee at the remote location. The latency required to access a resource close to the employee is especially high because datagrams must travel from the employee across the VPN to the organization on the West Coast and back to the resource on the East Coast. As a result, the round-trip requires a datagram to make four traversals of the continent.

Throughput. Another issue with a conventional VPN arises from the throughput available on the Internet. The problem can be important when using applications that have been designed for a high-speed LAN. In some organizations, for example, the web pages that employees use for internal company business contain extensive graphics. A LAN at the site provides sufficient throughput to make downloading web pages quick. For a remote user connected via VPN, low throughput can make waiting for a web page frustrating.

Overhead And Fragmentation. A third aspect of performance arises because tunneling adds overhead to a datagram. To understand the problem, suppose a site uses Ethernet and an application has created a datagram that is 1500 bytes long (i.e., the datagram is exactly as large as the network MTU). When a VPN router encapsulates the encrypted datagram in another IP datagram, at least twenty additional bytes are added for the outer datagram's header. The resulting datagram exceeds the network MTU, and will be fragmented before transmission. Because both fragments must arrive before the datagram can be processed, the probability of delay or loss is higher.

30.20 Security Technologies

A variety of security technologies have been invented for use in the Internet. Highlights include:

- *PGP* (*Pretty Good Privacy*). A cryptographic system that applications can use to encrypt data before transmission. PGP was developed at MIT, and is especially popular among computer scientists.

- *SSH* (*Secure Shell*). An application-layer protocol for remote login that guarantees confidentiality by encrypting data before transmission across the Internet.

- *SSL* (*Secure Socket Layer*). A technology originally designed by Netscape Communications that uses encryption to provide authentication and confidentiality. SSL software fits between an application and the socket API, and encrypts data before transmitting over the Internet. SSL is used on a web connection to allow users to conduct financial transactions safely (e.g., send a credit card number to a web server).

- *TLS* (*Transport Layer Security*). Designed by the IETF in the late 1990s as a successor to SSL, TLS builds on version 3 of SSL. Both SSL and TLS are available for use with HTTPS.

- *HTTPS* (*HTTP Security*). Not really a separate technology, HTTPS combines HTTP with either SSL or TLS and a certificate mechanism to provide users with authenticated, confidential communication over the Web. HTTPS uses TCP port 443 instead of port 80.

- *IPsec* (*IP security*). A security standard used with IP datagrams. IPsec uses cryptographic techniques, and allows the sender to choose authentication (i.e., validate the datagram's sender and recipient) or confidentiality (i.e., encrypt the datagram payload).

- *RADIUS* (*Remote Authentication Dial-In User Service*). A protocol used to provide centralized authentication, authorization, and accounting. RADIUS is popular with ISPs that have dialup users and with VPN systems that provide access to remote users.

- *WEP* (*Wired Equivalent Privacy*). Originally part of the Wi-Fi wireless LAN standard† used to keep transmissions confidential. Researchers at U.C. Berkeley have shown that WEP has several weaknesses. Thus, a replacement has been developed named *WPA* (*Wi-Fi Protected Access*).

30.21 Summary

Computer networks and the Internet can be used for criminal activities; major threats include phishing, misrepresentation, scams, denial of service, loss of control, and loss of data. Techniques used in attacks include: wiretapping, replay, buffer overflow, address and name spoofing, DoS with packet and SYN flooding, key breaking, port scanning, and packet interception.

Each organization needs to define a security policy that specifies aspects of data integrity (protection against change), data availability (protection against disruption of service), and data confidentiality or privacy (protection against snooping and discovery). In addition, an organization must consider accountability (i.e., how an audit trail is kept) and authorization (i.e., how responsibility for information is passed from one person to another).

---

†WEP applies to a variety of IEEE 802.11 protocols.

The set of technologies that have been created to provide various aspects of security include: encryption, hashing, digital signatures and certificates, firewalls, intrusion detection systems, deep packet inspection, content scanning, and Virtual Private Networks. Encryption is among the most fundamental technologies that is used in many security mechanisms.

Private key encryption uses a single key to encrypt and decrypt messages; the sender and receiver must keep the key secret. Public key encryption systems use a pair of keys; one key is kept secret and the other (the public key) is advertised widely. Digital signatures use encryption to authenticate messages. A key authority can issue certificates to validate public keys.

A firewall protects a site against attack by limiting the packets that can enter or leave. To configure a firewall, a manager devises a set of rules that give specific values for packet header fields. Intrusion Detection Systems that keep state information can identify attacks such as repeated SYNs.

Virtual Private Networks (VPNs) provide the benefits of confidentiality and low-cost. VPN technology allows an employee to telecommute. To keep information confidential, a sender can encrypt the payload, use IP-in-IP tunneling, or use IP-in-TCP tunneling. Tunneling has the advantage of encrypting packet headers as well as the payload. Some applications do not work well over a VPN because a VPN has longer delay, lower throughput, and higher overhead than a direct connection.

Many security technologies exist. Examples include: PGP, SSH, SSL, TLS, HTTPS, IPsec, RADIUS, and WEP.

EXERCISES

30.1   What is a firewall, and where is a firewall installed?

30.2   Name the technique used in security attacks.

30.3   List the major security problems on the Internet, and give a short description of each.

30.4   Why is deriving a security policy difficult?

30.5   Read about vulnerabilities in the WEP protocol. How does the WPA protocol avoid the problems?

30.6   Rewrite the firewall configuration in Figure 30.9 to allow an outsider to ping each of the three servers.

30.7   To what does *cryptography* refer?

30.8   Read about commercial IDS systems, and make a list of attacks the systems can detect.

30.9   If you and a friend each have a pair of public and private keys for a public key encryption system, how can you and your friend conduct daily communication without being tricked by a replay attack?

30.10   How can two parties use public key encryption to sign a contract that is then sent to a third party?

30.11   DoS attacks often send TCP SYN segments. Can an attacker also create a DoS attack by sending TCP data segments? Explain.

30.12   List and describe the eight basic security techniques.

30.13   When a VPN uses IP-in-IP tunneling, what prevents an attacker from reading the header of the original datagram?

30.14   Rewrite the firewall configuration in Figure 30.9 to move the email server to the computer running the web server.

30.15   Consider a DPI system that searches for a string of K bytes in each packet. If a packet contains 1486 bytes of payload, what is the worst case number of comparisons that must be made to examine the packet assuming a straightforward matching algorithm?

30.16   What is an access control list (ACL), and how is an ACL used?

30.17   Read about the *Data Encryption Standard* (*DES*). What size key should be used for data that is extremely important?

30.18   Suppose an attacker finds a way to store an arbitrary binding in your local DNS server. How can the attacker use such a weakness to obtain your bank account information?

30.19   If a password contains eight upper and lower-case letters and digits, how many possible passwords might an attacker need to try to gain access?

30.20   Suppose a company devises a security policy which specifies that only HR personnel are authorized to see payroll files. What type of mechanism is needed to implement the policy? Explain.

30.21   What are the two goals of a VPN system?

30.22   In some VPN systems, a sender adds a random number of zero bits to a datagram before encrypting, and the receiver discards the extra bits after the datagram has been decrypted. Thus, the only effect of the random padding is to make the length of the encrypted datagram independent of the length of the unencrypted version. Why is length important?

30.23   Suppose your friend has a public and private key for use with public key encryption. Can your friend send you a confidential message (i.e., a message that only you can read)? Why or why not?

30.24   List eight security technologies used in the Internet, and describe the purpose of each.

30.25   Why isn't deep packet inspection used on the highest-speed networks?

30.26   What are the three ways a VPN can transfer data across the Internet?

30.27   Many commercial firewall products allow a manager to specify packets to *deny* as well as packets to *accept*. What is the disadvantage of a configuration that allows denial?

30.28   What is a digital certificate?

Chapter Contents

31

Network Management (SNMP)

31.1 Introduction

Preceding chapters describe a variety of conventional applications that use the Internet. This chapter expands our study of network applications by considering network management. The chapter introduces a conceptual model used in industry, and uses the model to explain the scope of management activities. After explaining why network management is both important and difficult, the chapter describes network management technologies. It examines tools that are available, including application software that managers use to measure or control switches, routers, and other devices that constitute an intranet. The chapter explains the general paradigm used by management systems, and describes the functionality that such systems provide. Finally, the chapter considers a specific example of a network management protocol, and explains how software for the protocol operates.

31.2 Managing An Intranet

A *network manager*, sometimes called a *network administrator*, is a person responsible for planning, installing, operating, monitoring, and controlling the hardware and software systems that constitute a computer network or intranet. A manager plans a network that meets performance requirements, monitors operations, detects and corrects problems that make communication inefficient or impossible, and works to avoid conditions that will produce a problem again. Because either hardware or software failures can cause problems, a network manager must monitor both.

Network management can be difficult for three reasons. First, in most organizations, the intranet is heterogeneous — the intranet contains hardware and software components manufactured by multiple companies. Second, technology keeps changing, which means that new devices and new services appear constantly. Third, most intranets are large, which means some parts of the intranet are remote from others. Detecting the cause of a communication problem in a remote device can be especially difficult.

Network management is also difficult because many network mechanisms are designed to overcome problems automatically. Routing protocols bypass failures and intermittent packet loss can go unnoticed because TCP automatically retransmits. Unfortunately, automatic error recovery has consequences. Packet retransmission uses network bandwidth that could be used to send new data. Similarly, a hardware failure that goes undetected can become critical if a backup path also fails.

To summarize:

> *Although network hardware and protocol software contain mechanisms to automatically route around failures or retransmit lost packets, network managers need to detect and correct underlying problems.*

31.3 FCAPS: The Industry Standard Model

The networking industry uses the *FCAPS model* to characterize the scope of network management. The acronym is derived from recommendation *M.3400* published by the *International Telecommunications Union (ITU)*†. FCAPS is expanded into a list of five aspects of management. Figure 31.1 summarizes the model.

Abbreviation	Meaning
F	Fault detection and correction
C	Configuration and operation
A	Accounting and billing
P	Performance assessment and optimization
S	Security assurance and protection

Figure 31.1 The FCAPS model of network management.

---

†M.3400 is part of a series of standards that specify how a *Telecommunications Management Network (TMN)* should be configured and operated.

Fault Detection And Correction. Fault detection accounts for a major part of the operational aspect of network management. A manager monitors network equipment to detect problems, and takes appropriate steps to correct the problem. Possible faults include software failures (e.g., an operating system crash on a server), link failures (e.g., someone accidentally cuts an optical fiber), and equipment failures (e.g., the power supply fails on a router).

Often, users report failures by citing a high-level symptom such as "I just lost access to a shared disk." A manager must investigate to determine whether the problem lies with software, security (e.g., a new password), a server, or a link. We say that a manager performs *root-cause analysis*. Often, a manager can determine the cause by correlating many reports. For example, if many users at one site suddenly start to complain that a variety of services are unavailable, a manager might suspect that the problem lies in a shared connection that all services use.

Configuration And Operation. It may seem that configuration is a trivial aspect of network management because configuration only needs to be performed once — after it has been created, a configuration can be saved so a device automatically installs the configuration during a reboot. In fact, configuration is complex for three reasons. First, a network contains many devices and services, and the configurations must be consistent across all devices. Second, as new equipment and services are added or policies change, a network manager must consider all configurations to insure the entire network implements the changes correctly. Third, current tools allow a manager to configure individual devices and individual protocols; there is no easy way to configure a set of heterogeneous devices.

Accounting And Billing. In many corporate intranets, accounting and billing is trivial. The corporation charges the cost of running a network to a central account, much like the cost of electrical power or telephone service. In ISP networks, however, accounting and billing can consume more of a manager's time than any other aspect of management. For example, if an ISP offers tiered service with bounds on the traffic that can be sent, a system must account for each customer's traffic separately. Often, service agreements specify that the fee a customer pays depends on a measure such as the total bytes a customer sends per day. Thus, it is important to measure all of a customer's traffic and keep detailed records that can be used to generate a bill.

Performance Assessment And Optimization. A manager performs two types of performance assessment: *diagnostic assessment* to detect problems and inefficiencies and *trend assessment* that allows a manager to anticipate the need for increased capacity. Diagnostic assessment looks for ways to maximize the utilization of an existing network. For example, if a manager finds a path with low utilization, the manager might look for ways to shift traffic onto the path. Trend assessment looks for ways to increase the performance of the network to meet future needs. For example, most managers watch utilization on the link between their organization and the Internet, and make plans to increase the capacity of the link when the average utilization climbs above 50%.

Security Assurance And Protection. Because it crosses layers of the protocol stack and spans multiple devices, security is among the most difficult aspects of network management. In particular, security follows the weakest-link analogy: the entire security of a site can be compromised if the configuration is incorrect on one device. Moreover, because attackers continually devise new ways to break security, a network that is secure at a given time may be compromised later unless a manager makes changes.

31.4 Example Network Elements

Network management systems use the generic term *network element* to refer to any network device, system, or mechanism that can be managed. Although many network elements consist of a physical device, the definition encompasses services such as DNS. Figure 31.2 lists example network elements.

Manageable Network Elements	
Layer 2 Switch	IP router
VLAN Switch	Firewall
Wireless Access Point	Digital Circuit (CSU/DSU)
Head-End DSL Modem	DSLAM
DHCP Server	DNS Server
Web Server	Load Balancer

Figure 31.2 Examples of network elements that must be managed.

The industry uses the term *element management* to refer to the configuration and operation of an individual network element. Unfortunately, most available tools only provide element management. Thus, to create an end-to-end service, a manager must configure each network element along the path. For example, to create an MPLS tunnel across multiple routers, a manager must configure each router independently. Similarly, to implement a policy across an entire network, a manager must configure each element.

Of course, it is easy for a human to make a mistake when configuring many devices, which makes element management susceptible to misconfiguration. More important, to diagnose an error, a manager must examine one system at a time. The point is:

> *Because it only permits a manager to configure, monitor, or control one network element at a time, an element management system is labor intensive and prone to errors.*

31.5 Network Management Tools

Network management tools can be classified into twelve categories that character-ize their general purpose:

- Physical Layer Testing
- Reachability And Connectivity
- Packet Analysis
- Network Discovery
- Device Interrogation
- Event Monitoring
- Performance Monitoring
- Flow Analysis
- Routing And Traffic Engineering
- Configuration
- Security Enforcement
- Network Planning

Physical layer testing includes carrier sensor testing found on many LAN interface cards and wireless strength meters used to measure RF signal strength. *Ping* provides the best example of a reachability tool, and is heavily used by network managers. A *packet analyzer*, also called a *protocol analyzer*, captures and displays packets or statis-tics about packets; the *Ethereal* analyzer is available for download.

A network discovery tool produces a map of the network by probing devices. Often, a manager uses such a map to find the elements on a network, and then uses a device interrogation tool to access each element. Event monitoring tools produce alerts — typically, a manager configures a device to send an alert when certain thresholds are crossed (e.g., utilization of a link reaches 80%), and a monitoring tool displays an alert on a manager's workstation. Performance monitoring tools plot performance over time to help a manager spot trends.

Flow analysis tools, such as a NetFlow analyzer, also help a manager spot trends. Instead of merely reporting on overall traffic, a flow analyzer can help a manager spot changes in specific types of traffic (e.g., an increase in VoIP traffic).

Routing, traffic engineering, and configuration tools are related. Each helps a manager control elements. Routing tools control the configuration and monitoring of routing update protocols and the forwarding tables that result from routing changes. Traffic engineering tools focus on the configuration and monitoring of MPLS tunnels and related QoS parameters. General-purpose configuration tools allow a manager to install or change the configuration in elements. In particular, some configuration tools automate the repetitive task of making a change in a set of (usually identical) elements.

For example, if a firewall rule changes and a site has multiple firewalls, an automated configuration tool (often a Perl script) can install the same change in each.

Many security tools exist, and control a variety of security elements. Some security tools allow a manager to specify a policy, and the tool either attempts to configure devices to enforce the policy or attempts to measure devices to insure that the policy is in effect. A manager can use other security tools to test security — the tool attempts to attack devices or services, and reports to the manager whether the attack was successful.

Network planning is complex, and planning tools are among the most sophisticated. For example, tools exist that run linear programming algorithms to help a manager optimize network architecture or plan traffic management. Tools also exist that help a manager assess weaknesses (e.g., identify places in the network where two or more hardware failures will disconnect users from the Internet).

To summarize:

> *A wide variety of tools exist that help a manager configure, measure, diagnose, and analyze networks.*

31.6 Network Management Applications

Most of the tools described above operate over a network. That is, a manager remains in a single location and uses network technology to communicate with a given network element. Surprisingly, network management is not defined as an integral part of low-layer protocols. Instead, protocols used to monitor and control network devices operate at the application level. When a manager needs to interact with a specific hardware device, the manager runs an application program that acts as a client, and an application program on the network device acts as a server. The client and server use conventional transport protocols such as UDP or TCP to interact. Furthermore, instead of building a separate network, most managers send management traffic over the production network.

To avoid confusion between application programs that users invoke and applications that are reserved for network managers, network management systems avoid the terms *client* and *server*. Instead, the client application that runs on the manager's computer is called a *manager*, and a server that runs on a network device is called an *agent†*.

Using conventional transport protocols to carry management traffic may seem ineffective because failures in either the protocols or underlying hardware can prevent packets from traveling to or from a device, making it impossible to control a device while failures are occurring. Some network operators install separate hardware to handle management of highly critical devices (e.g., a dialup modem is attached directly to a high-speed router as a backup for a manager to use in case the main network is impassable). In practice, such systems are seldom needed. Using an application protocol for network management works well for two reasons. First, in cases where a hardware

---

†Although we will follow the convention of using *manager* and *agent*, the reader should keep in mind that they operate like any client and server.

failure prevents communication, a manager can communicate with devices that remain functional, and use success or failure to help locate the problem. Second, using conventional transport protocols means a manager's packets will be subject to the same conditions as normal traffic. Thus, if delays are high, a manager will find out immediately.

31.7 Simple Network Management Protocol

The standard protocol used for network management is known as the *Simple Network Management Protocol* (*SNMP*); the current standard is version 3, written *SNMPv3*. The SNMP protocol defines exactly how a manager communicates with an agent. For example, SNMP defines the format of requests that a manager sends to an agent and the format of replies that an agent returns. In addition, SNMP defines the exact meaning of each possible request and reply. In particular, SNMP specifies that an SNMP message is encoded using a standard known as *Abstract Syntax Notation.1 (ASN.1)*†.

Although the full details of ASN.1 encoding are beyond the scope of this text, a simple example will help explain the encoding: consider sending an integer between an agent and a manager. To accommodate large values without wasting space on every transfer, ASN.1 uses a combination of length and value for each object being transferred. For example, an integer between *0* and *255* can be transferred in a single octet. Integers in the range *256* through *65535* require two octets, while larger integers require three or more octets. To encode an integer, ASN.1 sends a pair of values: a length, *L*, followed by *L* octets that contain the integer. To permit encoding of arbitrarily large integers, ASN.1 also allows the length to occupy more than one octet; extended lengths normally are not needed for the integers used with SNMP. Figure 31.3 illustrates the encoding.

Decimal Integer	Hexadecimal Equivalent	Length Byte	Bytes Of Value (in hex)
27	1B	01	1B
792	318	02	03 18
24,567	5FF7	02	5F F7
190,345	2E789	03	02 E7 89

Figure 31.3 Examples of the ASN.1 encoding for integers.

---

†The name is pronounced *abstract syntax notation dot one*, and the abbreviation is pronounced by reading the characters, *A S N dot one*.

31.8 SNMP's Fetch-Store Paradigm

The SNMP protocol does not define a large set of commands. Instead, the protocol uses a *fetch-store paradigm* in which there are two basic operations: *fetch*, used to obtain a value from a device, and *store*, used to set a value in a device. Each object that can be fetched or stored is given a unique name; a command that specifies a fetch or store operation must specify the name of the object.

It should be obvious how fetch operations can be used to monitor a device or obtain its status: a set of status objects must be defined and given names. To obtain status information, a manager fetches the value associated with a given object. For example, an object can be defined that counts the number of frames a device discards because the frame checksum is incorrect. The device must be designed to increment the counter whenever a checksum error is detected. A manager can use SNMP to fetch the value associated with the counter to determine whether checksum errors are occurring.

Using the fetch-store paradigm to control a device may not seem obvious; control operations are defined to be the side-effect of storing into an object. For example, SNMP does not include separate commands to *reset* a checksum error counter or to *reboot* a device. In the case of the checksum error counter, storing a zero into the object is intuitive because it resets a counter to zero. For operations like reboot, however, an SNMP agent must be programmed to interpret a *store* request and to execute the correct sequence of operations to achieve the desired effect. Thus, SNMP software might define a reboot object, and specify that storing zero into the object will cause the system to reboot. Of course, SNMP objects are virtual in the sense that the underlying device does not implement them directly. Instead, an agent receives requests and performs actions that correspond to each *fetch* or *store* operation. To summarize:

> *SNMP uses the fetch-store paradigm for interaction between a manager and an agent. A manager fetches values to determine the device status; operations that control the device are defined as the side-effects of storing into objects.*

31.9 The SNMP MIB And Object Names

Each object to which SNMP has access must be defined and given a unique name. Furthermore, both the manager and agent programs must agree on the names and the meanings of fetch and store operations. Collectively, the set of all objects SNMP can access is known as a *Management Information Base* (*MIB*).

In fact, the definition of a MIB is not directly tied to SNMP. Instead, the SNMP standard only specifies the message format and describes how messages are encoded; a separate standard specifies MIB variables along with the meaning of fetch and store operations on each variable. In fact, separate standards documents specify MIB variables for each type of device.

Objects in a MIB are defined with the ASN.1 naming scheme, which assigns each object a long prefix that guarantees the name will be unique. For example, an integer that counts the number of IP datagrams a device has received is named:

iso.org.dod.internet.mgmt.mib.ip.ipInReceives

Furthermore, when the object name is represented in an SNMP message, each part of the name is assigned an integer. Thus, in an SNMP message, the name of *ipInReceives* is:

1.3.6.1.2.1.4.3

31.10 The Variety Of MIB Variables

Because SNMP does not specify a set of MIB variables, the design is flexible. New MIB variables can be defined and standardized as needed, without changing the basic protocol. More important, the separation of the communication protocol from the definition of objects permits any group to define MIB variables, as needed. For example, when a new protocol is designed, the group who creates the protocol can define MIB variables that are used to monitor and control the protocol software. Similarly, when a group creates a new hardware device, the group can specify MIB variables used to monitor and control the device.

As the original designers intended, many sets of MIB variables have been created. For example, there are MIB variables that correspond to protocols like UDP, TCP, IP, and ARP, as well as MIB variables for network hardware such as Ethernet. In addition, groups have defined MIBs for hardware devices such as routers, switches, modems, and printers†.

31.11 MIB Variables That Correspond To Arrays

In addition to simple variables such as integers that correspond to counters, a MIB can include variables that correspond to tables or arrays. Such definitions are useful because they correspond to the implementation of information in a computer system. For example, consider an IP forwarding table. In most implementations, the forwarding table can be viewed as an array of entries, where each entry contains a destination address and a next-hop used to reach that address.

Unlike a conventional programming language, ASN.1 does not include an index operation. Instead, indexed references are implicit — the sender must know that the object being referenced is a table, and must append the indexing information onto the object name. For example, the MIB variable:

standard MIB prefix.ip.ipRoutingTable

---

†In addition to generic MIB variables that work with an arbitrary device, many vendors define specific MIB variables for their hardware or software.

corresponds to an IP forwarding table†, each entry of which contains several fields. Conceptually, the table is indexed by the IP address of a destination. To obtain the value of a particular field in an entry, a manager specifies a name of the form:

standard MIB prefix.ip.ipRoutingTable.ipRouteEntry.field.IPdestaddr

where *field* corresponds to one of the valid fields of an entry, and *IPdestaddr* is a 4-octet IP address that is used as an index. For example, field *ipRouteNextHop* corresponds to the next-hop in an entry. When converted to the integer representation, the request for a next-hop becomes:

1.3.6.1.2.1.4.21.1.7.destination

where *1.3.6.1.2.1* is the standard MIB prefix, *4* is the code for *ip*, *21* is the code for *ipRoutingTable*, *1* is the code for *ipRouteEntry*, *7* is the code for the field *ipRouteNext-Hop*, and *destination* is the numeric value for the IP address of a destination. To summarize:

> *Although ASN.1 does not provide a mechanism for indexing, MIB variables can correspond to tables or arrays. To emulate a table or an array with an ASN.1 variable, the index for an entry is encoded by appending it to the variable name; when agent software encounters a name that corresponds to a table, the software extracts and uses the index information to select the correct table entry.*

31.12 Summary

A network manager is a person who monitors and controls the hardware and software systems that constitute an intranet. The FCAPS model defines the five basic aspects of network management to be fault detection, configuration, accounting, performance analysis, and security. A variety of tools exist to aid a manager in performing management functions. Because most tools only provide element management, a manager must handle tasks that cross devices manually.

Because network management software uses the client-server model, the software requires two components. The component that runs on a manager's computer and acts as a client is called a *manager*; the component that runs on a device in the network and acts as a server is called an *agent*.

The *Simple Network Management Protocol* (*SNMP*) is the standard network management protocol used in the Internet. SNMP defines the format and meaning of messages that a manager and agent exchange. Instead of defining many operations, SNMP uses the fetch-store paradigm in which a manager sends requests to fetch values

---

†Recall that a forwarding table was originally known as a *routing table*; the change in terminology occurred in the 2000s.

from or store values into variables. All operations are defined as side-effects of store operations.

SNMP does not define the set of variables that can be used. Instead, variables and their meanings are defined in separate standards, making it possible for groups to define a different set of MIB variables for each hardware device or protocol. The names of MIB variables are named using the ASN.1 standard; all MIB variables have long, hierarchical ASN.1 names, which are translated to a more compact numeric representation for transmission. ASN.1 does not include aggregate data types such as tables or arrays, nor does it include a subscript operator. Instead, to make a MIB variable emulate a table or an array, ASN.1 extends the variable name by appending the index information.

EXERCISES

31.1   What is a protocol analyzer?

31.2   Give an example of a protocol mechanism that hides an error.

31.3   Read about how ASN.1 encodes names and values. Write a computer program to encode and decode ASN.1 names such as the name assigned to *ipInReceives*.

31.4   If a user complains that they cannot access a given service, which aspects of FCAPS could the complaint potentially involve?

31.5   ASN.1 defines the exact format of an integer. Why doesn't the ASN.1 standard merely state that each integer is a 32-bit value?

31.6   What does a flow analysis tool help a manager understand?

31.7   Download free SNMP manager software, and attempt to contact a device such as a printer.

31.8   What are the two basic operations that SNMP uses?

31.9   If a firewall malfunctions, which aspect of FCAPS does the situation fall under? Why?

31.10   What is the chief advantage of appending index information to a name instead of using a conventional array that is indexed by integers?

31.11   It has been argued that one should not use a network to debug a problem in the network. Why does SNMP use the same network that it is debugging?

31.12   Find two examples of manageable elements other than those listed in Figure 31.2.

31.13   Write a program that reads an arbitrarily large integer in decimal, encodes the integer into the format illustrated in Figure 31.3, and prints the result.

31.14   What terms does network management software use instead of *client* and *server*?

31.15   Does SNMP define a name for each possible MIB variable? Explain.

Chapter Contents

32

Trends In Networking Technologies And Uses

32.1 Introduction

One of the most intriguing aspects of the Internet arises from the continual introduction of new applications and networking technologies. Applications that account for the majority of packets on the Internet have been invented in the past decade. Such applications were not feasible when the Internet was invented because they rely on new underlying technologies and infrastructure.

This chapter summarizes some of the trends in networking technologies, applications, and services. The chapter considers recent developments as well as longer-term research.

32.2 The Need For Scalable Internet Services

In a narrow sense, the client-server model of communication means that one application (a server) starts first and awaits contact from another application (a client). In a broader sense, the networking industry uses the term *client-server* to characterize an architecture in which many potential clients connect to a single, centralized server. For example, a corporation that runs a web server can expect contact from arbitrary users. The disadvantage of a centralized server arises from the resulting performance: as the number of clients increases, the server (or the access network leading to the server) quickly become a bottleneck, especially if each client downloads many bytes of content.

547

The server bottleneck problem is considered one of the most important limitations on Internet services. Consequently, both the networking research community and the networking industry have investigated ways to provide architectures and technologies that allow Internet services to scale and incorporate new trends; a variety of approaches are being used. The next sections describes several. To summarize:

> *A variety of technologies have been devised to allow Internet services to scale; although the approaches differ widely, each is useful in some cases.*

32.3 Content Caching (Akamai)

One of the first scaling technologies focused on caching web content. For example, ISPs often have a cache that keeps a copy of each static web page (i.e., a page for which the content does not change rapidly). If N of the ISP's users fetch the same page, only one request needs to be sent to the *origin server*; $N-1$ requests can be satisfied from the cache.

Companies like Akamai have extended the caching idea by offering a distributed caching service. Akamai has a set of servers located throughout the Internet, and an organization can contract with Akamai to preload the Akamai caches with content. To insure that caches remain current, an organization customer can update the Akamai caches periodically. Visitors to the organization's web site obtain much of the content from a nearby Akamai cache rather than from the organization's central server. As a result, load on the central server is reduced.

32.4 Web Load Balancers

Because utilization is high and many retail businesses depend on the Web for direct sales to customers, web server optimization has received much attention. One of the interesting mechanisms used to construct a large web site is known as a *load balancer*. A load balancer allows a site to have multiple computers each running an identical web server, and distributes incoming requests among the physical servers. Figure 32.1 illustrates the architecture.

A load balancer examines each incoming HTTP request and sends the request to one of the servers. The load balancer remembers recent requests, and directs all requests from a given source to the same physical server. To insure that all servers return the same answer to a request, the servers use a common, shared database system. Thus, if a customer places an order, all copies of the web server will be able to access the order.

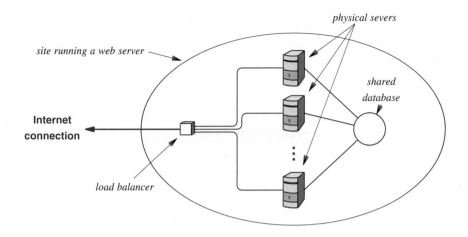

Figure 32.1 Illustration of a load balancer used for large-scale web sites.

32.5 Server Virtualization

Another twist on scalability arises from *server virtualization*. The motivation begins with an observation: many sites runs multiple servers (e.g., an email server, web
server, and a database server). In a conventional architecture, each server must be
placed on a physical computer. A performance problem can occur because the servers
running on computer *A* are all busy, but the servers running on computer *B* are idle.

Server virtualization solves the problem by allowing a manager to move a server
from one computer to another at any time. Of course, there are many technical details
to be handled, including changes in forwarding. However, the idea is straightforward:
run the server under a *Virtual Machine* (*VM*) system that support process migration. If
a given physical computer becomes overwhelmed, a manager can migrate one or more
processes to another computer.

32.6 Peer-To-Peer Communication

In the 1990s, several groups experimented with a general technique to increase the
speed of file download. Instead of fetching a complete file from a central server, a
client fetches individual pieces of a file. Furthermore, pieces of the file are placed on
servers throughout the Internet. Whenever a client needs a piece of a file, the client
chooses to fetch a copy from a server that is nearby. To increase the number of locations where a piece can be found, each client that obtains a piece of the file agrees to
act as a server that allows other clients to obtain the piece. The approach is known as a
peer-to-peer architecture (*p2p*).

Some of the most widely-known p2p systems have been created to allow the sharing of music files. For example, Napster and Kazaa both follow the p2p approach, and each has been popular among teenagers. Of course, a typical user does not care about the underlying technology — they only care that the system allows them to obtain copies of music files. Many users are unaware that when they use a p2p system, their computer agrees to propagate files to others.

32.7 Distributed Data Centers And Replication

Although load content caches, load balancers, server virtualization, and p2p architectures can each increase server scalability, some sites have so much traffic that another solution is needed: replication of an entire site. We use the term *distributed data centers* to characterize the approach.

As an example, consider the Google search engine. Google receives billions of contacts daily. To handle the load, Google has created multiple data centers, placed in various geographic locations. When a user enters the domain name *www.google.com*, the user is directed to the closest Google data center; the approach can be considered a form of load balancing among sites. Of course, to provide consistent service, Google must insure that a given data center returns exactly the same search results as its other data centers.

32.8 Universal Representation (XML)

One of the most interesting trends in networking arises from the widespread adoption of the *Extensible Markup Language* (*XML*). Initially, XML was designed to incorporate structure into web documents so the document could be understood by multiple applications. Instead of fixing tags, XML allows a programmer to choose arbitrary tags, making it possible to give each field an intuitive name. For example, one can assume a document that contains tags *<name>, <street>, <city>, <country>, <postal_code>* includes a record of a person's address. One of the key ideas behind XML is its ability to encode self-describing documents. That is, the document includes a *style sheet* that specifies legitimate document structure.

XML has become a de facto standard for representation, and is being used in a variety of new ways that were unanticipated in early designs. For example, XML is used on the interface between a web server and a database, and some load balancers have been created that can parse XML. In addition, XML is used to control downloads in mobile devices and to represent specifications used by network management systems.

32.9 Social Networking

In the early 2000s, Internet use shifted from a consumer model to one of social interaction among peers. Initially, most information on the Internet was supplied by *producers*, organizations such as media companies. An individual user consumed information, but did not produce it. By the 2000s, sites like Facebook, Myspace, and YouTube arose that allow any user to create content, which means that a typical user is uploading more data.

The shift in interaction is most noticeable among younger users. Many teenagers have created a blog or subscribed to one of the sites mentioned above. In the US, a nontrivial percentage of recently married couples met their mate through an online service. In addition, the use of online chat and other forms of person-to-person communication have increased.

32.10 Mobility And Wireless Networking

Mobile communication is among the most significant trends, and users expect to be connected to the Internet continuously. Most hotels offer Internet connections to their guests, and airlines are offering Internet service on planes. The author recently took a cruise, and was delighted to find that the Internet connection aboard ship worked so well that it could be used for VoIP telephone calls.

The demand for mobile communication has sparked interest in wireless technologies, and many wireless standards have been created. 802.11n technology provides higher throughput than its predecessor, 802.11b. The most significant change, however, has occurred in the cellular telephone industry: cellular phones will soon be converted away from other protocols to IP. In particular, once cellular carriers begin to use WiMAX, the entire system will be IP, meaning that cellular service and the Internet have converged.

Ironically, while the cellular industry has adopted IP as a long-term strategy, the technology known as *mobile IP* has not been adopted by the networking industry. Instead, most mobile users rely on Wi-Fi as a local access technology and use VPN software to connect to their businesses.

32.11 Digital Video

Cable providers are replacing analog transmission facilities with digital, and will soon be delivering content in digital form over packet networks. In fact, many providers are using IP as the packet protocol, and the term *IPTV* is used for the technology.

Using IP for video creates interesting opportunities. First, television and the Internet converge, making it easy to watch television programs on a computer or use a digital television as a computer display. Furthermore, IP makes it easier to deploy *on-demand* video, in which a user can access content when desired, control playback with pause and rewind functions, and capture live content for later viewing.

32.12 Multicast Delivery

Although Internet-wide multicasting has not enjoyed much success, the move to IPTV has stimulated interest in multicast. The motivation arises from a desire to optimize delivery. Although a provider may offer hundreds of channels of content, a given subscriber usually only has a few televisions displaying content at a given time. Furthermore, a few channels usually attract most of the viewers.

IP multicast allows a subscriber to register interest in a program by joining a multicast group for the program. Subscribers in a neighborhood connect to a logical LAN segment. Once a subscriber joins a group, the cable provider begins multicasting a copy of the program on the LAN segment. Multicasting continues as long as any of the subscribers on the segment are watching the program. The point is:

> With IP multicasting, only one copy of a television program needs to be sent across a logical LAN segment; multicasting of a program ceases once no more subscribers are watching the program.

32.13 Higher-Speed Access And Switching

At the edge of the Internet access technologies such as DSL and cable modems provide data rates of multiple megabits per second, two orders of magnitude more throughput than a dialup telephone connection. In some areas of the US, service providers are offering Fiber To The Home (FTTH), which increases the potential data rate to gigabits per second, three orders of magnitude beyond DSL and cable modems.

The Ethernet switches used in enterprise data centers provide 1 Gbps to the desktop. Higher capacity links operate at 10 Gbps, and it seems likely that speeds will increase to 40 Gbps. Such data rates are sufficient to support high-definition video.

32.14 Optical Switching

At the core of the Internet, the big question is: how can we combine optical and electronic technologies? Optical devices allow a provider to create an end-to-end light path that operates at 10 Gbps, often called a *lambda*. Although most current technologies require long times (multiple seconds) to set up a single light path, emerging optical technologies promise to reduce the time. As a result, it may be possible to set up a light path in less than a millisecond.

If a light path can be established quickly, how should it be used? Should an ISP use light paths to connect routers and then use packet technologies for access? Should an ISP set up a light path each time a user forms a TCP connection? The questions are the basis for an important research area; most large ISPs are convinced that optical switching will become increasingly important.

32.15 Use Of Networking In Business

Most large companies rely on computer networks for all aspects of business. However, networks are changing business in three ways. First, the availability of RFID technology is changing production, shipping, and inventory. Second, the availability of high-speed Layer 2 switches and packet technologies for voice and video are making it possible to replace travel with high-quality video teleconferencing systems. Third, many businesses are moving away from a strict command-and-control culture to a more collaborative style of management in which a team works together to make decisions. The availability of tools and network infrastructure that supports group interaction, such as wikis, is making it possible to collaborate over a network.

32.16 Sensors At Large And In The Home

Low-cost wired and wireless networking and low-power sensor devices have made it possible to build large sensor networks and connect such networks to the Internet. Sensors are being used to measure the environment (e.g., monitor air and water quality or gather weather information), track the movements of wild animals, help farmers monitor crops, monitor people in office buildings, and assess traffic on highways.

One particularly interesting use of sensors involves their use in residential buildings. It is already possible to install sensors that measure temperature and humidity, or monitor a home for dangers such as smoke and carbon monoxide. A home sensor network can be connected to the Internet, allowing an owner to monitor their home while traveling†. It will soon be possible to obtain low-cost sensor devices such as a sensor in every light bulb or a sensor on each appliance.

32.17 Ad Hoc Networks

Since the early days of packet networking, the US military has funded research on *ad hoc networks* that are self-organizing. That is, a set of wireless stations find neighbors, choose a topology, and establish routing that allows any station to reach any other. The military's motivation arises from an imagined operation where soldiers each carry a wireless network station, and the stations form a communication system automatically.

Ad hoc networking is becoming important in the civilian world as well, especially in rural areas and developing countries. In the US, farmers are using ad hoc technology to connect rural farms to the Internet. Each farmer sets up a wireless station (usually on a tall building, such as a silo), and the stations agree to forward packets, as needed. In developing countries, ad hoc networks are used as an inexpensive way to provide Internet access to an entire village.

---

†The author has created such a monitoring system for his home.

32.18 Multi-Core CPUs And Network Processors

High data rates pose a problem for networking equipment manufacturers: how to build systems that can process packets quickly. High-end routers must handle packets arriving over an interface at 10 Gbps. Special-purpose chips (ASICs) can be used, but such chips are expensive and take many months to design or revise. Conventional processors are sufficient for low-end networking devices such as a wireless router used in a home, but do not have sufficient computational power for higher data rates.

Chip vendors offer two solutions. First, chip vendors offer multi-core CPUs that each contain several processors. One approach distributes incoming packets among the N cores, which means that one core only handles $1/N$ of the packets. Second, chip vendors offer *network processors*. We can think of a network processor as a fast CPU that includes multiple cores plus special instructions to handle common packet processing tasks at high speed. The point is that equipment vendors are using more programmable processors in their equipment.

32.19 IPv6

No list of networking trends would be complete without a mention of IPv6. The original work began in 1993, and the design has been in place for many years. Originally, proponents claimed that IPv6 was needed because IPv4 could not handle audio or video, was not secure, and would run out of addresses. Each year since the creation of IPv6, various groups from academia and industry have predicted the doom of IPv4 and the rise of IPv6. Meanwhile, IPv4 has adapted, runs multimedia applications, and has as much security as IPv6. NAT and CIDR addressing have extended the IPv4 addressing capabilities. IPv4 continues as the fundamental protocol of the Internet. Some cellular operators, especially in Asia, see IPv6 as a way to allow IP addressing on cell phones, but operators also have the option of devising a layer 2 addressing scheme.

At this point, there is no technical reason to adopt IPv6. In fact, because IPv6 packet processing incurs more overhead, moving to IPv6 may limit the speeds with which packets can be sent. Thus, the motivation for IPv6 becomes an economic trade-off: it is possible to remove NAT from the Internet and have end-to-end addressing, but doing so will mean replacing all networking equipment and software. It is difficult to tell when customers will decide that the high cost justifies a change.

32.20 Summary

The Internet continues to evolve. New applications and technologies are invented constantly. Current trends include technologies for higher speed, increased mobility, and scalability. In terms of Internet applications, the trend has been toward social networking. In addition, new technologies have enabled average users to produce content.

Businesses are using tools that support collaborative management, and are using high-end teleconferencing systems to replace travel.

EXERCISES

32.1   Give examples of new networking trends for business.

32.2   Explain how content caching permits the Internet to scale.

32.3   Why are cellular telephone providers especially interested in IPv6?

32.4   A web site with N physical servers may not be able to process N times as many requests per second because shared resources can impose a bottleneck. Name two resources that are shared.

32.5   Where is a load balancer used?

32.6   In addition to permitting scaling, server virtualization may also allow a site to save energy during times when the load is low (e.g., on a weekend). Explain how.

32.7   Does a distributed data center approach make sense for a business in which each web request requires access to a central database? Why or why not?

32.8   What does digital video offer users?

32.9   Name three examples of social network applications.

32.10 With what general use is peer-to-peer computing often associated?

32.11 How are the Internet and cellular telephone systems converging?

32.12 When optical fiber is used to deliver data to a home or business, how much faster can data be sent than with DSL or a cable modem?

32.13 Name two technologies used to increase the speed of routers and switches.

32.14 Where are sensor networks being used?

32.15 What technologies are being used to provide remote access to villages?

Appendix 1

A Simplified Application Programming Interface

Introduction

Chapter 3 describes the socket API that programmers use to build clients and servers. This Appendix presents an alternative: a simplified API that allows a programmer to construct network applications without mastering the details of the socket interface. The Appendix is self-contained, and does not require an understanding of the Internet or TCP/IP. Thus, the Appendix can be read and understood before the rest of text has been studied.

The examples presented in the Appendix demonstrate an important idea:

> *A programmer can create Internet application software without understanding the underlying network technology or communication protocols.*

To make the point, we introduce a small set of library functions that handle communication, and show how the library functions can be used to write network applications. The example code from the chapter is available on the web site, and readers are encouraged to modify the examples or write additional applications.

A Model Of Network Communication

All Internet transfer is performed by application programs. When applications use the Internet, they do so in pairs. For example, when a user browses a web page, a browser application running on the user's computer contacts a web server application running on a remote computer. The browser sends a request to which the web server replies. Only the two applications understand the message format and meaning.

The Client-Server Model

To communicate across the Internet, a pair of applications use a straightforward mechanism: one application starts first and waits for the other application to contact it. The second application must know the location where the first application is waiting. The arrangement is known as *client-server* interaction. The program that waits for contact is a *server*, and the program that initiates contact is a *client*. To initiate contact, a client must know how to contact the server. In the Internet, the location of a server is given by a pair of identifiers:

(computer, application)

where *computer* identifies the computer on which the server is running, and *application* identifies a particular application program on that computer. Although application software represents the two values as binary numbers, humans never need to deal with the binary representation directly. Instead, the values are also assigned alphabetic names that humans use; software translates each name to a corresponding binary value automatically.

Communication Paradigm

Most Internet applications follow the same basic paradigm when they communicate. Two applications establish communication, exchange messages back and forth, and then terminate communication. The steps are:

- The server application starts first, and waits for contact from a client.

- The client specifies the server's location and requests a connection be established.

- Once a connection is in place, the client and server use the connection to exchange messages.

- After they finish sending data, the client and server each send an *end-of-file*, and the connection is terminated.

An Example Application Program Interface

So far, we have discussed the interaction between two applications at a conceptual level. We will now consider a detailed implementation. Computer Scientists define an *Application Program Interface* (*API*) to be a set of operations available to an application programmer. The API specifies a set of functions, arguments for each function, and the semantics of a function invocation.

To demonstrate network programming, we have devised a straightforward API for network communication. After describing the API, we will consider applications that use it. Figure A1.1 lists the seven functions that an application can call.

Operation	Meaning
await_contact	Used by a server to wait for contact from a client
make_contact	Used by a client to contact a server
appname_to_appnum	Used to translate a program name to an equivalent internal binary value
cname_to_comp	Used to translate a computer name to an equivalent internal binary value
send	Used by either client or server to send data
recv	Used by either client or server to receive data
send_eof	Used by both client and server after they have finished sending data

Figure A1.1 An example API consisting of seven functions sufficient for
most network applications†.

Note: our example code will also use an eighth function, *recvln*. However, *recvln* is not listed as a separate function because it merely consists of a loop that calls *recv* until an end-of-line has been encountered.

---

†Functions *send* and *recv* are supplied directly by the operating system; other functions in the API consist of library routines that we have written.

An Intuitive Look At The API

A server begins by calling *await_contact* to wait for contact from a client. The client begins by calling *make_contact* to establish contact. Once the client has contacted the server, the two can exchange messages with *send* and *recv*. The two applications must be programmed to know whether to send or receive — if both sides try to receive without sending, they will block forever.

After it finishes sending data, an application calls *send_eof* to send the end-of-file condition. On the other side, *recv* returns a value of zero to indicate that the end-of-file has been reached. For example, if the client calls *send_eof*, the server will find a zero return value from its call to *recv*. Once both sides have invoked *send_eof*, communication is terminated.

A trivial example will help explain the example API. Consider an application in which the client contacts a server, sends a single request, and receives a single reply. Figure A1.2 illustrates the sequence of API calls that the client and server make for such an interaction.

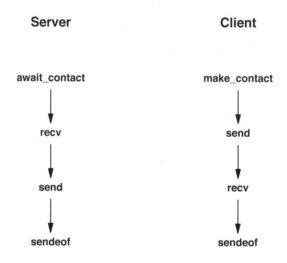

Figure A1.2 Illustration of the API calls used when a client sends one request and receives a reply from the server.

Definition Of The API

In addition to standard C data types, we define three types that are used throughout the code; using types keeps our API independent of any particular operating system and network software. Figure A1.3 lists the type names and their meanings.

Type Name	Meaning
appnum	A binary value used to identify an application
computer	A binary value used to identify a computer
connection	A value used to identify the connection between a client and server

Figure A1.3 The three type names used in our example API.

Using the three type names in Figure A1.3 we can precisely define the example API. For each function, the C-like declarations below list the type of each argument as well as the type the function returns.

The Await_Contact Function

A server calls function *await_contact* to wait for contact from a client.

```
connection await_contact(appnum a)
```

The call takes one argument of type *appnum* and returns a value of type *connection*. The argument specifies a number that identifies the server application; a client must specify the same number when contacting the server. The server uses the return value (type *connection*) to transfer data.

The Make_Contact Function

A client calls function *make_contact* to establish contact with a server.

```
connection make_contact(computer c, appnum a)
```

The call takes two arguments that identify a computer on which the server is running and the application number that the server is using on that computer. The client uses the return value, which is of type *connection*, to transfer data.

The Appname_To_Appnum Function

Clients and servers both use *appname_to_appnum* to translate from a human-readable name for a service to an internal binary value. The service names are standardized throughout the Internet (e.g., www denotes the World Wide Web).

> appnum appname_to_appnum(char *a)

The call takes one argument of type string (C uses the declaration *char* * to denote a string) and returns an equivalent binary value of type *appnum*.

The Cname_To_Comp Function

Clients call *cname_to_comp* to convert from a human-readable computer name to the internal binary value.

> computer cname_to_comp(char *c)

The call takes one argument of type string (*char* *), and returns an equivalent binary value of type *computer*.

The Send Function

Both clients and servers use *send* to transfer data across the network.

> int send(connection con, char *buffer, int length, int flags)

The call takes four arguments. The first argument specifies a connection previously established with *await_contact* or *make_contact*, the second is the address of a buffer containing data to send, the third argument gives the length of the data in bytes (octets), and the fourth argument is zero for normal transfer. *Send* returns the number of bytes transferred, or a negative value if an error occurred. Also see *send_eof*, which is used to send *end-of-file* after all data has been sent.

The Recv And Recvln Functions

Both clients and servers use *recv* to access data that arrives across the network.

int recv(connection con, char *buffer, int length, int flags)

The call takes four arguments. The first argument specifies a connection previously established with *await_contact* or *make_contact*, the second is the address of a buffer into which the data should be placed, the third argument gives the size of the buffer in bytes (octets), and the fourth argument is zero for normal transfer. *Recv* returns the number of bytes that were placed in the buffer, zero to indicate that *end-of-file* has been reached, or a negative value to indicate that an error occurred. The example code also uses a library function *recvln* that repeatedly calls *recv* until an entire line of text has been received. The definition of *recvln* is:

int recvln(connection con, char *buffer, int length)

The Send_Eof Function

Both the client and server must use *send_eof* after sending data to inform the other side that no further transmission will occur. On the other side, the *recv* function returns zero when it receives the end-of-file.

int send_eof(connection con)

The call has one argument that specifies a connection previously established with *await_contact* or *make_contact*. The function returns a negative value to indicate that an error occurred, and a non-negative value otherwise.

Summary Of API Types

Figure A1.4 summarizes the arguments used for each function in the example API. The table shows the type of each argument as well as the return type of the function. The last column of the figure specifies the type for arguments beyond the first two. Although *send* and *recv* each have four arguments, library function *recvln* only has three.

Function Name	Type Returned	Type of arg 1	Type of arg 2	Type of args 3&4
await_contact	connection	appnum	–	–
make_contact	connection	computer	appnum	–
appname_to_appnum	appnum	char *	–	–
cname_to_comp	computer	char *	–	–
send	int	connection	char *	int
recv	int	connection	char *	int
recvln	int	connection	char *	int
send_eof	int	connection	–	–

Figure A1.4 A summary of argument and return types for the example API.

The next sections contain examples of application programs that illustrate how client and server software uses our API to communicate. To reduce the size and make the code easier to read, the programs in this chapter use command-line arguments without checking their validity. An exercise suggests rewriting the programs to check arguments and report any errors to the user.

Code For An Echo Application

The first application we will consider is trivial: a client sends data and the server merely echoes back all the data it receives. That is, the client application repeatedly prompts the user for a line of input, sends the line to the server, and then displays whatever the server sends back. Although they are not useful to a typical user, echo applications are often used to test network connectivity.

Like all the applications described in this appendix, the echo application uses standard Internet protocols. That is, the client and server programs can run on arbitrary computers connected to the Internet as Figure A1.5 illustrates.

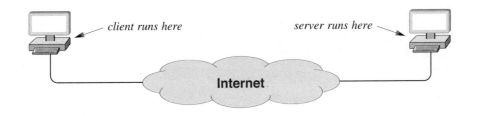

Figure A1.5 The echo client and server can run on arbitrary computers.

To invoke the server, a user must choose an application number between 1 and 32767 that is not being used by any other applications, and specify the number as a command line argument. For example, suppose someone using computer *arthur.cs.purdue.edu* chooses 20000 as the application number. The server is invoked by the command:

echoserver 20000

If some other application is using number 20000, the server emits an appropriate error message and exits; the user must choose another number.

Once the server has been invoked, the client is invoked by specifying the name of the computer on which the server is running and the application number the server is using. For example, to contact the server described above, a user on an arbitrary computer in the Internet can enter the command:

echoclient arthur.cs.purdue.edu 20000

Example Echo Server Code

File *echoserver.c* contains code for the echo server. Amazingly, even with comments and extra blank lines inserted for readability, the entire program fits on a single page of the text. In fact, after the program checks to ensure that it has been invoked correctly, the main body of the program consists of seven lines of code:

```
/* echoserver.c */

#include <stdlib.h>
#include <stdio.h>
#include <cnaiapi.h>

#define BUFFSIZE                  256

/*------------------------------------------------------------------
 *
 * Program: echoserver
 * Purpose: wait for a connection from an echoclient and echo data
 * Usage:   echoserver <appnum>
 *
 *------------------------------------------------------------------
 */
int
main(int argc, char *argv[])
{
        connection      conn;
        int             len;
        char            buff[BUFFSIZE];

        if (argc != 2) {
                (void) fprintf(stderr, "usage: %s <appnum>\n", argv[0]);
                exit(1);
        }

        /* wait for a connection from an echo client */

        conn = await_contact((appnum) atoi(argv[1]));
        if (conn < 0)
                exit(1);

        /* iterate, echoing all data received until end of file */

        while((len = recv(conn, buff, BUFFSIZE, 0)) > 0)
                (void) send(conn, buff, len, 0);
        send_eof(conn);
        return 0;
}
```

As we have seen, the server takes a single command-line argument that specifies the application number to use. In C, command-line arguments are passed to the program as an array of strings, *argv* along with an integer count of arguments, *argc*. The code extracts the command-line argument from *argv[1]*, and calls the standard C function *atoi* to convert the value from an ASCII string to binary. It then passes the result as an argument to *await_contact*. Once the call to *await_contact* returns, the server repeatedly calls *recv* to receive data from the client and *send* to transmit the same data back. The iteration terminates when *recv* finds an end-of-file and returns zero. At that time, the server sends an end-of-file and exits.

Example Echo Client Code

File *echoclient.c* contains code for an echo client application. Although not quite as short as the echo server, the client occupies only a few lines of code.

```
/* echoclient.c */

#include <stdlib.h>
#include <stdio.h>
#include <cnaiapi.h>

#define BUFFSIZE            256
#define INPUT_PROMPT        "Input   > "
#define RECEIVED_PROMPT     "Received> "

int readln(char *, int);

/*-----------------------------------------------------------------------
 *
 * Program: echoclient
 * Purpose: contact echoserver, send user input and print server response
 * Usage:   echoclient <compname> [appnum]
 * Note:    Appnum is optional. If not specified the standard echo appnum
 *          (7) is used.
 *
 *-----------------------------------------------------------------------
 */
int
main(int argc, char *argv[])
{
        computer        comp;
        appnum          app;
        connection      conn;
```

```
char            buff[BUFFSIZE];
int             expect, received, len;

if (argc < 2 || argc > 3) {
        (void) fprintf(stderr, "usage: %s <compname> [appnum]\n",
                        argv[0]);
        exit(1);
}

/* convert the arguments to binary format comp and appnum */

comp = cname_to_comp(argv[1]);
if (comp == -1)
        exit(1);

if (argc == 3)
        app = (appnum) atoi(argv[2]);
else
        if ((app = appname_to_appnum("echo")) == -1)
                exit(1);

/* form a connection with the echoserver */

conn = make_contact(comp, app);
if (conn < 0)
        exit(1);

(void) printf(INPUT_PROMPT);
(void) fflush(stdout);

/* iterate: read input from the user, send to the server,     */
/*          receive reply from the server, and display for user */

while((len = readln(buff, BUFFSIZE)) > 0) {

        /* send the input to the echoserver */

        (void) send(conn, buff, len, 0);
        (void) printf(RECEIVED_PROMPT);
        (void) fflush(stdout);

        /* read and print same no. of bytes from echo server */

        expect = len;
```

```
            for (received = 0; received < expect;) {
                len = recv(conn, buff, (expect - received) < BUFFSIZE ?
                            (expect - received) : BUFFSIZE, 0);
                if (len < 0) {
                        send_eof(conn);
                        return 1;
                }
                (void) write(STDOUT_FILENO, buff, len);
                received += len;
        }
        (void) printf("\n");
        (void) printf(INPUT_PROMPT);
        (void) fflush(stdout);
    }

    /* iteration ends when EOF found on stdin */

    (void) send_eof(conn);
    (void) printf("\n");
    return 0;
}
```

The client program takes either one or two arguments. The first argument specifies the name of a computer on which the server is running. If present, the second argument specifies the application number the server is using. If the second argument is missing, the client calls appname_to-appnum with argument *echo*.

After converting the arguments to binary form, the client passes them to *make_contact*, which contacts the server. Once contact has been established, the client issues a prompt to the user and enters a loop that reads a line of input, sends the line to the server, reads the reply from the server, and prints the reply for the user followed by a new prompt. When the client reaches the end of input (i.e., *readln* returns a zero value), the client calls *send_eof* to inform the server, and exits.

Several details complicate the code for the echo client. First, the client calls a function, *readln*, to read one line of input. Second, the client tests the return value from each function call, and exits when the value indicates an error occurred. Third, the client calls *fflush* to ensure that output is displayed immediately rather than being accumulated in a buffer. Fourth, and most significant, the client does not merely issue one call to *recv* each time it receives data from the server. Instead, the client enters a loop that repeatedly calls *recv* until it has received as many bytes as were sent.

The use of multiple calls to *recv* brings up a key point about our API:

> *A receiver cannot assume that data will arrive in the same size pieces*
> *as it was sent; a call to* recv *may return less data than was sent in a*
> *call to* send.

The text explains why *recv* behaves as it does: data is divided into small packets for transmission. Therefore, an application may receive the data from one packet at a time. Surprisingly, the opposite is also true: even if a sender calls *send* repeatedly, the network software may receive data from many packets before the application calls *recv*. In such cases, *recv* will return all the data at once.

Example Chat Server Code

The second application we will consider is a simplified form of the *chat* facility. Internet chat programs allow a group of users to communicate by entering text messages that are displayed on each others' screens. Our software provides a simplified version of chat that works between a single pair of users — when one user enters text, the text is displayed on the other user's screen, and vice versa. Furthermore, like the echo application described earlier, our chat software can be used between any computers connected to the Internet. One user begins by choosing an application number and running the server. For example, suppose a user on computer *guenevere.cs.purdue.edu* runs the server:

chatserver 25000

A user on another computer can invoke the client, which contacts the server:

chatclient guenevere.cs.purdue.edu 25000

To keep the code as small as possible, we have chosen a scheme that requires users to take turns entering text. Both the client and server issue a prompt when the user on that side is expected to enter a line of text. The user on the client side is prompted for input first. When a line of text has been received, the client sends the line to the server and the roles reverse. Users alternate entering text until one of them sends an end-of-file.

The code itself is straightforward. The server begins by waiting for contact from the client. It then enters a loop in which it obtains and displays a line of text from the client, prompts the local user, reads a line of input from the keyboard, and sends the line to the client side. Thus, until it receives an end-of-file, the server iterates between displaying output from the client and sending keyboard input to the client.

The client begins by contacting the server. Once communication has been established, the client also enters a loop. During each iteration, the client prompts the local user to enter a line of text, reads a line from the keyboard, sends the line to the server, and then receives and displays a line of text from the server. Thus, the client continues to alternate between sending a line of text that the user enters and displaying a line of text from the server.

File *chatserver.c* contains the code for the chat server.

```c
/* chatserver.c */

#include <stdlib.h>
#include <stdio.h>
#include <cnaiapi.h>

#define BUFFSIZE            256
#define INPUT_PROMPT        "Input    > "
#define RECEIVED_PROMPT     "Received> "

int recvln(connection, char *, int);
int readln(char *, int);

/*----------------------------------------------------------------------
 *
 * Program: chatserver
 * Purpose: wait for a connection from a chatclient & allow users to chat
 * Usage:   chatserver <appnum>
 *
 *----------------------------------------------------------------------
 */
int
main(int argc, char *argv[])
{
        connection      conn;
        int             len;
        char            buff[BUFFSIZE];

        if (argc != 2) {
                (void) fprintf(stderr, "usage: %s <appnum>\n", argv[0]);
                exit(1);
        }

        (void) printf("Chat Server Waiting For Connection.\n");
```

```
/* wait for a connection from a chatclient */

conn = await_contact((appnum) atoi(argv[1]));
if (conn < 0)
        exit(1);

(void) printf("Chat Connection Established.\n");

/* iterate, reading from the client and the local user */

while((len = recvln(conn, buff, BUFFSIZE)) > 0) {
        (void) printf(RECEIVED_PROMPT);
        (void) fflush(stdout);
        (void) write(STDOUT_FILENO, buff, len);

        /* send a line to the chatclient */

        (void) printf(INPUT_PROMPT);
        (void) fflush(stdout);
        if ((len = readln(buff, BUFFSIZE)) < 1)
                break;
        buff[len - 1] = '\n';
        (void) send(conn, buff, len, 0);
}

/* iteration ends when EOF found on stdin or chat connection */

(void) send_eof(conn);
(void) printf("\nChat Connection Closed.\n\n");
return 0;
}
```

Functions, *recvln* and *readln*, simplify the code — they each consist of a loop that iterates until an entire line or end-of-file is encountered. *Recvln* calls *recv* to receive from a network connection, and *readln* calls *read* to read characters from a keyboard.

The overall structure of the chat server is similar to the echo server we examined earlier. Like the echo server, the chat server expects a single command-line argument that is the application number to use. Once contact arrives from a client, the chat server prints a message for the local user, and enters a loop. At each iteration, the server receives a line of text from the network connection, prints the line on the user's screen, reads a line of input from the keyboard, and sends the line over the network. When it detects an end-of-file, the server sends an end-of-file and exits.

Example Chat Client Code

File *chatclient.c* contains the code for the chat client. As expected the client is slightly larger than the server.

```
/* chatclient.c */

#include <stdlib.h>
#include <stdio.h>
#include <cnaiapi.h>

#define BUFFSIZE            256
#define INPUT_PROMPT        "Input   > "
#define RECEIVED_PROMPT     "Received> "

int recvln(connection, char *, int);
int readln(char *, int);

/*-------------------------------------------------------------------
 *
 * Program: chatclient
 * Purpose: contact a chatserver and allow users to chat
 * Usage:    chatclient <compname> <appnum>
 *
 *-------------------------------------------------------------------
 */
int
main(int argc, char *argv[])
{
        computer        comp;
        connection      conn;
        char            buff[BUFFSIZE];
        int             len;

        if (argc != 3) {
                (void) fprintf(stderr, "usage: %s <compname> <appnum>\n",
                            argv[0]);
                exit(1);
        }

        /* convert the compname to binary form comp */

        comp = cname_to_comp(argv[1]);
        if (comp == -1)
                exit(1);
```

```
        /* make a connection to the chatserver */

        conn = make_contact(comp, (appnum) atoi(argv[2]));
        if (conn < 0)
                exit(1);

        (void) printf("Chat Connection Established.\n");
        (void) printf(INPUT_PROMPT);
        (void) fflush(stdout);

        /* iterate, reading from local user and then from chatserver */

        while((len = readln(buff, BUFFSIZE)) > 0) {
                buff[len - 1] = '\n';
                (void) send(conn, buff, len, 0);

                /* receive and print a line from the chatserver */
                if ((len = recvln(conn, buff, BUFFSIZE)) < 1)
                        break;
                (void) printf(RECEIVED_PROMPT);
                (void) fflush(stdout);
                (void) write(STDOUT_FILENO, buff, len);

                (void) printf(INPUT_PROMPT);
                (void) fflush(stdout);
        }

        /* iteration ends when stdin or the connection indicates EOF */

        (void) printf("\nChat Connection Closed.\n");
        (void) send_eof(conn);
        exit(0);
}
```

The client begins by contacting a server. Once communication has been established, the client enters a loop that reads from the keyboard, sends the data to the server, receives a line from the server, and displays the line on the user's screen. The iteration continues until the client receives an end-of-file condition from the server or an end-of-file from the keyboard (a return value of zero). At that time, the client sends an end-of-file and exits.

A Web Application

The final example application we will consider consists of client-server interaction for the World Wide Web. To run the server, a user chooses an application number and invokes the server program. For example, if a user on computer *netbook.cs.purdue.edu* chooses application number 27000, the server can be invoked with the command:

webserver 27000

As expected, the client specifies a computer, a path name, and an application number:

webclient netbook.cs.purdue.edu /index.html 27000

Although extremely small, our web server follows the standard protocols. Thus, it is possible to use a conventional (i.e., commercially available) web browser to access the server. For example, to use a commercial browser instead of our web client in the example above, one enters the URL:

http://netbook.cs.purdue.edu:27000/index.html

To keep our code as short as possible, we make a few simplifying assumptions. For example, the server only supplies three web pages, and none of the pages contains anything except text. Furthermore, each page is hard-wired into the code; the page can only be changed by recompiling the server (exercises suggest extending the server code to overcome some of the limitations).

The most significant limitation of our web application lies in the client. Unlike a conventional web browser, our client code does not understand how to format and display web pages. Instead, the client merely prints the source of the page. Despite the limitation, the client does interoperate with a commercial web server — it can be used to print the source of any page available on the Web.

Example Web Client Code

File *webclient.c* contains the code for the web client.

```c
/* webclient.c */

#include <stdlib.h>
#include <stdio.h>
#include <cnaiapi.h>

#define BUFFSIZE        256

/*-----------------------------------------------------------------------
 *
 * Program: webclient
 * Purpose: fetch page from webserver and dump to stdout with headers
 * Usage:   webclient <compname> <path> [appnum]
 * Note:    Appnum is optional. If not specified the standard www appnum
 *          (80) is used.
 *
 *-----------------------------------------------------------------------
 */
int
main(int argc, char *argv[])
{

        computer        comp;
        appnum          app;
        connection      conn;
        char            buff[BUFFSIZE];
        int             len;

        if (argc < 3 || argc > 4) {
                (void) fprintf(stderr, "%s%s%s", "usage: ", argv[0],
                                " <compane> <path> [appnum]\n");
                exit(1);
        }

        /* convert arguments to binary computer and appnum */

        comp = cname_to_comp(argv[1]);
        if (comp == -1)
                exit(1);

        if (argc == 4)
                app = (appnum) atoi(argv[3]);
        else
                if ((app = appname_to_appnum("www")) == -1)
```

```
                        exit(1);

        /* contact the web server */

        conn = make_contact(comp, app);
        if (conn < 0)
                exit(1);

        /* send an HTTP/1.0 request to the webserver */

        len = sprintf(buff, "GET %s HTTP/1.0\r\n\r\n", argv[2]);
        (void) send(conn, buff, len, 0);

        /* dump all data received from the server to stdout */

        while((len = recv(conn, buff, BUFFSIZE, 0)) > 0)
                (void) write(STDOUT_FILENO, buff, len);

        return 0;
}
```

The client code is extremely simple — after establishing communication with the web server, it sends a request, which must have the form:

GET */path* HTTP/1.0 *CRLF CRLF*

where *path* denotes the name of an item such as *index.html*, and *CRLF* denotes the two characters carriage return and line feed. After sending the request, the client receives and prints output from the server.

Example Web Server Code

File *webserver.c* contains the code for a (miniature) web server. The program contains three web pages plus the code needed to respond to a request:

```
/* webserver.c */

#include <stdio.h>
#include <stdlib.h>
#include <time.h>
#include <cnaiapi.h>

#if defined(LINUX) || defined(SOLARIS)
#include <sys/time.h>
#endif

#define BUFFSIZE        256
#define SERVER_NAME     "CNAI Demo Web Server"

#define ERROR_400       "<html><head></head><body><h1>Error 400</h1><p>Th\
e server couldn't understand your request.</body></html>\n"

#define ERROR_404       "<html><head></head><body><h1>Error 404</h1><p>Do\
cument not found.</body></html>\n"

#define HOME_PAGE       "<html><head></head><body><h1>Welcome to the CNAI\
 Demo Server</h1><p>Why not visit: <ul><li><a href=\"http://netbook.cs.pu\
rdue.edu\">Netbook Home Page</a><li><a href=\"http://www.comerbooks.com\"\
>Comer Books Home Page</a></ul></body></html>\n"

#define TIME_PAGE       "<html><head></head><body><h1>The current date is\
: %s</h1></body></html>\n"

int     recvln(connection, char *, int);
void    send_head(connection, int, int);

/*------------------------------------------------------------------
 *
 * Program: webserver
 * Purpose: serve hard-coded webpages to web clients
 * Usage:   webserver <appnum>
 *
 *------------------------------------------------------------------
 */
int
main(int argc, char *argv[])
{

        connection      conn;
        int             n;
```

```
        char            buff[BUFFSIZE], cmd[16], path[64], vers[16];
        char            *timestr;
#if defined(LINUX) || defined(SOLARIS)
        struct timeval  tv;
#elif defined(WIN32)
        time_t          tv;
#endif

        if (argc != 2) {
                (void) fprintf(stderr, "usage: %s <appnum>\n", argv[0]);
                exit(1);
        }

        while(1) {

                /* wait for contact from a client on specified appnum */

                conn = await_contact((appnum) atoi(argv[1]));
                if (conn < 0)
                        exit(1);

                /* read and parse the request line */

                n = recvln(conn, buff, BUFFSIZE);
                sscanf(buff, "%s %s %s", cmd, path, vers);

                /* skip all headers - read until we get \r\n alone */

                while((n = recvln(conn, buff, BUFFSIZE)) > 0) {
                        if (n == 2 && buff[0] == '\r' && buff[1] == '\n')
                                break;
                }

                /* check for unexpected end of file */

                if (n < 1) {
                        (void) send_eof(conn);
                        continue;
                }

                /* check for a request that we cannot understand */

                if (strcmp(cmd, "GET") || (strcmp(vers, "HTTP/1.0") &&
                                        strcmp(vers, "HTTP/1.1"))) {
```

```
                        send_head(conn, 400, strlen(ERROR_400));
                        (void) send(conn, ERROR_400, strlen(ERROR_400),0);
                        (void) send_eof(conn);
                        continue;
                }

                /* send the requested web page or a "not found" error */

                if (strcmp(path, "/") == 0) {
                        send_head(conn, 200, strlen(HOME_PAGE));
                        (void) send(conn, HOME_PAGE, strlen(HOME_PAGE),0);
                } else if (strcmp(path, "/time") == 0) {
#if defined(LINUX) || defined(SOLARIS)
                        gettimeofday(&tv, NULL);
                        timestr = ctime(&tv.tv_sec);
#elif defined(WIN32)
                        time(&tv);
                        timestr = ctime(&tv);
#endif
                        (void) sprintf(buff, TIME_PAGE, timestr);
                        send_head(conn, 200, strlen(buff));
                        (void) send(conn, buff, strlen(buff), 0);
                } else { /* not found */
                        send_head(conn, 404, strlen(ERROR_404));
                        (void) send(conn, ERROR_404, strlen(ERROR_404),0);
                }
                (void) send_eof(conn);
        }
}


/*-------------------------------------------------------------------------
 * send_head - send an HTTP 1.0 header with given status and content-len
 *-------------------------------------------------------------------------
 */
void
send_head(connection conn, int stat, int len)
{
        char    *statstr, buff[BUFFSIZE];

        /* convert the status code to a string */

        switch(stat) {
        case 200:
                statstr = "OK";
```

```
                break;
        case 400:
                statstr = "Bad Request";
                break;
        case 404:
                statstr = "Not Found";
                break;
        default:
                statstr = "Unknown";
                break;
        }

        /*
         * send an HTTP/1.0 response with Server, Content-Length,
         * and Content-Type headers.
         */

        (void) sprintf(buff, "HTTP/1.0 %d %s\r\n", stat, statstr);
        (void) send(conn, buff, strlen(buff), 0);

        (void) sprintf(buff, "Server: %s\r\n", SERVER_NAME);
        (void) send(conn, buff, strlen(buff), 0);

        (void) sprintf(buff, "Content-Length: %d\r\n", len);
        (void) send(conn, buff, strlen(buff), 0);

        (void) sprintf(buff, "Content-Type: text/html\r\n");
        (void) send(conn, buff, strlen(buff), 0);

        (void) sprintf(buff, "\r\n");
        (void) send(conn, buff, strlen(buff), 0);
}
```

Although the web server may seem more complex than previous examples, most of the complexity results from web details rather than networking details. In addition to reading and parsing a request, the server must send both a "header" and data in the response. The header consists of several lines of text that are terminated by the carriage return and linefeed characters. The header lines are of the form:

```
HTTP/1.0 status status_string CRLF
Server: CNAI Demo Server CRLF
Content-Length: datasize CRLF
Content-Type: text/html CRLF
CRLF
```

where *datasize* denotes the size of the data that follows measured in bytes.

Procedure *send_head* handles the chore of generating a header. When *send_head* is called, argument *stat* contains an integer status code and argument *len* specifies the content length. The *switch* statement uses the code to choose an appropriate text message, which is assigned to variable *statstr*. *Send_head* uses the C function *sprintf* to generate the complete header in a buffer, and then calls *send* to transmit the header lines over the connection to the client.

The code is also complicated by error handling — error messages must be sent in a form that a browser can understand. If a request is incorrectly formed, our server generates a *400* error message; if the item specified in the request cannot be found (i.e., the *path* is incorrect), the server generates a *404* message.

Our web server differs from the previous examples in a significant way: the server program does not exit after satisfying one request. Instead, the server remains running, ready to accept additional requests. That is, the server program consists of an infinite loop that calls *await_contact* to wait for contact from a client. When contact arrives, the server calls *recvln* to receive a request and calls *send* to send a response. The server then goes back to the top of the loop to wait for the next contact. Thus, once it is started, the server runs forever, just like a commercial web server.

Managing Multiple Connections With The Select Function

Although our example API supports 1-to-1 interaction between a client and server, the API does not support 1-to-many interaction. To see why, consider multiple connections. To create such connections, a single application program must call *make_contact* multiple times, specifying a *computer* and *appnum* for each call. Once the connections have been established, however, the application cannot know which of them will receive a message first. The application cannot use *recv* because the call will block until data arrives.

Many operating systems include a function named *select* that solves the problem of managing multiple connections. Conceptually, the *select* call checks a set of connections. The call blocks until at least one of the specified connections has received data. The call then returns a value that tells which of the connections have received data (i.e., connections for which *recv* will not block).

As an example, consider an application that must receive requests and send responses over two connections. Such an application can have the following general form:

Call *make_contact* to form connection 1;

Call *make_contact* to form connection 2;

Repeat forever {

    Call *select* to determine which connection is ready

    If (connection 1 is ready) {

        Call *recv* to read request from connection 1;

        Compute response to request;

        Call *send* to send response over connection 1;

    } if (connection 2 is ready) {

        Call *recv* to read request from connection 2;

        Compute response to request;

        Call *send* to send response over connection 2;

    }

}

Summary

It is possible for a programmer to create network applications that operate across the Internet without understanding how networks operate or how the underlying technologies carry the data between computers. The programmer must be given a set of high-level functions that form an Application Program Interface (API). This appendix presents a network API that contains only seven primitives, and reviews example applications that show the API is sufficient to construct software that correctly interoperates with commercial software.

EXERCISES

A1.1   The code examples in the appendix fail to check their command-line arguments carefully. Modify the code to add error checking.

A1.2   The *echo* service is a standard service available throughout the Internet. It has been assigned application number 7. Download, compile, and use the echo client to determine whether computers in your organization run a standard echo server.

A1.3 Modify the echo server so that instead of exiting after it handles one client, the server waits for another client. Hint: look at the web server.

A1.4 Download, compile, and test the example chat software by running it on two computers.

A1.5 Our chat software requires the users to take turns entering text. Rewrite the software to allow either user to type an arbitrary number of lines at any time. Hint: use threads.

A1.6 Modify the chat client to send a user name with each message, and modify the server to identify a user when displaying a line of output.

A1.7 Extend the above exercise so that instead of sending the user name with each message, the chat client and server exchange user names when they first make contact, remember the name, and display the name with each line of output.

A1.8 Why does the example code in the appendix use a mixture of calls to *write* and various forms of *printf*? Hint: does Windows treat sockets, files, and pipes identically?

A1.9 Devise software that permits an *n-way* chat session that allows users to join and leave the session at any time.

A1.10 Use telnet to contact a web server, send a *GET* request, and receive a reply.

A1.11 Try the web client program with an Internet web server. To do so, give the server's name, a path of *index.html* or *index.htm*, and application number *80*.

A1.12 Add another "page" to the web server.

A1.13 Modify the web server so it extracts the contents of each page from a file instead of having them hard-wired into the code.

A1.14 Expand the previous exercise to recognize file names that end in *.gif* and send them using a *Content-type* header with a value *image/gif* instead of the string *text/html*.

A1.15 (advanced) Build a client and server for a file transfer service.

A1.16 (advanced) Implement the Common Gateway Interface (CGI) from the specification found at:

http://hoohoo.ncsa.uiuc.edu/cgi/

A1.17 (advanced) Extend the web server so it can handle multiple connections concurrently. Hint: use *fork* or *pthread_create*.

A1.18 (advanced) Build a client that contacts an SMTP email server and sends an email message.

Index

Pearson Prentice Hall License Agreement and Limited Warranty

READ THE FOLLOWING TERMS AND CONDITIONS CAREFULLY BEFORE OPENING THIS SOFTWARE PACKAGE. THIS LEGAL DOCUMENT IS AN AGREEMENT BETWEEN YOU AND PEARSON EDUCATION, INC. (THE "COMPANY"). BY OPENING THIS SEALED SOFTWARE PACKAGE, YOU ARE AGREEING TO BE BOUND BY THESE TERMS AND CONDITIONS. IF YOU DO NOT AGREE WITH THESE TERMS AND CONDITIONS, DO NOT OPEN THE SOFTWARE PACKAGE. PROMPTLY RETURN THE UNOPENED SOFTWARE PACKAGE AND ALL ACCOMPANYING ITEMS TO THE PLACE YOU OBTAINED THEM FOR A FULL REFUND OF ANY SUMS YOU HAVE PAID.

1. GRANT OF LICENSE: In consideration of your purchase of this book, and your agreement to abide by the terms and conditions of this Agreement, the Company grants to you a nonexclusive right to use and display the copy of the enclosed software program (hereinafter the "SOFTWARE") on a single computer (i.e., with a single CPU) at a single location so long as you comply with the terms of this Agreement. The Company reserves all rights not expressly granted to you under this Agreement.

2. OWNERSHIP OF SOFTWARE: You own only the magnetic or physical media (the enclosed media) on which the SOFT-WARE is recorded or fixed, but the Company and the software developers retain all the rights, title, and ownership to the SOFT-WARE recorded on the original media copy(ies) and all subsequent copies of the SOFTWARE, regardless of the form or media on which the original or other copies may exist. This license is not a sale of the original SOFTWARE or any copy to you.

3. COPY RESTRICTIONS: This SOFTWARE and the accompanying printed materials and user manual (the "Documentation") are the subject of copyright. The individual programs on the media are copyrighted by the authors of each program. Some of the programs on the media include separate licensing agreements. If you intend to use one of these programs, you must read and follow its accompanying license agreement. You may not copy the Documentation or the SOFTWARE, except that you may make a single copy of the SOFTWARE for backup or archival purposes only. You may be held legally responsible for any copying or copyright infringement which is caused or encouraged by your failure to abide by the terms of this restriction.

4. USE RESTRICTIONS: You may not network the SOFTWARE or otherwise use it on more than one computer or computer terminal at the same time. You may physically transfer the SOFTWARE from one computer to another provided that the SOFTWARE is used on only one computer at a time. You may not distribute copies of the SOFTWARE or Documentation to others. You may not reverse engineer, disassemble, decompile, modify, adapt, translate, or create derivative works based on the SOFTWARE or the Documentation without the prior written consent of the Company.

5. TRANSFER RESTRICTIONS: The enclosed SOFTWARE is licensed only to you and may not be transferred to any one else without the prior written consent of the Company. Any unauthorized transfer of the SOFTWARE shall result in the immediate termination of this Agreement.

6. TERMINATION: This license is effective until terminated. This license will terminate automatically without notice from the Company and become null and void if you fail to comply with any provisions or limitations of this license. Upon termination, you shall destroy the Documentation and all copies of the SOFTWARE. All provisions of this Agreement as to warranties, limitation of liability, remedies or damages, and our ownership rights shall survive termination.

7. MISCELLANEOUS: This Agreement shall be construed in accordance with the laws of the United States of America and the State of New York and shall benefit the Company, its affiliates, and assignees.

8. LIMITED WARRANTY AND DISCLAIMER OF WARRANTY: The Company warrants that the SOFTWARE, when properly used in accordance with the Documentation, will operate in substantial conformity with the description of the SOFTWARE set forth in the Documentation. The Company does not warrant that the SOFTWARE will meet your requirements or that the operation of the SOFTWARE will be uninterrupted or error-free. The Company warrants that the media on which the SOFTWARE is delivered shall be free from defects in materials and workmanship under normal use for a period of thirty (30) days from the date of your purchase. Your only remedy and the Company's only obligation under these limited warranties is, at the Company's option, return of the warranted item for a refund of any amounts paid by you or replacement of the item. Any replacement of SOFTWARE or media under the warranties shall not extend the original warranty period. The limited warranty set forth above shall not apply to any SOFTWARE which the Company determines in good faith has been subject to misuse, neglect, improper installation, repair, alteration, or damage by you. EXCEPT FOR THE EXPRESSED WARRANTIES SET FORTH ABOVE, THE COMPANY DISCLAIMS ALL WARRANTIES, EXPRESS OR IMPLIED, INCLUDING WITHOUT LIMITATION, THE IMPLIED WARRANTIES OF MERCHANTABILITY AND FITNESS FOR A PARTICULAR PURPOSE. EXCEPT FOR THE EXPRESS WARRANTY SET FORTH ABOVE, THE COMPANY DOES NOT WARRANT, GUARANTEE, OR MAKE ANY REPRESENTATION REGARDING THE USE OR THE RESULTS OF THE USE OF THE SOFTWARE IN TERMS OF ITS CORRECTNESS, ACCURACY, RELIA-BILITY, CURRENTNESS, OR OTHERWISE.

IN NO EVENT, SHALL THE COMPANY OR ITS EMPLOYEES, AGENTS, SUPPLIERS, OR CONTRACTORS BE LIABLE FOR ANY INCIDENTAL, INDIRECT, SPECIAL, OR CONSEQUENTIAL DAMAGES ARISING OUT OF OR IN CON-NECTION WITH THE LICENSE GRANTED UNDER THIS AGREEMENT, OR FOR LOSS OF USE, LOSS OF DATA, LOSS OF INCOME OR PROFIT, OR OTHER LOSSES, SUSTAINED AS A RESULT OF INJURY TO ANY PERSON, OR LOSS OF OR DAMAGE TO PROPERTY, OR CLAIMS OF THIRD PARTIES, EVEN IF THE COMPANY OR AN AUTHORIZED REPRESEN-TATIVE OF THE COMPANY HAS BEEN ADVISED OF THE POSSIBILITY OF SUCH DAMAGES. IN NO EVENT SHALL LIABILITY OF THE COMPANY FOR DAMAGES WITH RESPECT TO THE SOFTWARE EXCEED THE AMOUNTS ACTU-ALLY PAID BY YOU, IF ANY, FOR THE SOFTWARE.

SOME JURISDICTIONS DO NOT ALLOW THE LIMITATION OF IMPLIED WARRANTIES OR LIABILITY FOR INCIDENTAL, INDIRECT, SPECIAL, OR CONSEQUENTIAL DAMAGES, SO THE ABOVE LIMITATIONS MAY NOT ALWAYS APPLY. THE WARRANTIES IN THIS AGREEMENT GIVE YOU SPECIFIC LEGAL RIGHTS AND YOU MAY ALSO HAVE OTHER RIGHTS WHICH VARY IN ACCORDANCE WITH LOCAL LAW.
ACKNOWLEDGMENT

YOU ACKNOWLEDGE THAT YOU HAVE READ THIS AGREEMENT, UNDERSTAND IT, AND AGREE TO BE BOUND BY ITS TERMS AND CONDITIONS. YOU ALSO AGREE THAT THIS AGREEMENT IS THE COMPLETE AND EXCLUSIVE STATEMENT OF THE AGREEMENT BETWEEN YOU AND THE COMPANY AND SUPERSEDES ALL PROPOSALS OR PRIOR AGREEMENTS, ORAL, OR WRITTEN, AND ANY OTHER COMMUNICATIONS BETWEEN YOU AND THE COMPANY OR ANY REPRESENTATIVE OF THE COMPANY RELATING TO THE SUBJECT MATTER OF THIS AGREEMENT.

Should you have any questions concerning this Agreement or if you wish to contact the Company for any reason, please contact in writing at the address below.

Robin Short
Pearson Prentice Hall
One Lake Street
Upper Saddle River, New Jersey 07458